Wiebe Nauta

The Implications of Freedom

Politics and Economics in Africa

Series Editors:

Robert Kappel and Ulf Engel

(Universität Leipzig)

volume 6

LIT

Wiebe Nauta

The Implications of Freedom

The changing role of land sector NGOs in a transforming South Africa

LIT

Cover Picture: Road and hills in the vicinity of Thornhill by: Wiebe Nauta

Bibliographic information published by Die Deutsche Bibliothek
Die Deutsche Bibliothek lists this publication in the Deutsche
Nationalbibliografie; detailed bibliographic data are available in the
Internet at http://dnb.ddb.de.

ISBN 3-8258-7798-1

© LIT VERLAG Münster   2004
Grevener Str./Fresnostr. 2   48159 Münster
Tel. 0251-620320   Fax 0251-231972
e-Mail: lit@lit-verlag.de   http://www.lit-verlag.de

Distributed in North America by:

Transaction Publishers
New Brunswick (U.S.A.) and London (U.K.)

Transaction Publishers   Tel.: (732) 445 - 2280
Rutgers University   Fax: (732) 445 - 3138
35 Berrue Circle   for orders (U. S. only):
Piscataway, NJ 08854   toll free (888) 999 - 6778

"The real truth, he suspects, is something far more –he casts around for the word– *anthropological*, something it would take months to get to the bottom of, months of patient, unhurried conversation with dozens of people, and the offices of an interpreter"

J.M. Coetzee, *Disgrace* (1999, p. 118)

Contents

List of Tables, Figures and Maps – ix
Abbreviations and Acronyms – xi
Preface and Acknowledgements – xiii

1. An Embedded Tale   15
Introduction – 15
'The Struggle', 'Freedom and Consultation' and 'New realism' – 16
The Struggle Era and the End of Apartheid – 17
'The Freedom and Consultation Era' – 23
The 'New Realism Era' – 34
Concluding Remarks and Overview – 40

2. Critical Reflections on NGOs   41
Introduction – 41
Critically Considering the 'NGO Literature' – 41
The Benefits of an 'Anthropology of Development' – 65
Concluding Remarks – 72

3. Land and Politics   75
Introduction – 75
Land and Colonialism in South Africa – 75
The Creation of Bantustans – 79
After the Elections: the Land Reform Programme – 91
Dilemmas of Local Government – 100
The Eastern Cape Land Sector after 1994 – 106
Conclusion – 107

4. MRA and the Dumped People of Thornhill   109
Introduction – 109
Reasons to Move to Thornhill – 111
The Birth of the Albany Resettlement Association – 115
Group Four – 117
Cooperative Arrangements Between ARA and Group Four – 119
ARA Becomes the Monti Rural Association – 124
Group Four Becomes Thornhill – 126
Conclusion – 129

5. Strategic Translations in Gasela   133
Introduction – 133
Gasela: an 'abandoned' farm – 133
The Involvement of the Monti Rural Association – 138
To Plough or Not to Plough… – 140
The Image of Gasela as a Potentially Thriving Agri-village – 145
A Market-Oriented Embrace and Strategic Translations – 151
The Fundamental Problem of Participation – 160
Conclusion – 162

6. MRA as a 'Learning Organization'   165
Introduction – 165
From 'Struggle' to 'Professionalism' – 165
Struggling with 'Development' – 167
The (im-)Possibilities of Organizational Learning – 180

Internal NGO Dynamics: 'racial issues' – 189
Conclusion – 196

7. The Government as Praying Mantis   199
Introduction – 199
NGOs as a 'Beacons of Continuity' – 199
Lobbying 'Comrades' in the Late Nineties – 211
Trapped by the Government's 'Market-oriented Embrace' – 221
Conclusion – 224

8. The Impact of 'New Realism' and the Role of Donors   227
Introduction – 227
The Impact of 'New Realism': MRA's sustainability drive – 227
Donors: Partners or Bosses? – 240
NGOs and Private Sector Consultants: eroded boundaries? – 248
Conclusion – 252

9. The Implications of Freedom   255
Introduction – 255
An Embedded Tale – 255
NGO Myths: a revealing case study – 261
Agendas for Future Research – 266
Observations about Land Sector NGOs and Land Reform in South Africa – 268

Appendix 1: Methodological Notes   273
Appendix 2: Archival Sources, Formal Interviews & Taped Exchanges   277
References   281
Endnote   291

List of Tables, Figures and Maps

Tables

Table 3.1: Restitution Figures 19.11.'99	92
Table 5.1: Age distribution and number of Gasela residents	132
Table 5.2: Area available for crop cultivation in Gasela	143
Table 5.3: Labour Requirements at Planting and Harvesting in Gasela	143
Table 6.1: New staff that left M RA in the period 1994 -1998	185

Figures

Figure 2.1: The three realms in society	48
Figure 2.2: The three overlapping realms	50
Figure 2.3: The market as part of civil society	51

Maps

Map 1.1: The Eastern Cape during apartheid	17
Map 3.1: The Xhosa and colonial advance	74
Map 3.2: British Kaffraria and Mission Stations	75
Map 3.3: Reserve Areas in 1913 and 1936	78
Map 3.4: Bantustans	79
Map 3.5: Eastern Cape with the Ciskei and the Transkei	81
Map 3.6: The Border Region	87
Map 3.7: Land Reform Pilot Projects	93

Abbreviations and Acronyms

ACLA	Advisory Commission on Land Allocation
ADC	Amatola District Council
ANC	African National Congress
ARA	Albany Resettlement Association
BKDF	Border Kei Development Forum
BOCCO	Border Civic Congress
BRAC	Bangladesh Rural Advancement Committee
CDDR	Commission for the Demarcation/Delimitation of Regions
CFRR	Committee For Rural Reconstruction
CGC	Ciskeian General Council
CLA	Ciskei Legislative Assembly
CLSB	Ciskei Living Stock Board
CNIP	Ciskei National Independence Party
CNP	Ciskei National Party
CODESA	Convention for a Democratic South Africa
COSAG	Concerned South Africans Group
COSATU	Congress of South African Trade Unions
CPA	Communal Property Association
CSO	Civil Society Organization
CTA	Ciskei Territorial Authority
DDA	Department of Development Aid
DLA	Department of Land Affairs
DOA	Department of Agriculture
DWAF	Department of Water Affairs and Forestry
ECNGOC	Eastern Cape NGO Coalition
ECSECC	Eastern Cape Social and Economic Consultative Council
ESTA	Extension of Security of Tenure Act
GEAR	Growth, Employment and Redistribution
GNU	Government of National Unity
GRA	Gasela Residents Association
GRADAC	Grahamstown Democratic Action Committee
GRO	Grassroots Organization
GRSO	Grassroots Support Organization
HUVO	Humanisten Voor Ontwikkelingssamenwerking
ICU	Industrial and Commercial Workers Union
IDP	Integrated Development Plan
IFP	Inkatha Freedom Party
IICU	Independent Industrial and Commercial Workers Union
ISER	Institute of Social and Economic Research
LAPC	Land and Agricultural Policy Centre
LGTA	Local Government Transition Act
LOGOPOP	Local Government Policy Project
LRC	Legal Resource Centre
LSC	Land Service Committee
MDM	Mass Democratic Movement
MK	Umkhonto weSizwe
MRA	Monti Rural Association
NAA	Northern Action Association
NCAR	National Committee Against Removals
NCBP	National Capacity Building Programme
NCOP	National Council of Provinces
NEDLAC	National Economic Development and Labour Council

NGDO	Non-Governmental Development Organization
NGFO	Non-Governmental Funding Organization
NGO	Non-Governmental Organization
NLC	National Land Committee
NNGO	Northern NGO
NP	National Party
NZV	New Zealand Volunteers
OFSC	Organization For Social Change
PAC	Pan Africanist Congress of Azania
PCG	Project Control Groups
PERA	Port Elizabeth Rural Association
PO	People's Organization
PSC	Public Service Contractor
PSC	Project Steering Committee
PTO	Permission to Occupy
RA	Released Area
RDP	Reconstruction and Development Programme
RSC	Regional Service Council
SA	South Africa
SAAU	South African Agricultural Union
SACC	South African Council of Churches
SACP	South African Communist Party
SADT	South African Development Trust
SANCO	South African National Civics Organization
SANNC	South African Native National Congress
SDA	Swiss Development Agency
SNGO	Southern NGO
SPP	Surplus People Project
SSA	Sweden Supports Africa
TA	Tribal Authority
TDF	Transkeian Defence Force
TEC	Transitional Executive Council
TLC	Transitional Local Council
TMC	Transkei Military Council
TNIP	Transkei National Independence Party
TOR	Terms of Reference
TRA	Thornhill Residents Association
TRC	Truth and Reconciliation Commission
TRC	Transitional Rural Council
TRDC	Thornhill Reconstruction and Development Committee
TrepC	Transitional Representative Council
UDF	United Democratic Front
UDM	United Democratic Movement
ULC	Umtata Land Committee
USAID	United States Agency for International Development
VO	Voluntary Organization
ZRA	Zweledinga Residents Association

Preface and Acknowledgements

This book is a revised version of my dissertation (Nauta, 2001). The research was conducted in the Eastern Cape Province of South Africa during 1996, 1997 and 1998, while I was employed by the Vrije Universiteit Amsterdam as a PhD researcher. In my application I had made it clear that South Africa, and especially the land sector, would provide an ideal setting to study the changing role of NGOs. These organizations could be studied against the backdrop of a society that was undergoing a major transformation on all institutional levels. Moreover, I believed that by using an ethnographic and actor-oriented approach –inspired by Norman Long and by Philip Quarles van Ufford– to study NGOs, more depth could be achieved than was normally the case in the 'NGO literature'.

During the research I was primarily based in the city of East London, where I was truly astonished by the level of cooperation I received from the NGO sector, the government sector and the academic community. I cannot express how welcome people made me feel in the NGO where I conducted my research. I would hereby like to thank everyone for his or her warmth, openness, friendship and support. Without them I would not have succeeded. Since this book also contains critical remarks about the NGO sector, I would like to reiterate that I admire the work that is being undertaken. I want to especially mention Ash and Lise, who became close friends; Gail and Russel, who managed to put up with me as a tenant; Danny and Lucy, who taught me a lot about parenthood; Mike and Barbara, who were always there on Sundays; Sibo, Phumeza and SisFan, who cooked Xhosa meals for me and helped integrate me in Eastern Cape society; Miriam and Ayanda. At the Institute of Social and Economic Research I would like to thank my colleagues Leslie, Ntobeko and Linda for their support and companionship.

My stay in the rural communities –especially Gasela and Thornhill– provided me with a unique opportunity to encounter the legacy of apartheid, and life in the (ex-)bantustan areas. Still today the lives of thousands of people, who have truly suffered during apartheid, are a daily struggle for survival. They scrape by on pensions, remittances and home gardens. I am extremely grateful for the warm reception given to me and Harriët in these communities and am truly humbled by the humanity – *ubuntu*– and lack of suspicion towards us as white visitors. I would like to especially thank Zolani, Nokuzola, Yanga, Uviwe and Toto and his family in Thornhill. In Gasela I would like to express my gratitude towards Zandisile and Mr. Lamani and his wife Lulama.

In the Netherlands I would like to thank my team of supervisors. Philip Quarles van Ufford was the driving force and always treated me as an equal. Bernhard Venema was always there when I needed him. Peter Kloos as the official promotor, allowed us the space we needed and gave me valuable comments on what I had written. Sadly, Peter passed away and never witnessed the end product. In 2000 Jan Abbink took over as promotor and still managed to make important contributions. I also want to mention my colleagues Peter and Els, with whom I shared more than a room. I am also grateful for the support received from the departmental secretaries: Paola, Gremina, Pien and Anouk. Furthermore I would like to thank the 'promotieclub' of Mart Bax for their inputs and the ZAIO's –Erik, Barbara and Julia–

with who I had stimulating South Africa sessions. This is also the place to express my appreciation for the support I received from CERES, and the people at KAIROS and HIVOS. Finally, I want to express my gratitude to those at the Faculty of Arts and Culture at the University of Maastricht –especially Rein de Wilde– who made it possible that I revised my dissertation and turned it into a book.

On a personal note I would like to thank Lolle for all his inputs. To Harriët I am grateful for providing me with the time to complete this project and for giving birth to Lotte and Nanne, who have become the joy of my life.

1. An Embedded Tale

Introduction

The term *non-governmental organization* is so widely used these days that it has effectively lost its meaning. Why then write a book about these organizations? I would argue that it is an attempt to put back flesh on what has become a very bare skeleton. Instead of theorizing for the umpteenth time *"what a real NGO is"*, this book describes a 'real' organization out there. Inspired by scholars like Ferguson (1990) and Long (1989, 1992), it is an attempt to (re-)introduce a *historical, political* and *socio-economic* dimension in the analysis of NGOs. Thus, I present, what I have termed, *an embedded tale*. A tale about a land sector NGO grounded in the historic, political and socio-economic context of the storm of transformation that engulfed South Africa in the last decades of the 20th century.

The Monti Rural Association[1] (MRA) is a land rights organization that originated during the anti-apartheid struggle and has operated since 1982 in what is now known as the Eastern Cape Province. Nowadays, it is still an active player in the land sector. By studying such an NGO in detail over a prolonged period of time and making use of ethnographic methodologies, much could be learned about internal organizational dynamics as well as the changing relationships with other development actors in the state, civil society and the market. To illustrate the complexity of these links the Monti Rural Association can be imagined as a small spider in several institutional webs that link and cut across local, regional, national and even international levels.

As a means to introduce the Monti Rural Association in this first introductory chapter, I have chosen to embed a concise history of the organization in a brief history of South Africa, mainly focusing on the 1980s and 1990s. By doing so, the first chapter not only reflects the aim to produce an *embedded tale*, but also provides the reader, who may know little about South Africa, with an overview of events and developments[2] which have strongly impacted on the 'birth' and 'life' of this South African land sector NGO[3]. Of course the author is aware that by presenting certain events and ignoring others, an interpretation of the history of the organization is given. As this book is not a work of history, it is not my aim to write an all-encompassing history of the Monti Rural Association. Instead, the main purpose of this chapter is to provide a 'quick tour', that will provide the reader with a 'feel' for the topic of this book: the changing role of the Monti Rural Association. Thus, the reader can see, for example, that it was no coincidence that two influential members of staff were arrested in late 1986, since in that year a nation-wide State of Emergency was declared in South Africa. More detailed historical facts about the organization can be found in the case studies. Chapter 4, for example, illustrates how the history of the organization is strongly interlinked with the history of Thornhill, one of the rural communities[4] it assisted over the years.

'The Struggle', 'Freedom and Consultation' and 'New realism'

Normally, when recent South African history is discussed only an apartheid and a post-apartheid period are distinguished. However, in my opinion it is crucial to move beyond this dichotomy, in order to improve our understanding of the complexities of the transformation processes South African progressive NGOs were involved in over the past twenty years. Therefore, I propose to recognize an interim period of great change –and also great confusion– as well. Thus, from the perspective of the progressive forces I identify three recent historical periods, that partly overlap.

Firstly, I identify the period of 'the struggle', as many call it. In my view that period covered the nineteen eighties and the early nineties. It was a period of a long and difficult struggle against an inhumane system held in place by an immensely powerful apartheid state. For that distinct period in history it is possible to identify, what I have called, a 'struggle discourse'. Pamphlets, reports, progressive people's rhetoric and actions were saturated with words and expressions like: 'struggle', 'mass mobilization', 'one man one vote', 'power to the people' et cetera. It is a discourse which was full of suffering and at the same time dynamically hopeful. Although we suffer today we are working hard to achieve change.

A second period can be identified when things are actually starting to change. Mandela is released and the period of struggle is slowly replaced by a period of euphoria and expectancy. In the early nineties, the progressive forces, but also the conservatives, begin to realize that the genie is out of the bottle. Thanks to Mandela's rhetoric of reconciliation and his firm believe in democracy, the progressive forces decide to enter into negotiations with the enemy and start to formulate plans and documents for a 'new South Africa'. Although it is still a difficult period, in which it is clear that the struggle is not yet over, a cautious optimism takes root. That optimism is followed by euphoria and expectancy when an agreement is reached on the interim-constitution in November 1993. In this period –from 1993 to 1996– a 'freedom and consultation discourse' emerges in which human reason, and a firm believe in negotiations gain currency. Terms like 'empowerment' 'consultation', 'negotiations', 'stakeholders' and 'consultation forums' become popular. In this regard, the formation of the 'Rainbow Coalition' became crucial, together with the formulation and publication of a document with a great impact: the Reconstruction and Development Programme (RDP) (ANC, 1994).

In 1996, several crucial things happen. Besides the fact that the National Party Leaves the Government of National Unity (GNU), the government also presents GEAR, its macro-economic Growth, Employment and Redistribution plan. From that moment onwards a 'new realism discourse' grips the national political scene. It is the beginning of a period of 'awareness', when the progressive forces that had joined the government realize that South Africa is part –and must be part– of a global economy. New terms are heard regularly: 'realistic expectations', 'international markets', 'global economy', 'exchange rate', 'monetary policies' et cetera. Thus, from the summer of 1996 until the end of the century new priorities take root and a 'new realism' discourse becomes dominant.

The Struggle Era and the End of Apartheid

In the late 1970s the situation in apartheid South Africa seemed to worsen every year. For example, after the killing of Soweto school children in 1976 and the establishment of the Transkei as independent bantustan, Steve Biko was murdered in detention in 1977. In the 1980's, therefore, the internal protest movement grew, while at the same time the foreign pressure on the regime, to implement reforms, increased. It was a period of great turmoil and repression, which I have termed the 'struggle era'. South Africa was led by the harsh P.W. Botha, or 'Groot Krokodil[5]', who publicly boasted about the reforms he had implemented –notorious is the establishment of the Tri-cameral Parliament in 1984 in which Whites[6], Indians and Coloureds were given separate chambers to debate legislation. However, his actions were neither taken seriously by the South African anti-apartheid movement, nor by most of the international community.

One of the leading organizations, in the internal struggle against apartheid, was the United Democratic Front (UDF), which established in 1981, the same year the Ciskei was granted independence as bantustan. The UDF was led by high profile figures like Alan Boesak and Patrick 'terror' Lekota. It was not a political party but an umbrella body that represented a large diversity of civic organizations. As van Kessel (2000) argued:

> "...the UDF must surely be unique in the heterogeneity of affiliates under its umbrella: from the Johannesburg Scooter Drivers' Association to the Northern Natal Darts Club, from the Grail to the Pietermaritzburg Child Welfare Society and the Medical and Dental Association" (p. 288).

The most concrete early issues that the UDF rallied around were the opposition to the tri-cameral constitution and the Black Local Authorities, that were instituted by the apartheid regime in the early eighties. Following the ANC's call to make the townships ungovernable the UDF stepped up its activities. It led to the typical 'struggle rhetoric' like: *"...the strength and sacrifice of our people, their will to be free, cannot be crushed"*[7]. The apartheid regime, however, answered by instituting consecutive states of emergency that led to an extremely polarized situation in the eighties. Particularly in the townships the situation got out of hand. Many areas did indeed become ungovernable. Although many protests were not violent –like consumer boycotts– the state's answer was frequently brutal, resulting in thousands of deaths. In some areas the anger of the activists could no longer be contained, which resulted in 'necklacing' –setting someone alight by hanging a burning car tyre around someone's neck– black councillors who collaborated with the apartheid regime. Although this violence was never condoned by the UDF leadership and heavily criticized by people like Archbishop Tutu, it occurred time and again.

By February 1988 the apartheid regime proceeded to ban the UDF and arrest thousands of activists. However, the groundswell of protests could no longer be contained. The struggle continued and within weeks the UDF had been replaced by the Mass Democratic Movement (MDM), backed by UDF supporters, ANC members and leaning heavily on the Congress of South African Trade Unions (COSATU), which was established in 1985. The UDM was essentially similar to the UDF, but the organization was even more loosely structured. More importantly, it did not have a permanent structure, which prevented it from being banned by the regime.

By early 1989, P.W. Botha was still in power and although cosmetic changes had been implemented, apartheid had not been abolished. At that stage, very few political commentators would have predicted the drastic political turn of events that was about to occur. Although the exact cause will never be clear, several factors led to growing problems for the apartheid regime. On the one hand, there were the international sanctions against South Africa that caused economic pain for an already shaky economy. The South African business sector, therefore, put increasing pressure on the regime to implement reforms. Furthermore, the iron curtain fell in 1989, which in the eyes of the apartheid regime reduced the 'communist threat' –used to justify many harsh internal and external measures. Additionally, the internal pressure, sustained by the Mass Democratic Movement (MDM), could no longer be contained. The country became paralyzed by strikes, rent and consumer boycotts and the ongoing township violence. As a result, the crocodile was replaced by the more flexible, globally thinking and 'progressive' F.W. de Klerk in the course of that same year. Subsequently, in early 1990 de Klerk went ahead to release Nelson Mandela and many other high profile political prisoners. Moreover, he unbanned most political parties like the ANC and the SACP. From that moment on a period of rapid change commenced. By 1993 most of these formerly banned parties joined de Klerk's National Party in what was called the Transitional Executive Council (TEC), a structure that preceded the first democratic government that would assume power after the first democratic elections in 1994. The struggle era seemed to have come to an end.

The Monti Rural Association (MRA) during the Struggle Era

During apartheid the black population experienced brutal restrictions that reduced them to second-class citizens and only allowed them access to the 'white areas' if they were part of a productive labour force. As the homeland –or bantustan– policy took shape, an entire machinery was devised to remove the black population from the 'white areas' in an attempt to create 'racially' and 'ethnically' homogeneous reserves. Consequently, many black communities in South Africa came under the threat of forced removal. Although the world had witnessed some of the harshest 'apartheid incidents', it was not aware of the extent of suffering caused by these forced removals. Moreover, within South Africa itself the ignorance concerning these issues –especially amongst whites– was also significant. What were the true motives behind these removals? Where did they take place? How many people were affected?

To answer these questions, the Surplus People Project (SPP) was established in February 1980. In several university towns in South Africa –Cape Town, Grahamstown, Durban, Pietermaritzburg and Johannesburg– concerned academics and community workers joined forces *"...to co-ordinate and initiate research projects into population relocation in South Africa"*[8] *(p. xix)*. Most importantly, the project aimed to publicize these research findings so that the world would become aware of the fact that 3,5 million people had been forcefully removed from their land since 1960 and many were still under threat. In 1983, after years of research, the project yielded a five-volume report, titled: *Forced Removals in South Africa*. The report, full of quantitative and qualitative data drew a complete picture of the extent of the suffering inflicted by the apartheid regime. Today it is still widely quoted.

However, as the project drew near its end, many of the participants felt that it was necessary to stay involved with the communities in which they had conducted their research. In some areas the people were still under threat of removal, while in other areas –for example, where black South Africans had been dumped in the new homelands– people were starving and even dying for lack of food, basic services and infrastructure. Particularly in the Eastern Cape many areas were affected as two homelands had been created: the Transkei in 1976 and the Ciskei in 1981 (see Map 1.1). Due to these developments boundaries were changed, large groups of people were forcefully resettled or incorporated into to these 'independent' bantustans, which effectively robbed them of their South African citizenship.

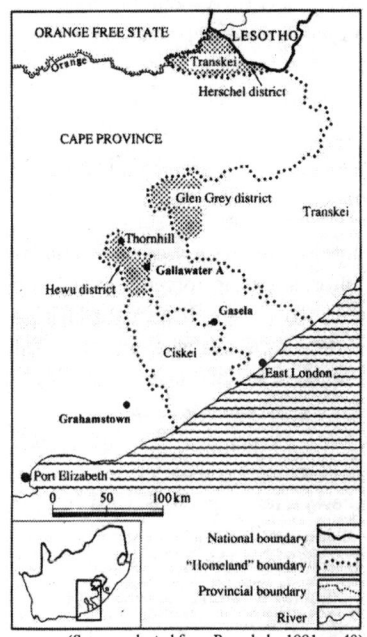

Map 1.1: The Eastern Cape during apartheid.

Thus, 'the Grahamstown Group', that had been responsible for the research in the Eastern Cape part of the Surplus People's Project, came together in Grahamstown –on Saturday 4 September 1982– in a preliminary meeting to set up an organization, provisionally called the Albany[9] Resettlement Association, *"with the broad aims of monitoring and giving up-to-date information on communities in the Eastern Cape who have been or may be resettled; serving these communities with information or any support possible (...); and co-ordinating the work of concerned organisations and individuals to these ends"*[10]. In the following meeting, on Sunday 26 September, other academics and several progressive organizations like the Black Sash and the Border Council of Churches were also invited to discuss the establishment and the future of ARA. Moreover, several reports were tabled on the situation in the rural areas, and strategies for the future were discussed with respect to finances, organizing workshops and publicity.

The publicity initiative was successful when, on Thursday 7 October, the first newspaper article appeared in the Eastern Province Herald under the heading: **"G'town group formed to monitor removals"**. The article quotes the group's first chairperson, associate professor[11] Deirdre Thompson, who explained how *"...ARA fieldworkers would make regular trips to communities under threat of removal and those who had already been resettled..."*[12] in order to gather information. This information would then be filed at a resource centre and made available to interested parties. Moreover, the newly established organization aimed to offer support to rural communities and inform them about their legal rights[13]. These communities were mainly situated in an area known as the Border –a corridor of South African territory between the Ciskei and the Transkei– and in the Ciskei (see Map 1.1 and Map 3.6).

Eventually the Surplus People Project yielded a string of land rights organizations[14], like for example, the Committee For Rural Reconstruction (CFRR) in Pietermaritzburg, the Port Elizabeth Rural Association (PERA) and the Northern Action Association (NAA) in Johannesburg. Countrywide these organizations became major players in the support of black communities against forced removals.

In May 1983, the Albany Resettlement Association published its first eight-page newsletter[15] with its first official logo: walking away from the reader is a Xhosa woman, with a small child beside her, carrying a large trunk (with their belongings?) on her head. This newsletter, that was sent around nationally and internationally –and could be subscribed to– contained maps, newspaper quotes, interviews with community members, pictures and detailed information on forced removal and forced incorporation areas in the Eastern Cape. It also contained a first reference to the 'Thornhill Camp', a re-located community that had been dumped in the bush in an area that had been incorporated in the Ciskei: *"...It is hard to see how people can keep alive, or to know how many have died here..."* (1983a, p. 5). With the people of Thornhill ARA would develop a long-standing relationship that is still strong to this day.

Surprisingly, in the second fourteen-page newsletter[16] –published half a year later– the first name-change of the organization was already announced. The word 'resettlement' was replaced by the word 'rural' so that it was still abbreviated ARA, but now stood for the Albany Rural Association. In the newsletter it was explained that it *"...marks a broadening of objectives. We still aim to monitor and publicise local relocation, but this has inevitably led on to a concern with all matters relating to the rural areas"* (1983b, p. 1).

After a promising start in 1982 and 1983, the Albany Rural Association experienced a few difficult years. According to the chairperson's report in 1984, the failure to consolidate the organization was mainly due to financial uncertainty and the fact that ARA volunteers all had full-time jobs. Therefore, only one newsletter was put out in 1985. Nevertheless, the volunteers tried to keep in touch with many rural communities. The situation somewhat improved as the first grants from foreign donors came through. As a result, a fieldworker was employed and an office was rented at the end of 1984. The new office, however, was gutted by fire in early 1985 and the first full-time fieldworker left the organization fairly soon. Only May Brown, a part-time fieldworker and an administrative assistant, remained.

In December 1984 these organizations founded a national umbrella organization, called the National Committee Against Removals (NCAR), that became a dominant voice in land debates on a national level. According to the ARA Newsletter[17] such a national organization was essential because *"...there is a national policy of removals; we must have a national response..."* (1985a, p. 3). In the early nineties this umbrella organization was renamed the National Land Committee (NLC), when it shifted its focus from the fight against forced removals to the support of marginalized black groups in their fight for land.

In 1986 the Albany Rural Association started functioning with renewed spirit. Jacob James, a new fieldworker, joined May Brown at the beginning of the year. However, as the political situation in South Africa deteriorated severely, a nation-wide State of Emergency was declared in June. As a result, the conditions under which the fieldworkers had to operate became extremely complicated. Security forces were everywhere and the organization was being watched. May Brown, more or less, went underground and Jacob James had to use all his skills in order to evade the security forces on his field trips. In his case –as a black man– it proved to be an advantage to have a 'white' name. Friends and (ex-)colleagues often recounted that the security police had enquired what colour this man was. Nevertheless, things went terribly wrong on 22 November 1986.

After several trips to Thornhill the Albany Rural Association went ahead to invite several community leaders from that area to Grahamstown in order to discuss future strategies for the 'dumped people'. However, the workshop in Grahamstown was raided by the security police –it had followed the leaders from Thornhill– and everyone present was arrested. Although most people were released the same day, Jacob James and May Brown –she had attended the meeting in disguise– were kept in detention. As they had both been detained before, May Brown was kept imprisoned for ten months, while Jacob James served exactly one year in prison. For the Albany Rural Association this meant an enormous setback as both fieldworkers were absent for most of 1987, a notorious year, in which the State of Emergency was continued. However, instead of being discouraged, the volunteers became extra motivated to continue the work of their detained comrades. After her release May Brown left the country because she was restricted in her activities by the authorities. Jacob James, however, re-joined his colleagues and became one of the driving forces behind ARA in the late eighties.

In early 1988 –in the same year that the UDF, COSATU and other organizations were banned– Jacob James re-joined ARA that had also appointed two new fieldworkers: Michael Ndlovu and John Carver. As the apartheid regime was actively engaged in promoting and supporting the Tribal Authorities in the Eastern Cape, ARA formulated a counter-strategy in which it was aimed *"(...) to help communities respond to this initiative... "*[18] and to *"(...) be generating self-sufficiency in the communities we work with... "* [19]. It marked the beginning of a period in which the organization 'blossomed'. The fieldworkers were extremely active and interacted on a regular basis with a large number of communities all over the Eastern Cape. A development sub-committee, together with area sub-committees, was very successful in generating information about communities in detailed newsletters –seventeen (!) newsletters were produced in three years. Topics included:
- forced removals in Cathcart from the old township to a new township;
- tensions between the newly established Residents Association versus the old conservative tribal authority structure in Kwelera;
- the forced removal of a community in Stockenstrom;
- the internal power struggles in Mgwali between the 'new' progressive Residents Association and 'old' Ciskei politicians;

- the quest for more and better land and basic services in Thornhill which had been promised by the Ciskei regime[20];
- et cetera.

Most of these cases resulted –directly or indirectly– from the process of 'consolidating' the Ciskei, which had been a loose aggregation of scattered areas since the late seventies and early eighties. In order to create one territory, many areas were identified for addition to the Ciskei. In other areas that were to remain white and within South Africa, the territory would have to be emptied of the black population. Many people under such a threat of forced removal objected to resettling in the Ciskei as they would lose their South African citizenship and the right to work in South Africa. For 'foreigners' –the inhabitants of these new homeland states would become aliens in South Africa– it would not be easy to get a work permit. Moreover, many feared losing their South African pensions.

As the ARA staff became more involved in communities that were politically divided, the work and publications of the organization increasingly became openly political. The ARA staff actively supported people in communities who intended to form so-called *residents associations*. These pro-democratic, anti-bantustan and anti-apartheid structures were set up to oppose the more conservative Tribal Authorities, which were the authority structures of chiefs and headmen in the bantustans. In the Ciskei –like in most other bantustans– the Tribal Authorities were strongly linked to oppressive Ciskei political system and its politicians. During interviews in 1997, some of the old staff of ARA explained to me how they had carried out a double agenda in the late eighties. On the one hand they did the land-related work for the organization, while on the other hand they had a clear anti-apartheid strategy. Some fieldworkers like Jacob James –who had ties to the underground ANC– actively pushed the formation of these democratic structures in order to create a broadly supported pro-democracy, anti-apartheid, anti-bantustan network in South Africa. These residents associations were also called 'civics' in South Africa, especially in the urban areas. To unite these forces a national umbrella organization was formed in 1992, called the South African National Civics Organization (SANCO). For a short while it became a powerful force in national political debates.

Another element in the struggle against apartheid was the national NCAR-coordinated 'Anti-Incorporation Campaign', largely initiated by ARA. The campaign was launched in October 1989 and yielded an ARA Newsletter which contained a Xhosa –the local language– text. It included a petition form in English and Xhosa that could be copied and multiplied in order to be signed by supporters. Not only did the petition demand *"...the end of forced incorporations into the bantustans"*, it also ended with the call for *"a unitary, non-racial and democratic South Africa"*[21]. It was the first time that the newsletter was used as an instrument to rally support in the communities and to deliver information in the local language.

These and other activities, organized predominantly by the Mass Democratic Movement (MDM), created and sustained an atmosphere of resistance in the Ciskei and the Border Area. As the tension rose the Ciskeian authorities declared a state of emergency. For example in Peelton –where ARA was active– there was a clampdown by the Ciskeian government, ordering the demolition of 70 homes and the arrest of over 100 residents. Consequently, many Peelton residents fled into South African territory to escape from the Ciskei security forces. Many similar incidents followed and the unrest in the Eastern Cape, and in South Africa as a whole, continued to spread, especially as rumours about impending major political changes grew. Finally, when President F. W. de Klerk announced reforms and the release of Nelson Mandela, the tension exploded in the Ciskei. On the fourth of March 1990, a coup was staged against the authoritarian homeland leader Lennox Sebe. Triumphantly. the ARA Newsletter[22] announced that the rural communities had been responsible for the rebellion that ultimately caused Sebe to be dropped from power. However, instead of the becoming more democratic, the Ciskei stayed in turmoil for several more years.

The new homeland leader, Brigadier Oupa Gqozo, proved to be as least as brutal and autocratic as Lennox Sebe. Since de Klerk refused to instate an interim administration in the Ciskei, on the grounds that it was an 'independent state', political oppression persisted. Thus, while in South Africa parties like the ANC were un-banned they remained banned in the Ciskei. To denounce this situation the progressive organizations, including ARA, organized a protest march on 7 September 1992. About 50,000 people marched on Bisho, the capital of Ciskei, against Brigadier Gqozo. The regime answered with a hail of bullets, killing 28 people and wounding many. The Albany Rural Association responded by publishing its ARA Newsletter[23] almost entirely in Xhosa, sharply condemning the *"Bisho massacre, Federalism and de Klerk's new South Africa"*. It took until a month before the first democratic elections of 1994 that Gqozo and other homeland leaders finally stepped down and South Africa effectively became one state again.

'The Freedom and Consultation Era'

The release of Nelson Mandela and others from prison in 1990, marked the beginning of a long and difficult negotiation process. The National Party (NP) of F.W. de Klerk entered the negotiations with the African National Congress (ANC), the Inkatha Freedom Party (IFP) led by Mangosuthu Buthelezi[24], and a host of other parties and representatives of bantustan governments[25], varying from the extreme right to the extreme left. Obviously, the negotiations were complicated by South Africa's extremely polarized history, in which racial tensions abounded. Especially the undercover activities by the security forces[26] that continuously instigated violence between black groups, led to extremely tense moments during the negotiations. Thus, the Convention for a Democratic South Africa (CODESA) deadlocked several times until it was replaced by the Multi-Party Negotiating Forum. In that forum the good chemistry between the young Cyril Ramaphosa, a trade union leader who led the ANC delegation, and Roelf Meyer, a coming NP man, led to a breakthrough.

One of the most difficult problems in the negotiations concerned the issue of federalism. The National Party, other white parties and the Inkatha Freedom Party vied for a federalist state in which the provinces would have quite an independent position. The white Conservative Party even formed a coalition with the black IFP and leaders of the homelands. This Concerned South Africans Group (COSAG) aimed to retain 'independence' for the homelands and to secure other ethnically defined areas. Thus, the whites hoped to establish a 'volksstaat'[27] while someone like Buthelezi expected a Zulu province. However, the ANC strongly opposed ethnically defined provinces. Instead, it wanted a multi-party democracy with a strong national government, as it was confident that it would play a significant role in such an administration. With regard to these discussions and the upcoming elections the establishment of boundaries for the new provinces took on a whole new significance. New borders would have a great impact on the constituencies contained in the new provinces, which would, in turn, affect the chance of winning for the various parties. Another contentious issue during the negotiations concerned the percentage of votes needed to change the constitution. Especially the National Party feared a situation whereby the ANC could too easily change the constitution, which would effectively result in a one-party state.

The negotiations yielded three important results: the Transitional Executive Council (TEC), an interim constitution and the intended formation of a Government of National Unity after the elections. The TEC, in which several parties participated, took over from the National Party government in December 1993 in order to prepare the road for the first democratic elections in 1994. Moreover, the interim constitution –which was approved by Parliament on 18 December 1993– provided the TEC with the constitutional framework to achieve a multi-party democracy and stipulated the re-integration of the 'independent' bantustans. Another important element was the intended formation of a Government of National Unity (GNU) after the elections. In order to allay fears by the opposition –especially the white and Zulu minorities– of an ANC dominated government, Joe Slovo, a former hardliner of the South African Communist Party (SACP), had proposed the establishment of a Government of National Unity after the first democratic elections for a period of five years.

Although it is somewhat arbitrary to identify an exact date that marked the end of the 'struggle era' and the beginning of the 'freedom and consultation era', I regard 18 December as such a turning point. The adoption of the interim constitution represented a watershed moment in South African history. Although formally the 'struggle' was not yet over, a 'freedom and consultation discourse' established a firm foothold in progressive South African political circles.

The Rainbow Coalition

> *"We enter into a covenant that we shall build the society in which all South Africans, both black and white, will be able to walk tall, without any fear in their hearts, assured of their inalienable right to human dignity –a rainbow nation at peace with itself and the world"* (Mandela, May 10, 1994).

With these words, from his presidential inauguration speech, Nelson Mandela expressed his wish in May 1994 to build a peaceful multi-racial society, in which the colours of the peoples would no longer stand for hatred, oppression and segregation but for the colours of a rainbow. The rainbow came to symbolize a nation in which peace, reconciliation, consultation and co-operation would be the central values. That nation would be led by the Government of National Unity: 'the Rainbow Coalition'. In the GNU the tripartite alliance –an alliance between the ANC, the SACP and the Congress of South African Trade Unions (COSATU)– was joined by de Klerk's National Party (NP) and Buthelezi's Inkatha Freedom Party (IFP). The tripartite alliance was –and still is– a unique feature in South African politics as it is a cooperative arrangement between two political parties –the ANC and the SACP– and a civil society organization, COSATU. COSATU and the SACP participated in the elections on the ANC ticket. Its merits and its complexities are extensively explored in this chapter.

The term 'rainbow coalition' is exemplary of the optimistic and euphoric 'freedom and consultation discourse' that dominated South African politics between 1993 and 1996. Its image of racial reconciliation and cooperation was also made visible in the new South African flag, in which the ANC flag and the old South African flag were combined. Moreover, it was made audible in the new national anthem that combined the black 'Nkosi Sikilel iAfrika' and the white 'Die Stem van Suid Afrika'. For the ANC the 'rainbow coalition' was an attractive compromise because the party feared the possibility of a 'race war'. Besides the threat of violence from white extremist groups, the party also feared possible violent eruptions in KwaZulu-Natal. This former homeland had witnessed some of the most violent eruptions of black on black violence, usually along 'ethnic'[28] lines –which were in fact often political in nature– between Inkatha Freedom Party Supporters and ANC supporters. Moreover, a Government of National Unity fitted in with one of Mandela's most important philosophies: his firm belief in reconciliation. Reconciliation involved (re-)creating trust, peace and understanding between the peoples that had been locked in a racial war for many decades. This meant that the ANC tried to avoid humiliating the National Party that had lost its position of domination, by reaching out to them and offering them a place in this transitional cabinet. However, besides Mandela's idealism there were also economic considerations involved in the idea of power-sharing as the ANC feared a massive white business exodus. By appointing De Klerk as Deputy-President and by appointing someone like the NP's Chris Liebenberg as Minister of Finance, the ANC hoped to alleviate white fears of extreme leftism and economic instability.

Failure of the Government of National Unity

Although it made a promising start, the Government of National Unity did not last the full five years. Since the National Party became an accessory to black empowerment and restoring black rights, de Klerk feared the declining support of whites. Thus, in June of 1996 the NP withdrew from the cabinet. Strategically, it coincided with the completion of the negotiations on the final constitution. Being at the centre of power during these negotiations, the NP was able to effectively influence the outcome of a document that would be crucial for all South Africans –including the white minority– in the coming decades. One of the most contentious issues, for example, was the so-called Property Clause. In the eyes of the National Party it was important to entrench property rights in the constitution as the ghost of widespread expropriation haunted them. 'The whites' feared losing the wealth they had amassed over the past centuries. Therefore, the National Party was intent on securing a property clause in the constitution that would protect property rights and prevent expropriation.

The ANC, on the other hand, felt that a democratic government should have the power to expropriate certain assets like land and property when it was for the common good. Especially in a post-apartheid situation where whites still held most of the country's assets and no equality between the races could be achieved without redistribution, expropriation was seen as a possible instrument. With regard to land, for instance, the black population had been systematically removed from more than 80% of the land over a period of centuries. As a result, the ANC did not see the need to protect the property rights of citizens in the new constitution. In fact, Mandela's party preferred to keep the section on property rights outside the constitution. However, during the negotiations on the final constitution in 1995 and 1996 it became clear that the National Party would not accept anything less than a property clause. Thus, when a property clause appeared to become unavoidable, the alliance did everything to make sure that the section on expropriation would spell out some exceptional circumstances that could justify it. In the end the property clause came to reflect both points of view. On the one hand it protected the property rights of citizens. On the other hand it reflected the ANC's point of view in that expropriation would be allowed under certain conditions –*for a public purpose*– which included *"...the nations commitment to land reform..."*[29].

This satisfied the NP, and, as the constitution was approved, de Klerk decided that the ANC could be best fought from the opposition benches. As a result, after only two years in government, the NP left the Rainbow Coalition. The ANC –the alliance– and the IFP remained behind. However, instead of a boost in support for the National Party its resignation from government signalled the beginning of a period of further decline and in-fighting. A year later, de Klerk resigned as party leader. Furthermore, some of the more 'progressive' members, like its top-negotiator Roelf Meyer, left the party. He teamed up with former homeland leader Bantu Holomisa –who had been kicked out of the ANC– in order to establish what they called, *"the first multi-racial party"*, the United Democratic Movement (UDM).

The Madiba Years
The first five years after the democratic elections could be termed 'the Madiba years'. It was the period in which Nelson Mandela –his clan name 'Madiba' was lovingly embraced by the whole nation– 'preached' reconciliation, reconciliation and reconciliation. This continued to be important as the NP quit the Government of National Unity since Mandela remained aware of the white minority's feelings of vulnerability. Wherever he made a speech and with whomever he debated, he always referred to the need for all the peoples of South Africa to live and work together for a common future. For Nelson Mandela this need to avoid polarization in a nation that was divided often involved walking on eggs. On the one hand he had to satisfy the demands of the 'black masses' that had suffered tremendously during apartheid. They did not only need an acknowledgement of that suffering, but also expected immediate and concrete improvements in their social and economic position. These high expectations led to great pressure on Mandela, the ANC and the cabinet. Especially after they had initially formulated some very ambitious targets, like the delivery of one million new low-cost houses in the first term of government. On the other hand he had to consider the position of the (white) establishment, both in government and in business, which held many of South Africa's bureaucratic and economic cards for the future. A major dilemma in this regard concerned the question of how to deal with the crimes that had been perpetrated against the oppressed during apartheid. How could the new government make sure that the perpetrators of crimes were punished without

antagonizing the white minority too much? The Truth and Reconciliation Commission (TRC) was seen as the right solution.

The TRC, headed by the charismatic former Anglican Archbishop and Nobel Prize winner Desmond Tutu, was appointed in 1995 to investigate the human rights abuses that had taken place during the apartheid years. In public hearings the direct and indirect victims were given the chance to speak and cry out. These frequently heartbreaking submissions were broadcast on radio and television and were meant to help cleanse the nation by giving a voice to the victims. Moreover, the perpetrators were given a chance to confess their crimes at these hearings. This frequently led to extremely emotional confrontations between the victim and the culprit. The scenes are etched in our memories: Tutu, in his purple robe, breaking down in tears after a particularly horrendous and emotional story told by a victim; the white, former security police officer who demonstrated some of his torturing tactics with an actor on the floor of the hearings building; the white interrogators of murdered black Eastern Cape activist Steve Biko, who told the audience that they had not beaten Biko with his head against the wall, but that he had fallen after a scuffle…; and, of course, the defiant ex-wife of Mandela, Winnie Madikizela-Mandela who maintained her innocence in the hearings concerning the killings committed by her team of bodyguards: 'the Mandela Football Club'.

Although the TRC was accused of a bias in favour of the black population –in my view it seemed only natural to devote more attention to the millions of blacks who suffered than to the relatively small group of whites who suffered at the hands of the ANC– also white victims of ANC attacks were given the chance to speak out. When the perpetrators asked for amnesty, a sub-committee –called the Amnesty Committee– proceeded to consider whether they had given full disclosure about the crimes they had committed. If this was the case the perpetrators were granted amnesty. If not, they remained in prison or were imprisoned. However, the amnesty committee made at least one gross mistake when it granted amnesty to a large group of highly placed ANC officials –some were government ministers– without having heard their submissions. Although the committee withdrew its amnesty grants within weeks, much damage had been done as it fuelled the opposition's accusations of being biased. When the final report came out in 1998 it all became quite messy when former president de Klerk managed to obtain a court ruling that prevented certain passages about him to be published. Moreover, to Tutu's dismay even the ANC tried to fight the publication of some sections. Although nationally the TRC's healing powers were hotly debated, Mandela's and Tutu's efforts to heal the nation earned them and their 'rainbow nation' high acclaim in the international arena.

Another instrument the Mandela government used for reconciliation and nation-building was sports. When the international bans against South Africa were lifted, following the first democratic elections, South African teams were allowed to compete again in the major sporting events of the world. The first significant sporting event that was hosted in South Africa was the rugby world cup in 1995. By personally supporting the national team –consisting mostly of whites– Mandela rallied the whole nation behind the team that eventually won the title. Moreover, South African athletes competed in the Olympics –a black South African won the marathon– and South Africa made an unsuccessful bid to host the games in Cape Town in 2004.

Furthermore, to the nation's excitement the national soccer team –'the bafana bafana'– represented their country in the soccer world cup of 1998. Ultimately, South Africa has high hopes of hosting the world cup in the 21st century. However, the nation's poor record on the crime front may endanger that bid.

Indeed, one of the most difficult problems the Mandela government faced concerned the worsening crime wave in the country. The crime situation is particularly worrying in the bigger cities. However, a spate of farm killings in the late nineties, whereby especially white farmers were targeted, also required the government's attention. Besides the fact that South African citizens feel insecure, the situation also adversely affects the tourism industry and foreign investment. In fact, it is such a serious problem that I am aware that it can hardly be discussed in a meaningful manner in only one paragraph. However, if the situation does not improve in the next decade, South Africa may well end up being shunned by the international community again. That would be disastrous for its emerging tourist industry and its international and cherished image of being 'the rainbow nation'.

In the international arena Mandela and his cabinet have tried their best to play a positive role. However, not all interventions proved successful. One of the first international efforts concerned the protest against the execution of Ken Saro Wiwa in Nigeria. The Nigerian regime was not amused and a long chill in the relations between the countries followed. Also Mandela's peace efforts in Zaire/the Democratic Republic of Congo did not yield the desired results. Moreover, Mandela's public praise of Mobutu and Kabila – *"two of Africa's great sons"*– during the negotiations could not be taken entirely seriously. However, the most serious glitch became South Africa's military intervention in Lesotho. After chaos had broken out, following the Lesotho elections in 1998, the South African military moved in without first seeking approval of the Lesotho king. To make matters worse, Mandela was out of the country during the intervention in which the South African military blundered.

Nevertheless, Mandela will also be remembered for some remarkable achievements. Through shuttle diplomacy he managed to solve the deadlock around the Lockerbie bombers, whereby he convinced Colonel Gadaffi to extradite the perpetrators to Scottish police on Dutch soil. Especially, Mandela's response – *"I am the master of my own fate"*– to Bill Clinton's criticism that he had dealings with a terrorist country, showed Mandela's deeply rooted sense of autonomy. Mandela and the ANC also tried to suggest ways of solving the Northern Ireland deadlock, for which former Prime Minister Major scorned them. However, a few years later Tony Blair went ahead and an ANC delegation was invited to share their experiences in peaceful negotiations with the Irish.

Furthermore, to underline the country's independent position and improve its economic situation, the cabinet sought close ties with Middle-East and Asian countries, like Saudi Arabia, Iran, Malaysia, Indonesia and China. Although admirable as 'South-South initiatives', the dealings with dictators and authoritarian regimes also led to much international and human rights groups criticism. The latter also criticized Mandela for bestowing South Africa's highest award on people like Gadaffi and Indonesian dictator Suharto.

The Tripartite Alliance
In order to form a strong opposition to the National Party government, Mandela and his party sought support from other parties when the ANC was unbanned in 1991. Moreover, as the ANC could not fall back on well-established party structures in the country, it needed to make use of the structures of other actors. As a result, the tripartite alliance was born, consisting of the ANC, the Congress of South African Trade Unions (COSATU) with its large membership base, and the South African Communist Party (SACP). As COSATU could mobilize its members, the alliance proved to be crucial when it was needed to flex some muscle during the CODESA negotiations. Subsequently, the three parties decided to run together on the ANC ticket in the first democratic elections. Moreover, it was decided to sustain their co-operative arrangement beyond the elections. In the arrangement, in which the individual parties continued to exist independently from one another, the ANC, COSATU and the SACP bundled their powers and resources under the ANC umbrella. In other words, the ANC would take part in the elections, whereby some of the candidates would originate from its own ranks, while others came from the ranks of COSATU and the SACP. This was not so extraordinary as many ANC members were members of COSATU and/or the SACP as well. Through this mechanism, COSATU and the SACP supplied parliamentarians and even government ministers in the Mandela cabinet.

Moreover, the ANC-led alliance worked together with other civic actors in drafting the Reconstruction and Development Programme, or RDP (ANC, 1994). The document that will be extensively discussed in the next section oozes a 'freedom and consultation discourse'. After it served as an election document, it was adopted by the Government of National Unity as a leading document, outlining South Africa's social, economic and political transformation. The alliance, in fact, symbolizes the ideology and rhetoric of the Reconstruction and Development Programme (RDP) that calls for a *"people-driven process"* (1994, p. 5). Although the trade union movement is said to belong to civil society, its participation in parliament and government structures through the alliance, gives civil society –or as some would say: 'the people'– a direct say in government affairs. However, other analysts believe that COSATU has been co-opted by participating in the alliance, as a result of which it lost its position of critical independence. In this view it is thought that by participating in government COSATU has dirtied its hands and granted the ANC too much leverage over its critical position in civil society. Moreover, COSATU itself regularly seems unhappy with the performance of the alliance, especially after the government adopted the macro-economic strategy GEAR (Growth, Employment and Redistribution) without thorough consultation of the alliance partners. In COSATU's view the adoption and implementation of GEAR endangered the implementation of the progressive RDP. Nevertheless, even after the 1999 elections, the alliance still continues to dominate the South African political scene.

Besides causing tension among its participants, the ANC-led alliance also causes confusion for the general public and analysts because of the blurring boundaries between the state and civil society. The mechanisms of control and consultation are vague and one gets the impression –see the above example– that it is just the ANC that rules. However, whenever it is convenient the ANC can claim alliance –read: civil society– support to justify its actions. Yet this support must be treated with caution as COSATU in a 1996 discussion paper has stated that *"...there have been very few substantial meetings of the Alliance"* (1996, p. 3). Of course the ANC-dominated cabinet is accountable to Parliament, in which the ANC-led alliance has the majority, but the ANC does not always seem to be accountable to its alliance partners. Although the ANC rhetoric is saturated with terms like 'consultation', 'empowerment' and 'the people must own the transformation process' it seems that in the case of the alliance the ANC does not take its own rhetoric too seriously.

Even nowadays the situation remains awkward for COSATU. After the elections in 1999, for example, it organized country-wide strikes for higher wages, while at the same time it was, through the alliance, part of the decisions in the Mbeki cabinet, against which it agitated. Thus, one could argue that the alliance weakens the strength and independence of South African civil society. Even for other civil society organizations, like the South African National Civics Organization (SANCO) and progressive NGOs, while not formally being part of the alliance, it is hard to regain their position of critical independence held before the 1994 elections, as this book will show. These organizations fought alongside the ANC, SACP and COSATU against the apartheid enemy and now find that they have to criticize their former comrades in government. This can lead to feelings of embarrassment, especially as this is also done by the new opposition –the National Party, the Democratic Party and some of the right-wing parties– in parliament. Thus, by voicing such criticism the civic organizations and NGOs may feel that they betray the ANC and 'the struggle' by being on the same side as the 'former enemy'.

The Reconstruction and Development Programme (RDP)
In my view the Reconstruction and Development Programme is the most crucial and influential document in the transitional years between 1993 and 1996. It was drafted in the same period in which the CODESA and the Multi-Party Negotiating Forum negotiations took place and it reflects the 'freedom and consultation discourse' of that period. The ANC published the programme in early 1994 and termed it a *"...coherent socio-economic policy framework..."* (1994, p. 1). It was the result of a long consultation process between the alliance partners and other civil society organizations like the South African National Civics Organization (SANCO). Before serving as the Rainbow Coalition's foremost policy document –a point of departure– it served as an election document for the progressive ANC-led alliance as it spelled out how the alliance planned to transform South African society in the post-apartheid era.

The 147-page booklet covers a wide variety of subjects, related to the reconstruction and development of South African society. Besides chapters on *Meeting Basic Needs* and *Developing Human resources*, it, for example, also contains chapters on *Building the Economy* and *Democratizing the State and Society*. It is a very optimistic document, as it was drafted just before the alliance came to power. Typical of the freedom and consultation discourse, it expresses high hopes for the possibilities of fundamentally transforming the country through consultation. A document full of visions, ideas, hopes, aims and plans for a better future for all. It was a time when the ANC still believed in many of its initial ideas, without having yet been disappointed by the actual difficulties of governing a nation in an increasingly globalized context. The RDP, therefore, oozes a freedom and consultation rhetoric that is hardly problematized:

> *"The central objective of our Reconstruction and Development Programme (RDP) is to improve the quality of life of all South Africans, and in particular the most poor and marginalized sections of our communities. This objective should be realised through a process of empowerment which gives the poor control over their lives and increases their ability to mobilise sufficient development resources, including from the democratic government where necessary" (ANC, 1994, p.15).*

Notwithstanding such flaws –who are these 'poor', and what does 'empowerment' entail?– the Reconstruction and Development Programme was eventually adopted by Parliament after the elections. Moreover, a separate Reconstruction and Development Ministry was established, to carry out the RDP.

The ANC-led alliance aimed to meet several concrete targets –others would call them promises in the light of the 1994 elections– in their first five-year term as part of a Government of National Unity (GNU). The most notorious target was formulated thus:

> *"At minimum, one million low-cost houses should be constructed over five years. These units should be specifically intended for low-income households and should include the rural areas" (p. 22).*

However, after several years in government the ANC realized that these targets should have never been spelled out so concretely, as they boomeranged back from the opposition benches and a disgruntled South African public. Especially during the first few years in government the GNU failed dismally with respect to housing delivery and other RDP targets. Therefore, the decision was taken in 1996 to do away with the separate RDP Ministry and transfer the responsibility for the programme to the Deputy President's[30] office. Although in later years the delivery rate somewhat picked up, the target of one million houses in five years was never reached and haunted the Mandela administration until the end.

The above may give the false impression that the RDP lacked all sense of realism. However the document, in fact, contains many valuable ideas and plans that found their way –albeit altered and adapted– to several Green Papers and White Papers published by the government in later years. Thus, some White papers can be discovered in the RDP in a rudimentary form. An example is the section on land reform in the RDP that states that:

> *"the land reform programme has two aspects: **redistribution** of residential and productive land to those who need it but cannot afford it, and **restitution** for those who lost land because of apartheid laws"* (p. 20).

The Green Paper on Land Policy, that was subsequently published by the Department of Land Affairs 1996, and which was followed by a White Paper on South African Land Policy in 1997, indeed identified these as two important pillars of land reform. However, tenure reform, as a third pillar, was added later. The RDP contained the rudiments, but the government could only fill in the details after it had become more acquainted with budgetary, legal and institutional bottlenecks.

To conclude, I would like to remark that the freedom and consultation discourse cannot be analyzed without taking into account the Reconstruction and Development Programme. The RDP, in turn, should be seen as the product of its era, when a progressive buzz of euphoria and expectation was in the air.

The Monti Rural Association during the Freedom and Consultation Era

As the political climate relaxed in the South African territories –as mentioned above the Ciskei areas remained problematic longer– the Albany Rural Association relocated to East London in 1993. This coastal city was situated in the Border area itself (see Map 1.1). Since the security forces were not as oppressive in white university towns, compared to the Border area, it had actually been an advantage to operate from Grahamstown during the early years of its existence. Now the time had come to move into its area of operation. As the move, in some way, marked a new start, the organization also changed its name into the Monti Rural Association (MRA). This name reflected its main area of operation, since *Monti* was the Xhosa name for the main city in the Border area: East London.

To mirror the fact that communities were no longer under threat of forced removal, as 'formal' apartheid had come to its end, the MRA logo was altered too. We still see a Xhosa woman with her child walking away from us, but instead of a trunk she is carrying a bucket –of water?– on her head. Thus, the logo now seemed to refer to issues of 'development'. This was in line with new structural and directional strategies of the organization that had been adopted in 1992 together with the establishment of the so-called Development Support Programme. Compared to the early 'development' work, that had been much more comprehensive, MRA's focus now shifted towards more 'classical' development initiatives: agricultural projects and the provision of infrastructure and services, like water, and pre-schools.

This new direction was also reflected in revamping the ARA Newsletter, which was renamed *Groundwork*. Again, it showed that the organization was changing its focus from resettlement and forced removals to rural development. Therefore, in the first Groundwork article – *"Putting the poorest first, why black rural communities need development"*– the organization gave its updated view on 'development':

> *"...Development is much more than (...) economic growth. The process should gradually improve living conditions (...). This is achieved through democracy (...). Domination and exploitation of the majority by a specific group or by outsiders is not development (...) all sectors of the community need to participate in the development business"[31].*

As more 'traditional' development issues were linked to issues of democracy, the organization, in 1993, mainly concentrated on the problems and policy issues that could be expected after the democratic elections. What should a land reform programme look like? How could the dispossessed black population (re-)gain access to land? What would be the role of women in the rural areas? What type of local government structures would be needed?

In addition, 1993 was the year of the *"Back to the Land Campaign"*[32], in which MRA played a significant role. The campaign aimed to put the issue of land on the national agenda. Therefore, MRA organized delegates from 18 Border communities to take part in demonstrations outside the national multi-party negotiations at the World Trade Centre in Kempton Park, in order to pressure delegates to take the plight of the rural poor seriously: *"There can be no peace until the emotional issue of land is settled"*[33].

In 1994 two events had a major impact on the work of the Monti Rural Association: the Community Land Conference and the first national democratic elections. On February 12 more than 1,000 representatives from rural communities all over South Africa were assembled by the National Land Committee (NLC)[34] affiliates. MRA became the main organizer in the Eastern Cape and ensured that many delegates from more than 20 communities were selected to represent the rural population. In a successful exercise the delegates debated the future of the rural areas. Moreover a *Land Charter* –compare the ANC Freedom Charter in the fifties– was formulated: *"We the marginalized people of South Africa, who are landless and land hungry, declare our needs for all the world to know..."*[35].

However the most significant event in South Africa's recent history took place from April 26 to April 29: the country's first democratic elections. Although one would not expect a land sector NGO to take part in the preparations for a national election, the significance of the event caused all the pro-democracy forces in South Africa to assume their responsibility. As a result, the MRA staff spent the large part of the month of April educating rural voters in the Border area. In that month the entire issue of Groundwork was devoted to the elections, containing pictorials of how-to-vote and explanations about the new political system in South Africa. Furthermore, MRA drew attention to the position of women: *"...the upcoming election on April 27 will be the first time black women will have the opportunity to put their cross on a ballot paper..."*[36].

After the elections NGOs like MRA spent much of their time and resources to study, discuss and comment on the new legislation and policies that the government put forward. It was a time when the boundaries between the NGO sector and the government blurred as so-called *Strategic Task teams* were set up to implement the government's Reconstruction and Development Programme (RDP). In these teams the government cooperated closely with the NGO sector in order to discuss the options for land reform and, for example, rural local government. MRA and other National Land Committee (NLC) affiliates had now become close, but critical, allies of Mandela's rainbow coalition. New national policies and legislation had become their number one priority. It was the future of South Africa that was designed –including a new constitution– and thus provided a historic opportunity to influence the country's destiny.

To make maximum use of this period of historic opportunity, the Monti Rural Association also stepped up its research efforts in 1994 and 1995. With a research staff of five and a British[37] visiting consultant several important research contributions were made, often in collaboration with other local research institutions. Amongst the most significant outputs were:

- an *Eastern Cape Regional Overview* for the newly formed Land and Agricultural Policy Centre (LAPC);
- the *Eastern Cape Land Reform Pilot Project Pre-Planning Report* for the LAPC;
- a submission on land tenure issues to the new government concerning the drafting of a Green Paper on Land Reform;
- a Thornhill Social Survey.

Most of these reports were well received and put to use by policy makers, academics and other NGOs. Thus, for the first time, a comprehensive database of communities and land-related issues in the Eastern Cape was created. It was valuable work that connected MRA staff directly to the highest government circles –like the Department of Land Affairs– where the future land reform programme was drafted.

Moreover, the Monti Rural Association continued to support rural communities in their quest for land. At the end of 1995 MRA could claim a historic victory as the Minister of Land Affairs, Derek Hanekom, handed over the Gallawater farm to members of the Zweledinga community. It made them the first beneficiaries of the Land Reform Programme in the Eastern Cape. Having made use of a new land Act[38], the community members were able to access government subsidies in order to purchase the farm from a white farmer. At the celebration the Minister said:

"...we are celebrating reconciliation, co-operation and successful negotiations between a landowner, a landless community and the state. And somewhere in between these three there is a small NGO called the Monti Rural Association, which played a vital role in bringing these three together and making it happen (...). The country and indeed the world is watching communities like Zweledinga...".

To which the MRA co-ordinator, Mavis Beechwood, added in her speech:

"...many eyes will be watching the progress of the Gallawater farm and the community has an enormous responsibility to make a success of sustainable farming for the sake of other communities who are hoping to benefit from land reform"[39].

The transfer of the land marked a hopeful development, and many expected great things for the future.

The 'New Realism Era'

As was discussed above, June 1996, can be identified as another watershed period in recent South African history. Not only did the National Party leave the Government of National Unity, it was also the time that the alliance and the IFP presented the new Minister of Finance –a post that had been filled by the NP before. The whole nation held its breath when they heard that the man to do the job would be Trevor Manuel, a man with a radical communist background. Many commentators feared widespread nationalizations and a much more radical socio-economic policy. However, the opposite was the case. On June 14, 1996 Manuel introduced a macro-economic strategy that was criticized by many as being South Africa's own neo-liberal structural adjustment policy. In my view, this introduction of the Growth, Employment And Redistribution (GEAR) strategy should be marked as another turning point in progressive South African politics. When GEAR was introduced it immediately became clear that the honeymoon was over. The ANC-led government, stepped off its pink cloud after two years of experience with governing the country and being exposed to the harsh realities of the world market. It marked the beginning of what I have termed 'a new realism era', which also yielded a new political discourse.

This 'new realism discourse' reflected the realities of governing a country with an emerging economy that inherited many apartheid problems: enormous inequalities between the 'races', a major unemployment problem and an export sector that experienced significant difficulties with competing in the world market. Thus, the progressive forces, which had become part of the government establishment, and had shed most of its 'struggle discourse', that had dominated the late eighties, were willing to consider another route. When GEAR was made public, they expressed the need to trade in their 'freedom and consultation discourse' that had inspired many in the early nineties, for a 'new realism discourse'. Below, I discuss the RDP, GEAR and the resulting conflicts and dilemmas as these exemplify some of the most difficult and fundamental problems faced by the first democratic South African government. Moreover, I believe that this 'new realism discourse' also led to a significant impact on 'the ground'. In later chapters it will be shown in detail how government departments in the field and NGOs found themselves confronted with policies, regulations and an 'atmosphere' that had thoroughly changed after the introduction of GEAR in 1996.

GEAR is what it states it is: a macro-economic *"...strategy for rebuilding and restructuring the economy..."* (Department of Finance, 1998, p. 1). The document contains sections on *Fiscal Policy* and *Monetary and Exchange Rate Policy*, but also a section on *Social and Sectoral Policies*. However, already in its first section the importance of the RDP is mentioned by stating that in the context of GEAR:

> *"...we can successfully confront the related challenges of meeting basic needs, developing human resources, increasing participation in the democratic institutions of civil society and implementing the RDP in all its facets"* (p. 1).

Nevertheless, GEAR led to a storm of protests from 'the left' who accused the government that it was South Africa's own internal neo-liberally inspired structural adjustment programme. In its 1996 Annual Report, for example, the Monti Rural Association (1996b) states that *"...GEAR is a classic neo-liberal policy document or self-imposed structural adjustment programme..."* (p. 7). In this regard it did not help that GEAR's introduction coincided with the decision to get rid of the RDP Ministry. It gave the impression that the RDP was no longer a guiding policy document.

It is true that the emphasis of GEAR is on the economic position of South Africa in a global context. It analyzes the economic situation and spells out what measures can be taken to stimulate growth and guard against economic decline. GEAR paints quite a bleak picture of the situation in 1996:

> *"...present trends in the economy lead to employment growth of 100,000 to 130,000 per year, with unemployment rising to 37 % by the year 2000..."* (p. 15).

To counter such negative trends, the government's main concern was to increase economic growth. GEAR outlined the need and the options for reducing the budget deficit, avoiding increases in the overall tax burden, abolishing exchange controls and stimulating job growth and foreign investment. Nevertheless the document also pointed to the need for public investments in education, health and welfare, and housing, land reform and infrastructure, because:

> "...progress in all these areas adds to the quality of life in communities, while simultaneously building productive economic capacity" (p. 14).

However, it stipulated that this must be done responsibly in order to avoid budget deficits, inflation and balance of payment difficulties. As a result, one of the major concerns voiced in GEAR is that the government prevents a wage-price spiral at all costs: *"...it is important that wage and salary increases do not rise more than productivity growth..."* (p. 18). For this reason its social partners, and especially organized labour, were asked to behave responsibly.

At the end of the GEAR document we find a crucial statement concerning the limits of consultation. Although the RDP saw no limits to the consultative process between the government and civil society organizations, GEAR leaves no doubt as to who is in charge. Indicative of a 'new realism discourse', GEAR clarifies who has the ultimate responsibility:

> *"Government has a clear policy coordination role. There are trade-offs amongst policy options and competing claims by different interest groups which need to be nationally resolved. Whilst institutions have been developed to aid this process, and Government is committed to an open and consultative approach, the ultimate responsibilities for a credible and coherent policy framework lies with Government"* (p. 19).

Thus, the GEAR document for the first time clearly indicated that the honeymoon was over. Ultimately, it is the responsibility of the government to coordinate and make decisions, especially in the light of competing claims. In the next section I explore whether the critics of GEAR do have a point.

GEAR versus the RDP

As was mentioned above, the Congress of South African Trade Unions (COSATU), one of the alliance partners, became one of the fiercest opponents of the GEAR strategy. Its criticism concerned the procedure of formulating the strategy as well as its neo-liberal content. According to COSATU (1996), GEAR was *"...presented to the Alliance as a fait accompli..."* (p. 4). Therefore, in its 1996 discussion paper the trade union accused the ANC of low democratic standards. It expressed that the RDP should continue to be the main policy framework and should not be replaced by GEAR:

> *"The programme of the democratic movement, the RDP, has been systematically undermined by a range of forces (...) from other political parties, as well as local and international forces, particularly business. (...) the logic of transformation, as contained in the RDP, has been overpowered by that of the forces attempting to halt transformation"* (p. 6).

In other words, *"...the RDP should remain the programme of the Alliance"* (p. 14). By 1999, COSATU's (1999) message remained unchanged: *"As a federation we must continue to oppose the GEAR strategy"* (p. 18) and *"discourage and oppose any form of neo-liberal approach in an attempt to resolve socio-economic problems"* (p. 19).

When examining these statements it becomes clear that COSATU was not satisfied with its role in the alliance. In the South African Labour bulletin Buhlungu (1997) noted this dissatisfaction of COSATU with its role. He suggested that COSATU should seriously study other options in order to regain some of its independence:
> "...trade unions, particularly those which are powerful, do have alternative ways of influencing ruling political parties..." (p. 77).

However, instead of retreating back to its position in civil society after the first five-year term in government, COSATU remained in the alliance after the second democratic elections in 1999 that brought Thabo Mbeki to power.

Closer analysis of the matter reveals some discrepancies and difficulties in COSATU's stance. First of all, it is problematic to present the GEAR-RDP controversy as an either/or debate as COSATU spokespeople frequently do. In my view the RDP is visionary document that was written as a guidance document –and election document– for reconstruction and development in post-apartheid South Africa. GEAR, on the other hand, outlines a macro-economic strategy that deals with the concrete economic parameters; possibilities and impossibilities. It stipulates a path, by outlining the financial, fiscal, monetary and budgetary constraints, for the responsible implementation of the main pillars of the Reconstruction and Development Programme. That is why in the GEAR document there is a constant reference to the RDP. One could say that the RDP is a 'dream document' while GEAR is an 'implementation document. True, GEAR sets a path for a South Africa (re-)entering the world market after years of forced isolation, while COSATU (1996), on the other hand, calls for a more interventionist state. COSATU envisaged a dominant role for parastatals and more public control of private funds and the Reserve Bank.

Secondly, not only does GEAR constantly refer to the RDP, the RDP itself actually contains many of the rudimentary ideas that guide GEAR:
> "The RDP will mean nothing if it cannot be financed (...). The existing ratios of deficit, borrowing and taxation are part of our macro-economic problem. In meeting the financing needs of the RDP and retaining macro stability during its implementation, particular attention will be paid to these ratios. The emphasis will be on ensuring a growing GDP" (ANC, p. 142-143).

Thus, it is not difficult to argue that GEAR is in fact the concretization of ideas that were already outlined in the RDP. Like the rudiments of many Green and White Papers, the rudiments of GEAR are present in the RDP.

Thirdly, it becomes clear, when analyzing COSATU's documents, that the federation has remained behind in time. Although they embrace the RDP with its 'freedom and consultation discourse', its own documents still ooze an eighties 'struggle discourse': *"how do we characterize this phase of our struggle?"* (1996, p. 9). It is a discourse that colours the type of solutions proposed by COSATU. For example, in order to solve the economic crisis and ensure the implementation of the RDP, COSATU called for the *"...mass mobilisation of our members..."* (1996, p. 27). In my view such 1980's rhetoric will not solve concrete socio-economic problems. However, although such solutions seem outdated and unrealistic, I believe that it is important that COSATU plays the role it does; fiercely opposing the neo-liberal side of the politics of the democratic government. For a well-functioning democracy several strong players inside and outside the government are necessary, representing extreme and opposing views. In that light one can question whether it is wise that COSATU is part of the government that it needs to monitor. With regard to democracy and civil society building they should, perhaps, consider leaving the alliance.

One of the forums in which the GEAR versus RDP debate features is NEDLAC, the National Economic and Development Council. It is an institutional arrangement –typical of the new South Africa and the RDP 'freedom and consultation discourse'– where government, organized labour, business, and, what the government calls 'community representatives' come together to negotiate economic development issues. Through consultation and consensus-building agreements are reached to facilitate economic progress. In its four chambers, 'Labour Market', 'Trade & Industry', 'Public Finance and Monetary Policy' and 'Development', separate but overlapping spheres of the economy are discussed. Non-governmental organizations were invited to take part in the fourth chamber. Although many applaud this consultative approach, others, like Friedman and Reitzes (1996), warn for similar problems as encountered in the tripartite alliance, where the government effectively seems to have neutralized and co-opted COSATU. Friedman and Reitzes see the emergence of a privileged group of civil society organizations, that is slowly neutralized and co-opted in a corporatist fashion. In their view this is a negative trend, since civil society constitutes more than a limited group of progressive organizations. A certain distance to government is needed to remain critical.

In conclusion I would argue that the publication of GEAR marked the advance of *'real politik'* in South Africa, whereby a 'new realism discourse' swept the national and regional political landscapes. This led to tensions within the alliance between those on 'the left' –who held on to values and ideals from the 'the struggle era' and the 'freedom and consultation era– and those who adopted a 'new' view of development, inspired by the realities of governing and South Africa's place in a global economy. The publication of GEAR also had a profound impact on the relations between former comrades in the NGO sector and those who had moved into government. The atmosphere changed and relations became more business-like. In the arena of land reform, for example, the focus changed from re-establishing the rights of Africans to land to an approach in which 'economic viability' became the keyword. Thus, in the land sector the honeymoon was ending as well.

The Monti Rural Association during the New Realism Era

Disappointingly, 1996 became a year of crisis for the Monti Rural Association. It became a watershed year in the history of the organization, at the end of which most of the 'old guard' had left the organization. From the moment the new government took office in 1994, an enormous demand for a progressive and well-trained workforce was created. As a result, NGO staff was 'head-hunted' by the government in order to replace apartheid bureaucrats. For MRA it meant that by the end of 1996 more than seven people had left the organization. Of course, such a tremendous 'brain drain' created many problems and added to the confusion that was caused by another restructuring exercise. Therefore, an external evaluation[40] commissioned by HUVO[41] –a Dutch funder– identified several weaknesses in the organization. Besides a lack of strategic direction it was stated that the restructuring process could draw MRA away from the essential roles it had once formulated: *"...policy, advocacy and, development support"* (p. 57). At the end of the crisis year even the coordinator had left the organization.

Dudley Eastwood, the new director, appointed in 1997, set out to get MRA back on track. Not only were all systems, policies and procedures overhauled, also an attempt was made to regain a political profile. In that respect the Farm Worker Campaign became crucial. This campaign –behind which MRA became one of the driving forces– was aimed to influence the Extension of Security of Tenure Bill, that was being drafted by the government. This legislation would have a significant impact on the rights of black farm workers and farm dwellers on white farms. MRA and other NGOs thought that these people deserved to obtain secure rights to the land that they had inhabited for many generations, but was formally owned by the white farmers. Moreover, the organizations saw a need to protect the workers against arbitrary evictions, which still occurred frequently.

The campaign entailed months of information dissemination and lobbying and advocacy whereby a large part of the farm worker population was reached in the Eastern Cape. It was a logistical nightmare as many of the farms were in remote areas and white farmers were often hostile. A second crucial step in the process entailed assembling these workers and dwellers at a two-day provincial summit in Grahamstown to discuss their demands. Subsequently, a delegation of farm workers delivered a submission to a parliamentary committee in Cape Town. The results of the campaign were somewhat disappointing. However, although, ultimately, many of the demands were not met, the MRA staff still believed that the final version of the Extension of Security of Tenure Act did give farm workers more rights, especially with respect to arbitrary evictions.

Besides the Farm Worker Campaign, the director initiated another restructuring exercise. The Monti Rural Association (1997a) formulated the *Strategic Direction 1997-1999*, and organized a *Funders Summit*. It was remarkable that an NGO took the initiative to discuss fundamental issues with its funders. The summit, where all of MRA's funders were invited, had two main aims: 1. the gathering of information regarding the future of funding in order to prepare a sustainability plan; 2. the rationalization and streamlining of reporting formats and procedures. Regarding the latter point, much progress was made which greatly eased MRA's reporting requirements. The first point, however, created much unrest and uneasiness in the organization, as the negative message with regard to the future of funding was quite unsettling. Several funders explained that they would pull out of South Africa after the transition period 1994-1999. As a result, MRA became temporarily rather preoccupied with its own organizational survival, especially since 'sustainability' had become yet another buzz-word in development circles.

Thus, a sustainability plan was drafted in which the possibilities for fundraising, income generation/cost recovery, cost reduction and even investment options were explored. It led to major changes in 1997-1998:
- MRA's work was divided in programme work and community-based work, whereby the latter would be undertaken through government contracts;

- in order to get easier access to government contracts, MRA changed its legal status from a Voluntary Association to a Section 21 Company (not for profit);
- as an investment the organization purchased business premises in order to reduce operating costs and increase fixed assets.

By implementing these changes the Monti Rural Association management believed that the organization would be able to survive in the development arena where the global market had taken root and private consultants competed for the same government contracts.

Concluding Remarks and Overview

After this 'quick tour' of the Monti Rural Association and South African history, it is now time to get immersed in the thick of things. First, Chapter 2, **Critical Reflections on NGOs,** discusses the problematic nature of the 'NGO literature' and explores the possible benefits of an 'Anthropology of Development'. Chapter 3, **Land and Politics,** is devoted to describing the history and the politics of land, and sketching the dilemmas, problems and opportunities that lie ahead. In Chapter 4, **MRA and the Dumped People of Thornhill,** another dimension is added to the *embedded tale*, by focusing on the intertwined history of the Thornhill 'community' and the Monti Rural Association. In Chapter 5, **Strategic Translations in Gasela**, the present-day methodologies and strategies of the NGO sector are illustrated. The intermediary position of NGOs ensures that they can engage in, what I have called, *strategic translations*. In Chapter 6, **MRA as a 'Learning Organization'**, it is explored whether an NGO, in its role as a civil society organization, can really be considered a *learning organization*. Chapter 7, **The Government as Praying Mantis**, is devoted to the relationship between NGOs and the government. It shows how an organization like MRA was 'rewarded' with a brain drain in the mid- 1990s, after having been a *beacon of continuity* for the South African government in the early years of the transition. Chapter 8, **The Impact of 'New Realism' and the Role of Donors**, is concerned with the increasing impact of the world market. It examines the market-related activities of NGOs and also their continuing dependence on donors. In the last Chapter, **The Implications of Freedom**, the benefits of an *embedded tale* are discussed. Moreover, it shows what NGO myths must be reconsidered and what agendas for future research may be drawn up. The book ends with –more personal– observations about land sector NGOs and the state of land reform in South Africa.

2. Critical Reflections on NGOs

Introduction
The last decades we have witnessed an expanding body of literature that has been brought about by the spectacular rise[1] of non-governmental organizations on all continents. In this chapter I discuss this 'NGO literature' critically. In the process I argue that it is heuristically helpful to make use of a model in which *the state, civil society* and *the market* are represented as overlapping realms. Moreover, I discuss the benefits of an 'anthropology of development' and its scope of better NGO research. However, I also discuss whether it is actually possible to distinguish neatly between an 'anthropology of development' and 'development anthropology', as it is proposed by some scholars.

Critically Considering the 'NGO Literature'
In my opinion much of the literature about NGOs could be labelled 'NGO literature'. It is often the product of 'development anthropology' and is largely produced and reproduced by 'insiders'[2]. When one is first confronted with this large body of literature on NGOs, one is likely to feel somewhat intimidated by the fact that 'NGO literature' seems rather inaccessible for a relative 'outsider'. It has characteristics of a jargon and seems to require some form of initiation.

Firstly, one notices that 'NGO literature' frequently has an 'activist flavour'. Although there is nothing wrong with activism, it does seem problematic when it is disguised as 'scientific analysis'. As the distinction between 'insiders' –NGO activists, NGO staff, academic consultants employed by the NGO sector– and 'outsiders' –disinterested parties who base their articles on independent and solid academic research– is usually not clear, much confusion may arise. For example, it becomes hard to distinguish between development reports and articles produced by the non-governmental sector –often written by academic consultants– and genuine scientific publications produced with the aim to further our understanding of such organizations. This is tricky as one must realize that texts and analyses, produced by 'insiders', contain 'symbolic capital' as Quarles van Ufford (1993) has argued:

> *"Definitions of development are vital 'symbolic capital', which is carefully tended by the agencies. These 'analyses' should not be seen as equivalent to a disinterested, scientific analysis. On the contrary, the capacity to control definitions of what is supposed to be happening locally is of the utmost importance to the agencies..."* (p. 140).

This has also been shown by Ferguson (1990), who described how World Bank reports should be read as 'political' documents. The 'development industry', in fact, becomes what he calls an *anti-politics machine* by disguising such reports and subsequent interventions in 'neutral', 'scientific', and 'technical' terms.

Secondly, many NGO authors feel obliged to come up with rather simple and straightforward solutions to very complicated issues: 'recipes for future success'. Even authors who seem to have analyzed the issues thoroughly, and have themselves stated that each context differs, feel somehow obliged to come up with advice that is applicable in any NGO context. Thus, 'NGO literature' is full of simple advice like:

"Southern NGOs should strengthen their grassroots links", or "NGOs should improve their performance measurement", or "we should establish a sense of global responsibility". Usually it is hard to distinguish between advice and outright 'wishful thinking'. In my view, after thorough analysis, one should either be concrete by providing solutions, applicable in a particular political and/or socio-economic setting, or one should simply refrain from engaging in such 'wishful thinking'.

Thirdly, it is problematic that this type of NGO discourse often seems to contain rather obvious contradictions. This becomes obvious when analyzing development policy documents with regard to the use of terms like 'empowerment' and 'participation'. Frequently it is argued that 'empowerment' and 'participation' should be 'given' or 'granted' to 'the people', or 'the poor' by governments, businesses or NGOs. Someone like Villarreal (1992) has exposed the inherent contradiction in such statements. It is the same type of development rhetoric that stresses that 'development' is a 'bottom up' process initiated by 'the people'. In the South African context, such 'participatory' development discourses have also pervaded the development arena.

Fourthly, the appearance of 'NGO literature' –although not inseparable from content– also seems to confirm that it is produced by and for 'insiders'. These texts are usually overflowing with abbreviations, to be deciphered in a glossary. Of course, there is nothing wrong with using the odd abbreviation. However, with regard to NGOs, authors frequently exaggerate their love of dense writing. Moreover, it seems to have become a sport to come up with the most ridiculous abbreviations. It is as if these exotic acronyms –BINGO (Big International NGO) or (Big NGO), QUANGO (Quasi-NGO), GONGO (Governmental NGO) or MANGO (Mafia NGO)– can give body to otherwise lightweight arguments. I, therefore, doubt whether the use of these *"monstrous terms"[3]*, as van Binsbergen (1993, p. 5) has labelled them, aids us to improve our understanding of non-governmental organizations and the way they operate. Rather, there is a danger that this type of 'NGO-speak', (re-)produced by 'insiders', may obscure our grasp of what goes on in the NGO sector.

A second observation regarding the appearance of 'NGO texts' concerns the fondness of seemingly straightforward lists. With the help of bullets many authors present changes, issues, features, influences and conclusions. In my view, such representations may also obstruct the ability to recognize the details and intricacies of development processes. Although the NGO sector usually criticizes large intervening parties, like governments and the World Bank, for similar behaviour, such –often politically correct– lists in the 'NGO literature' are just as problematic. Again, there is nothing wrong with using the odd bullet, but it must not become as dominant as in the case of Margarita Bosch (1997), who presented five such lists in a ten-page article.

Fifthly and lastly, I want to mention a point that holds true for much of the 'NGO literature', but also for many other social science texts. Not only are derogatory terms like 'third world' still used without reservation –predominantly by Americans–, but many authors also allow themselves to get carried away when discussing Africa. Even scholars who are critical of ethnocentric practices, make sweeping statements about 'the dark continent', that they would avoid making about Europe. For example, Bratton (1993) states:

> "In Africa where public resources are often allocated along personalistic or patronage lines, the most useful ties are informal ones" (p. 112).

Or Fowler (1991) claims:

> "...the paradox within the African state is its dependence on both formal and informal systems and dual moralities for its operation" (p. 54).

Naturally, it would be silly to deny that, in the case of Zambia, for example, both under president Chiluba and former president Kaunda, nepotism and corruption led to severe problems that affected the whole of society. Nevertheless, it is silly to generalize conclusions about the nature of organizational and institutional life in the whole of Africa. As if Egypt, Burkina Faso and South Africa are identical in this respect. It is hard to imagine that similar statements would be made for contexts as different as Ireland, Belgium, Greece and Portugal[4]. Historical sensitivity and a consideration of the political and socio-economic context of local arenas are important with respect to every continent.

Some of these shortcomings of the 'NGO literature' may be avoided when more empirical, actor-oriented and ethnographic research is conducted. In fact, some NGO scholars that have contributed to the 'NGO literature', have suggested themselves that more in-depth research is needed in order to understand NGOs. For example, Farrington and Bebbington (1993), seem sensitive to the fact that their analyses are based on a 'reported reality' by 'insiders':

> "...while there are some ethnographic and actor based accounts of the work and dynamics of government institutions (...), few have been written about NGOs. Our comments are based on our knowledge and the case studies written by the NGOs who participated in this study. We draw attention to this area as one urgently requiring research in the future as NGOs become responsible for ever larger amounts of social development expenditure" (p. 57).

Four years later Hulme and Edwards (1997) also call for more empirical research, concerning the so-called 'participatory methods' employed and propagated by NGOs:

> "detailed empirical research is needed to elaborate whether such approaches lead to changed interventions and whether such changes lead to improved outcomes" (p.10).

As such studies are still relatively rare, it is positive that new and young researchers are finally trying to employ such ethnographic approaches to study NGOs. A recent example of such an ethnographic NGO study was published in the Netherlands by Hilhorst (2000). Her doctoral thesis, *Records and Reputations: everyday politics of a Philippine Development NGO*, tries to examine the NGO through an ethnography of the organization. Another PhD project that will make use of ethnographic research methodologies has been initiated in 2001 by van Haren (unpublished). She aims to study South African housing NGOs and their role in democratization processes. I expect that such studies, together with this *embedded tale* about the Monti Rural Association –an ethnographic and actor-oriented study grounded in a historical, political and socio-economic context– will fill a much-needed gap in the literature about NGOs.

After these initial observations by a 'relative outsider', it is time to explore the definitional problems with regard to non-governmental organizations

Defining NGOs
When analyzing the term 'non-governmental organization' critically, it becomes quite apparent that it only tells us what such an organization is not: it is not part of the government. This severely limits the usefulness of the term as it covers organizations and institutions as different as businesses, philanthropic organizations, football clubs and churches. Although most scholars understand that businesses are not covered by the term NGO –in the USA the term 'non-profit organization' aids to avoid this confusion– the fact remains that we use the term so widely that it has effectively lost its meaning. If a term can both be used to refer to large international environmental organizations, like Greenpeace, or locally operating small-scale community organizations, much confusion may be the result. Or as Abdelrahman (2000) has argued: *"...the use of the term NGO to describe a broad range of organizations hides the widely different orientations and agendas of these organizations"* (p. 48).

Therefore, because this book is mainly concerned with types of organizations that are predominantly based in civil society and engaged in 'development' processes, it becomes imperative to find out how the term is used by the 'development industry'. However, this is a complicated exercise as well, since many development authors – both in NGOs and academia– have struggled to escape these definitional problems by coming up with new terms, abbreviations and definitions. Although in some instances this does seem helpful –the term non-governmental funding organization (NGFO) refers to NGOs, predominantly in the North, that fund local NGOs, usually in the South– as it limits the types of organizations included, the use of many such new terms may also add to the confusion. Examples of such definitional attempts are:
- Voluntary Organizations (VOs) and Public Service Contractors (PSCs) (Korten, 1990);
- People's Organizations (POs) and Non-Governmental Development Organizations (NGDOs) (Fowler, 1991, 1997);
- Civil Society Organizations (CSOs) (Blair (1997);
- Grassroots Organizations (GROs) and Grassroots Support Organizations (GRSOs) (Fisher 1998).

This list is in reality almost inexhaustible and together with the silly abbreviations, described above, complicates matters for the beginning NGO scholar.

In conclusion I agree with van Binsbergen (1993) who argues that the term 'NGO' is not an analytical and scientific term, but *"...an actor term used in a certain political culture..."*[5] (p. 7). Although van Binsbergen, subsequently, attempts to describe what an NGO is in sociological terms –for that he needs half a page– he proceeds to disqualify that attempt as he finds the definition too complex to be useful. Even so-called 'insiders', like Ball and Dunn (1995), face similar difficulties when defining NGOs. Although they base their definition on four, seemingly clear, characteristics of NGOs –Voluntary; Independent; Not-for-profit; Not self-serving in aims and related values–, these authors also need one whole page to explain exactly what is meant by these terms. In their view, for example, *not-for-profit* can include *for-profit* activities, as long as dividends are not paid to shareholders. What is important, therefore, is to learn more about the 'acquired meaning' of the term: how does the NGO literature –implicitly and explicitly– describe these organizations?

In order to do this in a systematic manner, I propose to use a 'working definition', based on recurrent themes in the 'NGO literature'. In order to understand what NGOs are we have to consider several aspects of such organizations:
1. their intermediary character;
2. to what extent they are value driven;
3. their relationship with 'the state';
4. to what extent they are non-profit organizations;
5. their dependence on donor funding.

I will use these five characteristics below to explore the NGO literature critically in order to clarify the myths, ideal-typical descriptions and uncharted territories.

The Intermediary Character of NGOs

In my view, the intermediary character of development NGOs is one of the defining features of this type of organization. Usually, the distinction here is between 'the people', or their organizations at 'grassroots', the development-oriented NGO at the intermediary level and the donors and government institutions on higher institutional levels. In this representation the NGO transfers certain resources –knowledge, services and/or funds– to people who are in need, while at the same time its activities are also directed the other way. Through, for example, advocacy and lobbying activities NGOs are engaged in aiding 'the poor' to get 'their voice' heard. Thus, it becomes clear that the intermediary character of NGOs is tied to their level of operation. Therefore, to avoid confusion, I would plead to distinguish between community-based organizations that originate and operate largely on the local level and development NGOs that operate on more intermediary levels.

Although in the NGO literature most authors follow a similar scheme, some confusion may arise as authors come up with new terms that are used interchangeably by others. For example, as was shown above, authors have come up with many different terms for community-based organizations, like Civil Society Organizations (CSOs), People's Organizations (POs) or Grassroots Organizations (GROs). On the more intermediate level terms like Grassroots Support Organizations (GRSOs) or Non-Governmental Development Organizations (NGDO) are employed. Usually the literature only ascribes these intermediary features to the more professional organizations at intermediate levels. Although I do wholly agree with the fact that the intermediary character of such development NGOs is a dominant feature, I disagree with the disregard of the intermediary characteristics of these community-based organizations. I would emphasize that these small-scale organizations do mediate between individuals in a local area and other institutional players. Moreover, when scholars fail to recognize these intermediary features, it increases the danger that they also fail to recognize divisions within communities.

In this regard it is also crucial to consider the question of membership. In order to distinguish between community-based organizations and the more intermediary NGOs, some authors automatically assume that the community organizations are membership-based 'people's organizations'. At the same time, it is assumed that the more professional NGOs at intermediate levels lack such a membership base. In such descriptions community organizations are seen to be created 'bottom-up' by 'the people' themselves in order to change things for the better in their communities, villages, townships or neighbourhoods. For example, Fowler, in his well-known 1991 article about the role of NGOs in changing state-society relations, defines People's Organizations as *"...institutions set up and controlled by (poor) people themselves..."* (p. 79: note 1), and NGOs as *"...non-profit-making development agencies which are not initiated, or controlled by the intended beneficiaries..."* (p. 78: note 1). However, to use such a membership-criterion to distinguish between the two types of organization is problematic. In the South African context, for example, it has led many to believe that these community-based organizations –called *civics* or *residents associations*– are 'democratic' as they were initiated by 'the people'. In the field, however, it becomes clear that many community organizations lack a membership base as they are established and led by the elite sections of a community and even lack democratic control. With regard to the issue of membership, it is, moreover, also crucial to recognize that there are examples of more intermediate NGOs that have a membership-base. For example, some of the large Northern co-financing NGOs are supported by a paying membership. Furthermore, huge international NGOs like Greenpeace could not exist without their members.

Nevertheless, without making absolute statements about their intermediary character or membership, I feel that the distinction community-based organization, versus non-governmental organization is helpful. However, several authors, like for example Fisher (1998), do not employ this distinction. Fisher defines both GRSOs and GROs as non-governmental organizations. What is more, she also defines informal and formal GRO networks and GRSO networks as NGOs. In my view such an approach, covering almost everything by the term 'NGO', effectively robs the term of its last crumbs of meaning. In my opinion all the organizations mentioned by Fisher can be earmarked as civil society organizations, but I would argue to uphold the distinction between community-based organizations and the more intermediate development NGOs. Thus, community organizations are based in villages, slums or townships, while the development NGOs are usually based in the neighbouring towns, cities or the capital. However, it is important to recognize that there is a grey zone in cases where, for example, a community organization grows to become a larger, more professional organization.

When we consider the intermediary character of development NGOs, we automatically stumble across issues of participation, accountability and democratization. The NGO literature generally recognizes the potential of NGOs to strengthen the role of 'people's organizations' and to facilitate beneficiary participation (e.g. Dawson, 1992; Bosch, 1997). The discourse of large development actors reflects these ideas as well, as is for example shown by Cox and Koning (1997), when they explain why the European Community supports NGOs:

> *"The EC's support goes both to NGO development projects in countries in the South and to their activities to mobilise public opinion in favour of development and fairer international relations between North and South. NGO are seen as vehicles by which official aid can reach the poorest and most marginalized people. The commission supports the role of NGOs in encouraging participatory*

development and the creation of a democratic base at grass roots level..." (p. 38, box 2.3).

The idea is that intermediary NGOs operate closer to 'grassroots' than state institutions, encourage participation of 'the people' in their own development, are more accountable to 'the people' and act as 'agents of democratization', both because on a national level they oppose undemocratic forms of governance, while on the local level they stimulate the emergence of civic groups and democratic forms of decision making. Below, I will return to the issues of democracy when discussing the relationship between NGOs and states. However, what must be stressed here is that critical research is needed into the relationship of NGOs with the beneficiaries or the people they often claim to represent. Several questions have to be answered. With which section of 'the community' does the NGO usually deal? To whom are they accountable? For example, quite often, elite factions play a dominant role. How do NGOs reconcile opposing views in 'communities'? Which role do NGO experts play in these so-called participatory methodologies? How exactly do NGOs exert influence on decisions taken by a 'community'? Are decision-making processes in such development arenas as democratic as is often claimed? As social scientists we have a duty, as 'relative outsiders', to carefully answer such questions through detailed case studies, instead of accepting the much-advertized NGO characteristics at face value. Only then will we be better able to understand and evaluate the role of NGOs.

A last aspect of intermediate development NGOs concerns the fact that these organizations are regularly 'geographically' categorized, as is illustrated by the above quote by Cox and Koning. Farrington and Bebbington (1993) employ the terms Northern NGOs (NNGOs) and Southern NGOs (SNGOs) as well, to differentiate between organizations that originate in the richer North and organizations that originate and are situated in the developing countries. Clearly, in this context, the terms North and South are not only neutrally geographic terms, but also refer to socio-economic divisions in the world. What complicates such definitional attempts, however, is the fact that, for example, China, India, Ethiopia, Venezuela and Nicaragua are actually Northern hemisphere countries. In that regard the North-South distinction is not straightforward, more so when one recognizes the fact that many Eastern European nations have also been added to the developing countries list. Nevertheless, for lack of a better terminology I also endorse the North-South distinction, especially as it ensures some sensitivity with regard to the socio-economic inequalities in the world. A related term, that also tells us something about the area of operation, is the term 'International NGO', which refers to organizations like Greenpeace and Amnesty International that operate on a global level.

In conclusion I would argue that for the student of development NGOs it is crucial to study the intermediary character of these organizations, while at the same it is important to avoid simplified characterizations. In this book I attempt to show that the intermediary position of NGOs guarantees them the possibility to engage in, what I have termed, 'strategic translations'. In that regard, it is important that scholars conduct their research on different levels in order to uncover how and when such translations take place, and what the consequences may be for the so-called participatory development processes NGOs are involved in.

NGOs as Value-driven Organizations

Since many non-governmental organizations get established because of a concern for others, it is commonly suggested that a defining characteristic of NGOs is the fact that they are 'value-driven'. In the definition by Ball and Dunn (1995), for example, this is one of the four characteristics of NGOs:

> "[NGOs are] *not self-serving in aims and related values: the aims of NGOs are:*
> a. *to improve the circumstances and prospects of disadvantaged people who are unable to realise their potential or achieve their full rights in society through direct or indirect forms of action; and/or*
> b. *to act on concerns and issues which are detrimental to the well-being, circumstances or prospects of people or society as a whole"* (p. 19).

In my view it is useful to take this definition as a point of departure because it illustrates the normative nature and concealing discourse of the 'NGO literature'.

First, I am critical of the normative nature of such a definition as it is, subsequently, used by authors to separate the 'good' NGOs from the 'bad'. In such a representation there are 'good' and 'real' NGOs on the one extreme, mostly concerned with other people's fates, and 'bad' NGOs, or 'pretend-NGOs', on the other extreme that have been primarily established to siphon off donor funds. In my view one should question the usefulness of such a dichotomy. Indeed, there are always bad examples of 'NGOs' that have mainly been established to tap into the swollen rivers of donor funds. But what is the use of declaring that these NGOs are not 'real' NGOs? Are organizations only labelled as NGOs when they are 90% value-driven? How does one measure this? Where does one draw the line?

In fact, I would argue that being –to a degree– funding-driven is as much a feature of 'the NGO sector' as being –to a degree– value-driven. Thus, I am critical of the fact that such definitions are concealing, and even disregarding the most fundamental contradiction in NGOs. On the one hand, these organizations are indeed concerned with the fate of others, as is proclaimed in mission statements. On the other hand, the NGOs –like any other institution– are legitimately engaged in activities that ensure their own financial and organizational survival. That is the reason why I would contest the type of definition drawn up by Ball and Dunn. It may cause one to overlook the fact that all non-governmental organizations have a self-serving side to them. Especially because NGOs themselves, frequently, downplay their self-serving side –usually the fact that they work wholly in the interests of 'the poor' or 'the people at grassroots' is emphasized– it becomes imperative that literature about NGOs does not make the same mistake. If the 'NGO literature', dominated by 'insiders', also 'sells' NGOs as being value-driven, there is a danger that we will lose sight of their other side. I would even go as far as to argue that NGOs need to be self-serving in order to carry out their work for others. However, it is the balancing act between these supposedly opposing aims, that is one of the great challenges for NGOs, as is illustrated by the case material presented in this book.

Another problem with such either/or dichotomies is that they lead to static representations. An organization is either value-driven or self-serving. Thus, we fail to see that NGOs go through different stages, belong to several institutional webs and are involved in a number of –frequently contradictory– organizational processes. For example, in the initial stages, when NGOs are established, they may usually more concerned with the ideals and purposes of the organization, as mission statements have to be formulated and contacts with 'the people' have to be sought. In another stage, where organizations go through their first organizational growth spurts, it may be expected that they are –for a certain period at least– more concerned with their own organizational future. Even during a financial year great fluctuations take place in the organizational processes of NGOs. For example, at the end of the financial year, when the annual report has to be finished for donors, or when grant applications have to be prepared, there is more emphasis on organizational continuity. Moreover, periods of crisis may occur, during which the financial survival of an organization is at stake, draining the organization for a while of much of its 'value-driven energy'. In my view, therefore, it is possible –both in the short term and the longer term– to identify periods of fluctuations in the dynamic balance between concern and effort for others and concern for the organization itself. In fact, it will always be the source of a certain amount of tension in NGOs, as it is rarely either or.

Korten (1990) also goes the dichotomy route by identifying two types of intermediary NGOs. The first is what he calls a Voluntary Organization (VO), a 'true' NGO that is value-driven and works with or for 'the people'. The second is what he calls a Public Service Contractor (PSC), a type of organization that is funding-driven and specializes in service delivery. According to Korten there is an increasing pressure on VOs, from donors and governments, to take over service delivery responsibilities from states. When a voluntary organization succumbs to such pressure, it transforms to become a PSC and in the process loses some of its key characteristics. Hailey (2001), for example, also argues that NGOs should actively protect and promote their core values, to keep them distinct from other organizations and institutions active in the field of development. From being largely value-driven these organizations then become largely funding-driven, according to Korten (1990). Again, I am critical of such a representation. Certainly nowadays, in a historical period where the market has become quite dominant, nearly all NGOs need to acquire some PSC characteristics. Moreover, as businesses increasingly have to present themselves as adhering to certain (moral) principles, values and/or practices –against child labour, environmentally friendly–, it will be hard to find a PSC in which values do not play any role at all. Thus, again, the dichotomy is not useful. As Korten (1990) realized this shortcoming, he coined the term 'hybrid organizations' to describe all kinds of crossovers that may emerge: *"...many organizations span the sectoral boundaries..."* (p. 104). However, in my opinion, most NGOs could then be described as 'hybrid organizations', as a result of which the terminology becomes rather redundant.

With regard to the research into the tension between the self-serving aspects and the more value-driven aspects of NGOs, it is important to stress that there can be large discrepancies between theory and practice. The task for social scientists, therefore, is to critically investigate and assess the relationship between the 'reported reality' and what really goes on in the organization and the field. Since it frequently happens that NGOs are only studied by analyzing reports of the organizations concerned, misrepresentations are bound to be the result. Of course, it is essential to study these reports, but it is another thing to accept uncritically what is reported.

Normally, the picture that is presented in these reports is quite different from what actually takes place in the field. Usually, there is nothing malicious about such a (mis-)representation, but it has everything to do with the audience for which reports are written. Obviously, NGOs consciously draft reports, and massage and knead the dough of their field activities into a certain mould for a particular audience. Moreover, in many instances, sections of NGO staff themselves are not fully aware of particular discrepancies between what happens 'out there' and what is reported. Take, for example, the common fact that management in an NGO is burdened with the reporting task, while there is a specialized group of field workers that actually spend time in the field. In such cases it is hard for management to be completely aware of the reliability of field data.

The above shows that it is, therefore, valuable that 'relative outsiders' research these issues. That is where the social scientist should come in. Not for a two-day evaluation and a questionnaire, but for a prolonged period so that short-term and long-term phases and dynamic processes are identified and described. Ultimately this could lead to a more valid longitudinal description –in all its nuances– of the mechanisms involved in balancing values and financial survival in a globalized context.

NGOs in Relation to the State
Non-governmental organizations are –by definition– not thought to be part of the state. Many NGO scholars, therefore contend that NGOs *"...are autonomous from government and political parties..."* (Bosch, 1997: p. 235). Others prefer the term *independence* to describe one of the major virtues of the NGO sector. To argue that NGOs are autonomous is to imply that there is no –or at least a very limited– relationship between these civil society organizations and states. In my view, however, this kind of ideal-typical representation is problematic. In fact, we cannot begin to truly understand NGOs if we fail to take into account their –frequently structural and intense– relationships with states. In order to begin to debate the nature and content of these relationships, which obviously vary according to country, region and/or socio-political context, there is a need to get familiar with the conceptual tools that social scientists commonly use.

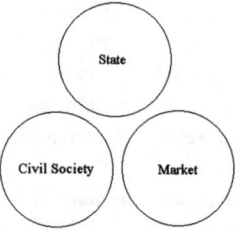

Figure 2.1: The three realms in society.

In order to understand 'modern' societies, usually three realms are identified, as is shown in Figure 2.1. While the state represents the realm of the government institutions, the market represents the realm of all commercial activities and civil society is the realm where citizens organize themselves in different associational configurations. Such models have regained currency since the early 1990s as the demise of the Soviet empire, and its satellite states, has spurred renewed interest in the concept of *civil society*. In my opinion *civil society* is a useful concept to aid us in understanding what goes on in the state, the market and 'the rest of associational society'. However, the concept is also problematic as it means different things to different actors, whether scholars, activists, state officials, or the aid industry. Moreover, it is also a contested concept. Nevertheless, I would argue that as long as we are aware of these pitfalls, it is a term we cannot do without, if only because it has become an actor term.

In this regard it is useful to reiterate what Lewis (2002) has stated:

"The potential usefulness of the concept of civil society can therefore be analyzed across two main dimensions –it can be 'useful to think with' and it may be 'useful to act with'" (p. 582).

Since it has, for example, inspired many resistance movements and NGOs to present themselves and act in certain ways, it has acquired –and is continually in the process of acquiring– new, or transformed, meanings. This is one reason why it is exceptionally difficult to come up with a definitive definition of civil society that neatly wraps up all loose ends. Therefore, Lewis (2002) argues[6] that we need to focus both on structure and process when analyzing civil society, in order to avoid representing the concept as a static and ahistorical concept. Already the renowned political philosopher Walzer has argued that he defends:

"...a complex, imprecise and at crucial points, uncertain account of society and politics", because he had no hope *"of theoretical simplicity, not at this historical moment when so many stable oppositions of political and intellectual life have collapsed* [after the end of the Cold War]", nor, did he suspect, would *"a world that theory could fully grasp and neatly explain (...) be a pleasant place"* (1995, p. 153).

Another problem with regard to the concept of civil society is that, for many, it has a prescriptive and normative, meaning. Especially the 'development industry' has shown renewed interest in the term as it pushed its 'good governance' agenda in the 1990s. In such a discourse, strengthening civil society came to be synonymous with building democracy and spreading neo-liberalism, as will be elaborated below. American NGO scholars, like Blair (1997) and Fisher (1998), seem to start from this premise as well. In order to understand where they come from it is, therefore, useful to show the model that lies at the basis of their analysis. In it only two (opposing) realms are identified, with the state on the one side and civil society on the other. However, civil society comprises the market (see: Figure 2.2).

Such differences in interpretations clearly lead to differences in opinion about the way in which NGOs function and relate to other institutions. For authors, who claim that the market is part of civil society (Figure 2.2), all activities in society that cannot be ascribed to the state are said to belong to the realm of civil society. Thus, in this view both profit and non-profit organizations are part of civil society. As a result, such authors do not necessarily understand non-governmental organizations to be non-profit. It is in this view, that a call for 'democratization' is usually directly linked to a call for 'free markets'. As Abrahamsen (2000) explains: *"...a near fusion of democracy and economic liberalism in the good governance discourse becomes apparent"* (p. xii).

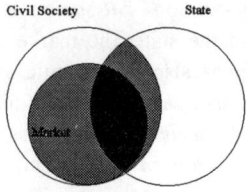

Figure 2.2: The market as part of civil society.

With respect to Africa these prescriptive and normative uses of the term civil society are especially problematic, because, according to Kasfir (1998), *"...using a normative concept of civil society to analyze African politics is likely to obscure more than it clarifies"* (p. 126). This is because such a use –as is often done by the development industry– causes a large part of African associational life not be recognized as being part of civil society. When using the prescriptive concept of civil society in Africa, aggressive, or anti-democratic, or ethnic or fundamentalist associational groups are usually excluded from civil society. Thus, donors and many development analysts push for a kind of sanitized and desirable form of civil society, that does little justice to the actually existing associational life in many African regions. According to authors like Kasfir (1998) and Lewis (2002) this creates difficulties. Therefore, they argue for a more inclusive definition that leaves room for a wider group of actually existing organizations and associations. According to Kasfir (1998):

> *"...it seems foolish to exclude ethnic associations, possibly the greater part of Africa's existing associations from any analytically useful explanation of the struggle for democracy (...). The better approach is to consider civil society as consisting of non-state organizational activity whether or not the organizations conform to the norm of civility"* (p. 144).

Lewis (2002) argues that it is a persuasive argument when some state that *"...the idea of civil society –whether explicitly recognized as such or not– has long been implicated in Africa's colonial histories of both domination and resistance"* (p. 575). This is quite clear in the South African context. Although most blacks were not regarded and treated as citizens by the apartheid regime –in fact the whole machinery was geared to label them as ethnic subjects, as Mamdani (1996) has shown– the anti-apartheid struggle by a large variety of groups with a very different background, shares characteristics very similar to resistance movements that emerged in other parts of the world –like Chile– and which are normally acknowledged as being classic examples of blossoming civil society. Thus, particularly in the African context, I would also argue in favour of a more inclusive use of the term civil society, which encourages the acknowledgement of a broader spectrum of organizations and associations.

I am, therefore, in favour of a model that is heuristically most useful, since it recognizes overlaps between the three realms that can be identified in society (see:

Figure 2.3). As states intervene in markets, civil society organizations buy and sell certain products or services and engage in political lobbying and businesses increasingly use ethical standards, or form cooperative arrangements with governments, such overlaps should also be represented in a model. Of course, for every context the relative sizes of the realms and the extent to which they overlap, may vary greatly. Only in extreme situations, as Lewis (2002), for example, describes the situation in Somalia where a state has been absent for years, one of the realms may be completely non-existent.

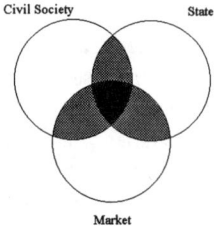

Figure 2.3: The three overlapping realms.

In the continuation of this section I intend to discuss the relationship between NGOs and states in three sub-sections: *Autonomy and Politics*, in which issues of independence and political involvement are discussed; *Substituting or Cooperating with the State* in which state substitution and cooperative arrangements are discussed; and, *'Good Governance' and 'the Franchise State'* in which I discuss how citizens may lose their rights due to 'good governance' measures.

Autonomy and Politics
The term 'autonomy' is a difficult term as it has an absolute flavour to it. Nevertheless, as was shown above, it is frequently mis-used in the 'NGO literature' by authors who claim that non-governmental organizations are autonomous from the state. Naturally, some NGOs are more autonomous than others, but to state bluntly that NGOs are completely autonomous is dangerous as it may obscure some of the more intricate aspects of NGO-state relationships. Therefore, I would rather use the term 'relative autonomy'. All organizations, governing bodies and institutions are to some degree influenced by their surrounding institutional arena. There is no NGO that does not take into account social, economic and political pressures when making strategic decisions.

When studying the 'relative autonomy' of NGOs, one comes across different ways in which states attempt to influence –or co-opt– NGOs. One of the most obvious cases is where state officials –a senior cabinet minister in a Zimbabwean example by Fowler (1991)– initiate or establish an NGO themselves. In such a case NGO authors would label the organization a GONGO (e.g. Korten, 1990), a term I have already critically discussed. As many NGOs are engaged in cooperative arrangements with states, it is much more useful to study, analyze and describe these arrangements than to disqualify them with such a crude label. It is understanding we should be after, not disqualification. Moreover, in some cases appropriation, cooptation and cooperation may not be so far apart. In this respect Fowler (1991) urges us to acknowledge the role of elites:

> "...the repertoire of state responses would suggest that the existing elites are both consolidating themselves within the voluntary sector and limiting its political impact by external control" (p. 73).

Indeed, in many developing nations it was noticed that ex-government staff moved into the NGO sector when the government bureaucracies were trimmed down. In this respect the South African case is interesting because the opposite happened. During the freedom and consultation era the NGO sector experienced a huge 'brain drain' as many joined the new government.

Another way in which governments attempt to extend their influence over NGOs is by registering them. Although in some cases it is purely for administrative or tax purposes, that may actually benefit NGOs, other cases reveal more sinister rationales. For example, when (authoritarian) states feel threatened by the presence of foreign-funded organizations, registration initiatives have more to do with controlling these NGOs and limiting foreign influence. Especially in cases where regimes are faced with reductions in foreign funding while at the same time noticing that Northern governments fund NGOs in their countries generously, tough action against NGOs may be the result. In such cases regimes are usually worried that these non-governmental organizations actively engage in (opposition) politics. Of course, the NGOs involved claim the contrary. In fact, for many NGOs active in development their involvement in politics is like walking a tight rope, especially when they confront an authoritarian regime. Officially they are neutral and independent, while in practice they are engaged in many oppositional political processes. Therefore, in such contexts NGOs may stress the technical side of their work in official reports while close scrutiny will reveal their political involvement.

Many actors in the 'development industry' truly believe –or make us want to believe– that development interventions are politically neutral acts. However, as was shown by Long and van der Ploeg (1989) in their article *Demythologizing Planned Intervention: an actor perspective*, such interventions are very political. Bratton (1990) also appears conscious of this fact with regard to the establishment of NGOs. He points out that "...*the construction of organizations is an unavoidably political act: it involves the exercise of power*" (p.91). But not only the act of organizing oneself is a political act. Bratton also convincingly shows that policy formation is a political process. It is hard to discuss meaningfully the political aspects of NGO engagement without referring to the role of politics and issues of democratization. In that debate, some authors ascribe politics only to the realm of the state, while others define politics much more broadly. Fisher (1998), who belongs to the latter, argues that NGOs have an important role to play at the forefront of civil society in a process that she calls 'political development', which is a more neutral term that she uses, for what others call 'democratization'. Fowler (1997), in a rather reifying statement, evidently sees NGOs and civil society in a similar light: "...*civil society is a political actor...* " (p. 231).

What I believe is crucial here is that we make a clear distinction between 'politics' and 'party-politics'. The first is an umbrella term for all political processes that I would ascribe to all three realms of society: the state, the market and civil society. The latter refers to a much more narrow process involving political parties that compete for power in the state. However, even in this interpretation, there remains a 'grey area'. Sometimes, although not necessarily openly, NGOs do affiliate to political parties. During apartheid, for example, many progressive non-governmental organizations in South Africa affiliated to the underground ANC. Moreover, according to Fowler (1997), amongst other sources of identity, some *"...Northern NGDOs have arisen from political affiliations..."* (p. 36). For Northern non-governmental funding agencies this can lead to a schizophrenic situation. In their country of origin they use their political image to rally support and accumulate funds, while in the Southern local development contexts they have to downplay their political image and stress the technical content of their support work, in order to avoid endangering their local counterparts. Therefore, I would conclude that we as social scientists must be aware of the fact that what organizations say they are is not necessarily what they are. To stress a non-political image may be a political act.

Substituting or Cooperating with the State

At the end of the seventies, development institutions like the World Bank and the IMF had lost most faith in the functioning of developing country states. Inefficiency, corruption, self-enriching elites, high levels of bureaucratization and wasteful parastatals were made 'the North' lose confidence in floundering developing country governments. As a solution, because it was recognized that markets could not deal effectively with poverty, civil society organizations were targeted to take over from developing country governments. These organizations would provide 'the people' and 'the poor' with services and resources that had been the responsibility of states. According to Robinson (1997), American and British political developments in the eighties have been a factor in bringing about a change of focus in the development arena. The age of Reaganomics and Thatcherism ushered in 'the lean government' in the North. These governments were trimmed by no-nonsense neo-liberal politicians, whereby especially the state's responsibilities in the welfare sector were strongly reduced. In the eyes of these politicians poverty was seen as a personal failure. Everybody could achieve 'the American dream' if they worked hard enough. As a consequence, charities and NGOs had to step in to take over tasks in welfare, health and education, resulting in a booming voluntary sector. I tend to agree with Robinson's analysis. Neo-liberalism swept the globe and as a result leading development institutions were more concerned with developing new and stronger markets than new and stronger civil society organizations. But as Kasfir (1998) has argued, *"...it is an idealized version not the actual practice of civil society in Western countries that* [analysts and donors]*wish to import"* (p. 143).

The structural adjustment programmes were instrumental in this respect. In their book, Hulme and Edwards (1997) identify three distinct historical periods in each of which a certain 'myth', shared by development experts, was dominant. Thus, they identify the 1970s as a period in which the 'myth of the state' predominated, followed by the 1980s, when the 'myth of the market' prevailed and lastly, the 1990s, when 'the myth of the market plus civil society' was dominant (p. 276-277). They use the term 'myth' to point out that in certain periods certain 'buzzwords' seem to dominate 'the development industry'. Although, the myth of the market plus civil society still seems at work in the 21st century, it seems as if states have slowly but surely been brought back into the picture. The buzzword nowadays is 'good governance', to which I will come back later. In this section I explore the arguments that are used when NGOs are compared to government institutions.

Usually it is argued that non-governmental organizations can deliver better results because they are smaller, closer to 'grassroots', more flexible, and more value-driven than government institutions. But there are critics as well who question the scale of operation of NGOs and who inquire what would happen if these organizations would grow explosively. Moreover, more fundamental questions are asked about the ideal-typical role of states, markets and civil society. In this discussion the most obvious criticism concerns the scale of operation of NGOs. For example, is it a realistic alternative to run an entire health sector, or educational sector, through NGOs? Edwards and David Hulme (1992) recognized this problem in their book *Making a Difference: NGOs and development in a changing world.* Therefore, they explored possibilities for 'scaling up' NGO impact. The two most significant solutions for increasing the impact of NGOs were *organizational growth –* or *'scaling-up'–* and *working with the government.* Below, some of the arguments are reviewed.

As was mentioned above, non-governmental organizations are often said to have advantages over state institutions, which have to do with size and flexibility. First, in my view, it is important to examine these claims critically. Subsequently, if these claims are true, it is crucial to explore whether these positive characteristics of NGOs get lost due to organizational growth, or take over from states. Do they face similar problems as large state or market institutions if they 'scale up'? Examining these claims seems especially useful when NGOs in the field regularly and strategically misuse them. For example, I have witnessed quite incompetent and fairly uncommitted NGOs, that, in order to explain their slow pace of progress, have said: we are slow to deliver because our high quality work method demands more time and more resources. Are NGOs indeed more flexible, more value-driven and do they have better relationships with 'the people'? In my view such arguments have limited value for an entire NGO sector. Although it can be of theoretical significance to compare 'the' state sector with 'the' NGO sector, such an exercise in the 'NGO literature' usually involves stressing the positive characteristics of the NGO sector against the background of a caricatural sketch –large, bureaucratic, corrupt– of the state sector. I would argue, therefore, that in order to make a meaningful assessment, we need to examine our arguments against well-documented case material.

However, there seems to be very little reliable and detailed case material available. And even if the 'NGO literature' does contain case material it is usually too sketchy. Actually, in many articles the cases are extremely short which makes it nearly impossible to judge the validity of the material. For example, in a twenty-page article by Bebbington and Farrington (1992), *NGO-government interaction in agricultural technology development,* more than fifteen one-sentence (!) cases are described to illustrate their arguments. The cases are so brief that it is not possible to take them seriously, let alone assess their value in the above argument. Moreover, many of the slightly longer cases in the literature seem to be based on material that has been collected during short field visits. In those instances, quite often, one can still identify the voice of the public relations officer. Concluding, one can say that it in view of the limited case material in the literature, it is hardly possible to critically asses the claims of NGOs and development experts who claim that these organizations are small, flexible and close to grassroots. What is needed is longitudinal, in-depth, ethnographic research.

However, if for argument's sake we accept these claims as being true, the question still remains whether non-governmental organizations are suitable to perform tasks that were formerly performed by states. Aren't small, flexible, close to the grassroots non-governmental organizations in a completely different league than government institutions that deliver services? The 'scaling-up' argument of Edwards and Hulme (1992) seems to confirm this view. When NGOs take over from states they will have to grow in scale in order to have an impact. According to Korten (1990) voluntary organizations (VOs) will also lose their value-driven character when they take over from states and become Public Service Contractors (PSCs), as was discussed above. Thus, it becomes imperative to research these claims with respect to these 'scaling-up' transformations.

When voluntary and small organizations evolve into bigger and more professional organizations with paid staff, they are bound to become more bureaucratic. More staff, offices, computers and cars normally mean a greater need for management, policies and procedures. One could argue, therefore, that there is an increasing danger that NGOs acquire similar characteristic as large state bureaucracies. However, one question remains: does increased growth, bureaucratization and accountability to funders automatically mean: less commitment to 'the people at grassroots' and less 'effectiveness'? I would argue that the contrasting of voluntary and committed staff in a small organization on the one hand, versus a more professional but less committed staff in a larger organization on the other, is not necessarily valid. Of course, there are situations where staff and organizations become engrossed in their own problems and, in the process, forget what they were about in the first place. On the other hand there are many small, flexible and committed organizations where volunteers are also worried about their own problems, like their car allowances. Furthermore, it is easy to imagine situations in which voluntary staff without experience can deliver shoddy work while well-trained paid staff does a good job. In conclusion it is important to reiterate that without detailed case material placed in a historical context it is hard to come to well-founded conclusions about the general impact of increased organizational growth on the work and functioning of NGOs.

Before discussing what is involved when non-governmental organizations and governments do work together, it is necessary to point out that the substitution of the state involves another possible danger as well. Kasfir (1998), for example, argues that a blossoming civil society which forces the state to retreat, may actually inhibit the state's ability to regulate civil society, thereby, ultimately, also weakening civil society and/or democratisation (p. 140-142).

As it emerged that NGOs were not always suitable to substitute governments in service delivery, it was explored by Edwards and Hulme (1992) whether, through more intensive cooperation between NGOs and states –*working with the government*– the advantages of both sectors could be utilized. However, with regard to the position of NGOs in such cooperative arrangements, it is generally believed that the NGOs will always play second fiddle. According to Edwards and Hulme (1992) *"...the constraints of the government system have to be accepted as a starting point"* (p. 17). Indeed, Kasfir (1998) points out that some non-governmental organizations *"...will decide they can achieve their formal objectives more successfully by quietly acquiescing in government injustices, even within their own field of operations"* (p. 138). Particularly, when NGOs are in the business of service delivery, it is said that their role is generally limited to carrying out government or donor instructions.

However, in my view, there are many different cooperative arrangements possible. Especially, at the local level, away from the centres of power, NGOs working with government structures can have a profound influence on the relationship. In this book I show, for example, how in the South African context after the political turn-around, non-governmental organizations attained a strong presence in certain fields. In the land reform arena land sector NGOs, for a while, even became what I have called 'beacons of continuity'. However, it is true that organizations must always be aware that the government usually has the final say.

In addition there are authors who point to the danger that NGOs, by working closely with governments, get contaminated by the dominant organizational culture in those countries. Wood (1997), for example, argues that *"...NGOs cannot easily insulate themselves from the prevailing organizational culture..."* (p. 87). Thus, it is argued that NGOs run the risk of becoming as inefficient, corrupt, bureaucratic and inflexible as the government institutions they work with. In my view, however, the South African case illustrates that the process may also work the other way, where NGOs influence the government departments they work with.

In the 'NGO literature', a more activist view, which argues that the initiative must come from the NGOs themselves can also be encountered. These authors are actually quite positive about the possibilities of NGOs to influence and even change the way governments work. For example, Fowler (1997) introduces the term 'learning for leverage' in order to point to certain mechanisms NGOs should develop to influence other institutional players, like the government. Through formulating development alternatives, policy advocacy, lobbying in political arenas, monitoring reports and applied research, NGOs themselves should become important players in the development arena. Thus, according to Fowler *"...a long-term aim for NGDOs and other civic organisations is to reach a position where governments and businesses acknowledge and respect citizen power as the complementary 'third force'..."* (p. 228). In Fowler's view networking then becomes an important strategy for civil society organizations and , what he calls, 'civic networks' may even *"...be the long-term key to gaining a balancing hold over states and markets..."* (p. 223).

Fisher (1998), also recognizes the power of such networks for scaling up NGO impact. However, she does not view these networks as being limited to civil society only. In her view *"...scaling up ultimately depends on the ability of NGOs of all types to scale out at the grassroots level through networking with other NGOs, local government, or local representatives of national governments"* (p. 170). Not only does she see possibilities for cooperative arrangements between NGOs and governments, but because she defines civil society more broadly whereby it also comprises the market sector, she also focuses on the possibilities for cooperation between NGOs and the market sector. Thus she states that:

> "...*not only are NGOs growing in numbers, promoting grassroots participation, and directly targeting issues of human rights and democratization, they are also (...) at the crux of the relationship between non-profit and for-profit sectors in the Third World*" (p. 172).

As Fowler does not include the market in his definition of civil society, he mainly sees a strong role for NGOs as brokers in the civic networks. Both authors, however, agree in that they see an international civil society emerging.

In my view, however, both authors are prominent examples of the kind of 'activist NGO discourse' that has permeated the 'NGO literature'. Although some ideas, like 'civic networking' seem interesting, I believe that it is more useful to thoroughly study such networks in concrete settings. In this book, for example, the National Land Committee –the national umbrella organization of land sector NGOs– will feature prominently. Through such studies the scope of 'civic networks' in the South African context can be assessed.

Another factor in predicting successful government-NGO cooperation in the NGO literature concerns the role of 'personalities'. Bratton (1990) puts his point across strongly when he states that "*whether or not NGO leaders are able to cultivate close personal contacts with the powers-that-be is one of the best predictors of major and sustainable impact*" (p.111). Edwards and Hulme (1992) agree with him as they consider that "...*personalities and relationships between individuals are a vital element in successful government-NGO partnerships*" (p. 17). This may be easier in cases where, through elites, an interpenetration has taken place of political society and civil society, as Bayart (1996) has argued. Although I would agree that such personal contacts could be of great benefit, it seems to me that other factors, like a historical opportunity due to a period of transformation must also be acknowledged. Furthermore, it must also be recognized that development success dependent on personal (elite) ties, carries an inherent danger as well. What happens, for example, when the individuals leave their organization? Are the 'grassroots' adequately represented in such a system? Moreover, these arguments must not only be put forward in the African setting where the occurrence of personalistic networks has been stressed by authors. In my view, the role of personal contacts seems relevant in many institutional environments, whether in government, business or the voluntary sector. In this book, for example, I show that a relatively small group of NGO staff and ex-NGO staff in government has had a relatively large impact on the development of policies in the land sector in South Africa.

'Good governance' and the Creation of 'a Franchise State'

Although much of the 'NGO literature' welcomes the idea that NGOs should substitute failing states, critical voices are heard as well. Robinson (1997), for example, makes clear that in cases where government contracts out certain services to non-governmental organizations, it is important that the state does retain a strong monitoring role. Without being kept in check, 'the development industry' has carte blanche and the beneficiaries may not get what they deserve. However, Robinson is realistic by arguing that "...*in the absence of detailed case studies or evaluations it is difficult to make any definitive statement about NGO performance when operating in a contractual mode..."* (p.77). Hopefully, this book will provide such detailed case material.

I tend to agree with authors like Robinson who are critical with regard to state substitution. In my view civil society organizations in general, and NGOs in particular, have a specific role to play. At the same time states have other responsibilities towards citizens, like for example, enforcing the law and formulating new legislation to protect citizens. Thus, functioning states are needed for non-governmental organizations to perform, as is also argued by Kasfir (1998). Bebbington and Riddell (1997) believe that the effectiveness of Southern NGOs indeed depends on the political and economic environment:

> *"their effectiveness will be enhanced by a relatively strong state with the capacity (and disposition) to provide services and to defend rights, and by markets which function in a manner which does not hinder or exclude the possible economic activities and market entry of SNGOs and poor people more generally..."* (p.110).

Thus, for a well-functioning NGO sector, that is part of a healthy civil society, it is important to have a well-functioning state and stable markets. Wood (1997) shares this view but, in analyzing the development discourse in regard to 'good governance', comes to a few interesting and rather cynical conclusions. One of which is the creation of *states without citizens*.

In recent years 'good governance' has become the new buzzword in 'the development industry'. The Dutch government, for example, has drastically reduced the number of countries eligible for development cooperation, by arguing that in countries where 'good governance' is absent, development cooperation is bound to fail. According to Wood (1997) this push for 'good governance' in developing countries, initiated in the North, has a perverse side to it, since:

> *"...part of the claim for 'good governance' is participation, a wider involvement of citizenry in managing their own affairs..."* (p.79).

Within the context of the United Kingdom Wood feels that *"...such a theme borders on a sick joke"* (p. 79). In his view, it is exactly this participation in government affairs that has been largely destroyed during the Thatcher years. In the eighties and nineties, for example, local government has been systematically undermined in the UK by the same forces that are now propagating good governance in the South. Kasfir (1998) argues in a similar fashion that the United Sates has shown a decline in civic activity over the past decades (p. 129)[7]. Thus, according to Wood, we are only left with the myths of democracy in the North, and 'good governance' is the attempt to make those myths a reality in other societies.

Wood signals the undermining of Southern states as a result of propagating 'good governance' and 'participation' in those countries. 'The development industry' –which is still dominated by the North– causes those states to lose some of their crucial functions, which are then replaced by sanitized, desirable types of NGOs, which are funded from abroad. Indeed, as Lewis (2002) has argued:

> *"much of the recent interest in civil society is clearly linked to the global dominance of neo-liberal ideologies during the past decade, which envisage a reduced role for the state and privatised forms of service delivery through*

flexible combinations of governmental, non-governmental and private institutional actors" (p. 571).
According to Wood (1997), these states are actually coerced to *franchise out* some of their essential service delivery functions. Not only does this lead to a fragmentation of delivery, also, in the process, political parties and unions are sidelined. Thus, *the franchise state* becomes a reality when the agents of delivery that have taken over from the state are insulated from universal accountability. Both Kasfir (1998) and Abrahamsen (2000) show that such processes usually result in what Kasfir calls an *elite democracy*, which *""...typically favours the wealthy* [and] *the organizations they form"* (p. 125). According to Abrahamsen *"this form of democracy (...) allows for the continuation of elite privileges and sanctions the persistence of suffering and deprivation among large sections of the population"*(p. xiii). Therefore, in Wood's own words:

> *"...the theme of 'good government' (...) risks self-contradiction by diluting these dimensions of responsibility and accountability through the creation of the franchise state as a solution to delivery incompetence (...). Citizens become consumers though often without meaningful access to a choice of suppliers. The loss of rights in the state is not adequately compensated for by acquiring them in the market"* (p.85).

In my opinion these authors are right to warn us for such developments. States and NGOs have specific roles to play.

A weakness in Wood's argument, however, is that he fails to acknowledge the fact that many developing country governments *are* corrupt, incompetent and authoritarian in the first place. In such contexts citizens already have few rights. Moreover, the solution Wood presents may not be too realistic as he suggests that the negative features of organizational cultures in developing countries need to be challenged. Through dialogue with sympathetic allies in the NGO sector and the state sector *"...an agenda of administrative reform..."* (p. 92) needs to be pushed. Personally, I have serious doubts whether such a dialogue works in situations where 'the rot' is pervasive.

NGOs as Non-profit Organizations
Usually the 'NGO literature' labels non-governmental organizations as the *non-profit* sector. Ball and Dunn (1995) and Fowler (1991), for example describe NGOs as *not-for-profit*, and *non-profit* respectively. When examining this claim superficially, there seems nothing wrong with it. Simply put, we identify market actors on the one end of the spectrum that have been established *for-profit*, while on the other end of the spectrum we identify NGOs that belong to civil society and are *not-for-profit*.

To examine what not-for-profit entails we must first look at what for-profit actually means. Making profit in the business world refers to the process whereby companies invest a certain sum in activities that yield more than they cost. These profits can either be re-invested –to expand the company and the profits– or they can, for example, be paid out as dividend to the shareholders. Logically, not-for-profit, then, would not entail any of such for-profit activities. However, as Ball and Dunn state in their definition of NGOs: *"NGOs may engage in revenue-generating activities. They do not, however, distribute profits to shareholders or members"* (p.

19). In other words, *not-for-profit* may also include *for-profit* activities! What is the use of such an argument and crooked definition? If it is clear, when we examine the non-governmental sector more closely, that many aspects of NGO activities involve outright *for-profit* activities, why still call them non-profit organizations in the first place?

What do such *for-profit* activities entail? NGOs active in development in the 21st century operate in a global context in which the market has become dominant. In such a context professionalization and *for-profit* activities become increasingly important. For example, NOVIB, a Dutch co-funding NGO that receives most of its funding from the Dutch government to disburse to Southern partners, has in recent years strongly developed a successful 'marketing strategy' in order to acquire additional private funds from the Dutch public. By using slick advertizing campaigns people are urged to support the organization by becoming a member and buy calendars and a whole range of other 'third world' products. The aim of these highly commercialized activities is to make a profit in a very business-like manner. However, the proceeds are, of course, not paid out as dividend, but are used to undertake the work they deem important and to keep the organization afloat. Highly professionalized international NGOs like Green Peace make use of similar strategies in order to generate funds for the causes they believe in.

Another example that illustrates the increasing importance of *for-profit* activities is the commercial manner in which Southern NGOs engage in service delivery activities. These organizations vie for the same government contracts in highly competitive arenas, together with commercial businesses and consultants. Besides the quality of the work, the government takes into account which organization delivers the services for the lowest price. Although, 'making a profit' may not be the only consideration for these NGOs to undertake these activities, the money made on these projects is welcome as it can be re-invested in the organization and its activities. As Korten (1990) rightly described, there is a continuous pressure from donors on non-governmental organizations in the neo-liberal development arena to take on such contracts. Moreover, the donors demand that NGOs do professionalize, especially in regard to financial accountability. Such pressures on NGOs may produce types of organizations that are faced with similar organizational problems as any other business enterprise. For example, organizational growth, linked to the contract mode may increase the demand for better-trained professional staff. Unless there are exceptional socio-political circumstances in which people are willing to volunteer for such jobs, this means that NGOs have to recruit such staff in the regular, often highly competitive, job market. This may result in another push for increased market orientation as the salaries and fringe benefits offered by the NGO have to become competitive. When in parts of such an organization a degree of voluntarism is retained, tensions are likely to occur between the volunteers and the new well-paid professionals. All these examples illustrate that the market is pervading in many institutional settings. The boundaries between for-profit and not-for-profit activities become less and less clear, and in some cases completely blur.

Concluding, I would like to remark that it is not acceptable to describe non-governmental organizations as being wholly not-for-profit as the global market has become so dominant. However, although these pressures have a profound impact on

NGOs, it should be remembered that the non-governmental sector still floats, for a large part, on donor funds. If by tomorrow all donor funds would dry up, very few non-governmental organizations around the world would be able to survive.

Dependence on Donors

Taking the considerable variety of donors into account, it is imperative that social scientists always spell out the type of donor they are analyzing and discussing. The term 'donor', or 'funder', can cover anything from a privately funded foundation (e.g. George Soros' Open Society), to Northern co-funding NGOs, Northern states (bilateral donors) and Multilateral institutions like the European Union and the European Investment Bank. What is clear, however, is that Northern states still play a major role in development assistance, both in bilateral and multilateral contexts and through the disbursement of funds to Northern NGOs. In this regard, Fisher (1998) draws attention to the fact that one could regard the Northern taxpayer as a donor. Although this view could be criticized, since individuals cannot make decisions concerning the destination of their taxes, it is true that especially Northern NGOs have to manage their public image quite carefully in order to please their membership and not antagonize the taxpayer. As was mentioned above, this can cause certain tensions in these organizations as their public image in the North may not correspond with their 'non-political' image in Southern development arenas.

In my view, when analyzing the relationship between Northern donors and their Southern 'partners', it is remains relevant that social scientists are aware of the major power differences between the North and the South. Although donors and development authors often try to obscure those differences by employing technical and neutral language, through terms like *development cooperation*, it is still the relatively powerful who donate and the less powerful who receive. In this regard it is fortunate that neo-liberal authors are quite open about the way in which they view the relationship between Northern donors and NGOs. Harry Blair (1997), for example, without a hint of irony discusses how Southern NGOs –he calls them civil society organizations (CSOs)– are 'directed' by Northern donors:

> "...*after their initial launching, the CSOs become, as it were, missiles that are largely internally guided, still subject to some direction from the ground (donors disbursing successive funding tranches when specific conditions are met)...*" (p. 32).

It must be said that such outright top-down and paternalistic statements are easier to analyze than other more politically correct development discourses in which the underlying ideas are the same but the language has been carefully adjusted to the most recent fashions in 'development speak'.

Focusing on the Northern NGOs that fund 'counterpart organizations' in the South, it is crucial to realize that although many Northern NGOs depend on Northern government funds, they themselves are the donors in their relationship with Southern NGOs. Bosch (1997) views these NGOs through Southern spectacles and calls them 'foreign non-governmental funding agencies'. This is exactly what they are, although I would prefer the term Northern non-governmental funding organizations (NGFO), in order to keep with the North-South and NGO terminology. An issue that is raised in the 'NGO literature' concerns the quality of this type of donor. Certain authors like

Fowler (1997), for example, regard these donors as fundamentally different from other donor agencies. They are said to have a different approach towards 'development' and regard the Southern NGOs much more as their 'partners'.

In Fowler's (1997) opinion the funding that is handled by those Northern non-governmental funding organizations is of a higher quality. It boils down to the discussion whereby it is said that there is an increasing pressure from donors generally –what Fowler calls 'the official aid system'– on NGOs to become more involved in 'service delivery' in substitution of Southern states, as was also argued by Korten (1990). The one group of donors that does not endorse this push are these Northern non-governmental funding organizations. According to Fowler these organizations fund Southern NGOs in a manner that truly strengthens civil society as these Southern 'partners' in turn support 'grassroots organizations'. To distinguish between funds from ordinary –read: push for service delivery– donors and Northern NGFOs, Fowler comes up with some interesting terminology. He contrasts the 'high quality' 'warm money' disbursed by Northern NGOs with the 'low quality' 'cold money' of other donors. In my view we need to assess this dichotomy critically.

As Fowler sees 'high quality' funds diminishing, he argues that Southern NGOs should be very careful in how they use these 'warm' funds. If there is no ocean of such funds, but only a respectable pond, 'high quality' funds should not be used for activities that replicate government delivery. Therefore, in his view, these funds should be used for types of core funding that ensure learning and more independence from 'ordinary' donors. According to Fowler (1997) such funding is increasingly concentrated in the hands of a few Northern non-governmental funding organizations –NGDOs in his terminology. As a result, whether they want it or not, these Scandinavian, English, German, Dutch and American organizations will become relatively more powerful. Thus, Fowler warns us that *"...this handful of Northern financing NGDOs will increasingly determine which NGDOs in the South and East enjoy higher levels of autonomy from government and the official aid system..."* (p.219). Nevertheless, Fowler is generally positive about the role of this limited group of Northern non-governmental funding organizations. 'Civic autonomy' is ensured when Southern NGOs are approached by Northern civic partners that speak 'the same language'. Moreover, Northern NGFOs are said to be more flexible so that they can also fund smaller Southern organizations.

I believe, however, that such arguments should not be taken for granted as Northern non-governmental funding organizations hold the purse that predominantly contains Northern government money. Like any other donor, Northern NGFOs are in a position to exert considerable pressure on their 'partner organizations' regarding the way in which 'business' is conducted. Certainly, according to Kasfir (1998), *"...donors rarely create autonomous organizations. Indeed, an aid-created* **independent** *civil organization comes close to being an oxymoron[8]"* (p. 134). What is needed, therefore, is thorough research to discover what elements of dependency play a role in such relationships. In this book, for example, I explore whether the Monti Rural Association recognizes these 'high quality' funders for what they are, and whether their modus operandi fundamentally differs from other types of funding agencies.

With respect to the five NGO characteristics, formulated in a 'working definition' and discussed above, it was shown that the 'NGO literature' should be critically considered for its flaws. 'Relative insiders' engage too often in wishful thinking and the echoing of myths about NGOs. Possibly, other approaches, that ensure a more critical distance by the social scientist should be considered. In order to expose the myths about NGOs there is a tremendous need for historically, socially, politically and economically embedded case studies.

The Benefits of an 'Anthropology[9] of Development'

In criticizing the 'NGO literature' I have suggested that these texts are primarily produced by non-governmental organizations, their representatives and, for example, academics hired as consultants to produce reports as well as 'scientific' publications. In other words, the 'NGO literature' is produced by relative 'insiders'. Grillo (1997) has shown that in recent discussions about the crisis in anthropology a distinction is made between *anthropology of development* and *development anthropology*[10]. In his words development anthropology is *"...engaged directly in application..."* (p. 2), while an anthropology of development is *"...primarily concerned with the socio-scientific analysis of development as a cultural, economic and political process"* (p. 2). Thus, the first refers to anthropologists being hired to evaluate projects or give policy advice, while the latter refers to a more independent form of scientific research, primarily concerned with gaining an improved understanding. An applied *development anthropology* is produced by relative 'insiders' while a more reflective *anthropology of development* is produced by relative 'outsiders'. In my opinion, therefore, the 'NGO literature' is a typical example of development anthropology.

Although I endorse the distinction between *development anthropology* and *anthropology of development* as sensitizing concepts, it must be noted that such a dichotomy is fundamentally flawed and, thus, has its limitations. On the positive side, it helps to sensitize us to the existence of different realms in which knowledge is (re-)produced. On the negative side, it may cause us to overemphasize the differences in order to reject one of the two bodies of knowledge. Moreover, it may cause us to ignore the fact that there is a large grey area. Gardner and Lewis (1996), therefore, warn us that *"...the 'anthropology of development' cannot be easily separated from 'development anthropology' (i.e. applied anthropology)"* (p. 50). This grey area is partly caused by the fact that some academics may switch freely between two roles – researcher and applied researcher, as was argued by Grillo (1997, p.2). This can lead to confusion, as it is sometimes not clear who plays which role.

When discussing the use of dichotomies in the social sciences some authors are very critical. Long (1992), for example, argues against the dichotomy *knowledge for understanding* versus *knowledge for action*:

> *"...such a dichotomy (...) encourages field practitioners and intervention experts to adopt a sanguine view of the possibilities of fundamental research contributing to the solution of concrete problems, and at the same time shields the researcher from having to struggle seriously with the issues of practical concern"* (p. 3).

In his view, therefore, theoretical and pragmatic activities are intertwined and should not be separated. Consequently, Long proposes an actor-oriented approach, whereby:

> "...its concepts are grounded in the everyday life experiences and understandings of men and women, be they poor peasants, entrepreneurs, government bureaucrats or researchers" (p. 5).

However, it remains unclear what can be done with such an 'improved understanding' gained through an actor-oriented approach. In an article with van der Ploeg (1994) Long gives us a hint:

> "We believe that an actor-oriented approach has implications for development practice in that it has a sensitizing role to play vis-à-vis researchers and implementors" (p. 82).

In other words, Long and van der Ploeg (1994) believe that an implementor, who has gained certain insights about the local level through an actor-oriented approach, will subsequently improve his interventions. However, I would argue that since (improved) knowledge is not the only factor in implementation, their hope may be vain.

Especially since the dichotomy is problematic, the problem remains how to distinguish between 'development anthropology' texts and 'anthropology of development' texts. Although 'fingerspitzengefühl' may be helpful, instances do remain where it is fairly unclear how to categorize the text under scrutiny. In some cases, for instance, 'anthropology of development' texts may contain 'development anthropological' assertions. In this regard it is interesting to mention Gardner (1997), who is evidently involved in 'an anthropology of development', but falls for an NGO myth: *"... 'empowerment' approaches still tend to rely heavily upon the 'expert' advice of outsiders (this is not, however, the case with NGOs, whose empowerment approaches are usually based on grassroots experience)"* (p. 154). To repeat such a myth is evidently quite problematic. Another problem with regard to the categorization of texts has to do with the fact that academia is not as 'pure' and 'independent' as some of us want to believe. Even academia is being increasingly funded by commercial agencies and a clear boundary between commercially funded research and 'independent' research is often hard to draw.

It is, nonetheless, encouraging to acknowledge that at least one of the bodies of knowledge seems excellently suited to expose the other. An 'anthropology of development' can expose the manner in which academics are 'co-opted' to produce a 'development anthropology' text. In this regard Ferguson's (1990) Lesotho study is an excellent example. Bringing back the 'political' and 'the historical' in his analysis of the World Bank intervention in Lesotho, he exposed how the academics, who had been hired by the bank, produced a report on Lesotho that ignored the (socio-political) history of the country and the fact that it was geographically and socio-economically embedded in South Africa.

It is this same author who actually makes an interesting contribution to the above debate. In his argument he does not discuss the relationship between 'development anthropology' and an 'anthropology of development', but points out the differences between a "development" discourse and an academic discourse: *"...I take the incompatibility of "development" discourse and academic norms as a point of departure..."* (p. 29). In his view, both discourses do not simply deal with 'the facts', *"but with a constructed version of the object"*. However, in his elucidation he also contends that no absolute schism exists. Nevertheless:

> *"the point (...) is to reveal (...) that the "development" literature is full of statements which would be unacceptable in most academic settings, while at the same time many observations and lines of thought commonplace in scholarly literature (...) are effectively excluded from the discourse of "development""* (p. 29).

Subsequently, if we accept that each body of knowledge is produced in its own social context –the first by and for 'organizations', the second by and for 'academia'– we have to deal with the problem of *translation*. That holds true in both directions. Implementing agents have to translate fundamentally scientific findings into applicable and politically acceptable measures, while academics may want to incorporate more applied findings –for example, produced by NGOs– into their 'anthropology of development' publications. The problem for implementing agents, however, is that they do not only have to combine knowledge gained from different sources, but they are also experiencing pressure from different directions. Political and financial pressures by donors, or a concern for the financial survival of an organization, may eventually have a stronger impact on development interventions than improved knowledge. However, and this is also significant, there are, indeed, instances in which NGOs and other development institutions are able to make use of the findings produced by an 'anthropology of development'.

In conclusion I would argue that 'NGO literature' is produced by 'relative insiders' and definitely has 'development anthropology' characteristics. However, we have to be careful not to interpret the distinction between 'development anthropology' and 'anthropology of development' as an absolute dichotomy. There is definitely an overlap and a grey zone. Not only because the same academics may produce both, but also because certain organizations are able to take into account –or translate– the results of more fundamental 'anthropology of development' research.

An Eclectic Approach

In this research project I have chosen not to follow one 'school of thought' rigidly, but to build eclectically upon a scholarly basis –'the Wageningen School'– and use other inspiring anthropological and development sociological sources. Moreover, I make use of other academic disciplines like (political) history, African studies, social geography and political science, to thoroughly embed the project.

First, I aim to describe my own academic background, or, to use a South African expression: "where I come from". Having been educated at the Wageningen Agricultural University, much of my academic development can be attributed to Norman Long and the 'Wageningen School' he established. Members of that 'school' are stimulating scholars such as Nuijten (1992, 1998), Villareal (1992), de Vries (1992a, 1992b), Verschoor (1992, 1997) and Hilhorst (2000). The foundation stone of this 'Wageningen School' is Long's (1992) 'actor-oriented approach', which:

> *"...aims to offer a flexible conceptual framework for comprehending development processes, including planned intervention but not exclusively. Its guiding analytical concepts are: agency and social actor, the notion of multiple realities and arenas of struggle where different life-worlds and discourses meet, and the idea of interface in terms of discontinuities of interests, values, knowledge and power"* (p. 271).

In trying to understand development processes Long focused on 'interventions', whereby he and van der Ploeg (1989) argued that:

> "...the concept of intervention needs deconstructing so that we recognize it for what it fundamentally is, namely, an ongoing, socially constructed and negotiated process, not simply the execution of an already-specified plan of action with expected outcomes" (p. 228).

Thus it should be realized that:

> "...interventions are always part of a chain or flow of events located within the broader framework of activities of the state and the actions of different interest groups in civil society" (p. 228).

The actor-oriented approach provided me with valuable insights into socio-scientific research and the unravelling of empirical situations. Besides the fact that the approach is critical of current concepts and methodologies, it also involves questioning the role of the researchers themselves.

With respect to this research project, an actor-oriented approach involves the unravelling of processes of development in which non-governmental organizations are involved. To study these NGOs as made up of social actors, means not only giving attention to the impact of 'larger' world relations in the local context, but also having an eye for local relations that influence the outcome. The approach does not involve easy simplifications, but tries to describe the mechanisms involved in development processes in all their aspects. Thus, it aids to identify different social worlds and especially arenas of struggle between these social worlds. In such interfaces negotiation and (non-)accommodation takes place between actors, representing distinctive interests, who are each part of networks of knowledge and power. My research, therefore, involved a multi-vocal, multi-level and multi-sited approach, whereby I have attempted to make sure that many actors were 'heard'. Not only have I conducted ethnographic research on the 'meso'-level of NGOs and the provincial government, but also on the local level and even on the national level. Of course, this involved fieldwork in many different sites to prevent a locational bias[11].

Another inspiring scholar is James Ferguson (1990). Like Long, Ferguson has shown that development processes should be analyzed in relation to wider socio-political, socio-economic and historical processes. In his influential and inspiring book about Lesotho, *The Anti-Politics Machine*, he showed how the World Bank, by employing a discourse that is full of *"...nation-fetishized 'development' talk..."* (p. 62), sweeps aside history as well as politics. It is clear that, like Long, Ferguson follows in the footsteps of Foucault by employing discourse analysis to study development processes. In a meticulous manner Ferguson scrutinizes the development discourse of the World Bank, which is veiled in neutral and technical language, thereby showing how the bank masks the profound political impact of its interventions. His textual analyses –linked to ethnographic fieldwork to look at practices– provide an inspiring example for the scope of such a methodology. According to Ferguson (1990) the World Bank analyzed and described Lesotho as a primitive agrarian nation-state, without taking into account its long history and its regional embeddedness. This 'trick' enabled the bank to present its own definition of Lesotho's development problems, followed by a recipe of remedies to overcome those problems. Moreover, Ferguson makes clear that political factions stood to gain from the World Bank's Thaba-Tseka Project, through which a whole region was opened up and bureaucratic state power was expanded by a central government that gained political and military footholds in the region. In Ferguson's view the World Bank became an *anti-politics machine.*

Ferguson teaches us two important lessons that can also be applied to the changing role of NGOs in a transforming South Africa. First, the need to consider the history of a region and its institutions, and, second, the necessity to be aware of past and present (socio-)political processes. Additionally of course, it is important to be conscious of socio-economic and geographic realities. This has prompted me to produce, what I have called, 'an embedded tale' about land sector NGOs in the Eastern Cape province of South Africa. In such a tale the historical, political and socio-economic elements feature prominently. Without understanding the history of a region, a country, a province and a local area, no adequate analysis of development processes is possible. Since many intervening parties (possibly intentionally) ignore the history of an area, it is up to the social scientist to (re-)introduce that dimension in his or her analysis. Thus, I have chosen to discuss how the struggle for land is intimately tied to South Africa's apartheid history. For example, the creation of the homelands, the popular struggle against apartheid, and the most recent history of political transformation in post-apartheid South Africa greatly impacted on the role of land sector NGOs in the region. Moreover, since there is hardly a society today that has become as politicized over the past few decades, the political dimension could hardly be ignored. During my fieldwork in 1996, 1997 and 1998 I became aware of the presence of political tensions just below the surface of nearly every human interaction. In South Africa, whether in casual conversation, academic debate or NGO workshops about pit latrines, (party-)politics permeates every discussion.

In the South African context, the apartheid regime was also very apt in presenting political measures with a severe impact in more neutral terms, in an attempt to conceal its hidden agendas. In this connection, the book edited by Boonzaier and Sharp (1988), *South African Keywords: the uses and abuses of political concepts,* is very useful and revealing. It shows, for example, how the South African government replaced a racial discourse with a cultural and ethnic discourse when it argued in favour of the creation of the homelands. In the context of the Ciskei and the Transkei, two former homelands that were created during apartheid with the aid of an ethnic discourse[12], I, for example, aim to argue that, although ethnicity played a role, the (party-)political struggle for power in the reserves had a much greater impact on the developments in the past decades. It may even be a moral duty of anthropologists to (re-)introduce the political and historical dimension in such a context as anthropologists in the past have worked closely with the colonial and apartheid regimes to do exactly the opposite.

Although relatively little has been published about the Ciskei as a homeland, the work by Switzer (1993), Anonymous (1989), Manona (1997) and de Wet (1997) is excellent material that provides great insight in the political dimensions of the struggle for power in a homeland. Moreover, Bundy (1988, 1977) and Beinart and Bundy (1987) have written influential works on the Eastern Cape peasantry in which they have managed successfully to do away with the colonial myth that African farmers have always been backward and in need of development, like the apartheid betterment schemes. Furthermore, authors like Bernstein (1996), Murray (1996) and Bank (1997) have published inspiring accounts about the post-apartheid agrarian situation and persistent present-day myths about the rural population that may cloud our understanding. Although several other authors who have published about South Africa have inspired me, I want to keep this list manageable by ending with Mahmood Mamdani (1996). His book *Citizen and Subject* should be mandatory reading for every scholar interested in Africa. Instead of stressing the uniqueness of the South African experience he shows us that apartheid had everything to do with colonial rule, through *decentralized despotism*.

Coming back to Ferguson (1990), it must be argued that he is also heavily criticized for presenting 'the development apparatus' in Lesotho as one powerful hegemonic entity. The World Bank in collusion with many development organizations and in partnership with central government is, according to Ferguson, engaged in the same development discourse. Thus, authors like Grillo (1997) and Gardner (1997) liken Ferguson to Escobar (1991, 1995) who is very outspoken about 'the development industry' as well. For example, in *Encountering Development: the making and the unmaking of the third world,* Escobar (1995) argues how the North has attempted to keep the South dependent in the post-colonial era through development assistance. Although it is useful that he reminds us of the great inequalities in the world, I am afraid that he overstates his case. His argument loses strength by presenting the development industry as one dominating entity with a sole purpose: continued hegemony of the North. In his own words: *"...development is the last and failed attempt to complete the Enlightenment project in Asia, Africa, and Latin America"* (p. 221). Therefore, Escobar sees a need for the Third World peoples to unmake and unlearn development, because, as he warns us in the last sentence of his book, *"...in many places there are worlds that development, even today and at this moment, is bent on destroying"* (p. 226). Such an apocalyptic and reified use of the term 'development' is in my view not suitable to come to interesting analyses and a deeper understanding. Although I am the last to deny that it is important to be sensitive to such inequalities, Escobar fails to see the many conflicting development discourses that exist, and have existed in all regions of the world.

This leads Gardner (1997) to state:

"Although writers such as Escobar and Ferguson are right to point out that the development industry largely draws upon a common pool of discourses peculiar to our age (cf. Ferguson 1990:9), we also need to understand how development knowledge is not one single set of ideas and assumptions. While at one level it may function hegemonically, it is also created and recreated by multiple agents who often have very different understandings of their work" (p. 134).

Although I agree with Gardner in her criticism of Escobar I do feel that it is unfair to place Ferguson in the same camp. Clearly, his study is so much more balanced and he shows that he is aware of the fact that there is not only one hegemonic development discourse in the world. Actually, he states that the development discourse he is describing *"...is bounded in time and space"* (p. 29). And this is exactly the reason why Ferguson seems to encounter a hegemonic development discourse in Lesotho. Firstly, because his research was conducted in the

1970's, a period in history when 'classical' development projects still dominated the scene and the World Bank had not yet allowed dissenting voices to be heard. Secondly, his study is concerned mainly with that large hegemonic institution: the World Bank. Thus, it is not surprising that Ferguson describes the more hegemonic aspects of that discourse.

Another factor that may have caused Ferguson and Escobar to be placed in the same camp is that they both plead to align themselves to more counter-hegemonic groups and social movements. Although I agree with Ferguson (1990) that we should try to participate politically in our own society, I feel that his call to align ourselves with *"...movements of empowerment..."* (p. 286) is scientifically dangerous, as it may lead to us become 'relative insiders' and lose the critical distance that is needed for good research, as the 'NGO literature' has illustrated. In our work it is understanding that we should be after rather than solidarity.

Gardner's statement above is useful as it points to several areas in development discourse analysis that we need to take into account. First of all, there are several levels on which to analyze discourses, whereby we must recognize that discourses at certain levels can also influence what is happening on other levels. A dominant national 'sustainable development discourse', for example, can have a great regional and local impact, but as discourses are reproduced and altered by actors on each level, local discourses of development may, in turn, have a profound impact on higher institutional levels. Secondly, discourses are peculiar to our age, or to state it more generally, the relevance of certain discourses is specific to certain periods in time and in history. Thirdly, I would like to add, discourses are situation specific, especially in more local arenas. The social scientist, therefore, should uncover and provide the context. In which social world (field) is the case embedded? Whose perspective does the development discourse express? Lastly, I would like to remark that it might not be appropriate to use the term 'development discourse' in every context. Since 'development' covers nearly everything, it might be useful to use a more precise terminology.

In the context of this book I have also made use of discourse analysis on several levels and in different realms. As was shown in Chapter 1 –and which will be elaborated in Chapter 3– I have distinguished three political discourses on a national level, linked to three periods in recent South African history. These political discourses –*a struggle discourse, a freedom and consultation discourse* and *a new realism discourse*– reveal the manner in which 'the progressive forces' in South Africa viewed the world. Moreover, those who engaged in development processes also expressed such discourses through their activities. Although these discourses originated in three consecutive periods in history, I argue that the use of these discourses was not limited to those specific periods. Even today social actors may make use of all three discourses, depending on the context, the audience and the development or political activity they partake in.

In order to end this argument, I would like to focus on the lower levels of analysis, and to what I referred to earlier: the need for ethnographic fieldwork. By linking ethnographic type of fieldwork at the organizational level, the project level or the grassroots level with analyses of higher institutional, political and socio-economic levels, much progress can be achieved. A recent EIDOS workshop in 2003 has shown interesting new contributions (Heaton, 2003; Nuijten and van Gastel 2003; Nauta, 2003). An older publication by the EIDOS group, *An Anthropological Critique of Development: the growth of ignorance*, edited by Hobart (1993), especially stands out. In that volume the clash between 'western knowledge' and 'indigenous knowledge' is explored and it is shown how western experts frequently dismiss local knowledge in favour of scientific knowledge and thereby contribute to a growth of ignorance. However, some authors also warn us against regarding 'indigenous knowledge' as something pristine.

An interesting contributor to the volume is Quarles van Ufford, who convincingly explains in which manner knowledge and ignorance are actively managed by participants in policy processes, both in a Javanese church and a Dutch development project. According to Quarles van Ufford, for some ignorance *"...can be an important asset..."* (p. 157). Not knowing what happens at certain levels in an organization may actually be a pre-requisite for particular managers to function in the organizational hierarchy. Already in his 1988 article, *The Hidden Crisis in Development*, Quarles van Ufford proved to be a true pioneer in the critical study of governmental and non-governmental development agencies. He, for example, argued that development institutions are using *definitions of development* that can link different social worlds:

> *"This brings me to a basic ambiguity inherent in all definitions of development. The definitions must present an analysis of social processes in the Third World, and also appeal to those who have an influence over funding decisions. Development goals, then, must relate with equal ease to quite different social worlds"* (p. 20).

Such insights have been a source of inspiration to me when faced with the task to research NGOs.

Concluding Remarks

In conclusion I would argue that the 'NGO literature' should be criticized for its jargon-like features. Although the working definition proved useful to explore the 'NGO literature', it emerged that much research into the role of non-governmental organizations is still needed. First, when examining the intermediary character of NGOs, it becomes clear that little is known about the exact mechanisms involved. For example, what means of 'translation' do NGOs use and how do they, for example, balance their commitment to grassroots with accountability obligations to donors? Second, although I have argued that we should not automatically assume that NGOs are purely value-driven, thorough case studies must be carried out to reveal how NGOs balance their 'value-driven' side with a more 'self-serving' side. Third, I have shown that NGOs cannot be adequately understood without taking into account their relationship with states. We need to understand how such relationships work and what overlaps, between the state sector and NGO sector, tell us about the role of both. In this regard it is heuristically useful to make use of a model in which the state, civil society and the market are represented as overlapping realms. Fourth, although I have already shown that the *non-profit* label is problematic, it is necessary that we discover more about the extent of the impact of 'the market' on the NGO sector. Last, it is important to assess the continued significance of Northern donors. Are we, for example, able to discern different types of funds –'high quality' and 'low quality'– as Fowler (1997) has argued?

I have also indicated that the dichotomy between an *anthropology of development* and a *development anthropology* is not straightforward. Nevertheless, I underwrite the use of the distinction, as it helps us to distinguish between an anthropology that is more concerned with 'application' and an anthropology that is more concerned with understanding. However, we do have to look critically at issues of translation. How can the 'relative insiders' –development anthropologists– make use of research results of 'relative outsiders' –anthropologists of development– and how can these 'relative outsiders' make use of publications produced by 'relative insiders'?

3. Land and Politics

Introduction
The emphasis, in this chapter, is on land and land-related political struggles, with the aim to sketch the background of the arena in which land sector NGOs are operating today. An NGO like the Monti Rural Association, for example, regularly has to mediate in situations of conflict that have their roots in the colonial and apartheid past. Furthermore, the chapter focuses on political processes in order to defuse the myths about African tribalism and ethnicity. Of course, nowadays, ethnicity, pseudo-ethnicity and colonial ethnic categories are still part and parcel of people's lives, as many authors have shown. However, as the history of the Ciskei will illustrate, so-called 'ethnic conflict' usually involved a struggle for political power and resources. Especially in the context of the former bantustans, ethnic arguments, invoking 'traditional imagery', were useful and are, even today, still regularly heard. During my fieldwork in 1996, 1997 and 1998, for example, local chiefs were still very skilful in referring to some mythical 'traditional past', without acknowledging that their Tribal Authority had been part of an authoritarian machinery, based on patronage, during the homeland era. This proficiency in obscuring the fact that they had been part of an oppressive apparatus, in which state salaries, administrative power and political allegiances were much more important than their 'ethnic identity' and 'traditional customs', prompted me to stress these politically coloured processes. I base myself, of course, on the excellent work undertaken by scholars like Mamdani (1996), Boonzaier and Sharp (1988), Vail (1989), Switzer (1993) and Beinart and Bundy (1987).

I end the chapter by presenting some rather bleak figures about the Eastern Cape that illustrate the extent of the apartheid legacy. Spatial absurdities, high unemployment and enormous disparities between the rich and the poor make the Eastern Cape one of the poorest provinces in post-apartheid South Africa. Moreover, I discuss whether most of the Eastern Cape's rural dwellers can actually be regarded as potential farmers. I end this chapter by focusing on some of the novel institutional arrangements that have emerged in the province after the first democratic elections. Especially in the land sector new cooperative arrangements between the government and the NGO sector have been tried. I begin now by looking at the early struggles over land.

Land and Colonialism in South Africa
According to Mamdani (1996) the South African state should be recognized for what it was: another example of the colonial state in Africa, ruling by means of *decentralized despotism*. It ultimately resulted in the creation of ethnically defined bantustans –or homelands–, and had a devastating effect on black land ownership. In the early nineteen nineties a population of fourteen million blacks, lived on 17 million hectares, or 13.7% of South Africa's land surface, while on the other hand 63% of the total South African land surface[1] –or 77 million hectares– was owned by only 77,000 white farmers (Department of Land Affairs 1996 and Auerbach 1990, cited by Minnaar 1994). Such disparities demand some background information.

As it is beyond the scope of this book, I will not discuss all the battles that took place over land during the past centuries. What is clear, however, is that the occupation of the land was essential to the colonial enterprise. Thus a quest for land and a quest for political power went hand in hand. Therefore, many authors regard 1652 –the year that Jan van Riebeeck founded a refreshment station on the shores of Table Bay– as the beginning of black land alienation in South Africa. Almost immediately after their arrival the Dutch began to fight the Khoikhoi, or 'hottentots' as they called them, in several consecutive wars. The Boers[2] then moved east and north where they encountered Nguni groups in the early eighteenth century.

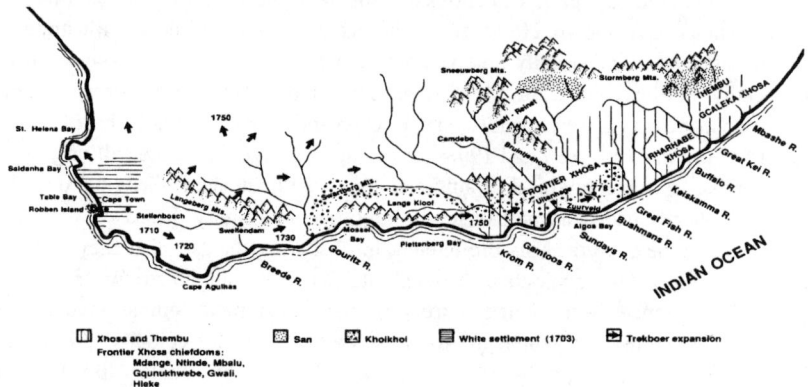

Map 3.1: The Xhosa and colonial advance.

Although, according to Switzer (1993) groups of Dutch trekboers initially even coexisted relatively peacefully with the Xhosa in the Zuurveld[3], they ended up fighting the Xhosa during several so-called frontier wars during the late eighteenth century in what would eventually become the Eastern Cape. The Xhosa, who belong to the Nguni linguistic group, were mixed farmers for whom cattle ownership played an important role in the constitution of society. Some Xhosa groups arrived in the south when they fled the northern areas during the expansion of the Zulu kingdom, 'the Mfecane'.

What is interesting to note here is that during all these battles over territory, different allegiances were formed and loyalties shifted (Switzer, 1993, Maylam 1986), although of course, in the end, the colonial powers prevailed. The Dutch, for example, also fought the British, that conquered the Cape in 1795, again in 1806, and became the official colonial power in 1814. The Xhosa fought amongst themselves as well, like for example the main Gcaleka and Rharhabe Xhosa factions[4]. During several conflicts between Xhosa factions, groups of Dutch Boers supported one of the Xhosa factions. For example, according to Maylam (1986), Coenraad de Buys, the leader of a group of Dutch trekboers who lived at the end of the eighteenth century, became a supporter of the powerful Rharhabe Chief Ngqika because he became the lover of Ngqika's mother. In other instances, groups of trekboers challenged the British colonial authorities, sometimes by trying to rally support among the Xhosa. However, finally, in 1811-1812, Boer commandos enlisted the help of the British to expel 20,000 Xhosa from the Zuurveld. Afterwards, a line of military forts was built, one of which was in Grahamstown, still a well-known settler town, where eventually the Albany Rural Association would be established.

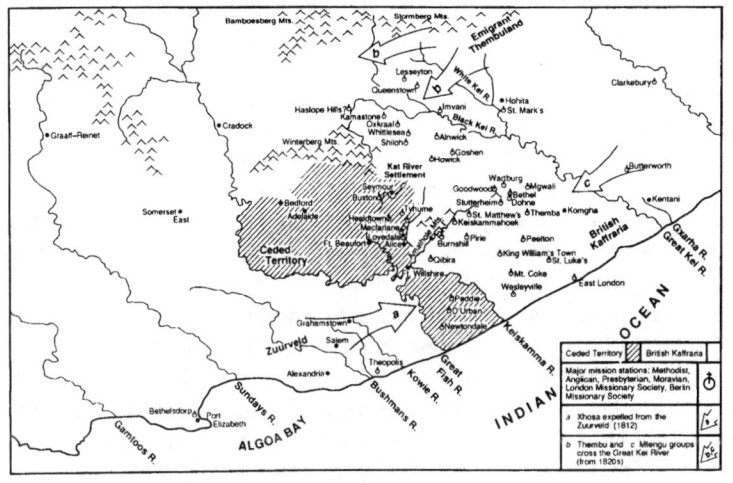

(Source: Switzer, 1993)

Map 3.2: British Kaffraria and Mission Stations.

Another example of an unlikely coalition is a large group of Africans that accepted the British colonial authorities after the frontier war of 1834-1835. This group, made up of various Nguni groups, became known as the Mfengu[5]. The British settled them east of the Fish river to act as a buffer between the Xhosa and the British. In successive frontier wars they fought at the side of the British troops. In 1847 the British managed to deal a powerful blow to their Xhosa opponents, as they succeeded to establish British Kaffraria[6] (see: Map 3.2), which was also known as Ciskei, between the Keiskamma and the Kei river. Thus, the British came to control a large part of the Xhosa territory and forced the Gcaleka Xhosa back across the Kei river.

In the period 1856-1857 another disaster struck the Xhosa, when the infamous 'cattle-killing' took place. Many see it as an important factor in the final demise and subjugation of the Xhosa. The cattle-killing marks one of the most traumatic episodes in Xhosa history and is nowadays still regularly referred to (See the Mail & Guardian excerpt). In the mid 1850s a fatal cattle lung disease swept the Xhosa territories and caused great havoc and social unrest. As a result, several prophets stood up to guide the Xhosa through this crisis. A young Xhosa girl, named Nongqawuse, prophesied that if the Xhosa were to kill their cattle and refuse to grow crops, in

> Tuesday, December 7, 1999
> **XHOSA ROYAL COUNCIL IN TALKS WITH BRITS**
> THE Xhosa Royal Council is meeting representatives of the British High Commission in Johannesburg on Tuesday. The Xhosa Royal Council seeks to establish talks about reconciliation with the British Royal Family in relation to the seven colonial frontier wars and the Nongqawuse incident (The Xhosa National Suicide of 1857) instituted by the British.
> Source: Mail & Guardian: www.mg.co.za/mg/za/news

77

attempt at purification, they could overcome the disease and a new age would dawn for their people. Most Xhosa believed her and many killed their cattle, ceased cultivating their fields and, subsequently lost everything they had. As a consequence, many died of starvation. Nowadays, a coherent explanation for this tragedy is still being debated by historians. Switzer (1993), for example, explains that by rejecting virtually everything they possessed, the Xhosa attempted to purify themselves while waiting for their ancestors –the New People – to bring them new and healthy cattle.

Yet, as the above Mail & Guardian (1999) excerpt seems to confirm, many Xhosa today, believe that the British were responsible for the incident by spreading rumour of the prophesy or even whispering the words in Nongqawuse' ears. Stapleton (1994), however, disagrees with both explanations. In Stapleton's analysis[7] the cattle-killing should be understood as a political act by commoners, who wanted to *"...overthrow their failed chiefs..."* (p. 192). He argues that commoners, who killed the herds of cattle they were caring for, but were owned by their chiefs, protested the collaboration of the chiefs with the British.

As I am not a historian, I am not in the position to judge who is right in this debate. What suffices in this context, however, is to acknowledge that the cattle-killing caused 20,000 people to die of starvation, and the British did their best to exploit the situation in order to finally defeat the Xhosa. Nevertheless, a last frontier war was fought in 1878 when another rebellion of the Xhosa was crushed. For many, however, the Xhosa were truly defeated by the prophesy of a Nongqawuse in 1856-1857.

The Mission Stations, 'Black Spots' and Reserves in the Eastern Cape

After the cattle-killing the influence of Christianity slowly increased. As many Xhosa were destitute and had lost faith in their own prophets, they converted more easily to the Christian faith propagated by the missionaries. Initially, the chiefs had not welcomed the missionaries, as they feared a challenge to their authority. However, as the British colonial pressure increased, according to Switzer (1993):

> *"...the chiefs became more amenable to the missionaries in the vain hope they would intercede on behalf of the Xhosa and somehow contain the expansionist settler community..."* (p. 113).

Thus, chiefs began allocating land to the mission stations. The missionaries attracted many who did not feel at home in their own communities. According to Switzer, mainly young women or widows who refused to (re-)marry, or people who were expelled by their chiefs sought refuge in the mission stations. In his view:

> *"...the missionaries assumed a chiefly role, allocating land and exhorting their people to obey the codes and rituals of belief and behaviour that were characteristic of Victorian Christianity"* (p.115).

Of course, eventually, instead of containing the expansionist settler community, the missionaries became actively engaged in undermining the authority of the chiefs. Switzer even describes how some missionaries led wartime commando units against Xhosa groups. Yet, the process of undermining chiefly power was often more subtle as, for example, missionaries played an administrative role in the taxation of Africans.

What may have had an even greater impact, however, were the ideological and cultural changes that the missionaries promoted. In the Christian tradition an individual work ethic linked to a nuclear family were seen as central values. Therefore, the missionaries promoted agriculture, rather than herding cattle, since that would install more of a work ethic in people. Thus, the dominant role of cattle in Xhosa society was rejected. Especially the fact that women were 'bought' by paying lobola during marriage, was seen as primitive and morally inappropriate. Moreover, although, according to Switzer, precolonial songs, dances, and poetry continued to exist independently, *"...increasingly the mission appropriated these messages and transformed their meaning..."* (p.118). By also capturing the Xhosa language in writing –'freezing' it by taking the dialect spoken by the Ngqika Xhosa– and translating the bible in Xhosa, the mission slowly increased its influence on Xhosa life and culture. Moreover, besides being granted land around the mission stations, a substantial group of Africans was being educated in the Christian tradition. Especially the Mfengu groups, who had aligned themselves with the British, benefited. Slowly, a well-educated Mfengu elite was formed that would eventually play a role in local politics and in the emancipation and struggle for rights of Africans[8].

The land being held by the Mfengu and by converted Xhosa, in the white-controlled areas on the mission stations, were usually individual garden and residential plots combined with communal grazing. For these individual plots people had to pay a yearly quitrent for which they received a quitrent title. In the next century these and other black areas would play a significant role as they would become known as the so-called *black spots*. These were black-owned parcels of land, that were surrounded by white areas from which the apartheid regime tried to remove Africans from the 1950s onwards. The most prominent mission stations that eventually became 'black spots' are represented in Map 3.3.

The Creation of Bantustans
At the end of the nineteenth century, after many armed conflicts, uprisings and revolts the British eventually controlled the Cape Colony and Natal, while the Boers had established themselves firmly in the Transvaal and the Orange Free State. However, in 1899 the South African war broke out between the British and the Boers, also referred to as the 'Boer War'. In this notorious and bloody conflict the two sides fought for hegemony and control of South Africa's resources. After the Boers eventually surrendered, a start was made with negotiations over a united South Africa, incorporating the four colonies. In 1910 the Union of South Africa was proclaimed.

This Union, however, did not herald positive news for black South Africans. Many more would lose the land that they had once inhabited, as Cecil Rhodes had already threateningly announced in the Cape House of Assembly in 1894:

"Every black man cannot have three acres and a cow (...). It must be brought home to them that in the future nine tenths of them will have to spend their lives in daily labour, in physical work in manual labour" (Beinart and Bundy 1987: p. 140).

Thus, also in the twentieth century, efforts continued to solve 'the African Problem'.

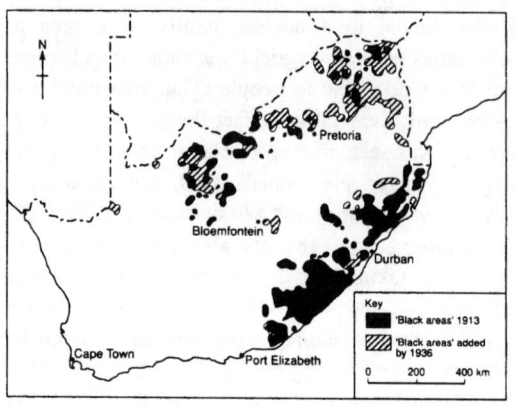

(Source: Worden, 1995)

Map 3.3: Reserve Areas in 1913 and 1936.

In 1913 the Natives Land Act was adopted, which made the rights to own, rent or even share-crop land in South Africa dependent on a person's race. The so-called 'scheduled areas', or black reserves, were created, outside of which black land ownership became prohibited. Millions of blacks were forced to leave their ancestral lands and were resettled in reserves that covered 7% of the land. In the Eastern Cape it led to several scattered black reserve areas that would later become the Ciskei and a larger area which would become the Transkei (Map 3.4). In 1936 the Native Trust and Land Act was adopted, that prohibited blacks to own land in the reserves and obliged them to utilize land administered by tribal authorities, appointed by the government. By then the area covered by the reserves, that served as a basis for what were later to become the 'homelands', was extended to a meagre 13.7% of South Africa's area.

After the National Party came to power in 1948 apartheid –based on an ideology of separate development for each 'racial group'– became an official policy that permeated every sphere of life, from education to marriage to economic life. Subsequently, the Bantu Authorities Act was passed in 1951 which laid the foundation for the road to 'independent' bantustans. In 1959, after the Promotion of Bantu Self-Government Act was passed, the government proclaimed that eight African 'national units' would be recognized. The pass-laws, like the 1955 Natives Urban Areas Amendment Act, made sure that Africans without a permit could no longer move freely into South African territory. Essentially, South Africa became a foreign country for millions of blacks (Beinart and Bundy 1987, Bundy 1988, Surplus People Project 1983a, Bernstein 1996, Department of Land Affairs 1997, et cetera.).

Black families owning freehold land before 1913 were initially exempt from the 1913 act and so-called 'black spots' remained in white farming areas. These black spots became the subject of a second wave of forced removals from 1960 to 1980. The South African state, through the South African Development Trust (SADT), bought land from white farmers that was used to enlarge the homelands only marginally. In that period 3.5 million people were removed from rural and urban areas into the bantustans.

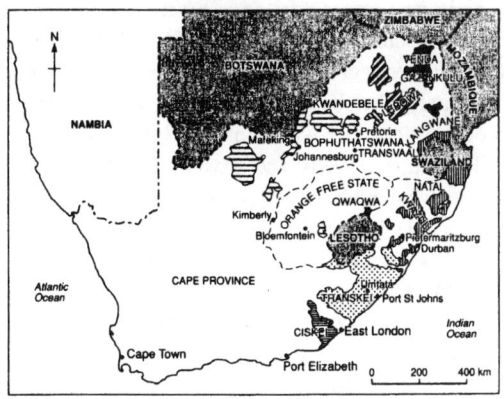

(Source: Worden, 1995)

Map 3.4: Bantustans.

According to the South African government these bantustans, were said to be based on the wish of each 'ethnic group' to govern themselves (see: Map 3.4). Thus, the Ciskei and the Transkei were established for the Xhosa, Kwazulu for the Zulu, Bophuthatswana for the Tswana, Venda for the Venda, Gazankulu for the Tsonga, KaNgwane for the Swazi, QwaQwa for the South Sotho, Lebowa for the North Sotho and KwaNdebele for the South Ndebele. It is clear that 'ethnicity' cannot be viewed in the South African context without looking at the role of the colonial powers and the apartheid regime. In many instances 'ethnicity', 'tribalism' and 'tradition' were created, re-invented –by state-employed anthropologists!– and strongly manipulated by those in power (Vail 1989, Mamdani 1996, Boonzaier and Sharp 1988, et cetera). This type of manipulation becomes quite clear when we study the so-called ethnic groups in the homelands. Without thorough study it is already apparent that other – plausibly more important– factors were crucial in the delineation of the boundaries between the 'ethnic groups'.

What was, for example, the logic behind two separate homelands for the Xhosa and two homelands for the Sotho? Why were all the major cities of South Africa outside these homelands? Why were most homelands aggregations of scattered pieces of unproductive and least fertile land? The answer is rather simple, the white government wanted South Africa for the white minority. It, therefore, created reserves governed by puppet regimes and dictatorial rulers for the black majority. Thus, white South Africa could continue to benefit from the abundance of cheap black labour while it effectively reduced 'the African problem' to a foreign problem. Wealth for the whites, sustained by access to cheap labour, neatly tucked away in unsustainable bantustans. During the apartheid era only four of these homelands were granted 'full'[9] political 'independence': the Transkei in 1976, Bophuthatswana in 1977, Venda in 1979 and the Ciskei in 1981. Although this 'independence' was never internationally recognized this did not change the situation of Africans living in the homelands. In the early 1980's, as more forced removals were planned, protests erupted around the country. This resulted in the Surplus People Project, out of which the Monti Rural Association emerged.

Also having an impact on the African occupation of the land, and linked to the establishment of the bantustans, was the policy of 'betterment' –the Afrikaans term for 'making better'. Betterment policy was veiled in a 'modernization' and 'conservationist' discourse, whereby the government argued that the African way of farming and livestock production was economically inefficient and ecologically harmful, ultimately leading to poverty and erosion. The first attempts at betterment were tried in the early twentieth century. Borrowing conservationist ideas from the USA, the government believed that Africans could be turned into progressive farmers. The whole argument, of course, was somewhat perverse. First the government robbed Africans of most of their land and forced them to live in reserves, which resulted in high population densities, land shortage and erosion. Subsequently, the government proceeded to scold Africans for being incompetent farmers.

Betterment planning involved the separation of arable land from grazing pastures –which were organized in anti-erosion grazing camps– and separating the residential areas from the agricultural areas. Thus, it also involved (forced) villagization, that suited the South African government in its attempts to get a firmer grip on the African population through the establishment of tribal authorities. Furthermore, it involved separating full-time farmers and those who combined farming with migrant remittances (Mamdani 1996). In this regard betterment policy also had a social engineering side to it, as the labour force that was created was also kept tied to the land in the rural areas. What was especially problematic was the enforced culling of cattle. As cattle was economically and culturally important to the Xhosa, this led to widespread rural protests. The first betterment schemes were introduced on black land at the mission stations and, according to Switzer (1993), the Ciskei reserve was turned into a betterment test-case. However, not deterred by the protests, the South African government stepped up its betterment implementation programme between the 1950's and 1980's. Especially in the Ciskei the situation in the villages worsened and led to severe tensions between landowners and the landless and between the tribal authorities and the victims of betterment (Switzer 1993, Westaway, 1997, Mamdani 1996). Moreover, much of the flexibility was removed from the farming systems, which, in many cases, led to even more erosion than before. Many people now lived further away from their agricultural lands and, eventually, abandoned farming altogether. In 2002, the Monti Rural Association, managed to convince the Minister of Land Affairs to include former Ciskeian betterment areas in the Land restitution Programme. This meant that such communities would become eligible for compensation (land or monetary) of land lost during betterment implementation.

In the area which is now the Eastern Cape, two bantustans, or homelands, emerged, the Ciskei and the Transkei (see: Map 3.5). In this chapter some of the relevant historical background information will be discussed as it aids us to understand the story of the Monti Rural Association and the communities it worked with, like Thornhill. Because the Monti Rural Association mostly worked in the Ciskei and the Border area –the white corridor between the Ciskei and the Transkei and the Ciskei–, the history of that region will be more extensively dealt with than that of the Transkei. However, I start with the Transkei because it was the first homeland to gain independence and its history is closely linked to the establishment of the Ciskei. In fact, the dumping of thousands of people in Thornhill was a direct result of Transkeian independence.

The Transkei
After having been a separate administrative unit in the Cape Colony, the Transkei became the largest African reserve in South Africa during apartheid. According to Peires (1992), the Transkei was always an exceptional homeland, because it was largely geographically coherent and:
> "...unlike all the other homelands, it is not inextricably economically interlinked with any specific South African city..." (p. 367).

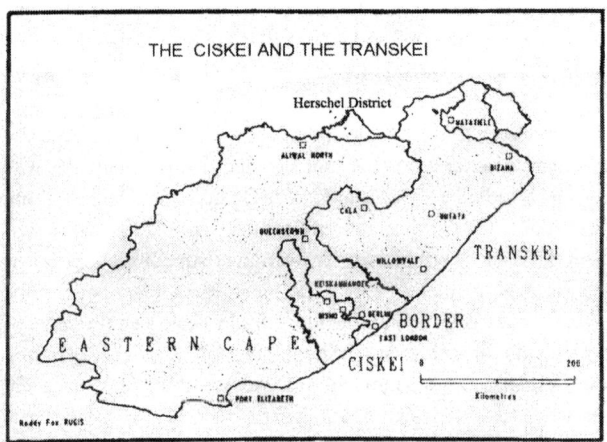

(Source: Adapted from Donaldson, Segar and Southall, 1992)

Map 3.5: Eastern Cape with the Ciskei and the Transkei.

In 1963 the Transkei Constitution Act declared the Transkei a self-governing territory in name. Maylam (1986) described how:
> "A six-man cabinet, presided over by a chief minister, was to be established, as was a Legislative Assembly, comprising sixty-four chiefs and forty-five elected representatives..." (p. 168).

In the ensuing elections, Kaiser Matanzima –who had studied with Mandela at Fort Hare University, but was a supporter of the idea of separate development and opposed the ANC and PAC– won and became the first chief minister. Within a few years, much of the opposition was thwarted and Matanzima's Transkei National Independence Party (TNIP) became the dominant political force. By 1976, the Transkei became the first 'independent' homeland after it had received several additional tracts of land. One of these was the Herschel district (see: Map 3.5), that was taken away from the Ciskei and granted to the Transkei in a consolidation attempt.

Herschel District was one of the reserve areas, created in 1913. It bordered the mountain state of Lesotho and had a large refugee Mfengu[10] population. In a well-known study, *The Rise and Fall of the South African Peasantry,* Colin Bundy (1988,

1977) described the developments that took place in the area between 1870 and 1920. It showed that Africans had actually been very successful commercial peasants in a period before the most constraining land laws took effect. Bundy described Herschel as a rich district in which African farmers flourished in the 1870s by exporting grain to mining areas. In Bundy's view the farmers were relatively successful because the population of Herschel, with its many small immigrant groups, did not have strong chiefs and were, thus, relatively free of constraints like paying tributes. However, as the pressure on the land increased, by encroaching white areas, increasingly fixed boundaries, immigration and an exploding population, the district went into rapid decline. In the early twentieth century the situation got progressively worse and erosion, economic depression and starvation became serious problems. When the district was allocated to the Transkei, thousands of people left Herschel and were dumped by the apartheid regime and the Ciskei regime in the area around Thornhill in the Ciskei.

After the consolidation of the Transkei, the regime of Kaiser Matanzima proved to be authoritarian and corrupt, but became firmly rooted because of several factors. Firstly, as Southall (1992) shows, the Transkeian Defence Force (TDF) – headed by a group of ruthless white military officers– played a crucial role in backing Matanzima. Secondly, the South African government supported the regime financially and economically[11]. Nevertheless, on a political level there was some room for independent views. That is, homeland leaders could –to a certain degree– be critical of particular elements of apartheid. Matanzima, for example, was critical of the system of Bantu education –separate inferior schools for black children– and even broke off diplomatic relations with South Africa in 1978. Lastly, one could say that the Transkei was ruled and exploited by a large elite group in which chiefs and headmen played a considerable role.

Peires (1992), however, warns us that this elite should be analyzed correctly, as he does not agree with those who either state that the homeland leadership and the local bourgeoisie's interests were identical or assume that the latter were the immediate clients of the South African State. According to Peires the homeland leadership was in the hands of chiefs, who:

> *"...cannot be regarded as a 'traditional' ruling class because they have entirely ceased to represent the dominated remnants of the pre-colonial order ..."* (p. 384).

Significant, in this respect, is the fact that the South African government created a Paramountcy in Emigrant Thembuland by dividing Thembuland –a region in the Transkei– in two in the late fifties. By giving Matanzima the title of Paramount Chief of Emigrant Thembuland his political position was strengthened.

Moreover, according to Peires, the homeland governments should be seen as being part of the South African government apparatus, without implying that they are simply part of the South African government bureaucratic command structure. He identifies the homeland regimes as being part of patrimonial *"clientelist networks"* (p. 385):

> *"The homeland leadership is neither the puppet of the South African state, nor does it represent the interests of the homeland bourgeoisie. Rather it is the intermediate link between the two in a clientelist chain of command"* (p. 385).

I agree with Peires that one cannot speak of 'one bourgeoisie'. I would say that the history of the bantustans has proven that powerful (pseudo-)ethnic, or political elite factions have been in constant competition with each other for the political control of scarce resources and South African support. This last point is important as it was always South Africa that played a dominant role in homeland politics, either openly or covertly. Sometimes the policy boomeranged, for example when Bantu Holomisa came to power in the Transkei.

In 1986, the South African government, being fed up by the corruption going on in the Transkei, replaced Kaiser Matanzima with his brother George. A period of confusion and infighting followed, in which even a coup attempt against the Ciskei regime was staged. In a short space of time several leadership changes followed, that ended in another coup in 1987 that brought Bantu Holomisa to power. This young military officer who had been detained by Kaiser Matanzima, and been made a general in the Transkeian Defence Force by Kaiser's brother George, established the Transkei Military Council (TMC), which did as it promised. As Southall (1992) describes, the TMC instituted two commissions of inquiry into corruption. Therefore, the Pretoria government was initially quite pleased with the new ruler. However, that soon changed as Holomisa made an unexpected move.

Holomisa's move, in November 1989, involved a show of solidarity with a legendary Transkei opposition figure. Holomisa staged the reburial of an old adversary of Kaiser Matanzima –pro-ANC Thembu Paramount Chief Sabata Dalindyebo– who had been accused in the late seventies of treason by Matanzima. In 1980 Dalindyebo had fled to Zambia and died there in exile in 1986. Originally, when the body returned home it had been placed in a commoner's grave by Kaiser Matanzima, which had gravely offended the Thembu. According to Southall (1992), Holomisa organized a reburial to *"...correct Matanzima's abuse of customary practices..."* (p. 6) and align himself with Dalindyebo and his pro-ANC ideas. The ceremony became a large political rally, attended by thousands of people, including some high profile ANC members like Winnie Mandela. To the dismay of Pretoria, Holomisa in his speech then proceeded to announce his plans to organize a referendum to determine whether the people were in favour of reincorporating the Transkei in South Africa. Furthermore, Holomisa held talks with the banned organizations and soon after the funeral:

> *"...and some three months before President de Klerk took similar action in South Africa, the TMC unbanned the ANC and PAC along with 13 other national and local opposition groups"* (Southall, p. 6).

From that moment onwards, things changed fast and Holomisa proved to be a useful ally for the ANC, since he was one of the few bantustan leaders who publicly declared his willingness to return the Transkei to a united South Africa.

The early nineties witnessed at least three coup attempts against Holomisa, supported by elements of the former ruling elite in concurrence with South African covert forces. They all failed and in 1994 the Transkei was officially reincorporated into South Africa. Holomisa went on to become a popular ANC figure, but was expelled from the organization after he made public accusations against prominent ANC members concerning alleged corruption.

In the next section I discuss the other homeland in the Eastern Cape: the Ciskei.

The Ciskei and the Border Corridor

As was mentioned above, the name 'Ciskei' first surfaced after the establishment of British Kaffraria in 1847. The name 'Ciskei' refers to land 'this side' –west– of the Kei river, as opposed to 'Transkei', meaning across the Kei river. The reserve area was at first a conglomeration of scattered areas in what is now the Eastern Cape province and was only consolidated into one geographical entity in the early 1980s. As Anonymous[12] (1989) describes, the Ciskei government evolved out of the Ciskeian General Council (CGC) that had been established in 1934. According to Switzer (1993), the CGC, also referred to as 'Bunga', only represented the eight local councils for Africans, including the Glen Grey District Council[13]. The Bunga, that was mainly advisory in nature, was even weaker than its Transkeian counterpart, because the local councils in the Ciskei largely controlled their own revenue. Both the Bunga and the local councils were chaired by white commissioners, who largely controlled the agenda. According to Switzer, councillors were explicitly "...*forbidden to discuss 'political' matters...*" (p. 227). Thus, the Bunga mainly concerned itself with issues like health, roads and anti-erosion measures.

After the bantustan legislation was passed in the 1950s, the Bunga was dissolved, and a three-tiered system of government was introduced. This included Tribal and/or Community Councils at the lowest level, followed by Regional Authorities at the intermediate level and the Ciskei Territorial Authority (CTA) at the highest level. The CTA, or 'New Deal', was formed in 1968 and headed by an executive committee, consisting of six ministers, that was supported by a civil service. The first Chief Councillor was Justice Mabandla, a Mfengu chief. As was explained above, the Mfengu were a collection of several groupings that had migrated into the area during the time of Zulu King Shaka. They had converted to Christianity and fought on the side of the British against the Xhosa in the frontier wars. Thus there was always a certain amount of tension, as the Rharhabe Xhosa had always resented the Mfengu for their part in the war. These Rharhabe had actually taken the opportunity to take back the control they had lost to the Mfengu in the rural areas, when the National Party began its policy of retribalization in the 1950s. According to Manona (1980), the white Commissioner-General, Hans Abraham, who represented the South African government in the Xhosa homelands at the time of Mabandla's New Deal, actually dominated the Ciskei political scene, by making effective use of ethnic tensions in the Mfengu-Rharhabe relationship to control the territory.

According to Anonymous (1989), the Rharhabe were annoyed by the dominance of Mabandla, because of his Mfengu roots. Thus, when Lennox Sebe, who had been minister of education in Mabandla's cabinet, was demoted to the position of minister of agriculture, he decided to run against Mabandla in the next elections for the Ciskei Legislative Assembly (CLA), the successor of the CTA. Sebe mobilized influential businessmen and several Rharhabe chiefs in a group that called itself *Ikhonco*[14], which means 'link' in Xhosa. According to Charton and kaTywakadi (1980), Sebe effectively rallied around Rharhabe ethnic sentiments against the Mfengu. One issue which was exploited was the fact that many Mfengu were now the landowners –they had received land that had belonged to the Xhosa when the British defeated the Xhosa– while many Rharhabe refugees were landless. To the utter dismay of Mabandla, Sebe's strategy worked and, thus, in 1973 Lennox Sebe became the first Chief Minister of the Ciskei. Sebe, is cited by Charton and kaTywakadi, as having stated after the victory:

> "... The reason why I now find myself in his post [i.e. Chief Mabandla's] is the fact that we belong to different tribes. Chief Mabandla is a Fingo and I am a Rharhabe..." (p. 126).

Most authors, however, also emphasize the fact that the South African government supported Sebe, as irregularities were reported during the elections.

At a local level the people in the Ciskei were ruled through the Tribal Authorities. A Tribal Authority (TA) was not simply an ancient but revived 'traditional' institution, but rather, as Manona (1997) convincingly argues, an efficient top-down ruling structure in which consultation with the people and consensus-building had largely been scrapped. Linked to the establishment of TAs were the South African government's betterment planning policies, that were discussed above and which involved (forced) villagization. Councillors of the Tribal Authority were not elected by the people, but appointed by the TA. Although in earlier times, chiefs only made decisions after consulting the people and an inner circle of advisors, in the new political situation, "...*the chiefs generally were no longer directly responsible to their people, but were civil servants with specific obligations to the government...*" (p. 58). In that sense Manona (1997) seems to agree with Peires (1992) who stated that the Ciskei government was dominated by chiefs who were *"...part of a state apparatus which is centred not in the homeland itself but in Pretoria"* (p. 385). Thus, the chiefs had absolute power and would only be challenged in the eighties when locally organized residents associations were formed by the indignant youth.

Pseudo-ethnicity
After having been elected as Chief Minister, Lennox Sebe proceeded to establish himself firmly at the helm of government. First of all he formed his own political party, the Ciskei National Independence Party (CNIP), while Mabandla formed the Ciskei National Party (CNP). However, since the parties almost equalled each other in size, Sebe had to devise a strategy to gain more support. According to Switzer:

> *"Sebe could strengthen his party in the Ciskei Legislative Assembly (CLA) only by establishing new tribal authorities. Nine were created between 1973 and 1976..."* (p. 332).

This included one for himself. Anonymous (1989) tells us how Sebe, after a first failed attempt, finally established himself, with 23 landless families, as Rharhabe chief on a white farm, called Ndevana, that had been added to the Ciskei for consolidation purposes. By 1979 40,000 refugee farm workers had been resettled on the farm, according to the SPP report (1983b) for the Eastern Cape. This suited Sebe – who was rarely present– as more inhabitants meant more power and a higher chiefly salary.

Moreover, it also appears that the ceding of Herschel and the Glen Grey districts to the Transkei in 1975 was part of Sebe's strategy to gain absolute control in the Ciskei Legislative Assembly. Several groups of refugees from Herschel and Glen

Grey, for example, were allowed to establish their own Tribal Authorities. In the case of Thornhill, three Herschel chiefs established themselves in the resettlement camp and subsequently became active supporters of Sebe and MPs in the CLA. Although, some authors would describe the immigrant groups that had originally settled in Herschel in the 19th century as 'Mfengu', in this context, it is important to make a distinction between the Mfengu that were settled by the British in the area East of the Fish River and those that had settled in northern areas like Herschel. Thus, Sebe was able to convince the Herschel chiefs to support him in his struggle against Mabandla, a Mfengu. Switzer (1993) describes how, as a result, Lennox Sebe won an overwhelming victory in the 1978 elections. Moreover, he proceeded to appoint Mfengu ministers which convinced the CNP opposition, including Mabandla, to cross the floor and join the CNIP. Thus, according to Anonymous, the Ciskei became, effectively, a one-party state based on patronage. Lennox Sebe, subsequently, became President for Life.

After Sebe had successfully exploited ethnic sentiments to come to power, and the tables had turned when Mabandla joined his cabinet, the new ruler did everything to discard the ethnic discourse. Anonymous (1989) argues that this was not difficult because, *"...in as much as the CNIP was an ethnic party (...) it was truly a party of like-minded individuals working for common goals..."* (p. 403). In order to mend relations with the opposition Sebe now concentrated on Ciskei nation-building:

> *"President Sebe now aimed to build a new and united nation owing allegiance to neither Rharhabe nor Mfengu ethnic loyalties, but united in a single Ciskeian nationalism"* (p. 402).

Sebe, in the process, replaced governing by party –which he had done very successfully– with governing by patronage. According to Anonymous, *"...dropping his anti-Mfengu rhetoric was a small price to pay for the broadening of his support"* (p. 403). Nevertheless, Sebe continued to get rid of people whom he deemed too powerful. For example, a descendant of the great chief Maqoma, was sacked from the cabinet and exiled from the Ciskei.

One of Sebe's most obvious attempts at nation-building was the construction of a national shrine at Ntaba kaNdoda ('the mountain of man'), a small mountain in the Ciskei that featured in a well-known Xhosa poem. According to Anonymous (1989), Sebe built a conference centre, an 18,000-seat arena and a heroes cemetery. Every government employee was required to attend the party gatherings at least once a year, and Sebe's security apparatus made sure that anyone who did not attend received a salary cut or even lost his job. Moreover, at Ntaba kaNdoda the population was regularly invited to make contributions to Sebe's party coffers; money that was frequently used by Sebe for private purposes.

Although King William's Town was supposed to become the capital of an 'independent' Ciskei, Anonymous (1989) described how its white residents fought incorporation and managed just before the 1981 elections in the Ciskei to block the addition of the town to the Ciskei. As a result Sebe was 'given' a new capital city, just seven kilometres away from King William's Town. The new capital, named Bisho, reflected Sebe's megalomania, by boasting statues, impressive ministerial buildings, a sports stadium and a presidential palace. Moreover, Sebe deemed it necessary to construct an international airport –suitable for Boeings– that was never used except for his own presidential jet.

What most troubled Lennox Sebe, though, was the fact that the Ciskei, unlike the Transkei, had never been unmistakably one territory, and, thus, lacked legitimacy. Moreover, the Ciskei lacked natural resources, was not particularly suitable for farming as it was quite dry, and lacked an economic base. Therefore, during its whole existence, the Ciskei remained the hinterland of cities and regions that remained part of the South African Republic. The Ciskei's border reflected this problem. For example, although, it would have been obvious to the neutral observer to add East London and King William's Town to the Ciskei, the South African government decided that these white urban centres should remain within South Africa. Therefore, the border of the Ciskei bantustan weaves ingenuously around these towns, in such a way that only their townships were made part of the Ciskei (see: Map 3.6).

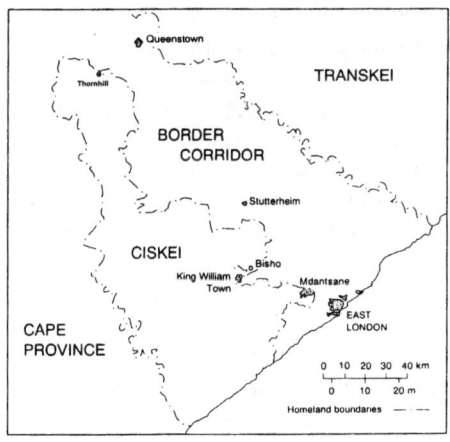

(Source: Adapted from Buckle, 1995)

Map 3.6: The Border Region.

As a result, East London Africans were for a large part removed to a newly built township called Mdantsane, located 25 kilometres from the city centre, which, according to the Surplus People's Project (1983b), had a population of around 200,000 in 1980 and which is nowadays one of the largest townships in South Africa. In that sense the Ciskei was a true labour reserve, as thousands of commuters had to travel from the Ciskei to South Africa –from Mdantsane to East London– every day. Many of these people, were politically conscious and had a history in the labour unions, as can be expected after having become acquainted with Eastern Cape history[15]. Mdantsane, therefore, was always a source of trouble for the Ciskei regime.

Moreover, as the Surplus People Project (1983ab) reports have shown, the Ciskei was a convenient dumping ground for the 'excess' black population, which was removed from South African soil. During the late seventies and eighties many so-called 'black spots' in the Border area, between the Ciskei and the Transkei, were earmarked for removal. These areas, frequently around the old missions stations, were the last vestiges of black land ownership in the white corridor. The aim was to remove the black population when the Ciskei territory was consolidated. Furthermore, white farmers evicted thousands of 'excess' farm workers to what was to become the 'independent' Ciskei. Many protests and successful campaigns of rural people were the result, in which organizations like the Monti Rural Association played a dominant role as is shown in the following chapters.

Independence and Decline

Although a commission appointed by Sebe himself advised against 'independence', Sebe went ahead and is said to have manipulated a referendum in 1980 to get a mandate by the people. Thus, in December 1981, the Ciskei became independent, after ceding Herschel and Glen Grey to the Transkei and receiving large tracts of white farmland, that consolidated the Ciskei geographically. However, rather symbolically, the flagpole capsized when the Ciskei flag was raised during the independence ceremony (Anonymous, 1989). Sebe was now in absolute control of his own country, assisted by his brother Charles, who was in charge of the Ciskei Intelligence Service. As the story of the Thornhill community shows in the next chapter, the oppression by the security forces was particularly brutal. According to Peires (1992), Lennox, subsequently, got rid of Charles in 1984 as he feared his younger brother was becoming too powerful. Sebe's paranoia continued to grow as the discontent in the Ciskei increased and civic associations and labour unions caused unrest. By 1986 frictions between the Ciskei and the Transkei even led Matanzima to stage a coup against the Ciskei. Although the Transkeians managed to free Charles Sebe from prison and kidnap Lennox Sebe's only son, the coup failed when the Transkeian troops were defeated at the Ciskei Presidential palace during a full-scale military attack.

However, a few years later, another coup attempt followed that was successful. According to Peires (1992), the Sebe regime was toppled by Brigadier Oupa Gqozo on 2 March 1990, only a month after Nelson Mandela's release. As the popular protests –by the UDF-aligned civic organizations and labour unions– in the Ciskei had increased in intensity during this period, nearly everyone interpreted the coup as a transition to democracy. As a result, waves of joyous demonstrations swept the region when Sebe was overthrown. In a special issue of the Albany Rural Association's newsletter of March 1990, for example, the downfall of Sebe was mainly attributed to the rural unrest that had been simmering:

> *"...it was the struggle of the people of the Ciskei, especially in the rural villages, that made Sebe's survival impossible..."* (p. 1).

Moreover, Oupa Gqozo initially appeared to be a democrat. He aligned himself with the ANC, adopted a democratic style and dismantled the Tribal Authorities as model of local government.

However, Peires (1992) has shown that Gqozo reversed his decision with respect to the Tribal Authorities not long after the coup. Moreover, he refused to meet the powerful Mdantsane Residents Association for talks. As the Thornhill example shows in the next chapter, Gqozo also failed to live up to his promises to the residents associations in the rural areas. In fact, Gqozo proved to be as brutally oppressive as his predecessor and possibly even worse. As a result, questions were asked to determine who Gqozo actually was and where he had come from. According to Peires

Gqozo had only returned to the Ciskei three weeks before the coup from Pretoria where he had been a military attaché to the Ciskei embassy. Nobody knew him and Peires is convinced that he was *"...a stooge, entirely dependent on Military intelligence..."* (p.380). It was the South African government that *"...had sent Gqozo to the Ciskei..."* (p. 380).

Nevertheless, although he did not even have the little legitimacy Sebe had enjoyed, Gqozo, counting on his brutality, remained in power until the end. In 1992 it even led to the 'Bisho Massacre'. During a peaceful mass demonstration for democracy, Gqozo's security men proceeded to fire upon the crowds at the Bisho stadium, killing twenty-nine people and wounding over two hundred. The incident confirms that Gqozo remained defiant and refused to re-incorporate the Ciskei in South Africa. He held out until the end, and only when his 'colleague' Lucas Mangope of Bophuthatswana was forced by the South African Military to hand over his homeland, Gqozo agreed, only weeks before the first democratic elections, to relinquish his position. With the demise of the Ciskei, the Eastern Cape province was born.

After the Elections: the Land Reform Programme

When the new government came to power, Derek Hanekom –a white ANC member– was appointed as Minister of Land Affairs[16]. His Department of Land Affairs faced the challenge of bringing back the balance in land ownership and land access. The Green Paper on Land Policy, based on the Reconstruction and Development Plan (RDP), was published in February 1996. It was the result of a lengthy process of public consultation that was typical of the freedom and consultation era in the first few years of the 'new democracy'. First, a Framework Document on Land Policy was produced in May 1995. This document was critically commented upon by over 50 organisations, which led to a draft Statement on Land Policy and Principle. This draft was then debated at the National Land Policy Conference in August '95, attended by over a 1,000 people, ranging from NGO staff to community representatives and (white) commercial farmers. At that conference the Monti Rural Association, together with other National Land Committee affiliates and representatives from black communities played a dominant role. Subsequently, the Green Paper was re-written to serve as a basis for the White Paper on South African Land Policy that was published in April 1997. It contains the guide-lines for land reform in South Africa. The goal of a land policy for the country is:

- *"...to deal effectively with:*
- *the injustices of racially based land dispossession of the past; the need for a more equitable distribution of land ownership;*
- *the need for land reform to reduce poverty and contribute to economic growth;*
- *security of tenure for all; and*
- *a system of land management which will support sustainable land use patterns and rapid land release for development"* (Department of Land Affairs 1997: p. 7).

In order to achieve the above goals, the White Paper proposes a land reform programme consisting of the following three pillars:
- *Land Restitution, which involves returning land (or otherwise compensating victims) lost since 19 June 1913 because of racially discriminatory laws.*
- *Land Redistribution makes it possible for poor and disadvantaged people to buy land with the help of a Settlement/Land Acquisition Grant.*
- *Land Tenure Reform (...) aims to bring all people occupying land under a unitary, legally validated system of landholding...*" (Department of Land Affairs 1997: p. VI).

However, although the White Paper was the result of processes of country-wide consultation and was generally regarded as a well-prepared and well-researched piece of legislation, many difficulties would be encountered during the implementation phase. As will be shown below, this proved extremely challenging for each of the three pillars of land reform. On a very basic level already problems had to be faced. For example, when the Green Paper was published in 1996, nobody knew how much land the South African State owned. According to the Department of Land Affairs (1996), "... *The total area of public land is unknown, which itself is very unsatisfactory (...). Roughly 26% of the surface area of the RSA is believed to be state land –some 32 million hectares*" (p. 68). Although, by 1997 the situation had become much clearer, the exact amount of vacant state land was still not yet known, according to the White Paper. Since the State is one of the largest stakeholders in the redistribution and restitution processes such information is clearly vital.

Furthermore, in the early period after the elections there was much confusion concerning the responsibilities of different government departments and tiers of government. Not only did ambiguities exist between the levels of government – national, provincial and local– also between departments responsibilities were not clearly spelled out. Every government department was transforming and grappling with a new constitution, new legislation, procedures and policies and a large number of new staff. As a result, the Green paper, contained many proposals for administrative reforms. By 1999 responsibilities, procedures and policies had drastically improved. Instrumental in this respect was the formulation of the *Development Facilitation Act* of 1995 to facilitate and streamline land delivery and development in both former South African and former homeland areas. What remained difficult, however, was how to deal with other legislation that impacted on land and land reform. Crucial in this respect were questions around local government, communal land and the position of 'traditional leaders'.

Restitution

At face value the first pillar of the land reform programme seems straightforward. One makes a list of people who lost their land in the post-1913 period and either returns the land back to them or compensates them with another piece of land. That is what the new government must have thought when they made public the time schedule by which the restitution process was supposed to be finalized. Citizens would have three years to lodge their claims, the Land Claims Court would then have five years to process the claims and after ten years all the court orders would have to be implemented. Thus, it was imagined that the process would be completed in a maximum of eighteen years.

However, already in the first phase severe problems were encountered. In order to assist the Land Claims Court, a Land Claims Commission was instituted in every province to administratively assist the preparation of restitution claims. The tasks of the Commission included receiving claims and processing and researching them in order to supply the Court with correct information. However, by 1996 –two years after the elections– only 5,000 restitution claims had been lodged and, thus, it became obvious that the rural and urban poor could apparently not be easily reached to inform them about their right to submit a claim. Moreover, to actually stake a claim involved the necessary paperwork and know-how of the restitution process, which most people lacked. Although the amount of claims increased slowly over the years, it stayed worryingly low. By 1998 it became obvious that the May 31 cut-off date –after which no new claims would be accepted– would be too early for large numbers of people. Especially the NGOs affiliated to the National Land Committee, including the Monti Rural Association, realized that the institutions responsible for the restitution programme had done a poor job. Many people would miss a huge opportunity. Thus, they successfully lobbied the government to get the cut-off date extended to 31 December 1998. Subsequently, under the slogan: *"Claim Your Land Rights!"*, a national campaign was launched by the National Land Committee and its affiliates, Department of Land Affairs and the Land Claims Commission to encourage people to lodge their claims. By the end of the year a total of 63,455 claims had been received by the Commission, almost doubling the amount of 36,000 claims that had been in by May '98 (Department of Land Affairs 1999a,b).

The second phase, processing, researching and judging a claim, proved to be even more problematic. The new government had completely underestimated the slow turning of the bureaucratic and legal wheels. In order for the court to come to a final judgement, and award a claimant the land or compensation, the proof had to be beyond reasonable doubt. Therefore, some of the earliest claims that were lodged, were rejected because of the shoddy research and paperwork. Moreover, the situation on the ground proved to be far more complicated than initially imagined. Especially in cases where claims went back a long time, or where claims overlapped each other. For example, in the urban areas –80% of the claims are urban claims– many people may have rights to the same parcel of residential land: the first black owners, the white owners, the tenants and in some cases even the sub-tenants and later the squatters that invaded the land. In these cases detailed research of a high standard was needed to disentangle the web of overlapping rights. Whose rights should prevail? And how to deal with the other claimants?

However, in the first years it became clear that the quality of the research by the Land Claims Commission was sub-standard. Moreover, the fact that the commission was severely under-staffed also led to much criticism from the NGO sector. As a result of all these problems, only 264 restitution claims had been settled (see: Table 3.1) in the first five years of government, according to the Department of Land Affairs (1999a). This sad result was a dismal 0.4 % of the total amount of claims received. As Hanekom was not particularly impressed by the result, a Ministerial Review of the Restitution Programme was ordered in 1998 to speed up the delivery.

Total number of claims received	63455
Total amount of compensation paid (SA Rand)	13,416,681
Total amount of land restored (ha)	264,615
Total number of claims resolved	264

(Source: DLA (1999a), internet http://land.pwv.gov.za/Restitution/new_stats_rest(graph).htm)

Table 3.1: Restitution Figures 19.11.'99.

To conclude, I want to make a few general remarks about the work of non-governmental organizations in the restitution field. Sadly, as the NGO sector was involved in many of the restitution cases, the meagre 264 resolved claims in a way also reflects the result of five years of NGO involvement. Since the NGO sector worked closely together with the new government in the land reform field during the first five years of democratic rule, many of the government's failures are also the NGO sector's failures. In the case of restitution, for example, some of the early claims really served as 'trial and error cases' to learn about the type of research that was needed and the legal procedures involved. In the process, therefore, the NGOs made many mistakes as well. Moreover, much of the initially overly optimistic rhetoric concerning restitution, by the first new government officials in the Department of Land Affairs, can be traced to the NGO sector, where many had their roots. Nevertheless, although many claims have not been processed yet, the NGO sector deserves substantial credit for the way in which it made urban and rural people aware of the restitution process in the *Claim Your Land Rights* campaign. Actually, many of the claims were prepared by the NGOs on behalf of black communities. Without the NGO sector the government would have never succeeded in receiving as many claims as it did. What remains, however, is processing and resolving them, something which is not in the hands of non-governmental organizations.

By 2003 the rate of restitution had speeded up dramatically. According to the Commission on Restitution of Land Rights, it had become clear *"that the court driven process was antagonistic and painstakingly slow, hence the settlement of only 41 land claims between 1995 and March 1999"* (Commission on Restitution of Land Rights, 2003: p. 2). Therefore, a new administrative approach was introduced in 1999 that *"resulted in a phenomenal and exponential increase in the number of claims settled to date, in excess of 36488"* (Ibid: p. 3), out of a total of 79,000[17] valid claims. However, critics of the government point to the fact that *"the DLA has made much of the recently rising number of settled restitution claims in its efforts to counter growing criticism by civil society about the wider crisis of the country's land reform"* (Hargreaves and Eveleth, 2003: p. 86). According to these critics, it is *"a land restitution programme that is rapidly delivering statistics, but very little land"* (Ibid.: p. 86). Indeed, when scrutinizing the figures it is revealed that the DLA, through its new approach, has solved most cases –mainly small urban claims– through financial compensation. Nevertheless, it must be admitted that the dismal results of the late 90's have indeed improved.

Redistribution
The second pillar of the land reform process is the Land Redistribution Programme. While restitution entailed returning land to the rightful owners, redistribution involved giving the 'African' population the opportunity to (re-)gain access to land. In the initial phase of this programme the Land Reform Pilot Programme was launched at the end of 1994:

> *"Its purpose is to develop equitable and sustainable mechanisms of land redistribution in rural areas, as a kick start to a wide reaching national programme"* (Department of Land Affairs 1996: p. 4, box 1.2).

In these pilot schemes, that were set up in all the new provinces, 'the stakeholders' –a popular and widely used term in the government's new 'freedom and consultation discourse'– were stimulated to negotiate a solution for a more equitable land distribution in their region. White farmers, farm workers, communities, tenants, NGOs, the commercial sector, local government departments and others were encouraged by the government to cooperate. Thus, as it was envisaged in the RDP, land was to be redistributed in a more equitable fashion through consultation. In the Eastern Cape the pilot scheme comprised the area around the city of Queenstown (see Map 3.7).

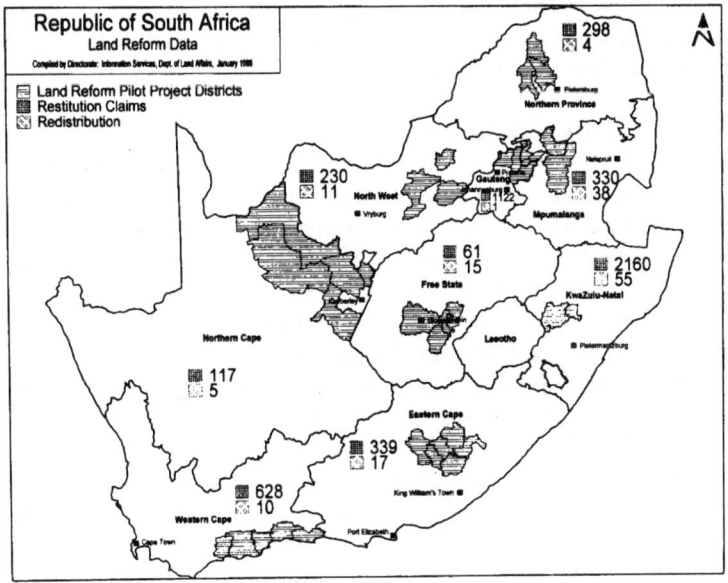

(Source: Department of Land Affairs, 1996)

Map 3.7: Land Reform Pilot Projects.

This included Thornhill, an area densely populated by a dumped community the Monti Rural Association had close relations with. However, already in 1997 the pilot schemes ceased to be pilots and were re-integrated into the regular land reform programme. This decision was taken as the Department of Land Affairs had already learned enough and could no longer justify delaying the regular redistribution programme until the full result of the pilots had come in.

Like the restitution programme the redistribution programme also proved to be much more difficult, slow and complicated than initially envisaged. Keeping in mind that millions of 'blacks' had no access to land, only 427 redistribution projects – involving 295,451 people– were in the implementation phase by 31 March 1999, according to the Department of Land Affairs (1999c). An inhibiting factor in the redistribution programme was the mechanism by which the land would have to be transferred from the 'haves' to the 'have-nots'. As the National Party had fought successfully for the inclusion of a property clause in the new South African Constitution, expropriation was no longer an easy option for the Rainbow Coalition. White farmers were, thus, protected by the constitution:

"(1) No one may be deprived of property except in terms of law of general application, and no law may permit arbitrary deprivation of property.
(2) Property may be expropriated only in terms of law of general application - for a public purpose or in the public interest; and
subject to compensation (...).
(4) For the purposes of this section - the public interest includes the nation's commitment to land reform, and to reforms to bring about equitable access to all South Africa's natural resources"[18].

However, as point 4 indicates, the National Land Committee (NLC), including its affiliates like MRA, and the ANC could also claim a small victory, since the constitution in its final version, at least, recognized the possibility of expropriation for land reform[19].

However, although the government had the power to redistribute "in the public interest", it was decided not to antagonize the white farmers, as they played an important role in South Africa's food security and export sector. As a result, the Department of Land Affairs opted for the *willing-buyer willing-seller* (DLA, 1997) arrangement. However, as 'the poor' generally lacked the funds, an elaborate Settlement/Land Acquisition Grant scheme was set up for households. In the scheme 'a household' –a difficult term as it hides power imbalances and can easily favour powerful family members– is entitled to a maximum of R.15,000[20] (± $ 2,400). This grant could be used to purchase land and, or, to realize improvements to land or housing. However, the amount was heavily criticized by the progressive NGO sector for being insufficient. Moreover, many thought it unfair that whites could receive payment for land that is, in the eyes of many blacks, not rightfully their own. The government, nevertheless, does believe that it is fair to compensate white farmers as most of them have bought the land they farm.

The government had understood at an early stage that it was necessary to (re-)introduce South Africa into the world market and, thus, it seemed obvious to try to redistribute land through the market. Although at first sight many will wonder why commercial South African farmers would be willing to sell their land, many of them are indeed interested to sell out because a large number of them cannot make ends meet. As the South African agricultural sector had been one of the most heavily subsidized sectors, many farmers got into trouble when subsidy systems were abolished after the new government came to power. As South Africa sought to abolish subsidies and to break down its tariff barriers in order to (re-)gain access to world markets the South African farmers, quite abruptly, found themselves in an impossible situation. While their production costs stayed the same –or grew due to the wage increases they were forced to pay–, the prices for their produce fell drastically. Furthermore, many had already struggled, for several years, through severe droughts in the early nineties. As a result, a lot of South African commercial farmers became heavily indebted and are, thus, willing to sell their farms.

The prospective buyers, however, especially the really poor, have few resources besides the settlement grant at their disposal. Thus, they can never buy such farms on their own. In order to solve this dilemma, the government and the NGO sector came up with the concept of Communal Property Associations (CPAs). The idea is that, say 100 poor households, who have an interest in farming, can form a Communal Property Association in order to buy a farm from a white farmer. In the first years after the elections various CPAs were, thus, formed and land was transferred to them. However, one does not need to be a bright economist to figure out that a farm, which is hardly economically viable and which has barely sustained one white farmer and his family, will not yield sufficient income and resources to sustain around 500 people[21] belonging to a CPA. Not to mention the fact that many farms are even more expensive and would require even larger CPAs. Even if the farms would sustain such a large population, huge management problems can be expected with so many owners. Lastly, the high cost of farms does not leave the new owners much cash for investments and improvements. Thus, CPAs may gain access to land but since little resources are left to buy equipment and inputs, farming the land productively may still be impossible. As a result many of the early CPAs have failed dismally, like, for example, the Gallawater A farm in the Eastern Cape. In the mid-nineties the Monti Rural Association played a crucial role in supporting the community to acquire that farm. The story of Gallawater A's rise and decline and the role MRA played in it, is told in Chapter 6. It is illustrative of the role of South African land sector NGOs and the relationships that developed between such organizations and community structures.

Concluding, one can say that redistribution remains a difficult process. The disappointing results also reflect badly on the work of NGOs that have cooperated closely with the government. Just like in the process of restitution, both the government and the NGO sector have had to learn about redistribution through trial and error. Many mistakes were made and little concrete progress –that is land transferred to people– was achieved. However, the procedures, laws and regulations have become much clearer now, and better progress is expected. Nevertheless, the more fundamental problems concerning CPAs have not been resolved. There are even indications that the government is becoming more and more cautious of transferring land to the poor with little or no resources. Especially after the elections in 1999, when a new Minister of Land Affairs, Thoko Didiza, was appointed, the focus is said to have shifted from 'the poor' and 'the landless' to supporting emergent black commercial farmers –the not so poor. However, the changes proposed and implemented by Didiza have also been criticized. A new programme, the Land Redistribution for Agricultural Development (LRAD), that was launched in 2001 (National department of Agriculture, 2001), is:

> *"...designed to provide grants to black South African citizens to access land specifically for agricultural purposes. The strategic objectives of the sub-programme include: contributing to the redistribution of 30 % of the country's agricultural land over 15 years; improving nutrition and incomes of the rural poor who want to farm on any scale; de-congesting overcrowded former homeland areas; and expanding opportunities for women and young people who stay in rural areas"* (p. 2).

Through LRAD beneficiaries can access grants –the minimum is R. 20,000–, as long as they also contribute –a minimum of R. 5,000– in kind or cash, themselves. Although even critics agree that redistribution figures have improved, because *"...land delivery through LRAD is accelerating"* (PLAAS, 2003), it is said that the targets set by the Minister in 2001, have, so far, not been met, as only 2% of agricultural land has been transferred. Moreover, the poorest groups seem to lose out, as *"...the big winners under LRAD would appear to be small groups with substantial resources of their own"* (Ibid., p. 4). Again, just as in the case of restitution, the government is criticized by the NGO sector for going the market route, and not taking a more interventionist –rights-based– approach that delivers substantial amounts of land to the poor.

Tenure Reform

The third pillar of land reform, the Tenure Reform Programme, may be even harder to implement than the Restitution and the Redistribution Programmes. According to the White Paper:

> *"...tenure reform must build a unitary non-racial system of land rights for all South Africans"* (Department of Land Affairs 1997, p. 60).

In other words, the South African government envisaged to create one system of land holding which (re-)defined all forms of land tenure. Tenure reform initially entailed replacing all forms of formal and informal landholding that had developed during the colonial and apartheid period. Permission to Occupy (PTO) certificates, Quitrent titles, but also access to communal lands and squatter rights were to be brought under one system. No longer should race, gender and/or ethnicity play a role with regard to land rights.

At the outset the, the new government opted for a system of land tenure that was rooted in the market, just as restitution and redistribution. In the process all types of landholding titles would ultimately become freehold titles. This was criticized by authors like Marcus, Eales and Wildschut (1996) who claim that *"...a major consequence of the freehold system of tenure is its expense (...). It requires accurate survey and registration (...). It also supports an expensive (...) professional class of estate agents, surveyors and conveyancers feeding off the system"* (p. 177). Not only is it expensive, as the authors argue, it also requires a well-functioning bureaucracy which has the capabilities to deal with such a sensitive operation. Especially when the rights of people to the same piece of land need to be disentangled. In many rural areas of the former homelands, for example, people were informally awarded pieces of commonage during the apartheid years. Such people never became the actual owners, but in an informal, practical sense they became and remained the users. In some cases such users –with, for example, a PTO certificate– have sold their rights to certain parcels of land to others. Others have transferred their rights through inheritances. In many areas such transactions occurred although they were formally prohibited. Tenure reform has to find solutions that are acceptable for all these types of owners, semi-owners or users of land. An extremely complicated process indeed.

In order to ensure that the informal occupants of land –frequently large communities of squatters who (re-)occupied land illegally during apartheid after they had been forcefully removed– did not lose their rights, the *Interim Protection of Informal Land Rights Act* was adopted in 1996. Moreover, it was later extended to 31 December 1999. Furthermore, mainly to make progress in the Redistribution Programme, the *Communal Property Associations Act* was also passed by Parliament in 1996. This was also crucial for the tenure reform programme as it created the possibility for large groups of individuals to get the ownership title for one piece of land, like for example community commonage. Another piece crucial of legislation that was brought before Parliament was ESTA, the *Extension of Security of Tenure Act*, of 1997. This act was an important achievement as it formalized the rights of farm tenants, farm workers and/or farm dwellers on white farms and others in cities who lived on someone else's land, in order to protect them against arbitrary evictions.

The enactment of ESTA by the South African government partly determined the role of land sector NGOs during the period of fieldwork conducted for this book. According to the Department of Land Affairs (1999c) the ESTA affected the lives of about 6 million people. While the act was being drafted by government, the affiliates of the National Land Committee, including the Monti Rural Association, aimed to positively influence the final outcome. In their view, the act would have to award farm dwellers ownership rights to the land they had occupied for decades on white farms. The government, on the other hand, principally aimed to protect farm dwellers against arbitrary evictions. In the last phase, the Department of Land Affairs joined hands with the NLC affiliates and paralegal NGOs to 'consult with' and 'inform' farm workers in what was called 'the Farm Worker Campaign'. In Chapter 7, it is shown that this consultation process during the campaign, although it had positive aspects, did not lead to a fundamental modification of the bill. Ultimately, the Farm Worker Campaign illustrated that the government and the NGO sector, despite initial cooperative arrangements, had slowly begun to drift apart.

Due to the extremely complicated situation on the ground, one can say that progress in the tenure reform programme is slow and much research is still needed in order to solve the issue of overlapping rights. In many communities, NGOs have been instrumental in carrying out such research in the late nineties. These so-called Tenure Test Cases, have yielded much information about the complications that need to be overcome. In many communities, the situation concerning these land rights can be extremely volatile. During my fieldwork, for example, I have witnessed how the mere mentioning of a possible change in status of quitrent titles led to angry conflicts between villagers –between the title holders and the landless– that bordered on the violent.

In 2003 new developments with an impact on tenure led to heated debates between the government and the progressive NGO sector. First of all the government tabled the Communal Land Rights Bill in October, which contained proposals for dealing with communal lands in the former bantustan areas. As it was ultimately deemed impossible –too difficult and too expensive– to register and divide all communal lands into privately owned parcels, as was already predicted by Marcus, Eales and Wildschut (1996), the bill proposed to transfer powers over communal land administration and ownership to, so-called *traditional councils*, in which 'traditional leaders' have a major say. These *traditional councils* are a new invention, proposed in the Traditional Leadership and Governance Framework Bill that was also tabled before parliament in late 2003. Confronted with both pieces of new legislation, critics from the NGO community have reacted with shock. The National Land Committee (NLC) and the Programme for Land and Agrarian Studies (PLAAS) have even placed an advertisement in a national newspaper (Business Day, 10.11.2003) in which they call to *"stop the Communal Land Rights Bill"*. Although the legislation contains provisions to ensure that one-third of the members of traditional councils are women and 25% of the members are elected, critics argue that traditional leaders will become more powerful than ever before. The Tribal Authorities, remnants of the colonial and apartheid-era oppressive machinery, will regain much of their influence that seemed lost after the first democratic elections. According to the critics, the legislation effectively revives the Bantu Authorities Act of 1951, that played an essential role during apartheid (Cousins and Claassens, 2003). Moreover, they argue that it endangers the position of women, while at the same time it is *"deeply anti-democratic (...)* [as] *it gives extraordinary powers and almost unlimited discretion to the minister of agriculture and land affairs to make decisions on the nature and content of people's land rights"* (Ibid.).

These recent developments illustrate the fact that when one is contemplating the role of land, it is important to consider, not only ownership, but also administration and local government (Ntsebeza, 1999). Inevitably, in the South African context, this also means focusing on the role of 'traditional leaders'.

Dilemmas of Local Government
In a country like South Africa, with a history of profound divisions –between white and black, rich and poor, the Republic and the bantustans, the urban and the rural– the most important aim of the new government was levelling the playing field in all spheres of life. Besides the economy and the land sector, the field of local government was another sphere in which the apartheid legacy was particularly felt. Apartheid and its policies of racial segregation resulted in different institutional arrangements for different areas. White South Africa had well-developed and democratic local government structures –solely for the white population– and as a consequence relatively well-managed metropolises, cities, towns and rural villages. Black, Coloured and Indian areas, however, each had their particular form of local (non-)government. Especially in the former bantustan areas, where in most places Tribal Authorities were effectively still in power, a new system of local government was greatly needed after the elections.

Before I continue to discuss local government in detail, it may be useful to explain the system of government that was established in South Africa after the first democratic elections. In the 'new' South Africa the Executive, or the Cabinet, which is headed by the President, is held accountable by Parliament, consisting of elected members. Besides Parliament there is a second chamber called the National Council of Provinces (NCOP). In 1997 the NCOP had its first session when it replaced the Senate in terms of the new constitution. In the council each of the nine provinces has a single delegation of ten members. The NCOP deals with any law that affects the provinces, while the National Assembly (Parliament) deals with laws of national importance. Moreover, on the national level a Council of Traditional Leaders was instituted with an advisory function to the national government and the President. On a provincial level a similar government structure was established, whereby the Premier of the Province presides over a Cabinet that is held accountable by the Provincial Legislature. Moreover, a Provincial House of Traditional Leaders was instituted with an advisory function. Thus, formal political power came into the hands of elected officials. All levels of government below the level of the provinces is considered local government in the South African context.

Local Democratic Government

Just like the higher levels of government, local government will ultimately be entirely democratically elected. In 1995 South Africa held its first local government elections. However, after a typical 'freedom and consultation era' consultative process, the White Paper on Local Government was published in March 1998. The Ministry for Provincial Affairs and Constitutional Development (1998) published it with the aim to sketch the future of more permanent local democratic government structures.

An important goal of the new plans was to re-integrate 'black areas' into white and industrial areas. During apartheid, black areas had been systematically removed or cut-off from white and industrially developed areas, and thus from a viable tax base. The taxes from the developed areas could thus be used for the rich white municipalities only. Thus, the Community Councils, instituted in 1977 in the African areas, besides having very limited powers, did not have the resources to govern their communities effectively. Moreover, their legitimacy was severely criticized by the black population and many councillors were regarded as collaborators. That distrust and hostility worsened when the Community Councils were replaced by Black Local Authorities in 1982. The resulting wave of violent protests, and the establishment of the UDF in 1983, which opposed the Black Local Authorities, can be seen as an important phase in the struggle against apartheid, as was described above. The tools of protest included rent and service charge (electricity and water) boycotts, consumer boycotts, and sadly, the 'necklacing' of collaborating councillors. According to the White Paper on Local Government the popular struggle slogan during those days was: *"One City One Tax Base!"*.

During the period of negotiations after Mandela's release, local government became one of the important issues. In 1993 *the Local Government Transition Act* (LGTA) was negotiated by the Local Government Negotiating Forum:

"The process put forward in the LGTA was essentially a locally-negotiated transition and it has resulted in a wide diversity of forms of local government"

(Ministry for Provincial Affairs and Constitutional Development 1998, p. 3).

The LGTA laid the foundation for a phased transition in local government. In the pre-interim phase local forums were established to negotiate the appointment of temporary councils, that would govern until the first local government elections. After those elections the interim phase would begin, in which a permanent form of local government would be designed and legislated. At the end of 1999, South African local government was still in that interim phase. In the final phase, a permanent local government system would be established in South Africa.

In many areas the first democratic elections were conducted on a '50:50' basis. Of the councillors 50% were drawn from the statutory side, while 50% were drawn from the non-statutory side. This compromise had been fought for by the National Party during the Kempton Park negotiations, and protected 'the whites' from losing all influence at the local level. Nevertheless, the local government elections in 1995 led to a major turnaround in local political arenas, as many townships were re-integrated in white cities and towns, Such transitions led to new opportunities for the formerly oppressed but also to racial tensions. For example, in formerly white towns where a black major was appointed. For most black communities the reintegration led to much needed improvements. Yet, in many areas it was problematic that the same tax base, that used to be sufficient for the white area, now had to serve a much larger area and population. In fact, it proved to be a micro version of the macro problems in South Africa: how to bring the whole population up to the same standard of living as was previously enjoyed by the whites.

In the interim phase, the highest tier of local government was formed by the District Councils. According to the White Paper they vary considerably in size, budget and staffing. In some areas they are completely new and in others they are amalgamations of former white and black (or Coloured or Indian) areas. In many areas, especially in the former homeland areas, the former dumping grounds of forced removals and the immense squatter areas, the District Councils directly provided services to the public. In such areas there was hardly a tax base and/or management capacity to administer to the needs of the people. Therefore, in those areas, the lowest tier of local government is absent, or highly dependent on the District Council.

The tier below the District Councils still takes different forms until a permanent system of local government is established in the final phase. In the meantime there is a clear difference between the urban areas and the rural areas. In the urban areas, that is in the cities and smaller towns, local government is made up of Transitional Local Councils (TLCs), that function relatively well. However, in the rural areas and the smallest rural towns the systems of local government are still more ambiguous. According to the White Paper:

- *"...there are three forms of government in the rural areas:*
- *Transitional Representative Councils (TRepCs).*
- *Transitional Rural Councils (TRCs).*
- *District Councils with Remaining Areas"* (Ministry for Provincial Affairs and Constitutional Development 1998, p. 7).

TRepCs mainly have a representative function, while only a few powers have been devolved to them as they generally lack the administrative and financial capacity. District councils play an important supportive role in these cases. TRCs are similar to the urban Transitional Local Councils. However, although they do have taxing powers, they are frequently too small to generate sufficient funds. As a consequence many of the TRCs are also dependent on District Councils for grants. Thirdly, as was mentioned above, there are the areas where District Councils directly provide services to the people, the District Councils with Remaining Areas. In the interim phase, the District Councils play quite a dominant role, either by being completely responsible for local government in certain areas, or by playing a supportive role. In the Eastern Cape, the three District Councils that cover most of the area in which the Monti Rural Association operates are: The Amatola District Council, The Stormberg District Council and the Drakensberg District Council.

After the elections in 1994, the whole institutional environment was in flux. Every level of government experienced overlapping transformation processes, frequently leading to situations in which nobody seemed to know how to implement certain policies anymore. In many instances NGOs had to step in as *beacons of continuity* in order to train local government officials to understand and work with their own rules, regulations, policies and legal frameworks. Therefore, the Monti Rural Association established a Local Government Unit, that aimed to support, train and critically study the local government structures and developments in the Eastern Cape. Although the Monti Rural Association regularly provided courses for District Council staff, MRA was mainly concerned with the improvement of capacity of the lowest tier of local government. In many communities this has taken the shape of workshops and training sessions on a very basic level: how to hold meetings, how to take minutes, how to abide by democratic principles et cetera. Such emergent local government structures in the communities were usually formed by the former residents associations or 'civics', that will be discussed in the below.

Civics
Residents associations, or 'civics' –a South African term for a locally organized community groups– were formed in South African urban and rural communities during the eighties. These ward committees, village committees and other aggregations of citizens liaised with the UDF and were established by community members taking matters of local rule in their own hands as they opposed the distrusted, and often collaborating, Black Local Authorities and Tribal Authorities. Civics were seen as the only legitimate and 'democratic' structures by the progressive forces and 'the people'. Frequently, these civics or residents associations were established with the help of progressive NGOs. An organization like the Monti Rural Association, for example, helped to organize such committees all over the rural Eastern Cape, as will be illustrated in Chapter 4. These NGOs recognized that a mass movement against apartheid was needed to de-stabilize the country. As a result, urban and rural civics and residents associations became a political force.

In many areas the civics also formed their own regional umbrella organizations. In the Eastern Cape, for example, the Border Civic Congress (BOCCO) was established in 1987 in which ARA staff like Jacob James and Michael Ndlovu also played a role. In 1992 the BOCCO was amalgamated into the South African National Civics Organization, or SANCO (Manona 1997), that became a strong national player. However, although the organization helped to draft the Reconstruction and Development Programme (RDP), together with COSATU and the ANC, it progressively lost some of its strength and political relevance after the political parties had been unbanned. After those parties were unbanned many of the civics leaders got involved in overt local politics. In most areas this led to cooperative arrangements between SANCO and the ANC (or PAC or IFP). In other areas, however, civics stayed more or less autonomous. As a result substantial overlaps between SANCO and the political parties occurred, which led to tensions around the question of which organization was the legitimate representative of 'the people'.

When these 'new' civics or residents associations were established, during the struggle era, they were perceived as a threat by 'traditional leaders' and their Tribal Authorities (TAs). Especially in the rural areas of the homelands these tensions led to serious and sometimes violent clashes between the predominantly young and angry generation that embraced 'the struggle' and the predominantly older and obedient authoritarian generation[22]. 'The young' demanded democratic change, while 'the old' expected deference and respect for their 'tribal' leaders. Even in the late nineties, these tensions still played a role in local politics. For many NGOs, working in the rural areas, these tensions resulted in taking sides. In most cases the progressive NGOs chose to support the young, who were advocating democratic change, as it fitted in with the 'democratization project' of the NGO sector, as will be shown in the next chapters.

'Traditional Leaders'
During the apartheid era 'traditional leaders' were used to manage what could be termed local government in many black rural areas. This mode of indirect rule was labelled *decentralized despotism* by Mahmood Mamdani (1996). In his book *Citizen and Subject* he shows how this form of racial domination functioned. Through tribally organized local authorities a racial identity was reproduced in citizens –the mostly urban whites– while at the same time it created an ethnic identity in subjects –the rural blacks. Mamdani argues that by separating blacks in their own bantustans, administered by colonially- and apartheid-manipulated 'traditional structures', South Africa can be regarded as a prime example of the colonial state in Africa. A state dependent on forms of indirect rule.

Usually such leaders had 'royal blood', being a descendant of a King or a chief. However, whenever such 'traditional leaders' became too powerful or too critical of the regime, they were strategically replaced. People like loyal soldiers in the great wars –WW I and WW II– or headmen could then be appointed as chiefs. Authors like Mamdani (1996), Boonzaier and Sharp (1988), Vail (1989) and Beinart and Bundy (1987), have all shown how the institution of traditional leadership was subordinated, changed and perverted by the colonial and apartheid powers in South Africa. Thus, authoritarian and relatively rigid systems of rule were established in the former homelands. Although not all 'traditional leaders' simply became apartheid puppets, decades of selection did result in a relatively loyal group of rulers. Therefore, what we nowadays encounter as 'traditional leadership' bears some resemblance, but actually little correspondence to what it once was.

When the final constitution was drafted, after the first democratic elections in South Africa, much debate followed on the position of traditional leadership. In the final version it is clear that although it stipulates a democratically elected form of local government, it also recognizes the importance of 'traditional leaders'. Since in some (rural) areas –for instance, in rural Transkei– the systems of tribal rule were still recognized as legitimate by the people, they could hardly be eliminated by the stroke of a pen. Even in areas where the Tribal Authorities have little legitimacy, they are usually still strong bastions of ethnically defined political power. For the new government this created quite a dilemma. Clearly, these authoritarian structures could not be regarded as democratic structures. On the other hand they could hardly be ignored, especially as many of the powerful 'traditional leaders' carried political weight. Moreover, as many of the black democratic political leaders themselves, were born and raised in areas where 'traditional leaders' were powerful and part of the 'cultural heritage', they kept a certain respect for the kings, the chiefs and their institutions. Thus, although people like Mandela have been extremely critical of collaborating chiefs, they have not completely turned their backs on 'traditional leaders'. Therefore, when Patekile Holomisa –a powerful ANC MP– was installed as a Xhosa chief in April 1999, most of the politicians were seen to be present. On such occasions 'politics' seems to be put aside. For example, Mandela was seen walking arm in arm with Chief Kaiser Matanzima[23], the former Transkei ruler who had been heavily criticized in the past by Mandela for collaborating with the apartheid regime. This conflicting relationship is one of the most difficult problems in the local government arena that needs to be resolved by the ANC.

The White Paper on Local Government recognizes the problem:

"...Chapter 7 of the Constitution provides for the establishment of elected local government across the country, while Chapter 12 of the Constitution recognizes traditional authorities and states that national legislation may provide for a role for traditional leadership as an institution at local level on matters affecting local communities..." (Ministry for Provincial Affairs and Constitutional Development 1998, p. 75).

Nevertheless, the constitution is quite clear about the position of traditional leaders in relation to the elected local government bodies:

"The traditional leader of a community observing a system of indigenous law and residing on land within the area of jurisdiction of an elected local government referred to in Chapter 10, shall ex officio be entitled to be a member of that local government, and shall be eligible to be elected to any office of such local government" (Constitution of South Africa, Chapter 11, section 183).

Although the constitution seems quite clear by stipulating that traditional leaders can only be ex-officio members of a local government structure unless they are democratically elected, in practice, that is on the ground, the constitution has not been implemented yet.

Thus, in many rural areas the chiefs have effectively stayed in power. Although not all the tasks of traditional leaders correspond with that of local municipalities, it is clear that there is a substantial overlap. For example, in many areas the allocation of communal land, for all practical purposes, still remains the responsibility of the chiefs. This conflicts with the constitution that stipulates democratic control. Other stipulations, like for example the law against gender discrimination, may, potentially, also have far-reaching consequences for the institution of traditional leadership. It is now up to the Mbeki government to come up with concrete plans that will define the role of traditional authorities.

As was described above, in the section on land tenure reform, it took the Mbeki government until 2003 to come up with new legislation that outlined the future of traditional leadership. Together the Communal Land Rights Bill and the Traditional Leadership and Governance Framework Bill seem to propose reviving Tribal Authorities, through the institution of *traditional councils*. Although some measures seem to have been taken that both ensure the representation of women, *"vulnerable community members"* (Communal Land Rights Bill 2003, subsection 23(4)), and elected members, critics point to the fact that this revived position of 'traditional leaders' is incompatible with the constitution (Cousins and Claassens, 2003). The future will reveal whether the democratic forces prevail in rural South Africa. It is clear, however, that chiefs at the local level are not going to give up their privileged positions without a struggle (Ntsebeza, 1999), as is also illustrated in the case of Thornhill (Chapter 4).

The Eastern Cape Land Sector after 1994

The Eastern Cape is sub-divided in six districts, that are each, in turn, sub-divided in municipalities. According to the 1996 census figures (Stats SA, 1996) the province has a largely rurally-based (63%) population of 6,3 million. Its provincial capital became the defunct city of Bisho, the Ciskei's former capital. The first Eastern Cape Premier, Raymond Mhlaba, was soon replaced by Reverend Makenkhesi Stofile as the ANC was not satisfied with the rate of progress in the province. At times, however, it is still speculated whether the national government should intervene to redress problems in the fields of education, health and the chaotic situation around pension pay-outs.

The Eastern Cape Province is still one of the most problematic and poorest provinces in South Africa, which can largely be attributed to the two former homelands that it incorporates within its borders. These former homeland areas are still the site of tremendous social, economic, political and ecological problems. According to Nel (1997), the following figures illustrate the grave situation in the Eastern Cape:

- *"the lowest level of participation by potential workers in the country (42,6% of those able to work cannot find jobs); (...)*
- *highest level of male absenteeism (31,3%);*
- *second lowest personal income level;*
- *second highest dependency rate (...);*
- *lowest life expectancy; and*
- *lowest human development index"* (p. 10).

Furthermore, as in other areas in South Africa, the province has to redress the huge disparities between the rich and the poor.

Apartheid has left spatial scars as well. Mdantsane, the Eastern Cape's largest township with at least 200,000 inhabitants[24], is still as far from the city of East London as it ever was. Moreover, a serious problem, nowadays, is created by the fact that people have taken matters in their own hands and massively flock into the urban centres. There, squatter areas are mushrooming, with all the problems usually associated with such areas: overcrowding, crime, lack of hygiene et cetera. In the town of Butterworth, for example, Bank (1997) reports an increase of shacks from 700 in 1989 to 5,000 in 1995. Not only are people voluntarily leaving the townships to be closer to the cities, white farmers have, on a large scale, forcefully evicted thousands of farm workers and their families, as they feared the new Extension of Security of Tenure Act (ESTA) which would give farm workers more rights.

Although 63% of the population is still rurally based, these people should not necessarily be regarded as peasants, livestock farmers or agricultural producers. Besides the fact that much of the land is still in the hand of white farmers and much of the black male population is absent (working in the mines and in the cities), large groups of people are still residing in the former dumping grounds of the Ciskei. These masses of rural dwellers can be described as a 'rural proletariat'. Illustrative, in this regard, is the fact that many of these rural dwellers are dependent on some form of welfare grant. Especially pensions and disability grants are important in that respect. Sometimes an entire (extended) family lives on grandmother's pension.

During my own fieldwork, many of the people I interviewed in the rural areas like Thornhill, Gallawater A and Gasela proved to have had long periods of urban experience in the metropolises on the Rand (mineworkers) or in Cape Town and Durban. However, as Bank (1997) argues, frequently, it is not either/or. People seem to oscillate between the urban and rural areas, spending much time in both. According to Bank "...*large numbers of informal settlement households survive neither in town nor country, but between the two...*" (p. 26).

Another complicating factor with regard to agriculture is the fact that an urban-based ex-bantustan elite owns farms in the former homelands, especially in the Ciskei. They were often associated with the corrupt Ciskei regime, and benefited when Sebe and Gqozo distributed the white farms that were received from South Africa in order to consolidate the Ciskei. Frequently, these farms are only used to graze the elite's cattle. Thus, this land is not in the hands of people who want farm and use the land more productively. Besides these social and economic factors, it must be said that the Eastern Cape is a difficult area when farming is concerned. Droughts, erosion and inland winter frost make it hard to survive as a farmer. Moreover, low world market prices for produce like wool –once one of the Eastern Cape's main products– have hampered commercial farming. Additionally, stock theft, related to high levels of poverty, is nowadays another major problem in the Eastern Cape.

New Institutional Arrangements
In fact, this whole book is devoted to the novel institutional arrangements that emerged in the Eastern Cape in the mid- and late nineties. In the following chapters detailed case material dealing with the benefits and the problems of these new institutional arrangements will be presented. Here it is my aim to introduce most of the institutional actors in the land sector in order to get the reader acquainted with land reform in the Eastern Cape.

Since the 1994 elections the political playing field has completely changed. The new political dispensation has brought another group of actors to power. As the ANC came to power in the province, progressive people rapidly gained influential positions in government. Since most of these people –'comrades'– knew each other from the struggle era, and the rainbow coalition preached change, consultation and empowerment through its 'freedom and consultation discourse' in the years 1993-1996, several joint initiatives were taken in the first years after the elections.

Without a doubt the Provincial Department of Land Affairs was –and still is– the most important actor in the land sector of the Eastern Cape. Little happens without this department being involved. Minister Derek Hanekom initially stimulated close cooperation with the NGO sector in the early days of the transition. Its Provincial Office, has a head-office in Port Elizabeth and a smaller office in East London. Novel institutional arrangements emerged as the Monti Rural Association seconded staff to the department in the mid-nineties. Moreover, MRA played an important role in the Eastern Cape Land Reform Pilot Scheme and cooperated closely with the department in various so-called 'Steering Committees'. In this respect, the establishment of the Land Reform Steering Committee is worth mentioning. This group of influential people, in the government and the NGO sector, met on a regular basis to identify and resolve bottlenecks in land reform. Eventually, several MRA staff took up permanent positions in the Department of Land Affairs (DLA). Not only in the Eastern Cape, but also in all the other provinces and in the National department of Land Affairs, ex-NGO staff ended up in influential positions. Most significant in the Eastern Cape context is the fact that John Carver, ex-director of MRA, assumed the position of head of the East London Department of Land Affairs Office, and in 1998 became the overall Provincial Director of the department. Also in local government departments, like the Amatola District Council, ex-MRA staff took up high positions.

In order to solve and redress the inequalities with regard to land, the Department of Land Affairs carried out a land reform programme in the Eastern Cape which is similar to the national programme: restitution, redistribution and tenure reform. One of the areas which is still a focus area of the Department of Land Affairs is the former Land Reform Pilot Area around Queenstown, which includes Thornhill. Yet, land reform is as slow as in other provinces and many feel that more radical forms of redistribution and restitution are required. However, the department is also dependent on other government departments like the Department of Agriculture (DOA)[25], the Department of Water Affairs and Forestry (DWAF) and the Department of Housing and Local Government.

Another prominent example of a novel institutional arrangement in the Eastern Cape was the formation of the Eastern Cape Social and Economic Consultative Council (ECSECC), based in Bisho and closely linked to the Premier's office. The organization was tailored after NEDLAC, the National Economic Development and Labour Council at the national level. ECSECC includes representatives from labour, business, government and the NGO sector. It simulates and initiates consultation on provincial development issues and disputes, in order to speed up economic development and government delivery. Although such initiatives have had a significant impact in the first few years after the elections of 1994, it seems that the room for such novel institutional arrangements has decreased after the national government published its macro-economic strategy GEAR, as a result of which a 'new realism discourse' slowly trickled down to the provincial and the local level.

Other land sector actors are the NGOs active in the Eastern Cape, of which the Monti Rural Association is a significant actor, especially in the areas of the former

Ciskei and the Border. In the late nineties there were three National Land Committee affiliates in the Eastern Cape, each covering another geographical part of the province[26]. The Port Elizabeth Rural Association (PERA) operated in the south, while the Umtata Land Committee (ULC) covered most of the area formerly known as the Transkei, in the north. Although the three affiliates frequently cooperated on an ad hoc basis in committees and campaigns –for example in the Farm Worker Campaign (Chapter 7)– the NGOs did not come to a more institutionalized cooperative arrangement[27]. Around these NGOs operated a number of Legal Resource Centres (LRCs) in the Eastern Cape. These paralegal organizations assisted rural dwellers with legal problems like, for example, farm evictions. Another NGO that MRA frequently worked with is Land Service Committee (LSC), an NGO that concentrated its activities on appropriate technology in the field of water delivery and capacity building to maintain the delivered infrastructure.

Besides NGOs, there is an ever-increasing group of consultancy firms active in the land sector. In fact, in the late nineties the number of consultants far outnumbered the non-governmental organizations in the 'land business'. In this mushrooming sector many small consultancy firms were actually established by ex-NGO staff. These consultants try to combine what they have learned in the NGO sector with a more business-like mode of operation, while benefiting from the contacts they have established during their NGO stints. They often vie for the same government contracts as the NGOs. Thus, 'comrades' have become competitors in the market.

In short, it can be said that the whole land sector in the Eastern Cape, varying from the government departments to the NGOs and the consultancy firms, fundamentally transformed in the nineties. Although the government attempted to coordinate and implement these transformation processes in an orderly fashion, confusion reigned in the mid- and late nineties. As –frequently contradictory– transformation processes occurred on every level, in every sector and in all institutional realms, the result was sometimes discouraging. However, in the land sector NGOs like the Monti Rural Association often played a positive role. In some instances these organizations even became, what I have termed, *beacons of continuity*. Eventually, however, the 'comrades' of yesteryear became bosses, leading government figures and competitors in the market.

Conclusion

In conclusion I would like to reiterate some of the issues touched upon in this chapter. First of all, it is important to realize that one cannot understand development problems and processes in an area like the Eastern Cape without taking into account of its long history of colonial and apartheid domination. However, what has also emerged in this regard, is that Africans, like the brutal homeland leaders –aided by their security forces and many of the tribal authorities– have also played a significant collaborative role during the times of oppression and subjugation. Moreover, I have attempted to explain that many conflicts, which are frequently only described in tribal or ethnic terms, have a strong political or economic component in which struggles for power and resources have played a critical part. Nowadays, many of these past struggles that concerned land still impact, in one way or another, on the activities undertaken by

NGOs in the land sector. In fact, the apartheid legacy is particularly felt in the Eastern Cape, as it is one of the two poorest provinces in South Africa.

This legacy has also perpetuated the myth –that is still prevalent amongst many development experts and government agencies– that most rural dwellers in South Africa are potential small-scale commercial farmers. However, many of these rural people, in fact, constitute a 'rural proletariat'. This can lead to major problems when the land reform programme is implemented –through new institutional arrangements which are discussed in the next chapters– in the Eastern Cape.

4. MRA and the Dumped People of Thornhill

Introduction
In this chapter I focus on the local level, and specifically on the evolving relationship between the Monti Rural Association and the 'community' of Thornhill. As part of the *embedded tale*, I show that their respective histories are strongly intertwined and can hardly be separated. Naturally, I concentrate on the struggle for land, which had a specific dimension in Thornhill, as the 'refugees' –or immigrants– from Herschel never received what they were promised by the Ciskei and South Africa. The changing relationship between the Thornhill community and the Monti Rural Association is explored around the issues that were faced by Group Four, a group that arrived in Thornhill without their chiefs.

As I have stated before, it is only useful to separate 'the national' from 'the regional' and 'the local' when it aids us to analyze the role of non-governmental organizations and how they have changed over the past decades. Interestingly, one of the lessons we learn in this chapter is that the struggle for land and political power at the local level in Thornhill was closely linked to the anti-apartheid struggle on a national level. Although no one will dispute the fact that the struggle against apartheid on the national level was a political struggle, the political details of the Thornhill case seem to have been lost over the years. Therefore, I try to determine which hidden agendas were involved. Why did Sebe lure thousands of people from their homes in Herschel? What reasons might the people, and especially their chiefs, have had to leave everything Herschel behind and trade it for the Thornhill dustbowl? And, what hidden political agenda shaped the MRA interventions?

These findings are important as they shed light on the significant role land sector NGOs played in South Africa as political agents for democratic change in the struggle against apartheid. However, it also reveals the complexity of NGO interventions in communities, especially when these are politically divided. More often than not, sides are taken in (political) power struggles and, thus, NGOs lose the independent position that they often claim to have.

The Ceding of Herschel
Thornhill, near the town of Queenstown (see Map 3.6), is a notorious place in the Eastern Cape because it became a dumping ground for people from the Herschel district who are said to have fled their homes in 1975 in order to escape incorporation into the Transkei. As was explained in the previous chapter, the Transkei received two Ciskeian districts before it was granted 'full' independence. Since the Ciskei was then 'a self-governing homeland' it still fell under the authority of the Republic of South Africa and, thus, gave Ciskeians the right to South African citizenship. Nevertheless, the collaborating Ciskei Legislative Assembly (CLA) agreed to cede its Herschel and Glen Grey districts to the Transkei in 1975. However, the Ciskei only agreed after it had been promised large tracts of white farmland in the north-east in return, which would aid its own consolidation. Yet, ultimately, it transpired that the Ciskei received much less land than it was originally promised. After the political decision had been made in 1975 to cede the two districts, the people in both Herschel and Glen Grey

were given an individual choice whether they wanted to move to new land in the Ciskei or remain behind to become part of an independent Transkei. As this chapter is about the people of Thornhill, the focus here will be on Herschel.

As was described in the previous chapter, Herschel was an extraordinary district. Not only had it been a district with a relatively successful African farmer population in the 19th century, as was described by Bundy (1988, 1977), it had also been a *"...cultural melting pot..."*, according to Beinart and Bundy (1987, p. 224). This 'cultural melting pot' consisted of six major tribal groups, headed by chiefs.

When the people were given the choice to leave Herschel, only three of these six chiefs decided to move to Thornhill, while the others resolved to stay behind in Herschel. Chief Malefane of the Basotho tribe[1] left with a part of his followers as did Chief Hinana of the Amaqwati and Chief Bebeza of the Amavundle tribes. However, as not all people moved along 'ethnic' lines, many also remained behind. Moreover, a substantial group of people that decided to move originally belonged to the tribes whose chiefs remained behind: the Amahlubi, Myemane and Bathlokwa tribal authorities. Their respective chiefs, Mehlomakulu, Manxeba and Kakudi respectively stayed in Herschel with a large part of their followers. Eventually, this fourth group of people that moved to Thornhill –the people without chiefs– would become known as 'Group Four'. Thus, relatively soon after the people of Herschel were informed, 40,000[2] people from these four groups were moved to a desolate transit camp called Thornhill, about thirty kilometres from Queenstown. However, instead of the houses, schools and clinics they were promised, the people only found tents in Thornhill, and too few at that. For three years this desolate camp in the bush became their common home until Chief Malefane and Chief Hinana were granted their own lands. However, for many –most of the Amavundle Tribal Authority and Group Four– this heavily eroded and windswept place would become their permanent home.

From the mid-eighties the Monti Rural Association –in those days still the Albany Rural Association– became active in Thornhill. It was one of the first organizations to publicize –nationally and internationally– the plight of the people of Thornhill and their struggle for survival. It was a time of droughts, epidemics, social and political tension within the community and political repression in the whole of what is now known as the Eastern Cape. The Ciskei government, supported by the tribal authorities, was brutally repressive, and remained so after Nelson Mandela was released. Nevertheless, the democratic forces in the Eastern Cape slowly gained influence and as the tables turned the tribal authorities lost much of their legitimacy and power. In this process residents associations were formally established, to administer to the needs of 'the people', and local branches of the political parties sprung up. These shifts in power led to severe conflicts in Thornhill that eventually also caused controversy in the Monti Rural Association, as a result of which, a member of staff was dismissed. In the mid-nineties, 'democracy', 'development' and 'stakeholder consultation' became the new buzz words. 'Freedom and consultation' impacted on every level and penetrated every fibre of society, and, as can be expected, affected the relationship between NGOs and local communities.

Reasons to Move to Thornhill
When conducting ethnographic research in Thornhill the overwhelming majority of people told me that they left Herschel to escape Transkei independence. This is also the message that is conveyed by NGO reports and, for example, journalists who wrote about Thornhill[3]. The Thornhill residents either said that they feared becoming subjects of Chief Matanzima, who would become the first leader of the Transkei, or mentioned that they wanted to retain their South African citizenship. The latter was true for many as they were dependent on the South African labour market as migrant workers. However, as an outsider I got the feeling that there must have been other motives behind the move in order to explain why between 30,000 and 50,000 people came to Thornhill, a desolate transit camp in the middle of nowhere. Moreover, the above mentioned reasons do not seem to explain the relative lack of protest in Thornhill when the Ciskei became an independent homeland in 1981. Why did people, who had left everything behind in Herschel to retain their South African citizenship, not strongly protest the loss of that privilege five years later? In order to explain this it was necessary to dig deeper and examine closely what was at stake here.

Political Struggles Disguised as Tribal Conflicts
When I asked Zandisile Teka, an active ANC member and principal of the Amavundle primary school in Thornhill, what motives Chief Lennox Sebe might have had to lure the Herschel people to the consolidated Ciskei, he answered:
> "before, he beat Justice Mabandla with one vote margin. He needed the extra electoral support of 'new' chiefs. That is why he promised them new land, schools, houses, et cetera...".

Indeed, during the seventies, a prolonged struggle for political power took place in the Ciskei between Lennox Sebe and Justice Mabandla, as was recounted in the previous chapter. First, Lennox Sebe rallied political support by evoking ethnic anti-Mfengu and pro-Rharhabe sentiments, which, when he won the elections, he later replaced by a nation-building discourse in which Ntaba kaNdoda ('the mountain of man') featured prominently. Also the ceding of Herschel and Glen Grey to the Transkei, seems to have been related to this power struggle between the two opponents, according to Switzer (1993) and Anonymous (1989).

Indeed, the ceding of the two districts had three positive effects on Lennox Sebe's power base. First of all, the Sotho and Thembu, who predominantly stayed behind in Herschel and Glen Grey respectively, lost their political significance in the consolidated Ciskei. Secondly, the chiefs that did move became supporters of Sebe as he offered them land and political positions. Even though some authors would describe the Herschel tribes as 'Mfengu', these were not the same Mfengu that supported Mabandla, as was shown in the previous chapter. Thus, the chiefs that did move from Herschel and Glen Grey were granted privileges and high positions in the Ciskei hierarchy after they joined the Ciskei National Independence Party (CNIP). Thirdly, although Sebe was not of royal blood, he created a chiefly position for himself at another resettlement camp in order to attain some ethnic Rharhabe legitimacy. Ultimately, these machinations produced the desired result when Sebe defeated Justice Mabandla. Instead of forming a strong opposition, Mabandla, then, proceeded to join Sebe's CNIP in 1978, effectively turning the Ciskei into a one-party state.

During the time of the move, the chiefs that were planning to leave Herschel actively engaged in a rallying campaign to ensure that many of their followers joined them so that their new tribal authorities would not become too small. People meant power. The chiefs joined a government that was largely organized along tribal lines, however, as Manona (1997) states:

> "...the Tribal Authorities that had been created constituted local administrative units of this government. The ruling party was the Ciskei National Independence Party (CNIP) [and] (...) in fact Tribal Authorities were largely reduced to vehicles for CNIP programmes, fund-raising ventures, and directives..." (p. 53).

Thus, as Manona suggests, the 'tribal' became the 'political' and vice versa. The chiefs became part of the Ciskei government apparatus at both the national and the local level. Therefore, although they sometimes publicly complained, it explains why they failed to fundamentally criticize that same government for all the promises that had been broken. They had become the government...

Betrayed by their Chiefs, Lennox Sebe and the South African Government

As the 'refugees' poured into the Thornhill 'transit camp' in 1976, they realized that something had gone wrong when they only encountered tents. The expectations had been high as Mrs. Mnyamani, secretary of the Thornhill Reconstruction and Development Committee (TRDC), related in an interview:

> "the government promised us land, houses and things like hospitals. Each person would get a key and open a house when they arrived...".

These expectations were not at all unreasonable as promises had indeed been made in a meeting on April 24 1975[4] at the Magistrates' Office in Herschel. This meeting, to inform the Herschel population about the options open to them, took place only 24 hours (!) before the Ciskei issued its proclamation announcing the excision of Herschel and Glen Grey. In the meeting South African government officials and Ciskeian government ministers had met the Herschel Chiefs and members of their tribal authorities[5]. The issues around the resettlement had been explained and elucidated by a Mr. Uys, the South African Deputy Secretary of Bantu Administration and Development:

> "4.(b) Area of resettlement shall be prepared in a way to attract and comfort the wishful occupants.
> (c) The infrastructure e.g. Schools, Clinics et cetera would be ready prior to resettlement.
> (d) Houses would be ready having taken regard the nature of that particular area in the case of a Township" (p. 3).

Later in the meeting Mr. Uys went on to reiterate:

> "The underlying basis in this whole project is that people must not suffer physically, morally and financially..." (p. 4).

However, no clinics, schools or houses were built before the people arrived in Thornhill. The only arrangement that was made by the South African and Ciskei governments, in an area overgrown with thorn bushes, was the provision of tents.

To make matters worse, there were not enough tents to cater for everybody, as Mr. and Mrs. Kwinini explained in an interview:

> "...people were transported in buses while their things were transported in trucks. The truck brought our things here and others got tents. We didn't get tents. Thornhill was full of bush, there was no place to sleep, there was no time to cook, there was nothing. It was raining hard and there was water on the ground everywhere. We had to use our furniture to make a shelter and put the zinc[6] on that furniture. We lived like that for about four days".

Whereas the situation was very bad in the first few weeks, people hoped for the better. That hope, however, turned out to be fruitless as the circumstances continuously deteriorated as more people arrived. Livestock died, due to the stress of the move and the lack of feed, much of people's belongings like furniture was destroyed by the rain and the primitive circumstances, and soon after, in January 1977, the first epidemic of gastro-enteritis broke out.

Thus, on the seventh of January the Daily Dispatch[7], a regional newspaper, reported *"...the death of at least 10 babies on the refugee farm Thornhill"*. And although a make-shift clinic was set up, a rapid inoculation programme followed and money was allocated for improvements, it became clear that the situation was out of control, as is illustrated by a quote of Chief Malefane in the Daily Dispatch[8], ten days later:

> "...we know we should have arrived in smaller lots of 1,000 at a time but those who had no transport just walked here, or organized their own and our number was soon 20,000 before Chief Minister Sebe or Bantu Affairs was ready for us. That is why there is all this confusion and chaos...".

Malefane's statement shows two things: one, Sebe and the Tribal Authorities that moved had been much more successful in rallying people than they had expected; and, two, they had lost control. However, it is clear that besides having underestimated the number of people and having lost control, the chiefs, Sebe and the South African government had done nothing to prepare for the arrival of the refugees. There were no houses, no roads, no schools, no clinics and there was little water and hardly any food. The situation had become dramatic and most people were despondent.

Chief Sebe, however, refused to acknowledge any responsibility and put all the blame on South Africa. However, the Ciskeian opposition tried to take advantage of the situation by attacking Sebe in the press. A quote from Chief Justice Mabandla, in which he openly criticized the Ciskei Government in the Daily Dispatch[9] for its role in the *"Thornhill scandal"*, indeed seems to confirm that there were political interests at stake. According to Mabandla Sebe was responsible and:

> "...this whole scandalous issue is a typical outcome of political ambition. Against vigorous opposition and demonstrations, Mr. Sebe arrogantly steered a motion in the Ciskei Legislative Assembly to hand over Herschel and Glen Grey to Transkei and what followed is now history".

For the chiefs themselves, however, the situation soon improved as houses were built for them. Moreover, through the chiefs and their headmen provisions were distributed to their followers, although the people did not receive adequate housing. However, for the people that came without chiefs the situation remained hopeless for much longer as they found it much more difficult to get access to provisions and services. Nevertheless, people stayed and endured the hardships because they expected to eventually leave the transit camp and be allocated some of the excellent farmland that their leaders had been shown.

The Quest for Land
Besides the political reasons and the anxiety of ordinary men and women to lose their South African citizenship, it was clear to me that there might have been another important factor behind the move. Land in Herschel had become scarce, population pressure had steadily increased over the past century and erosion had been a problem for decades. Therefore, the promise of new horizons and unspoilt farmland in the Ciskei might have lured many of the 'refugees'. Although others claim it was never the main reason behind the move, Frank Tikile, South African National Civics Organization (SANCO) officer in Thornhill, had a clear opinion that seemed to confirm my suspicion:

> "...for me the whole thing was not about the Transkei business. It was land I wanted. The soil was washed away, there were dongas[10] [in Herschel]. We needed new land (...). Now the people say that we were running away for the Transkei but the truth is only that we wanted better land. I was under Chief Hinana who didn't want to stay (...). Even for the chiefs the main reason was the land, more ground...".

Indeed, in order to convince the chiefs, their councillors and headmen that leaving Herschel would benefit them, South African and Ciskeian government officials had taken them on an organized two-day bus trip in 1975. Not only were they shown the prosperous white farms next to the Queenstown –Tarkastad road (not far from Thornhill), but also the impression was created that these farms would ultimately become theirs when that whole area would be added to the Ciskei. As Mr. Tikile explained:

> "The people were disappointed because the land they were given was not as much as was promised (...). On the bus trip they promised the spread of people (...). The officials were very clear, they said: this will be the Ciskei, under Whittlesea, not under Queenstown...[11]".

Thus, it was clear to me that the quest for land might have also played a decisive role in convincing the people to move.

This was, again, confirmed when I conducted an interview with the three chiefs that had moved to Thornhill. At one stage, a vocal councillor from one of tribal authorities, stood up, and using strong Xhosa imagery, had this to say about the promises that were made in regard to land:

> "The land in Herschel was too small, not enough to plough. We wanted all the young ones to buy cattle, to keep them. Matanzima wanted land, he was given Herschel (...). Then Sebe said: I have got land, those who want land should follow me. The land which I have for you is three times as big as the land in Herschel. We had to follow the cow that was going to give us a lot of milk...".

Thus, even though the chiefs and their Tribal Authorities received land and benefited from the positions they held in the Ciskei, they still consider themselves cheated.

Promises were broken and the amount of land they received was too little. As the councillor concluded:
> "Our pain now is here (...), if we moved we could get three times the land in Herschel (...). It did not happen (...), this land is too small for the three chiefs".

However, although the chiefs were never granted what they were promised, the three tribal authorities at least received land for settlement. Chief Malefane moved to Midfort, Chief Hinana moved to Tentergate where they and their followers each received additional farmland. Chief Bebeza was granted Thornhill and, additionally, received the two farms Zola and Phakamisa. The only group of people that never received any land and which can therefore be considered the real loser in this sad chapter of South African history was 'Group Four'. But before discussing the specifics of Group Four it is necessary to look at one of the major public responses to these developments in South Africa: the Surplus People's Project and the ensuing 'birth' of ARA.

The Birth of the Albany Resettlement Association

At the end of the seventies a group of South African academics, mainly from English speaking universities, saw the need to investigate, document and publicize the plight of the victims of the wave of forced removals and relocations that had swept the country in those years. Subsequently, as was referred to in Chapter 1, in February 1980, 'the Surplus People Project' was officially launched as a research project. In its elaborate five volume report (1983a) it is explained that there was a need:
> "...to focus on forced removals throughout the country, particularly in the rural areas where access was difficult, resulting in relocation unknown to outsiders" (p. xix).

Eventually the initiative became instrumental in focusing national and international attention on a particularly brutal episode of apartheid history. According to the report 3,5 million people have been forcefully removed or relocated since the 1960's. These kind of telling quantitative data –the volumes contain many figures for the different regions– were accompanied by qualitative data. Thus, through this project the victims were given a 'face', as the volumes contained pictures, and a 'voice', as the life histories of the people were recorded. Furthermore, after the report was published in 1983, the participating academics in the different regions believed that more work was needed. Many felt that they had only scratched the surface of what was happening to black and 'coloured' people in South Africa and the bantustans and therefore saw the need for more in-depth work in these communities. Others felt that they could not go back to the their academic ivory towers during a time of such upheavals. They felt something more substantial had to be done. As a result a string of organizations was founded in the towns where the English-speaking universities were situated.

Thus, 'the Grahamstown Group', that had been responsible for the research in the Eastern Cape part of the Surplus People's Project, came together on Saturday 4 September 1982 in a preliminary meeting "...to set up a body provisionally called the Albany Resettlement Association..." (ARA):

> "...with the broad aims of monitoring and giving up-to-date information on communities in the Eastern Cape who have been or may be resettled; serving these communities with information or any support possible (...); and co-ordinating the work of concerned organisations and individuals to these ends"[12].

In the meeting plans were discussed to be tabled at the first main meeting that was to be held on Sunday 26 September in the Ichthyology Department of Rhodes University. That Sunday, other academics and several organizations like the Black Sash and the Border Council of Churches were invited to discuss the establishment and the future of ARA and several reports were tabled on the situation in six different areas like Mgwali and Frankfort. Furthermore, the strategies for the future were discussed with regard to workshops to be organized, finances and publicity.

Ten days later the publicity initiative resulted in the first newspaper article to appear in the Eastern Province Herald[13] under the heading: *"G'town group formed to monitor removals"*. The article quotes the group's first chairperson, associate professor Deirdre Thompson in the Department of Political Science at Rhodes University, who explained how:

> "...ARA fieldworkers would make regular trips to communities under threat of removal and those who had already been resettled...".

The idea was to gather information, which would then be filed at a resource centre and made available to interested parties. Moreover, the newly established organization aimed to make information on legal rights available to communities and offer them support. In order to communicate with communities and interested parties, it was also decided to regularly publish a newsletter. In the first newsletter[14] of May 1983 –with a Rhodes University address– it is reiterated that the committee:

> "...has developed out of the need to continue aspects of the work initiated in the Eastern Cape by the Surplus People Project. It sees as one of its major aims the monitoring and publicising of local relocation..." (1983a, p. 1).

In that first newsletter a small passage was already devoted to the situation in Thornhill:

> "As for the Thornhill camp, where tens of thousands still hang on –they came in a mass of some 40,000 political refugees from Herschel in 1976/77– this desolate, dead tract of ground, far from everywhere, dry, all the bushes gone, is the worst possible base for survival, let alone development" (1983a, p.5).

Furthermore, a rough map of the area was added to give people an idea where this disaster area was situated.

In December 1983 the second newsletter[15] was published in which the first name-change, –to Albany Rural Association– was explained. It:

> "...marks a broadening of objectives. We still aim to monitor and publicise local relocation, but this has inevitably led on to a concern with all matters relating to the rural areas" (1983b, p. 1).

However, in an interview in 1998, one of the first committee members, Jack Green, explained to me that the name change had everything to do with deflecting security police attention away from the organization:

> "instead of a name that worked as a red rag, we wanted a more neutral name...".

Although the start was promising, it took several years for the organization to really get established and become somewhat effective.

During this first period most of the volunteers were not as active as they should have been, since all had full-time positions. According to Dave Pine, the Chairperson of the committee, in the 1984 Chairperson's Report (ARA, 1985b):

> "...the uncertainty around our financial situation and the problems of full-time work, and shortage of money all served to prevent us from establishing ourselves as a more permanent and efficient working group..." (p. 1).

Therefore, as soon as the first grant came through from abroad it was decided to employ fieldworkers, who could spend more time in the field and who were proficient in Xhosa so that lines of communication with the rural communities could be improved. Thus, slowly but surely ARA became a force to be reckoned with in the Eastern Cape and community involvement was expanded and intensified. In Thornhill the first actions were taken around the issues faced by Group Four.

Group Four

As was explained above, a fourth group –the people without chiefs– came to Thornhill. This group, of which the majority belonged to the Amahlubi tribe, while a minority belonged to the Bathlokwa and Myemane tribal authorities, was not a distinct group from the beginning. 'Group Four' slowly came into being as the people realized that they were treated differently. Moreover, during this process of becoming one, several factions emerged. In the days of the move to Thornhill, the people without chiefs soon found out that the Ciskei had no intention of allowing them to remain without chiefs. In fact, the only option presented to the members of Group Four was to join one of the existing chiefs. This led to much resentment as people claimed, referring to the meeting in which the excision of Herschel was discussed, on April 24 1975, that they had been promised a choice. According to the minutes of that meeting Mr. Uys, in his answer to a question posed by Chief Hinana, had indeed stated that:

> "No body will be forced to break away from his Chief or rather to join or live with a certain Chief. It is a matter of personal choice; it depends on the individual" (p. 5, 1975).

Thus, after their arrival in Thornhill, the people without chiefs felt cheated by this forced tribal incorporation. Basically, it led to three responses:

1. A large number of Group Four people sought incorporation with one of the tribal authorities that had moved. Thus, they pledged allegiance to another chief in order to get access to provisions in the early days, and sites, land and services in the following years;
2. another group resisted tribal incorporation, but for different reasons:
   a. one faction was outspoken in its rejection of the other chiefs and insisted that it had been promised to elect its own chief with all the privileges like land and services that came with it;
   b. another faction, that consisted of those who could be termed the 'democrats' or 'progressives', fundamentally rejected the institution of chieftainship.

By presenting the facts in this manner, it appears that these three sub-groups of Group Four could be easily distinguished at all times. However, this is not the fact. People switched occasionally from sub-group to sub-group and allegiances arose and were discarded whenever it was suitable. For example, several leaders of the Amahlubi tribe in Group Four, who wanted their own chief, decided to join the Thornhill Amavundle Tribal Authority at an early stage for practical purposes and, as a result, even became tribal councillors. Nevertheless, in the mid-nineties, after having been part of the Amavundle Tribal Authority for almost two decades (!), these people proceeded to regroup and form the 'Break-away Group Four'. This group, subsequently, not only denied being a part of the Thornhill community but also (re-)voiced its original demands to form their own tribal authority. This demand was, of course, not taken too seriously by the new democratic authorities in the Eastern Cape.

One of the most active Group Four members in the early days was Albert Lobese, who would, eventually, be employed by the Albany Rural Association. He returned to the community, after having worked in Johannesburg from 1977 to 1985, when his mother informed him about the hardships. Hence, because he became very critical of the Tribal Authority in Thornhill and the Sebe regime, he proceeded to start a shop with more than one objective:

"...I applied for a general dealer license. It was hard to talk to people[16] but when you have a shop, people have an excuse to come and see you. My mother talked to the elders and we started a kind of committee, a Group Four committee, to represent the people".

The main aim of the committee was to get their rights recognized and to break the power of the Tribal Authority in Thornhill. In Albert Lobese's own words:

"The Tribal Authority was very strong in those days. In order to discredit them you needed people who could stand up in their meetings and who would question everything in the meetings. By doing that people would approach us. We had to use elderly people who were aligned with the Tribal Authority but who were supporting us. We couldn't use the youth then, because they had no influence".

In the meantime, however, the youth had also been meeting in secret.

Although the youth was not yet recognized as a major force in those days, Sipho Teka –nowadays the Chairman of the Thornhill Reconstruction and Development Committee (TRDC)– in an interview revealed how the youth also started to become active around 1985:

"...I was a student in standard eight when we started with a school boycott. Later on we also held sit-ins at Bisho[17] and Queenstown because there was no water and not enough land in Thornhill".

Slowly the group around Albert Lobese found the right strategies to rally people around. They wrote letters to the Ciskei and the South African government to complain about their lost rights. Furthermore, they targeted the involuntary but obligatory payments that had to be made by members of the community towards the Ciskei government:

"...we used the Development and Security Fund. We thought of a strategy to boycott these payments and boycott the Ntaba kaNdoda meetings. These meetings, twice a year, were held at the mountain near Bisho where all

Ciskeians had to be present and contribute about ten rand. Nobody told you what happened with this money. We felt that we had to resist that. We found strong pensioners to resist that. As we were successful, people realized that no one would be arrested if they didn't pay this money".

Although these first protests were certainly noticed by the traditional leaders, they didn't lead to a major shift in how the community was ruled. For that to happen the participation of more people was imperative.

Cooperative Arrangements Between ARA and Group Four

In 1986 the Albany Rural Association employed Jacob James, a black activist from the Transkei, who had escaped Kaiser Matanzima's security police. Moreover, the structure of the organization was revised, as the workload had increased. By employing several 'professional' field workers and an administrator, who managed the office, the voluntary –mostly academic– staff distanced themselves somewhat from the practical work. Thus, the volunteers formed 'the committee' that regularly met with the employed field staff to discuss the work and the strategies. A step, that can be seen as one of the first steps in a long process of increased professionalization. As Jacob James had his roots and many contacts in the Queenstown area, members of Group Four managed to contact him. They explained their predicament and together a new impetus was given to their struggle.

Arrests and Torture

However, it didn't last as a nation-wide State of Emergency was declared and the security police in Grahamstown became aware of ARA's activities. As Jacob James recounted in an interview:

"Then came the Thornhill people with their problem during the state of emergency and we had no way out but to assist them. So I had to go out to Thornhill and come nearer Queenstown where I knew that the police were looking for me[18](...). So, I had to travel by car but I wouldn't come near Queenstown, I would make a detour to Thornhill (...). I survived about five months working in that fashion...".

However, his luck ran out and events took a dramatic turn as the security police traced his calls and followed members of Group Four as they drove to Grahamstown for a workshop organized by ARA:

"In the midst of a workshop the security police came in and we were all arrested, but others were released the same day. It was only myself and May Brown[19] –in fact, May was in disguise at the time– who were detained. May was detained for nine months, I was detained for a year.... So those were my beginnings within the Albany Rural Association".

The Thornhill people were also released, but the incident signified the beginning of a period of intensified oppression. From that moment on Albert Lobese and others were closely watched by the security forces.

Nevertheless, despite the intimidation and with the support of the voluntary committee members, Albert Lobese continued his activities. As a result, in June 1987, he had one of the most traumatic encounters in his life when the security police raided his home. In an interview he related how the police showed up at his house and:

> "...five black police men came with guns and two bakkies[20]. They threw me in the van like a potato bag (...). When we arrived at Whittlesea, no one was asking questions but they all had to beat me: 'you think you are clever, you think you can come and terrorize Ciskei, we'll show you!' I decided not to resist because the Ciskei police had a bad history of killing people...".

The police then went on to severely torture him with electric shocks that left burn marks everywhere. In 1998 these marks were still visible as he showed me his damaged legs during an interview.

> "They handcuffed me with a chain and the chain was wrapped around me to the feet. And then a small wire was connected to my hands. Now they switched on the electricity. It was like shaking your heart like this...it is not painful but it is shaking you like this (simulates the shakes). You realize that you are becoming dry throughout your body, I then started crying, really I had to cry (...). That happened for 45 minutes without stopping...".

Luckily, his wife had succeeded to call a lawyer in Grahamstown who, in turn, had managed to contact the authorities in Bisho. As a result, the torture was halted and the police released Albert Lobese after three days. However, instead of giving up and hiding away he contacted the Albany Rural Association and sought publicity. The City Press newspaper carried a cover article[21] with a photo of his burns of which it took him weeks to recover. When he finally did, instead of being discouraged he became more determined to do something about the appalling situation in Thornhill. In spite of the fact that his wife threatened to divorce him. He explained to her:

> "I can't stop now, because when I stop now, those people will be pleased. It shows that we are doing something important. That is why they arrested us".

The stories of Albert Lobese and Jacob James illustrate how the histories of the Monti Rural Association and the Thornhill community are intertwined. The brutal measures failed to discourage them. In fact, their horrific experiences reinforced their belief that they were fighting a just cause. As Albert Lobese said above, the oppressive measures showed them that they were doing something important.

Renewed Mobilization and the Hidden Agenda of ARA

Although Jacob James was still in jail in 1987, Albert Lobese kept in touch with the voluntary members of the ARA committee. He gathered as much information as possible about what had happened in Herschel before the move. Soon after Jacob James was released from jail the two of them got together again and a new strategy was devised. In an interview Jacob James –who is now one of the highest officials in the Department of Land Affairs in Pretoria– revealed his modus operandi during the eighties:

> "I was an ANC underground operative (...). I had a double agenda when I was working for ARA. One, it was to achieve the aims and objectives of ARA as an organization which was working against forced removals (...). But I saw that in the context of the overall struggle against apartheid. And in order for ARA to effectively fight against forced removals the rural people themselves needed to be organized. I took it upon myself as a task (...), both as an ARA employee, as well as a political activist, (...) that people should have their own formations to take up issues that are bothering them on a daily basis".

Furthermore, ARA became involved in the formation of the Grahamstown Democratic Action Committee (GRADAC), which itself affiliated to the United Democratic Front (UDF). Moreover, on an international level a network of support was also created like, for example, the United States –South Africa Sister Community Project. Thus, ARA, in an intermediary role[22]:

> "...established formal links between Thornhill and Wichita and between Peelton and Phoenix. (...) These linkages involved ongoing communication with the local groups in the cities in the USA. It also involved advising them on strategies vis-à-vis pressurising the SA government..." (p. 1)

This would make it more difficult for the apartheid regime to ignore what was going on in Thornhill.

Within Thornhill, however, the activities were also stepped up. According to Albert Lobese, Jacob James had a great talent as a communicator and helped resolve many conflicts in Group Four. Moreover, he helped to sustain the spirit of opposition. For example, after the traumatic incidents in 1987:

> "...people were afraid to be arrested...but Jacob brought us together again. He said: 'unless you organize the youth very little will happen, because old men will take much longer'. Then we started organizing the women and later we organized the youth".

However, as described above, the youth had already been active since 1985/86. According to Lungisile Qakaza, vice secretary of the Thornhill Reconstruction and Development Committee (TRDC):

> "the uprisings in Gauteng[23] made us want to do something here. We held meetings at night in someone's house with eight to twelve people to set up our programme (...). We wanted to convince the Tribal Authority and especially the headmen that they were being used by the previous government. We met to discuss the strategies to convince those people. But they didn't take us seriously".

Thus, Albert Lobese was surprised when he eventually found out how organized the youth was:

> "...the youth easily understood our position. We never knew that they were so organized. But we felt that we had to control them...".

In 1989 the Thornhill Youth Organization was formed. And according to Sipho Teka, who became the first vice-president:

> "...the youth, were the most active in those days".

Subsequently, the youth group became one of the most important factors in resisting the chiefs and the authoritarian regime in the Ciskei. Most of the elderly people had been brought up to respect these institutions, but this new generation had other things in mind. Severe inter-generational tensions were the result, whereby the youth came to represent democratic changes while most of the older generation kept defending the Tribal Authority.

It was now a matter of bringing all the forces together in order to show the Tribal Authority and the Ciskei regime that their dominant position was no longer accepted. According to Jacob James the best option to achieve this was the establishment of a residents association:

> "...that would serve as a forum so that all the people within a particular community are able to come and talk about issues that they have to deal with as a community".

In other communities he did the same. He even went a step further as he believed that the strategy of affiliating these residents associations to the United Democratic Front (UDF) would lift regional protest to a higher level:

> "...I started to move very forcefully in terms of ensuring that those communities, those community organizations, start affiliating to the United Democratic Front and start participating in the activities of the UDF".

Moreover, the MRA staff became involved in setting up a regional umbrella organization for local civics, called the Border Civic Congress (BOCCO)[24]. In that manner, although indirectly, people within those organizations were linked to the banned ANC as Jacob James contends:

> "...we started to use that leadership to make a kind of web of underground structures of the ANC and start recruiting people from those communities".

As a result, the protest activities broadened and became more forceful. However, the state's response became even harsher as well. Therefore, when Albert Lobese and the others proceeded to organize a march of pensioners against the Ciskei regime, many were arrested yet again. Nevertheless, the youth was undeterred and continued to hold a sit-in at one of the churches in Queenstown and demanded land and fulfilment of the broken promises. Albert Lobese remained in detention for several weeks and even went on hunger strike until the authorities finally released him.

By the time de Klerk held his speech in Parliament, announcing the release of Mandela and the unbanning of the ANC, the situation in the region had become quite grim. Also within Thornhill conflicts broke out, especially when the youth resorted to more extreme measures. On several occasions the anger boiled over and shops and cars were burnt of people who –in their eyes– were collaborating with Pretoria and the Ciskei regime. In fact, a wave of protests swept the Eastern Cape and especially the Ciskei, until, early in March 1990, President Lennox Sebe was ousted in a coup. The new leader, Brigadier Oupa Gqozo, promised to discard the tribal authorities and work together with the newly formed democratic structures. He even came to Thornhill where he got together with members of the various committees and promised Group Four that their problems would soon be solved.

De Klerk's speech had an enormous impact in South Africa on both the national and the local level. In Thornhill, for example, it led to the formal establishment of the Residents Association and the creation of an ANC branch. Subsequently, according to Albert Lobese, the Tribal Authority became marginalized:

> "...we defeated the Tribal Authority at that time. We even took the tribal office and used it (laughs). The Tribal Authority got stuck (...) and we continued the administration of the area. We also formed the ANC branch and I was the chairman while I was the general secretary of the Residents Association. We did very well...".

Clearly, the members of the residents association felt that they had finally won the battle and they expressed their joy freely. In fact, the quote indicates that they openly humiliated the Tribal Authority by confiscating their office. In that period, besides holding the positions in the RA and the ANC, Albert Lobese was also employed as field worker by the Albany Rural Association. As a result, he became responsible for other communities as well. Thus, he was now wearing several different hats.

The people who wanted change in Thornhill had become more confident now and because of the political breakthroughs new powers were unleashed. However, after several months, it turned out that Oupa Gqozo did not live up to his promises. Not only did Gqozo fail to provide the community with land, he also reversed his decision to do away with the Tribal Authorities. Thus, the need was felt for a new strategy in order to realize their demands.

Invading New Land: occupying Merino Walk
Through ARA Group Four had been brought in contact with the lawyers of the Grahamstown Legal Resources Centre, an association of progressive lawyers. They helped the group to write letters to the Ciskeian and South African authorities[25] in order to communicate their demands concerning land. However, this correspondence that had lasted for several years had not yielded any meaningful results. And as neither the conditions in Thornhill had improved much over the years, nor Gqozo had issued them new land, Group Four felt that more drastic measures were necessary. Therefore, the decision was taken to forcefully occupy land in the vicinity of Thornhill.

For several years, the South African government had designated a large area, consisting of white farms, to be added to the Ciskei for its consolidation. Although, this area, named Released Area 60 (RA 60), had been purchased by the apartheid regime in 1980, it had never been turned over to the Ciskei since part of the territory had been used by the South African Defence Force. another reason why RA 60 was never released had to do with the fact that the land was claimed both by the people of Hewu, who had lived in the adjoining overcrowded area, and by the members of Group Four.

After monitoring the farms in RA 60, Albert Lobese and others belonging to Group Four decided to target Merino Walk farm for invasion. They decided not to inform the Albany Rural Association and other organizations as to minimize the risk of the security police becoming aware of their plans. As Albert Lobese recounted:

"...after three weeks of monitoring the farms (...), we took people with trucks and we occupied the land of Merino Walk. The farm workers ran away and they told the police that people are occupying land. Sixty people and the youth followed and we all stayed in the house. Unaware that the Ciskei soldiers are hunting us...".

The following day ARA was contacted and, subsequently, Jacob James accompanied the occupants to Bisho where they entered into negotiations with the Gqozo regime. However, not much was achieved and the group was prohibited to be present during the official negotiations between the Ciskei and South Africa concerning their occupation of Merino Walk.

A week later the Ciskei police and army moved in and the illegal occupants were evicted. Again, Albert Lobese and the other leaders of the Residents Association were arrested and put in prison. However, they were bailed out after four days by their lawyers and returned to Thornhill where, they regrouped and devised another strategy. Jacob James advised them to operate in the open the next time and to make sure that the press was aware of their actions. Thus, they immediately informed the press when they re-occupied Merino Walk successfully in January 1991. Subsequently, the South African Minister of Development Aid, Piet Marais, even came to Merino Walk where he promised them that they could stay on a temporary basis and would not be evicted. However, when they met him again in East London several weeks later, and the minister had nothing substantial to offer, the Thornhill residents walked out of the meeting and publicly denounced him[26].

What ensued was a long legal and psychological battle in which the Thornhill occupants were continuously harassed, but ultimately endured. One of the South African government's strategies was the trusted tactic of divide and rule. Thus, South African officials informed the Hewu community that the land the government had designated for them had been occupied by people from Thornhill. At a meeting where the resulting tensions between Hewu and Thornhill were supposed to be discussed – and where the Thornhill residents refused to be present –even a bomb went off. Notwithstanding these experiences, a part of Group Four persisted and settled permanently at Merino Walk. By 1999, many were still there and had managed to develop their settlement.

ARA Becomes the Monti Rural Association

The nineties also signalled the dawn of a new age for the Albany Rural Association. However, the first years of the decade were not easy as the Gqozo regime proved to be as oppressive as the Sebe regime had been. Nevertheless, the organization continued to play a strong role in Thornhill and in Merino Walk. In order to be more effective in Thornhill the organization offered Albert Lobese a job as fieldworker in mid-1990, as was mentioned above. It was a logical step for the organization that was still based in Grahamstown. Having a member of staff who lived in the community ensured that the situation in Thornhill could be monitored much more closely. However, it presented problems as well.

By employing a community member, who was part and parcel of the conflicts in Thornhill, ARA lost the little independence it had retained. This was exacerbated when, after the unbanning of the ANC, Albert Lobese also became a dominant figure in the local ANC branch. Combining a position as an ARA fieldworker, being responsible for other areas as well, with his work for the Residents Association and the local ANC branch became an increasingly difficult balancing act. As he had become one of the most powerful men of Thornhill, others became envious of his success. Especially in the circles of the Tribal Authority the critique grew. Several accusations followed, which were referred to by a conservative figure in an interview in 1998:

> "Albert was even sent to California by ARA (...). They [Albert and ARA] once promised to buy a combi[27] to take the old people to the pension pay-out centres. Up until today we haven't received anything, some people are transported there by wheelbarrow. And that while Albert was given a car, a Cressida. Now he has a Corolla. But where was the combi they promised us"?

Also within ARA, the tension grew. Especially after 1993, when the organization moved offices from Grahamstown to East London and adopted a new name: the Monti Rural Association.

During the time of apartheid it had been quite useful to retain the office in Grahamstown. Although the police in this university town in the Republic of South Africa had monitored the group, it had not been as repressive as in the Border area and the areas immediately adjacent to the Ciskei. However, as the winds of change swept the nation, and much of the repression was eliminated, it was decided that an office in East London, in the Border area itself, would be useful. Furthermore, the ARA Newsletter was revamped and renamed *Groundwork*, becoming a newsletter with a broader focus on land and land-related issues. However, although the organization had officially moved to East London, in practice, staff worked for MRA from four (!) locations in 1993. Some staff remained behind in Grahamstown, a researcher was temporarily based in Umtata, the Transkei, and the satellite office in Queenstown was retained. Moreover the organization grew so rapidly –in early 1994 the staff consisted of fourteen people– that the coordinator could hardly manage anymore on his own. As a result, a decision was taken to form a Coordinating Committee, consisting of the coordinators of the organization's programmes. According to Joy Molo[28], who joined MRA in the mid-nineties:

"*...it was a process of transition from being an organization that was run more as activists, to an organization that was run more as an organization...*".

The larger the organization became, the more difficult it was to simply be 'activists'. Thus, it became increasingly difficult to sustain this more informal way of operating, which had been sensible in the period when the organization was small and when the security police monitored ARA's activities closely.

However, Albert Lobese did not agree with the new approach to the work, as he explained in an interview:

"*They told me to plan more new work but I felt that I had to do follow-up work. I believe in spending a lot of time in the community rather than an hour. I don't think I can be effective if stay only an hour in the community. (...) The new director had a different approach: the management approach. I had a leadership approach. The management approach forces something, which is different to what we were doing...*".

Thus, Albert, in a way, became a relic of the old days. However, the fact that he combined so many roles also seemed to impact negatively on the quality of his work.

Nevertheless, the organization went ahead with the new approach, particularly because it was changing its focus. From 'anti-removal' and 'anti-forced-incorporation' support the focus shifted to the support and implementation of the Land Reform Programme that had been formulated by the new government. Less emphasis on support, more emphasis on development issues. One issue which was hotly debated, in this regard, was whether MRA employees themselves would be allowed to benefit personally from the new land legislation. The majority in MRA decided against that, and, thus, the situation became even more complex for Albert Lobese, as he belonged to Group Four which was aiming to get land. His simultaneous wearing of several hats continued to provoke severe criticism and, ultimately, his integrity came under attack from his ARA colleagues. Thus, in 1996, as a result of a controversial decision, he was sacked as he refused the ban on accessing a government subsidy for land. Nowadays, although rather anonymously, he still lives in Thornhill and has a moderately successful brick-making business.

However, between the time ARA became MRA and the moment he was sacked in 1996 Albert Lobese remained active in Thornhill and managed, together with Zandisile Teka, to broaden the struggle for land of Group Four into the struggle for land of the whole of Thornhill, as will be discussed in the next section.

Group Four Becomes Thornhill

As was described above, the Group Four committee was formed by Albert Lobese and others in the late eighties. Its leaders, however, also became the leading members of the Thornhill Residents Association (TRA) that was established a few years later to challenge the Tribal Authority. Thus, in the early nineties these two bodies, the TRA and the Group Four committee, had quite an overlap in both aims –more land and better housing and services– and members. In fact, during this period the struggle of Group Four became the struggle of Thornhill as a whole. Which mechanisms were at work here?

The most active people in Group Four were ANC-minded people. They believed in and fought for democratic change, and were generally opposed to the dominant position of the Tribal Authority. When these people, like Albert Lobese and youths like Sipho Teka, took the opportunity to form a Residents Association, it obviously meant that they ultimately aimed to administer to the needs of the whole of Thornhill. Therefore, when the ANC was unbanned and residents associations were allowed to operate in the open, the association was named the Thornhill Residents Association (TRA) and not the 'Group Four Residents Association'. Its goal was to take over from the Tribal Authority and become the legitimate administrating body of the area. As Albert Lobese explained:

> "...some people didn't want to get rid of Group Four while on the other hand we set up the TRA. So I had to move out of Group Four and be part of the residents association.... Gradually Group Four disappeared because in order to get what we wanted it was necessary to organize everyone. That was our position. The elderlies couldn't understand, but gradually they followed us and Group Four perished".

When, subsequently, they succeeded in undermining the Tribal Authority (TA), many people crossed the floor and joined them. However, although the majority of people now supported the Thornhill Residents Association, a substantial group of people still supported the Tribal Authority. Moreover, because of the recent history, the new democratic leaders were also reluctant to approach the Tribal Authority in order to seek cooperation. Too much had happened.

However, the fact that many who had preciously supported the tribal Authority had now crossed the floor meant that the emphasis shifted even more from Group Four to the whole of Thornhill. One of those who joined was Zandisile Teka, the Amavundle Primary School principal. He is still critical of the fact that the Tribal Authority was completely side-lined in the process of setting up the TRA, and that the residents association humiliated the TA by taking over their tribal office:

> "...when Group Four members started the Residents Association for the first time, they never approached the other side [the Tribal Authority]. I remember a meeting when I told the Group Four leaders that this should be for everybody: 'I don't like the stress on Group Four'. It seemed as if they were

> *throwing stones to the other side saying: 'look, you have been benefiting in the Sebe era, it is our turn now'. I said: 'unite the people'".*

Nevertheless, when the land and development claims were pursued by the Thornhill Residents Association in the following years, it slowly became the mouth-piece of most of the community. Moreover, it became recognized by the new government structures and Non-Governmental Organizations. However, within Thornhill, it never lost its reputation of being anti-Tribal Authority and therefore never attained complete legitimacy.

A similar problem hounds the Monti Rural Association. Although the organization has evolved over the years and although there has been a high staff turn-over, it is still distrusted by the members of the Tribal Authority in Thornhill. In their eyes the organization supported the opposition to the traditional leaders in the eighties and early nineties. Thus, the chiefs and their councillors claim that MRA brought dissent and conflicts to the community. In their view the organization has caused much harm and left the Tribal Authority more or less powerless. They feel betrayed by MRA and will, therefore, always perceive the organization in that light. Also in other communities the Monti Rural Association encountered similar problems. Trying to cooperate with such tribal structures in the late nineties remained difficult.

The Establishment of the Thornhill Reconstruction and Development Committee (TRDC)

When, after the elections in 1994, the new government introduced the Reconstruction and Development Programme (RDP), the Thornhill community welcomed a new opportunity to form a truly legitimate local structure. Headed by Nelson Mandela, the 'Rainbow Coalition' preached unity and stakeholder consultation at every level. Even in the most remote rural areas this 'freedom and consultation discourse' impacted and, as a result, stakeholder forums were formed in order to negotiate, discuss and implement the reconstruction and development challenges that lay ahead. In Thornhill the stakeholder forum that was established became known as the Thornhill Reconstruction and Development Committee (TRDC).

One of the driving forces behind the establishment of the Thornhill Reconstruction and Development Committee was Zandisile Teka, who felt that he could bridge the gap between the Thornhill Residents Association on the one side and the Tribal Authority on the other side. He was one of the people who saw that – despite the fact that some had benefited more from the Sebe regime than others– all had been losers and all had suffered because of the promises that had been broken. Moreover, he recognized the fact that many of the original Group Four members had become part of the Amavundle Tribal Authority, like himself. These people had pledged allegiance to the chief in order to get access to a site in Thornhill. In an interview he related:

> *"Yes, I played a big part in establishing the Thornhill Reconstruction and Development Committee. We called the chief and his people and asked the people who surround the chief to be part of this committee. During '90-'91 when Sebe was disposed, we had the problem of one group [Group Four] dominating and claiming that they were the only ones who had been*

suppressed. So we had to fight that and say: let us unite and fight together for more land...".

Zandisile Teka worked together with his younger brother Sipho Teka[29] to establish the new committee. The history of these brothers is interesting as the older brother had been part of those in Group Four that supported the Amavundle Tribal Authority, while the younger brother had always been active in the youth movement that opposed the tribal authorities. In this phase, however, they worked closely together and Sipho Teka explained how inclusive the TRDC had become:

"We said that all organizations must submit one name. In total 22 organization were listed as founders. Everybody did, the disabled, the skilled workers, the police et cetera We then proceeded to draft a constitution which would bind us".

During that phase the Monti Rural Association played a key role:

"...to develop a document in which we agreed on the criteria to be used to admit members. Most importantly, organizations had to submit proof of having a constituency and proven interest in development".

After a lengthy process the TRDC finally became a legitimate and respected structure through which all development activities in the community were processed. According to Zandisile Teka:

"...The tensions in the community abated after the TRDC was established in 1995".

Since then the TRDC meetings have become the only place where all stakeholders meet and where open and sometimes very critical discussions take place. And although the most influential committee members are the youth activists of yesteryear, there is now at least an understanding with the Tribal Authority that major community decisions will have to be taken in the TRDC. Thus, even the old partners from the struggle era do not escape critical scrutiny. In 1998, for example, I witnessed that the Monti Rural Association was heavily attacked in this forum. In the eyes of the TRDC the organization was partly responsible for delays in the submission of a report to the Department of Water Affairs and Forestry (DWAF).

After 1995, when the local government elections were held, the area witnessed the birth of yet another structure. This Transitional Rural Council (TRC) –of a form of local government as discussed in Chapter 3– consisted of several councillors. However, it does not have its own budget and one of the councillors has a seat in the Stormberg District Council. Although the TRC closely cooperates with the TRDC, many feel that the latter is the true legitimate structure of the people. Especially as genuine local issues are discussed in the Thornhill Reconstruction and Development Committee. Therefore, Zandisile Teka feels that:

"For Thornhill, as we ourselves have established the TRDC, that should be our local government, that is where all the local issues should be discussed".

In the next decade these overlaps will have to be sorted out as local government is still in flux.

At the end of the nineties there was only one faction, referred to above as 'the break-away Group Four', that is still refused to acknowledge that it was part of the Thornhill community. Moreover, they did not recognize the fact that a democratic form of local government would have to be implemented. Although their number is small and their chances limited they believed that as original Group Four members they still had the right to establish their own Amahlubi Tribal Authority. Their spokesman, David Manyingisa, said in an interview:

> "We are Amahlubi, the problem is that we don't see ourselves belonging to the people of Thornhill. We would like to have our own traditional way of doing things which is different from the three chiefs that came here".

However, very few take this group seriously as these were the people who had pledged allegiance to the Amavundle Chief in Thornhill and even served as tribal councillors during the Sebe years. Nevertheless, one could say that 'Group Four', in yet another appearance, was still alive in 1999.

As for the Monti Rural Association, most of the old staff had left the organization in the mid-nineties. After MRA had been active in voter education and the new government had been brought to power many of them proceeded to take up high positions in the government, particularly in the Department of Land Affairs. Notwithstanding this critical 'brain drain', the organization was still playing a major role in the Eastern Cape. Whereas it has lost much of its original unique position in the community it was still one of the agencies that was active in Thornhill, by assisting the people to achieve all that was promised more than twenty years ago: enough land, houses, clean water and services.

Conclusion

This chapter has illustrated that the history of MRA can hardly be understood without understanding the political struggles that took place in Thornhill and vice versa. With regard to these struggles, I have aimed to show that the daily political battles for power and resources in South Africa were often disguised and regarded as 'ethnic conflict'. Especially in an area like the Eastern Cape the various 'tribal' actors were, in fact, engaged in the struggle for their slice of the political Ciskei cake. As Sebe was most successful in his machinations he eventually came out on top. Subsequently, the tribal authorities were used to rule the rural areas. Again, an excellent example of what Mamdani (1996) has called *decentralized despotism*.

The case of Thornhill has revealed several hidden agendas. Not only did many proceed to leave Herschel in order to retain their South African citizenship, they also left their homes because they were seeking new and fertile land. Sebe, on the other hand lured these people because it suited him politically. Besides getting rid of people through the ceding of Herschel and Glen Grey, he also gained the support of the loyal chiefs that moved. Moreover, it provided him with an opportunity to create his own chiefdom. But also the Monti Rural Association staff had a hidden agenda. The field workers of the Monti Rural Association, like Jacob James and May Brown, were actively involved in the liberation struggle. This struggle informed the community interventions of MRA. The establishment of residents associations in the Eastern Cape, which became affiliated to the United Democratic Front, and the manner in which groups that opposed the Tribal Authorities were supported, had everything to do with the broader anti-apartheid struggle. The MRA staff linked these local level struggles to the national fight for freedom.

Lastly, the chapter has illustrated how NGOs can be tainted by earlier interventions. MRA's work in the late nineties is, for example, still burdened by an image that originated in the eighties and early nineties. It is one more argument against the idea of neutral interventions by outside agencies. Non-Governmental Organizations always side more with some groups than with others, as communities are internally divided. Such divisions, sometimes resulting in factions, are quite frequently obscured in the discourses of NGO intervention. Although the term community has been criticized on many occasions, both in academia and in the non-governmental sector, it is a term –like 'household'– with connotations that can hardly be weeded out. What is interesting about the Thornhill case is that it reveals two things. One: the community is and was divided. Two: during the course of the past decades changing coalitions were often crucial in tipping the balance of power. Whether during apartheid or during the new dispensation, coalitions withered and bloomed, influenced by –and influencing– the political situation in Thornhill.

Ultimately, the Thornhill Reconstruction and Development Committee (TRDC), in which all the 'stakeholders' were represented, offered the community a chance to form a new forum where all local development issues could be debated. After its inception the tensions in Thornhill soon abated. Nevertheless, some of the conflicts are still smouldering under the surface and it is possible that these tensions erupt when the face of local government is given a more permanent character. In this regard, the unclarity with regard to the position of chiefs in South Africa is an explosive issue, nationally as well as locally. Thus, in many areas, like Thornhill, two systems of local governance coexisted in the late nineties.

5. Strategic Translations in Gasela[1]

Introduction
In this chapter I discuss the intermediary role of the Monti Rural Association and its ability, as NGO, to engage in *strategic translations*. I aim to show how the organization, quite pragmatically, adopted a political strategy in which it became necessary to depict the Gasela residents as potential commercial farmers. These rural dwellers –a rural proletariat?– with few agricultural skills and a lack of resources had to be portrayed as potential farmers in order to convince the Department of Land Affairs to transfer the land to the community. Thus, both MRA and the Gasela residents came to be held in a 'market-oriented embrace' by the government.

I will try to elucidate how the intermediary position of the land sector NGO provided the staff with the opportunity to make, what I have called *strategic translations*. Thus, I agree with Nyamwaya (1997) who has stated about the health sector:

> *"...while in theory communities are supposed to play a leading role in the health-development process, the process is still largely controlled by government and NGO development 'experts' who do not allow communities to play major roles"* (p. 184).

In my opinion, such processes of control also take place in the land sector in South Africa. Research, workshops and NGO reports are important tools in these strategic translations.

The case material, presented in this chapter, furthermore, illustrates that participation is a fundamental problem in NGO strategies. Although NGO ideology acknowledges the need for community participation in development processes, the political processes and battles the NGO engages in on behalf of 'the people' can frequently do without. In fact, in many cases a certain distance from the people eases these strategic translations. Keeping certain 'grassroots views' out of the NGO reports is often crucial to achieve what is aimed for. This is easiest in those cases where, as the Monti Rural Association Media Officer stated *"...we are the connection between voiceless communities and the outside world..."*. The gatekeeper holds the key...

Gasela: an 'abandoned' farm
On the road from East London to Johannesburg, eight kilometres before the town of Stutterheim –founded by German settlers– a large signpost to the left of the road points to the Gasela railway station. A bumpy dirt-road not only leads to this small rural train station but also to Gasela, a farm that was once called 'Mooifontein' (Pretty Fountain/Spring) and that is situated between the road and the railway. Significantly, this railway line was once, in the nineteen-eighties, not only a boundary between two parts of Mooifontein farm, but also the 'international border' between the Republic of South Africa and the Ciskei.

One of the most remarkable features in the morning is the quiet. One hears the traffic on the road, but the entire farm seems deserted. The colonial-style red-roofed farmhouse is surrounded by a prison-like two and a half meter barbed wire fence. The gate is locked and the house seems abandoned. The roof over the braai[2]-area has fallen down and the garden is overgrown with high grasses and weeds. However, on closer inspection some activity can be observed in the yards of the thirty odd 'African' huts and mud houses that surround the farmhouse. A few women are hanging clothes to dry on fences, some are cooking, small children are playing in the dust. Men seem virtually absent. In the afternoons, however, Gasela seems to come to life. The many children have returned from school and usually the younger ones are playing soccer on a dusty patch in front of the barbed wire fence, while young men practice rugby on a relatively well-maintained rugby field next to the farmhouse.

What is surprising is the fact that few farming activities seem to take place. Indeed, there are several small well-kept gardens with maize, beans and pumpkins – one could probably call them 'subsistence' plots– next to some of the huts. Furthermore, some cattle roam the farm during the day and a few households keep chickens and pigs. But there is no sign of intensive agriculture or stock-keeping. The fields lie fallow and are partly overgrown with bushes and young trees and the cowsheds near the farmhouse are empty and look dilapidated. Moreover, apart from a broken-down tractor and an old diesel water pump, most farm implements seem to have vanished. No ploughs, harrows, not even shovels and hoes. Walking around one wonders whether this is the farm that the Monti Rural Association has described as a potentially thriving agri-village.

MRA has been involved in Gasela since 1993, when the ex-farm workers feared to be evicted and encountered many problems with the lessee, a white farmer who had maltreated several community members. Since 1996 there is no longer a white farmer on the farm, and only the ex-farm workers remain. According to figures presented by the Monti Rural Association 218 people can be regarded as Gasela residents (see: Table 5.1).

AGE	NUMBER	%
0-20	110	50,4
21-40	70	32,1
41-60	27	12,3
61-80	11	5,2
Total[3]:	218	100

(Source: MRA, 1997b, p.11-12)

Table 5.1: Number of Gasela residents and Age Distribution.

These residents occupy thirty of the 52 residential sites on the farm.

In its 1996 report, *Gasela Proposal to the Department of Land Affairs*, the Monti Rural Association (1996c) is very clear about the agricultural potential of the land and the aspirations of the community:

"...*MRA proposes that Gasela be treated as a **pilot project for the establishment of an agricultural settlement** which aims to meet the food requirements of the community as well as provide a cash income which provides residents with a livelihood...(...). The Gasela community is a stable and cohesive community who want a rural lifestyle where their main source of income is agriculture...*" (p. 8-9).

Thus, it is concluded that:

> *"The Gasela community should be given ownership rights to the land on which they reside –Portion 1 of Mooifontein (89 ha)..."* (p. 12).

However, as the Department of Land Affairs was not convinced by the arguments in MRA's first report it was reluctant to transfer the land. As a compromise, it appointed the organization again for follow-up research. Based on much more thorough research, the Monti Rural Association (1997b) subsequently presented the results in its *Report on Gasela November 1997*. In it, MRA was more critical and did actually query the skills available:

> *"Although there are different interests in Gasela, the majority of respondents prioritise agricultural enterprise, both as a productive option and in terms of the settlement ramifications. Although there is some level of agricultural skill in the community, especially in vegetable production and soil preparation, it should be acknowledged that there is a shortage of the range of skills that is required for a successful commercial enterprise"* (p. 14).

Nevertheless, the Monti Rural Association, still saw a good opportunity for farming as it expected that:

> *"...if 20 hectares is allocated to cabbages and 20 hectares to potatoes then the resulting estimated annual gross margin will be R320 974.00^4 per annum (...). It is clear that the transfer of agricultural land to the Gasela community will lead to a substantial improvement in their quality of life. In very hard, material term, if one divides the projected cash flow by the number of extended households, then each extended household will benefit by approximately R10,000 per annum..."* (p. 25).

Thus, the organization still remained convinced, in its main recommendations, that *"Gasela should be swiftly transferred to its residents"* (p. 28).

As a social scientist and an agricultural scientist, I believed that the image of Gasela –a potentially thriving agricultural settlement for its income mainly dependent on agricultural production– which MRA presented in its reports, was not consistent with what I encountered on the farm. At first sight, I saw very little farming going on, a dominant presence of older women, a high level of illiteracy. Not the obvious kind of community that one would imagine to be very successful at commercial farming. This led me to seek answers to many questions. For example: What was the background of these people? What were their experiences, as 'a community' with communal activities Why were they not cultivating –or 'ploughing'^{5} as the people themselves would say– the land on a larger scale? In order to answer some of these questions it is useful to go back a few years.

The Early Years

Mooifontein, or Gasela as it is referred to nowadays, was a typical white-owned farm in the sixties and seventies. The white farmer, a mister Johan Klaas, and his family lived in the large 11-roomed house, while the black farm labourers, with their families, lived in a cluster of roundavels^6 and mud houses at a distance of about seventy-five meters from the main house on a rocky patch of land. The men worked as labourers while some of the women worked as a maid or a kitchen help in the main house. According to Mr. Xolani Dubeni, who was born on the farm in 1960, *"Life was not right in that time, we were growing up with suffering, my father worked for 2 rand a month...".* Or as Mr. Vuyo Yako, also born in Gasela in 1964, talked about his mother and her work for the farmer's family:

> "...*She used to start working at five o'clock [a.m.], often till late at night, sometimes even till ten o'clock. She didn't have time to herself, time to get out. My grandmother used to take care of us. In Gasela in those days the six households made up a population of between 60 and seventy people. About ten of those were working...".*

The *baas*[7] was omnipotent in those days and ruled over the workers twenty-four hours a day. He even made demands on them in their leisure time and sometimes these demands were rather peculiar. For example, Johan Klaas taught the boys and young men how to play rugby so that his sons Pieter and Japie, who were in the school rugby team, would get regular rugby practice on the farm. A few years later, after the Klaas family left a regular rugby team was established on the farm. According to Mr. Vuyo Yako it was called *"'Vuzumzi': awake the home...".* Nowadays, Gasela's rugby team is still the pride of the community and partakes in the regional rugby competition.

An 'International Border' Across the Farm

In April 1978 the Klaas family left for a farm on the other side of Stutterheim and the Ciskei Living Stock Board (CLSB) took over Mooifontein. In that period of roughly two years the CSLB expanded the territory of the farm as it was intended to eventually incorporate it into the Ciskei, the new homeland in the making. Nevertheless, in 1980, in preparation of Ciskei's independence, it was decided that the railway line would become an 'international border'. The part of the farm that was situated on the other side of the railway track became part of the Republic of Ciskei, while the part between the main road and the railway remained in the Republic of South Africa. During this time quite a few people moved to the 'good side' of the farm in order to retain their South African citizenship.

In 1980 the apartheid government –by all respondents referred to as GG ('Gee Gee'), or General Government– took control over the South African part of the farm. One of the departments that arrived was the Department of Development Aid[8]. It was the start of a period of relative prosperity and an abundance of work for the Gasela residents, said Mr. Vuyo Yako:

> "...*GG was very nice to us, they helped us with food and transport of sick people and the rugby team and they employed us with about 500 other people...".*

However, for many others in the surrounding areas it marked the onset of a period of great suffering as it was the time of homeland consolidation and forced removals. This meant that many areas were cleared of the superfluous 'blacks' to create 'all-white' areas. Those that were removed were consequently dumped in the bantustans. For example, a large part of the population of Mgwali, a mission station and a so-called 'black spot'[9], was removed to an area near Gasela. These new areas of high influx were then serviced from Gasela by the South African government. It used the farm as a base in the Republic of South Africa to 'aid and develop' these areas in the Ciskei –across the railway line. Hence, its hypocritical name: Department of Development Aid.

According to Mr. Vuyo Yako, this programme of assistance involved, amongst other things, the building of houses:

> "...the Department of Development Aid came to assist people that suffered without houses. If people's houses broke down, the government gave them tin houses. Many people in Ndakana are from Mgwali. GG helped them, they were mostly right-hand people supporting Sebe".

It was clearly part of a political deal between Sebe and the apartheid regime where the latter provided much of the infrastructure.

As mentioned above, this period of prosperity and an abundance of work on the farm and in the neighbouring areas led to a great influx of new labourers. Some of the new arrivals came to settle permanently as Mrs. Nomntu Stuurman described:

> "We came to Gasela and my husband received R. 300 per month, me 150 rand. I was working in the house of the umlungu (...) because I know the job of the kitchen (...). We built a house (...) and we started ploughing a garden".

However, a large part of the 500 labourers, who were from different tribes like the amaXhosa, amaSotho, amaNdebele and amaZulu, did not reside on the farm permanently. They stayed in a camp of tin shacks that was built under the gum trees, while others stayed on farms in the neighbouring areas. During this whole period the farm was cultivated to provide the labour pool with food. Crops like maize, beans and potatoes were grown and the people who stayed on the farm were allowed to graze their cattle.

Fear of Forced Removal

When, finally, in the beginning of the nineties, the winds of change began to sweep the country the General Government was no longer needed in Gasela as the era of the bantustans was clearly coming to an end. Thus the white personnel with some of the more skilled black staff, like truck and tractor drivers, were transferred to East London and the tin shack settlement was destroyed when the labourers were sacked. The original Gasela residents –and a few new arrivals who stayed– were left to their own devices and to make matters worse, the community itself came under threat of removal. In February 1993, when the last whites left, the remaining labourers were told to leave the farm within a month. However, one of the community leaders, Mr. Jim Dabani, who had lived and worked in Gasela since 1983 as the foreman of the watchmen, took action. He obtained oral permission, by government officials in East London and the local commissioner of police, for the Gasela residents to stay on the farm. Nevertheless, it marked the beginning of a period of severe insecurity, complicated by the fact that most people were now unemployed.

In that same year, 1993, the Department of Agriculture took control of the farm and the situation became even more complex as this department leased the farm to a white farmer, a Mr. Steen. Instead of working together with the farm labourers, or properly employing them, this farmer abused people and threatened the community. According to community members he bossed people around, prohibited grazing on the farm, used the occasional violence and threatened them with eviction. As Mrs. Bukelwa Qongwana described the situation:

> "Mr. Steen wanted us to work for him for nothing, he claimed that the land was private land and that he was the owner. He was lying (...). He was a silly

man. *He abused someone in Gasela. He beat him with the back of his gun and broke his arm because he didn't want to fetch firewood for Mr. Steen".*
And according to Mr. Dabani *"Mr. Steen was bad. He threatened to shoot our cattle and bulldoze our houses...".* During this period of threats and confusion several residents asked a white lady from Kei Road –who came to Gasela regularly to sell 'utywala' (alcohol)– for advice. She subsequently contacted the Monti Rural Association and passed on the request for help.

The Involvement of the Monti Rural Association
When MRA fieldworkers arrived in mid-1993, they encountered a tense situation. Although two community leaders were active, there seemed to be little sense of direction. Therefore, one of the first things MRA did was to advise the people to improve their standard of organization. Moreover, the NGO helped them to establish links with other structures to improve their capacity and strengthen their bargaining position. As a result, the Gasela Residents Association (GRA) was set up which was, subsequently, linked to the sub-regional committee of SANCO[10] in Stutterheim. Furthermore, the Monti Rural Association attempted to mediate in the conflict between the lessee and the Gasela farm dwellers, and also formally complained to the Department of Land Affairs (DLA) about the continuous harassment of the community by the lessee.

Nevertheless, the process was slow and it took several years for the situation on the farm to reverse. One of the first victories was recorded in 1994, after Mr. Steen had cut off the water supply to the residents of Gasela. When MRA was informed about the matter they took Derek Hanekom, the newly appointed Minister of Land Affairs, to Gasela when he visited the Eastern Cape in October 1994. Hanekom was appalled and assured the community that they would not be evicted. He also made sure that the water supply was soon reconnected. At last the Gasela residents felt that the balance of power was tipping. There was a chance that iPilisi would ultimately be defeated. However, in early 1995 another conflict arose as community members cut firewood on the farm and were subsequently arrested. When MRA was called, the fieldworkers involved SANCO from Stutterheim in order to mediate between the community and the lessee. It resulted in the release of those arrested, and soon afterwards the Department of Land Affairs terminated the lease of Mr. Steen. Nevertheless, he was allowed to stay on the farm as 'care-taker' until the department removed him altogether in 1996.

The Fight for Land
Apart from assisting and facilitating the establishment of the Gasela Residents Association (GRA), the Monti Rural Association also informed the people about the possibilities of land acquisition. In a first attempt MRA helped the GRA to submit a land claim to the Advisory Commission on Land Allocation[11]. One of the main arguments in the claim, in the eyes of the community (and MRA), concerned the fact that *"...the community has been settling on the farm since 1960...",* and *"...they do not have any land to practice farming...".* After a lengthy procedure, in the course of which the Advisory Commission on Land Allocation was succeeded by the Commission on Land Allocation and eventually by the Commission on Restitution of

Land Rights and during which time several new laws and procedures evolved, the Gasela Residents Association received a negative response on April 10, 1996[12]. It read:

> "While the Commission on Restitution of Land Rights is very sympathetic to the needs of landless people, we are unfortunately not in the position to assist with general applications for land, such as you have made (...).
>
> The new Commission on Restitution of Land Rights was established to assist those who lost their rights through racially discriminatory laws after 1913, to claim back such rights (...).
>
> Unfortunately, your application for land does not fall within the mandate of the Commission as outlined in the act. There are, however, other land reform programmes which may be able to meet your needs...".

In short, the Commission on Restitution of Land Rights determined that the people of Gasela could not qualify for a restitution claim as it did not concern land that they had lost under racially discriminatory laws.

After the initial disappointment, MRA, in consultation with the Gasela Residents Association, decided to pursue another avenue. Instead of a restitution claim, it was now expected that the Land Redistribution Programme would yield the desired result. This programme, as was described in Chapter 3, was formulated to transfer white-owned land to the black majority on a *willing-buyer willing-seller* basis. However, as the land was already owned by the state, and no white farmer had to be compensated, MRA argued that the people of Gasela should be granted the farm, so that they could use their settlement subsidy to purchase an additional portion of land. Therefore, in its 1996 report, *Gasela Proposal to the Department of Land Affairs*, that was quoted above, the Monti Rural Association (1996c) concluded:

> "In summary, in the interests of regional stability and in line with DLA's stated priority of redistribution of state land, MRA proposes that Portion 1 of the farm Mooifontein be granted to the Gasela community and that settlement subsidies and the option of purchasing an additional portion of land be made available to them" (p. 8).

Following the submission of this proposal to the provincial Department of Land Affairs (DLA), it became clear that the department remained sceptical about the transfer of the land. Two major obstacles remained. First of all the director of the provincial DLA, John Carver, who –until a few years earlier– had been the director of MRA, was still not convinced that the Gasela community had the actual will, the capacity, the skills, and the resources to farm the land successfully. He doubted the economic viability of the plan. Secondly, a Stutterheim District plan was to be formulated in order to investigate the settlement options for the wider region. In such a plan it would be investigated whether various black communities would have to be amalgamated into several large and well-serviced rural settlements. Therefore, it was not at all clear whether such a District Plan would leave room for small autonomous agri-villages like Gasela. Thus, in such a scenario, the Gasela residents would probably have to leave the farm in order to be offered housing in township-type settlements in the area. During a meeting of Gasela stakeholders[13] in August 1997[14] Mr. Carver referred to both obstacles:

"We were not actually sure whether people would be actually interested in farming. Moreover, it is necessary to look at the area in relation to the surrounding areas...".

Later on in the meeting he furthermore stated:

"My personal guess is that we might have to think about three satellite settlements in the area. In the end we might have to make some hard decisions...".

Nevertheless, although the Department of Land Affairs was not at all convinced that the transfer of land to the Gasela residents was desirable, it postponed making a hard decision since work on the Stutterheim District Plan would take several years. Moreover, the Gasela residents had rights to stay on the land due to the Interim Protection of Informal Land Rights Act[15], that gave them short term tenure security. As the Monti Rural Association did not share the apprehension of DLA, in regard to capacity, skills and will of the community, the department –in the meantime– awarded MRA another research contract to prove the contrary. That research, which built on the research in 1996, yielded the *Report on Gasela November 1997*, that was quoted above and which, although more realistic in regard to problems around lack of agricultural skills, still argued in favour of land transfer.

As could be expected, the Department of Land Affairs did not fundamentally alter its position after it received the 1997 report. However, they did make clear that they would not object if the community started cultivating the land in order for them to prove that they could exploit the resources on the farm successfully. Over and above the land on which they resided, the people of Gasela were also granted permission to make use of another portion of the farm on the other side of the road. In this manner the Gasela residents could use the time, needed by the departments to sort out all the intricacies of the Stutterheim District plan, to demonstrate their eagerness and ability to farm in order to convince the government. Subsequently, in early November 1997 the Monti Rural Association informed the Gasela residents that they had permission to cultivate the land.

Consequently, rapid cultivation of the land became crucial for the people of Gasela and for MRA. Why was it then that almost a year later the land had not been cultivated? Was it a question of lack of resources, did people indeed lack the skills, or were there community dynamics that the NGO might have overlooked?

To Plough or Not to Plough...

In August 1998, when the author was last in Gasela, the farm's large fields yet had to be cultivated. Although, as in other years, nearly every household had cultivated a 'garden'[16], not one of the larger fields had been ploughed, either communally or privately. Nevertheless, the 'ploughing' issue was an important issue that frequently cropped up in community meetings. Moreover, practically all the community members, who were active in one of the Gasela structures, mentioned it as a priority; not only in their conversations with outsiders. Then why was no ploughing done?

The most frequently heard explanations by the Gasela farm dwellers had to do with the difficulty of finding a tractor for a reasonable price. For their private gardens people usually hire a tractor from the neighbouring village as Mr. Xolani Dubeni explained in an interview:

> *"Sometimes when we are going to plough, we ask a tractor to plough for us from Ndakana. A garden costs 35 rand to plough. I sow the seeds myself by hand...".*

But according to Mr. Mbulelo Mfene this was not possible in November for the farm's large fields:

> *"In November we didn't find a tractor, the Ndakana tractors were busy when MRA came to give us this place (...). We have no ox ploughs. If we have support, the government can borrow us a tractor. We did plough our gardens but that was also difficult. It took place in the evenings (...), and on Saturday and Sunday. Costs are 60 rand for a small garden. People are waiting for their pensions. Few people work here and there is too much weeds and grass to plough by hand...".*

Subsequently, several community leaders went to a neighbouring white farmer who indicated that he would be willing to plough for them, as Mrs. Nomntu Stuurman recounted:

> *"We were preparing to plough but we were asking the white man to plough. He wanted to charge 4,700 rand, the second time we asked [it was] 5,000 rand...".*

This clearly was an amount of cash that could not be raised by the community since the main source of income is pensions and disability grants. In a last attempt –it was now already March 1998– some of the men, who worked for the Döhne Agricultural Research Station, tried to borrow a tractor there as Mr. Mbulelo Mfene explained:

> *"I am busy to get a tractor from Döhne. We are waiting for April, if the Döhne budget comes, they can plough for us...".*

But also this attempt failed and thus most of the farm remained uncultivated.

When analyzing these answers it becomes clear that community members view the lack of access to a tractor as most problematic. However, several factors seem to be involved in this lack of access. First, there seems to be a shortage of available cash. Although the Ndakana tractors seem much cheaper than the white farmer's tractor, that might actually prove to be an illusion. Sixty rand for one tenth of a hectare (the approximate size of a garden plot) also translates to 6,000 rand for ten hectares. Such astronomical amounts of cash are very hard to cough up for a group of rural dwellers like the Gasela residents. Second, Mr. Mfene also suggested that time was a complicating factor. Not only were the available tractors busy on other fields during the ploughing season, the community members also lacked the time during the week. Work in the fields mainly had to be done in the weekend or in the evenings. This also suggests, as a third factor, problems around labour, especially during activity peaks. Additionally, the conversations I had with people about the ploughing issue and the meetings I attended suggested a 'culture of dependency'. These were people who primarily seemed to look for help from outsiders when confronted with problems. In my view this was related to their history as farm workers and the oppressive machinery of the apartheid state that had marginalized them. However, a last factor also seemed to be at play here: the difficulty of managing a common resource. In Hardin's (1968) classical article *The Tragedy of the Commons*, he explains how herdsmen will keep as many cattle as possible on a common pasture, since the damage caused by adding an extra cow is shared amongst all herdsmen. The benefit, however, is mainly reaped by the individual. Eventually, according to Hardin, this will lead to a tragedy, an ecological disaster. In Gasela another –but related– mechanism seems at play, which may remind us of the problems on the old Soviet collective farms: why invest privately –time, energy, money or other resources– in managing a common resource, while others –even those who invested less– will also reap the benefits.

The Women's Project
After having been in the field for several days and thinking that besides a tractor other resources, like fertilizer and seeds, might also be hard to come by, I discovered another 'agricultural project' in Gasela. The questions about seeds prompted community members to mention the 'women's project' which turned out to be an agricultural project located at the back of the main farm house. To my surprise, such a project had never been mentioned in any of the MRA reports about Gasela. It was a flat piece of land of about fifty metres long and twenty metres wide that had been neatly fenced off and was overgrown with weeds. Although it had obviously been a while ago, the land was once cleared of bushes. However, the seeds that were to be planted had not found their way into the soil but lay in a dark cupboard in the second kitchen of the farmhouse; that is –as was discovered later– most of the seeds. As a researcher I hoped that this project could provide some more clues for the failure to cultivate the large fields.

Several years ago, around 1995, a group of women from Gasela had been to a workshop in Stutterheim where they were encouraged to start an agricultural project. Mr. Nakase, a local councillor in the Transitional Rural Council (TRC), explained that the national and provincial ANC Women's League had organized these workshops:

> "...advising women in the villages to start community gardens (...). We provided the women with seed, not from the council but from the Lutheran church in Stutterheim. We helped them distribute...".

However, it seemed that the workshop had not entailed more than a stimulating speech about farming and the handing over of the seeds, as the project almost immediately ran aground.

During my fieldwork in Gasela the following conversation took place when I asked Mrs. Nomntu Stuurman, whether she was part of the women's project:

> "Yes, (laughing) we are ploughing a 'useless plant'[17], we found the implement of ploughing too late".

For two years?

> "I don't know. The thing of many people is not right. Everyone has a different view so it ends up in conflict".

What don't people agree about?

> "First the TRC[18] gave us seeds, but the secretary of the women's league took the seeds for herself because we were not united".

What did you differ about?

> "Andiazi[19]...".

What do you feel when you see the land unused?

> "I feel unhappy...".

Other women also complained about the project and some accused the secretary of the ANC's women's league, Mrs. Nomphelo Mbutana, of 'stealing' some of the seeds for her own use. According to some, this was one of the main reasons that led to the breakdown of the project.

However, in an interview with Mrs. Nomphelo Mbutana herself, who seemed quite annoyed, she explained that they had ploughed this year in the women's project:

"We didn't have money to buy seeds".

Why did you not use the seeds that are available?

"We have a problem of the residential committee and we don't plant seeds because of the rain. There was too much and we were too busy with our gardens...".

For two years?

[becoming quite angry] *"I am asking you: your question is nice, but you can collect all of us and ask us why we do not plough. It is better when everyone is present. We started to collect ten rand of the people but not all of them wanted to contribute. They said they don't have".*

What do you think is the solution?

"I said earlier that we went home to home to collect ten rand to plant... We want to plough. But I promise you that this year we are going to plough...".

Clearly, even in this small version of a communal agricultural project in Gasela there were conflicts, irritations and misunderstandings around the use of resources. More specifically, there was the obvious tension between the private and the common domain that led to distrust and tensions.

The main priority for every household was to get its own garden ploughed and planted and only after that was achieved could people think about common agricultural goals. But even those goals are subordinate to private goals like sending children to school and clothing them. Undoubtedly, the ten rand contribution to the project was too much too ask of many of the Gasela women.

What did the women's project tell us with respect to the chance of success of an even larger scale agricultural project? First, it can be predicted that raising more than one hundred rand per family, for ploughing alone, will be even more difficult, if not impossible. Especially as the average monthly household income was only 460 rand, according to MRA's 1997 Gasela report. Moreover, if there are already problems around cooperation, between approximately twenty women in the women's project, would the participation of the whole community not lead to even greater problems? In fact, in my opinion, it is safe to assume that some of these same mechanisms apply to the (non-)cultivation of the farm's large fields. Although several people are enthusiastic, they are somewhat reluctant to invest privately in what is seen as a common resource. This is explicitly illustrated by a statement by Mr. Vuyo Yako who explained why people would be hesitant to use their own cattle for ploughing. Apart from the fact that oxen are not kept anymore he stated that:

"People don't want to use animals to plough, because it makes the cattle weak, (...) the cows are not used to that. That is why we need a tractor. Also, I can't give the community my cow, if someone else uses it, they can hit it and push it so hard it can die".

Besides the difficulties with regard to managing a common resource, the women's project points to another set of problems in Gasela: weak committees and weak leadership.

Organization and Leadership

Although the list of community structures established from 1993 onwards, like the ANC youth league, the ANC Women's League, the ANC 'proper', the Gasela Residents Association (GRA), the Crèche Committee, the Water Committee and the Police Community Forum, seems impressive, most of these structures are rather ineffective. Moreover, the GRA and the ANC proper are one and the same and fraught with leadership struggles for the past few years.

A residents association affiliated to SANCO is ideal-typically an organization that unites people outside the sphere of party-politics. However, in Gasela there were no other political parties active besides the ANC. As Lindile Msukwini, secretary of the ANC and the Gasela Residents Association explained:

"The role of Sanco is to unite all organizations in the villages, but here we are only one. The [ANC] meetings are every week but sometimes it skips a week when the community needs to discuss something as SANCO. The ANC committee is the same as the SANCO committee".

He, furthermore, added:

"A village is no village without SANCO...".

Thus, the committee that was the ANC in one week was SANCO in the next. Nevertheless, although the committee seemed quite active and although there were no party political struggles in the community, it appeared that a lack of experience, combined with a lack of leadership left the community in a rather vulnerable position.

Since Mr. Jim Dabani, a vocal old man who was the first elected chairperson of the GRA, retired in 1996, a leadership vacuum existed in Gasela. His successor, Xolani Dubeni, was soon voted out, since *"...he was rude in his position and used abusive language to older people in many meetings"*. Subsequently, Mrs. Nolindili Bhatyi became the first woman chair, although her husband, who is a church minister, seemed to pull strings in the background. However, the committee seemed quite directionless and Mrs. Bhatyi was far from vocal on the important issues. For example, she stayed in the background during meetings and was not the kind of person that would easily contact outside agencies as she didn't speak English or Afrikaans. This is not necessarily related to the fact that she is woman, as some of the other women were much more vocal and strong-minded in meetings than she is –also in discussions with men.

In my opinion this lack of effective leadership, combined with a lack of resources, management skills, and a reluctance to invest private resources for the common good, made me even more sceptical about the possible (commercial) success of Gasela as a thriving agri-village. Before going on to discuss other fundamental problems in the Monti Rural Association plans, it is useful to look in detail at some of the figures, assumptions, proposals and recommendations that were put forward by the organization.

The Image of Gasela as a Potentially Thriving Agri-village
As we saw in Table 6.1, the Monti Rural Association put the number of Gasela residents at 218. These people live in what MRA calls 'the settled area' where they have their huts and small gardens. In its *Report on Gasela November 1997*, the organization presented the basic figures and facts that supported its recommendation to turn Gasela into a commercially oriented agri-village. Of the total area of approximately 89 hectares (see: Table 6.2) it was proposed to reserve 40 hectares for commercial vegetable production.

TOTAL AREA	89.24 ha
SETTLED AREA	10.2 ha
FORESTED AREA	12.7 ha
STEEP AREA	9.0 ha
REMAINING AREA	57.34 ha

(source: MRA, 1997b, p. 24)

Table 5.2: Area available for crop cultivation in Gasela.

On this land MRA envisaged the community to cultivate 20 hectares of potatoes and 20 hectares of cabbages. Another 15 hectares would, subsequently, be reserved for subsistence cultivation.

This means that the remaining 21.7 hectares –12.7 ha of forested area and 9.0 ha of steep area– would be reserved for grazing. According to the MRA report (1997b, p. 13) half of the households own cattle, 38% own chickens and 21% own sheep and/ or goats, while in total, there are 62 heads of cattle, 2 sheep, 13 goats and 91 chickens.

With respect to labour, the Monti Rural Association expected the requirements for planting and harvesting to be 120 hours per hectare for both cabbage and potatoes. That is 800 working days for 40 hectares, which translate into ten days of work for eighty labourers (see: Table 6.3).

Crop	Hrs/ha	Area (ha)	Time required (days)			
			80 labourers	50 labourers	30 labourers	20 labourers
Potatoes	120	40	10.00	16.00	26.67	40.00
Cabbages	120	40	10.00	16.00	26.67	40.00

Table 5.3[20]: Labour Requirements at Planting and Harvesting in Gasela.

These research results and proposals were subsequently presented and discussed with the community in a workshop.

'Workshopping' and Reporting the Research and the Proposals
In a workshop on 20 November 1997 –at which the author was also present– the results of the Monti Rural Association research project in Gasela were discussed with members of the community. Furthermore, MRA's proposals regarding commercial vegetable production were 'workshopped', as it is called in NGO jargon. The workshop was attended by 53 people: 31 women and 22 men.

After presenting its research findings and tabling its land-use proposals the Monti Rural Association staff asked the community to break up into three groups, or commissions. The men, the women and the youth, then, proceeded to discuss the presented research findings and land-use options. The men showed preference for both crops and livestock farming, while preferring the crops with the highest returns: cabbages and potatoes. As to livestock, the men indicated that they preferred cattle only, which would be their responsibility. The women also showed a preference for both livestock and crop farming. However, they identified an additional cash crop: beans. Moreover, they showed an interest in a whole range of subsistence crops that they also deemed important: from maize, to sweet potatoes and spinach. The youth preferred only crop farming, especially cash crops like potatoes and cabbages and a few subsistence crops like maize and beans. Furthermore, they believed that livestock should not be regarded as an option.

At the end of the workshop Dwight Rover, the agricultural expert of the Monti Rural Association, in a concluding speech for the community stated:

> "...so, the option that we presented is alright. You've indicated that you want more crops, which I think is good. We'll incorporate your ideas into the final report, which will then be presented to DLA. If they like it and agree that you can farm, then we'll recommend to DLA that the land is transferred to the community (...). We'll let you know as soon as DLA gives us an answer".

Although Mr. Rover did indeed acknowledge the inputs made by the community members, and promised to incorporate them in the final report, he did not indicate how. However, his overall conclusion seemed to be that the Gasela residents endorsed the MRA plans. This '*strategic translation*' of the view of the community was even more simplified in the 1997 report, where the stance of the community members was rephrased as follows:

> "The whole community are in favour of MRA's research findings. Crop farming is the top priority as it will alleviate poverty in the area. In particular, crops such as cabbages and potatoes are seen as a realistic option..." (1997b, p. 33).

In very clear terms this example shows how an NGO is able to strategically translate the situation on the ground in a manner which suits the political strategies of the organization. In this way two issues were left out of the conclusions: what to do with livestock and how to incorporate a larger diversity of crops.

In my view, however, especially problems around livestock and labour could be expected.

Livestock and Labour

When discussing the issue of livestock in Southern Africa, one needs to be especially vigilant as cattle ownership means much more to Africans –and the Xhosa– than a narrowly defined economic value. Status, *lobola* (bridewealth), slaughtering for ceremonies, and a form of 'traditional' banking are some of the functions of cattle, besides the more direct values like milk, meat or draught power. In other words, livestock, and especially cattle, is a significant part of the cultural fabric of society. This is the case with many South African livestock-keeping African peoples[21].

This is relevant because the Monti Rural Association plans did not acknowledge the livestock that was kept by the most influential community members in Gasela. If we limit this discussion to the 62 heads of cattle that were held on the farm, then there is no way that these could be kept on the land if 40 hectares of cabbage and potato production would be realized. In its 1997 *Report on Gasela* MRA, therefore concluded that *"...due to the lack of available area at Gasela extensive livestock production is not recommended..."* (p. 22). However, in the above workshop, the organization chose to be rather vague about the livestock issue. At no stage did any MRA member make it crystal clear that a choice for commercial vegetable production would automatically imply doing away with most heads of cattle. However, only five days later, in a meeting[22] with other supporting organizations and institutions, and without any community members present, the MRA staff explained that the people would not keep any livestock on the farm.

Initially, a Mr. Sgenu, from the Department of Agriculture in Stutterheim, had remarked that *"...on the 21 ha remaining land, which is the steep land and forest, a maximum of 7 heads of cattle can be kept. Maybe one should say: no cattle"*. Answering him the MRA staff –to my surprise– stated that *"people will not keep livestock, but it is not clear how they are going to get rid of the livestock that is present..."*. This caused Mrs. Mondli of the Amatola District Council to remark: *"don't force your view on the community!"*, which led to a significant answer by Bongani Matsila, a prominent MRA staff member: *"we won't, we believe in a participative process..."*.

Then why was this fundamental issue of livestock keeping not thoroughly discussed with the people concerned during the workshop in Gasela, five days earlier? What does this teach us about the way in which the interests of the Gasela residents are represented by the MRA staff members and about the participative process during workshops? Before attempting to answer these questions I look at another weak point in the plan: the issue of labour.

Without discussing the more complicated issue of skilled labour and management expertise, it may be useful to look critically at the amount of labour available for a 40 hectare commercial vegetable production scheme. Without going into all the details, it becomes clear that very few people are available to work in agriculture full-time. If one subtracts the absent, the old, the sick, the school-going and the women who have to run their households and have to cultivate their gardens, only about 35 people would be available for working in the project. Theoretically, taking into account the labour peak figures, presented by MRA in Table 6.3, that might be just sufficient.

However, having been in Gasela for longer periods during my fieldwork, I came to doubt the figures that the Monti Rural Association presented about the number of Gasela residents. Although they might be correct in an absolute sense, I would suggest that far fewer people live there during the week. During my own survey, my field assistant and I encountered only 76 Gasela residents above the age of 12. At least sixteen were too old to work and only a few men and women were not working or not attending school. That would put quite a strain on relatively few people, especially during the labour peaks.

More fundamentally, however, one needs to question whether the Gasela residents can be considered agricultural producers.

Agricultural Producers or a Rural Proletariat?
As Gasela is a place with a definite rural feel to it, many outsiders will be inclined to describe it as a 'farming community'. However, as Bank (1997) described in his essay, *Town and Country: urbanisation and migration*, many of the rural villages close to the towns in the Eastern Cape are:

> "...quiet and deserted during the week. The only obvious evidence of productive activity is the movement of older women working at their daily chores of housekeeping, firewood collection, and attending to gardens (...). In the deeper rural areas of the province (...), there are more deserted homesteads and unattended fields" (p. 24).

Such observations, therefore, make it imperative to look closely at what went on in Gasela and determine who these people are. Although, indeed, a large part of the community consists of ex-farm workers, many of the men and women have a very diverse background. Therefore, in order to get more clarity, we will look at several categories in the community:

- the older generation of ex-farm workers;
- the younger generation who are active elsewhere;
- the young generation of school-going adolescents.

Although the Monti Rural Association also acknowledged the problem of lack agricultural and management skills in its 1997 report, it, nevertheless, appreciated the fact that many in the community had a farm worker background:

> "...virtually all of the interviewees mentioned that they have skills in vegetable growing and soil preparation..." (1997b, p. 14).

However, in my view, this is less positive than it seems because many farm workers had a specific and limited task when they were employed by farmers. In fact, the MRA report mentioned some of these tasks: milking, fence mending, welding, tractor driving et cetera. Furthermore, many of the ex-farm workers are the old men and women who can hardly be expected to work in the fields because of their age. Lastly, I want to stress that it must be remembered that apartheid was a 'successful' attempt to keep people ignorant and on the fringe of society. That has clearly left a huge mark on the people, especially on those who spent their whole life on white farms as farm labourers. In the eyes of many of this older generation the silent suffering, subservience and ignorance can still be seen.

Thus, it can be said that the older generation had several problems. First of all, most of them were too old to actively farm. Secondly, their skills were too specific and limited. Being able to drive a tractor or mend fences does not ensure being able to successfully manage a farm. Thirdly, this generation was not well educated and in the course of their lives had many bitter experiences and were frequently intimidated. Lastly, the people who were still active as farm workers, like Mr. Mfene, a tractor driver at Döhne Agricultural Research Station, did not have much time to farm their own fields. Thus, this generation might be willing, but hardly able to farm commercially. Their number one priority was security of tenure and protection against eviction.

The second group, or the younger generation, consisted of the grown-up children of the ex-farm workers. It is this group on which the success of the commercial agricultural project would depend. However, in my view, this generation especially seemed to have a focus with regard to work, and a cash income, that was directed outwards. To illustrate this I could use many of the informants as an example. Yet, here I present a short working history of Mr. Vuyo Yako, who left Gasela for the first time in the late seventies, at sixteen.

In Cape Town Mr. Yako, while staying with his cousin's sister, attended night school and worked as a 'till man' in a shop for several years. During Gasela's 'boom time' in the eighties he came back to work as a carpenter and a painter for the General Government, that is in '83, '84 and '86. In between, in 1985, he tried his luck in the Welcome Goldmine in Gauteng. After 1986 he went to Pretoria but didn't succeed there, but in 1988 he found work with the municipality in Glencoa, Natal. That didn't last long either and at the end of the same year he returned to Gasela where he stayed for the next two years. But in 1991, as he himself described:

"...I went to the Transkei where I was employed by Sadac Kriel and Sali Avenas, who were Muslims, and who taught me bricklaying and carpentry. They were good people. I returned to Gasela in '92 and I started working for a security firm in Bisho^{23} for Gqozo^{24}, where we received training at Amapase base. Every month-end I came to Gasela to pay my sisters (...). When the peace force left [Bisho] I started working for Red Alert Security from April '94 to '95. However, we were paid a low salary, we didn't get permanent positions and we were not paid regularly. Our coloured manager, Thomas, took our money. I then joined the Peace Force in Johannesburg until September '96 and lived with my sister in Alexandra. But the Peace Force deserted us and I joined Prestige Cleaning Services in Sandton square. I am always working, I am always looking for money...I am hungry, I am not educated. In total I spent 2 years in Johannesburg. In September '96 I came back to Gasela, in 1997 I had no work, no jobs...".

This extraordinary life story of a young man, who was thirty four years old in 1998, is not-so-extraordinary after all.

In fact it exemplifies how many black men and women move all over the country in search for economic opportunities; and have done so for decades. Although older women generally stay behind in Gasela to run the home and bring up the youngest children, even some of the young women try their luck in Cape Town, Johannesburg or Pretoria. In those cases the children are usually left with their grandparents in Gasela. In my view, this younger generation of people in their prime, would need to provide the backbone for a successful commercial agricultural project. However, as the example illustrates, this is usually the generation with an outward, urban focus in search of a cash income. This is the generation that perceives the rural area of Gasela as home, where they are able to leave their children with grandparents and where they will eventually return to retire. I believe that it will be very difficult to motivate these people to seek their fortune at home in Gasela, let alone start their own 'communal enterprise'. They are not agricultural producers, but rather part of a 'rural proletariat' who are seeking their fortune in the economic centres.

Nevertheless, there are some women who do stay in Gasela and who are quite vocal about farming their gardens. For example Mrs. Nozimo Vukaphi, in an interview made clear that she wanted more land which she wanted to cultivate. When I asked her whether she knew how to grow crops she answered:

"Of course I know, I am a Xhosa baby. I would like to grow cabbage, carrots, beans...everything...".

Yet, this ethnic Xhosa imagery seems especially related to the subsistence gardens that are kept by the women. Whether such motivation is enough for a commercial project to succeed remains to be seen. Especially since these are the women who already have a heavy workload as mentioned above. In any case, there is definitely a demand from these women for larger private gardens.

For the even younger generation, the ones in their teens and early twenties, the situation in the late nineties, was slightly different when compared to the past. Unlike the generation preceding them, who left young to seek paid work, many now stayed in Gasela longer to attend secondary school in Ndakana village. However, although these boys and girls are staying in Gasela, their school work prevented them from doing a lot of work on the farm. In fact, in an interview with some of the young men they stated that only about fifteen of them neither attended school nor were employed. However, very few in the group actually regarded farming as a serious future 'career' option. Although some indicated that they would want to work in agriculture most dreamt of becoming a soldier or a doctor and rather seek paid work than farm for themselves.

In conclusion, one can say that the history of Gasela illustrates many of the mechanisms that adversely influenced the lives of the South African black population. Apartheid has left deep moral, social and economic scars and although Gasela is located in a rural area, the people who live there do not have an exclusive rural focus. In fact, like many black South Africans they have, to some degree, been alienated from the land. Gasela does not seem to differ much from the rural areas on the urban fringe, that were described by Bank (1997). Although people are interested in land, and especially in security of tenure, they may not be the ideal agricultural producers that the government wants them to be. Gasela is a place where children can grow up, where one can return in times of adversity and where one retires and buries the dead. But for economic opportunities people venture into the 'real' world. The garden is ploughed to provide some food, but cash in the form of pensions or remittances stays of the utmost importance to keep the household afloat. Moreover, livestock plays an important role in their lives, which is, thus, not something they will be inclined to give up easily. In my view, therefore, Gasela may not become the thriving commercial agri-village that the Monti Rural Association will want it to be.

What remains then in this chapter is to seek an explanation of why the community is portrayed as a potential farming community, by an organization that knows better and is staffed by people who really want to make a positive contribution.

A Market-Oriented Embrace and Strategic Translations

In my opinion, the Monti Rural Association came to represent the Gasela residents as potential thriving farmers, as it came to be locked in a 'market-oriented embrace' by the Department of Land Affairs. MRA was dependent on other, more powerful actors, like the Department of Land Affairs, that laid down the rules of the game and kept shifting the goalposts. In fact, these shifts were so fundamental, that although the goal is still in the field, one wonders whether the same game is still played.

The Gasela case clearly highlights the complex dynamics a non-governmental organization gets involved in as an intermediary organization. In order to get more clarity I will focus on the three dominant actors in this tale: the Department of Land Affairs, the Monti Rural Association and, lastly, the people who lived in Gasela. Each of the actors agreed that the people of Gasela should get access to land. The Gasela residents wanted the land they lived on in order to have tenure security and, thus, be safe from eviction threats. Any additional land was welcome as it relieved the pressure and would result in more space for each family. The Department of Land Affairs was also cognisant of the fact that the community deserved tenure security. However, the department was not sure whether it was wise to grant the people of Gasela the farm, as it had serious doubts as to the economic viability of the plan. The Monti Rural Association, lastly, followed a pragmatic approach: the land would have to be transferred to the community –whatever way possible– as the organization believed and fought for tenure security of the rural poor.

For an NGO, like the Monti Rural Association, it was not easy to support communities in their claims to land after the first democratic elections. One of the main reasons why these applications for land have been so extremely complex is that the laws, the acts, the procedures and the government policies constantly changed. Moreover, the players involved changed. In fact some institutions completely disappeared, while others were fundamentally transformed. Such changes and uncertainties have caused much confusion, in the communities, in the NGO sector, as well as in the relevant government departments. As a consequence, often quite pragmatically, MRA has steered through these rough and unpredictable seas, taking one route this month and when finding it was blocked, taking another route the next. In MRA's pragmatic approach only one thing remained constant: ensuring a land transfer for the Gasela residents. Thus, after the first restitution claim had been rejected, MRA had to confront DLA, as state land fell directly under the Minister of Land Affairs.

The Impact of 'New Realism' on the Department of Land Affairs

In early 1996 DLA seemed quite benevolent, especially since MRA's director had just moved to the department to become a regional director. However, several factors contributed to a change of attitude in the department. Significant in this regard is the fact that the Gasela residents lived on a potentially productive commercial farm in an area with a fine climate, good soils and an excellent infrastructure. It was not a dry patch of land in the vicinity of a township that has hardly any economic value.

Initially, when the land reform programme was conceived, after the new government came to power, there was a strong emphasis on 'rights' and consultation, inspired by the ANC's struggle against apartheid and the newly formulated RDP (see:

Chapter 3). It was a time when the 'freedom and consultation discourse' was dominant in the South African political arena. The land reform programme was designed in such a way, that implementation, consultation, learning and adaptation of the programme went hand in hand. Significant in this regard, was the establishment of the Land Reform Pilot Programme, with schemes in every new province, in order to gain experience. This emphasis on 'rights' and 'consultation' prompted white farmers' representatives, when the *Green Paper on South African Land Policy* was published in 1996, to actually state that the term 'redistribution' had a socialist flavour.

However, at the same time, the political choice not to antagonize the white farmers, by opting for a *willing-buyer willing-seller* approach, led to a strong market component in the land reform programme. Moreover, after 1996, this was reinforced by a GEAR-inspired 'new realism discourse' in South African politics. This dominant position for market rhetoric in South African public debate had a strong impact in all policy fields, including land reform. As a result of the *willing-buyer willing-seller* strategy 'community members' were stimulated by the government to form trusts or Communal Property Associations (CPAs) in order to access subsidy schemes that made it possible to purchase white farms. Soon, however, concerns arose as to the viability of such schemes. CPAs were fraught with problems around leadership, management, access to resources, the ability and willingness to farm, and a reluctance to invest privately in what was regarded as a common good. Frequently, this led to a situation in which the farm was not used productively. In a country where parts of the population were still malnourished that seemed not right. Thus, over the years the government came to regard such land transfers as a waste of productive capacity. Consequently, much of the land reform programme came to be redefined with a strong emphasis on economic viability. Not 'rights to land' but 'ability to farm commercially' became dominant in South African land reform.

Also locally, in the Eastern Cape, the experience with the first land transfers proved not too positive. Sadly, one of the problematic schemes was realized with the aid of the Monti Rural Association: Gallawater A farm. This formerly white farm was transferred in 1996, but became a notorious failure, as will be shown in Chapter 6. Thus the Provincial Department of Land Affairs came to regard Gallawater A as the prime example of what should be avoided in land reform: wasting productive capacity. Also the Monti Rural Association staff realized that the Gallawater A case would have a negative impact on the benevolence of the Department of Land Affairs. In December 1998 MRA produced a report[25] in which it was stated that the difficulties experienced in Gallawater A:

> "...*have had a considerable impact on land reform in the Eastern Cape. In DLA there is a growing reluctance to establish communal legal entities, there is a weariness of the creation of new settlements, and it is now more difficult for resource-poor people to benefit from land reform than it was in 1995...*" (p. 18).

Planning processes on other institutional levels also complicated the potential decisions of the Eastern Cape Department of Land Affairs. According to the White Paper on Local Government, for example, every municipality was urged to prepare Integrated Development Plans (IDPs). Moreover, regional plans like the Stutterheim

District Plan were in the making, which would have to take into account environmental and population issues in an integrated manner. Therefore, DLA could hardly transfer a farm to a group of farm workers without such a plan being in place.

In conclusion, it can be said that the above-mentioned factors together reinforced the Department of Land Affairs' reluctance to transfer the land to the Gasela farm dwellers. Below, I examine the effect of DLA's stance on the Monti Rural Association.

The Monti Rural Association Engaging in 'Strategic Translations'

During the years that the Monti Rural Association was involved in Gasela the organization's approach was mainly pragmatic and informed by its mission statement formulated in 1993 (MRA Interim Report January– July 1993c):

> *"MRA aims to assist rural communities and families, and in particular landless and marginalized groups, in the Border region to gain access to and possession of land; to access resources so as to develop their settlements; to build and strengthen the capacity and efforts of rural communities to assume control of their own development; and through these activities and processes, to contribute to the formulation of just policies at local, regional and national levels"* (p. 2).

Therefore the organization's number one priority was to get the land occupied by the Gasela residents legally transferred to the community. In a first reference made to Gasela, in the minutes of a 1993 MRA evaluation and planning meeting[26], it was stated that *"...MRA also told them that the land is state owned and they can make a claim on the land via ACLA[27], they must set up a community structure..."*.

However, as was explained above, that land claim failed and the Department of Land Affairs became the main custodian of the land. Initially, this was seen as positive within MRA and actually led to a feeling of expectancy as it was the former MRA Director, John Carver, who had become the Regional Director in that department. At that stage it was felt that having former comrades in powerful positions would benefit MRA and the communities it worked with. In fact, the government seemed to have become a close ally of the NGO sector in the early years after the transition. For example, according to the *1996 Green Paper on South African Land Policy*, published by DLA:

> *"The land reform programme emphasises the key role of the non-governmental sector in supporting rural and urban development and land reform policies. Organisations in this sector have established strong links with communities involved in land struggles and have been instrumental in enabling communities to articulate their demands for land"* (p. 78).

It was clear that DLA acknowledged the important role of land sector NGOs. Thus, especially with a small communities like Gasela, most communication between DLA and 'the people' took place through MRA. With many of the larger communities, like Thornhill, the department itself had direct and regular contact.

Especially from 1994 until 1996 very close cooperation between the National Land Committee and its affiliates (like MRA) and the Department of Land Affairs led to new initiatives like the Eastern Cape Province Land Reform Steering Committee, where NGOs and representatives of several government departments were invited by the Department of Land Affairs to discuss bottlenecks in land reform on a regular basis. However, as time progressed and all parties learned as they went along, the government departments became more confident and eventually retreated into their original niche. Thus, the government departments became more matter-of-fact and cautious after the experiments of the initial years. Since everybody in the NGO sector had felt that having one's former colleagues and comrades in powerful position would be of benefit, very few had reckoned with two consequences of a more business-like and distant government. First, as the government became more government, and the initial euphoria wore off, the comrades of yesteryear shifted their loyalty. The state and its institutions, laws and policies became their foremost point of reference. As a result, many people who remained in the NGO sector felt betrayed by their former colleagues. Second, having come from the NGO sector, these ex-NGO people in government knew exactly what the weaknesses of the non-governmental organizations were. Subsequently, some became the fiercest critics of the NGO sector, or at least developed a healthy suspicion towards the work methods and quality of their former colleagues. John Carver, the DLA Director in the Eastern Cape, for example, knew exactly the mistakes that had been made and the problems that had been encountered in Gallawater A during the time when he had been a leading figure at MRA. As a result he became (over-)cautious in regard to the Gasela land transfer. A prudence that was also reinforced by the 'new realism discourse' that trickled down from the national level.

This somewhat less loyal, less cooperative, and more cautious government left the management team at the Monti Rural Association quite insecure. They worried about the possible loss of their preferential status and, they realized that the quality of their work would have to improve. This insecurity had two repercussions, one positive and the other negative. The positive effect was that an organization like the Monti Rural Association saw the need to shape up and, thus, improve the quality of their work. For years, especially during the apartheid era, the organization had largely operated in an institutional void, with few checks and balances, especially when they had operated partially illegally. However, the negative effect was that this concern for the quality of the work became tied to a concern for its own prestige vis à vis their former comrades at the Department of Land Affairs. The MRA management wanted to prove to their ex-colleagues in government that they were capable of delivering high quality research based on 'hard facts'. Thus, in my opinion, the Monti Rural Association became trapped in DLA's 'market-oriented embrace'.

By 1997, the feelings of expectation within the Monti Rural Association with regard to cooperation with government had been replaced by feelings of frustration. It seemed to them as if the Department of Land Affairs kept them on a string, especially since their 1996 report on Gasela had been received critically by DLA. In fact, in late 1997[28], in a strategic planning meeting with his staff, the MRA Director, Dudley Eastwood, pointed out that there were macro-economic issues at stake here. He stated that:

> "...the basic assumption of the Department of Land Affairs is that giving arable land to the poor leads to a waste of economic resources. Don't be confused or idealistic about land reform in South Africa, you have got to go back to GEAR to understand why the department behaves like this...".

Later on senior staff member Bongani Matsila remarked:
> *"For Gasela John (Carver) seems to push for a solution whereby people will be placed in settlements with services and gardens..."*.

This was the greatest fear of many rural dwellers. They would be rounded up from the scattered patches of land where they lived, to be placed in rural townships where the government could provide housing, infrastructure, services like water and electricity and schools and clinics. However, Dudley Eastwood still saw a possibility to convince DLA to transfer the land:
> *"We're going for a major showdown with the Department of Land Affairs around Gasela..."*.

This 'showdown' would involve fighting the department on its own turf and in its own terms whereby 'economic viability' became the defining notion. Thus, through the Department of Land Affairs the 'new realism discourse' penetrated the work of the Monti Rural Association. Subsequently, in this political game, to convince DLA to transfer the land 'hard science' became the political instrument. In this battle with DLA, MRA would consciously move beyond the soft type of research they had conducted in the past –social surveys, community skills assessment et cetera. The management team was convinced that only by adding hard facts –soil survey, labour requirements, predicted cash flows et cetera– they would be able to convince DLA. A fighting spirit took hold of the organization to ensure that they found the right arguments in facts about soils, rainfall and production figures, against the background of images of a community consisting of rural agricultural producers in Gasela. As a result the 'scientifically' argued *Report on Gasela November 1997* was produced. Thus, the Gasela case became a mix of a desire to regain lost prestige and respect of the Department of Land Affairs and a concern with the plight of these rural residents. In this political struggle the plight of the Gasela residents came to be reduced to a pragmatic and bare minimum: the transfer of the land.

Another factor which contributed to this strategy by MRA was a realization that 'professionalization' of the organization was needed in order to survive in the post-apartheid cut-throat NGO environment. MRA, like the government, became more aware of a market rhetoric. NGOs were confronted with an environment in which Northern donors not only diverted their funds to the now legitimate government, but also stressed the need for professionalization (see: Chapter 8). As a result, many NGOs were forced to vie for contracts in the market place and some NGOs even went so far as to set up subsidiaries that could engage in profit-making activities. For MRA this reinforced the impact of the 'new realism discourse' that had already penetrated their work through their close contacts with the Department of Land Affairs. In the case of the Monti Rural Association, this strategy involved, amongst other things, hiring technical experts. Thus, a small group within MRA, led by the director, Mr. Eastwood, a newly hired agricultural and soil expert, Dwight Rover, and a successful Transkei farmer, Themba Mangaliso, came to define the terms in which the Gasela project was handled. This group of technically inclined staff came to stress 'the technical' in their effort to convince DLA. For the time being it suited them, politically, to ignore the 'social reality in the field'. The number one priority became securing the transfer of land.

The Tools of Translation
In order to convince DLA, three instruments were of importance to an intermediary organization like the Monti Rural Association: 1. Its mode of research; 2. The method of interaction with the beneficiaries through workshops; and, 3. The reports that were produced. These instruments, or 'tools of translation' were crucial in the political process the Monti Rural Association was engaged in.

The Research
First of all, let us look at the research methods employed by NGOs. It is clear that research in any context should be critically evaluated, more especially in contexts where the actors stand to gain from the results of the research. Many non-governmental organizations engage in research activities that are enveloped in the same 'objective' and 'scientific' formats and discourse as academic research projects. However, there are distinct differences. The main difference is that the research conducted by NGOs, frequently, has an activist purpose. The research is part of a political process and is usually conducted to prove a certain point. Although academic research may also be influenced by those that pay the grants –especially in these times dominated by 'market thinking'– academic institutions in most parts of the world still try to protect their positions of scientific independence. NGOs, however, are less concerned with issues of 'objectivity'. In fact, these organizations can be quite blunt about the way in which they conduct research. I came across a clear example in a discussion with the Director of MRA concerning another MRA research project, that I was involved with in an advisory capacity. In his view, I approached the topic too academically:

> "We are setting a precedent with this rights enquiry[29]. MRA has political objectives, more than the Department of Land Affairs. Our research is not neutral research, we need particular types of information...".

This was also the case in Gasela.

The Monti Rural Association focused strategically on the economic and physical intricacies of the plan in order to be able to convince the Department of Land Affairs that was preoccupied by its own 'economic viability' discourse. This technocratic and (pseudo-)scientific approach, stressing agricultural production factors, was enhanced by making use of images of the Gasela residents as rural agricultural producers. In much of Southern Africa such images are used by the development industry to justify agricultural development interventions. In many instances, like in the case of Lesotho (Ferguson, 1990), the rural residents with decades of experience in the cash economy and an urban outlook, are represented as 'traditional farmers'. The persistence of such images is related to a dominant and widespread belief that Africa is the one remaining continent where man is still close to nature and 'traditionalism' is prevalent.

In conclusion, it can be said that the research carried out by MRA should be regarded as an instrument in the political struggle with DLA to get the land transferred to the Gasela residents. As the Department of Land Affairs was preoccupied with an 'economic viability discourse', MRA, tried everything, in its research efforts, to describe the situation in Gasela in those terms. Not the rights to tenure security but their ability to farm would have to convince DLA. In my view they were not entirely aware of the complicated situation in Gasela as their research efforts, more or less, neglected 'community dynamics'. However, even if they had been aware, the organization might have consciously decided to neglect it, as it would have weakened their stance. Problematic community dynamics did not fit in their strategy to attempt to convince DLA.

The Workshops
The workshops conducted by MRA in Gasela were instrumental in the NGO strategy to create an image of Gasela as a possible thriving agri-village. Standard interaction between NGOs and their beneficiaries frequently takes this form. Also in the case of Gasela interaction between MRA and Gasela community members mainly took place in this manner. It is usually a lively happening in which information is gathered and disseminated. In fact, it is possible to distinguish between two types of workshops:
1. the information dissemination, or teaching, workshop;
2. the consultation and participation workshop.

In the first type of workshops community members are informed or taught about a diverse range of topics, ranging from information on what land reform entails to the way in which community meetings should be conducted, or the way in which votes should be cast during election times. The second type of workshop is the type whereby, under the banner of 'consultation' and 'participation', the community is asked to share 'its' opinion about a range of topics. However, although both types make use of dynamic methods of interaction, the workshops leave much room for interpretation, errors and, what I call, 'strategic translation'.

The information dissemination workshops can be quite problematic, as it is usually the NGO that decides what type of information should be disseminated during these workshops. When very basic workshops are conducted about bookkeeping, how to conduct meetings, or how to vote during elections problems rarely occur. However, in cases where the NGO briefs the community about important strategic issues, like for example around land, problems may arise. As it generally is the NGO that holds the trump cards, the organization can easily paint a picture of the situation that strategically suits them. Here we come to an important point. The intermediary status of NGOs, especially in countries or areas where 'the people at grassroots', and often even the government officials themselves, lack very basic knowledge, leaves room for these organizations to engage in, what I call: 'strategic translations'. In other words, as these NGOs are usually the link between 'the people at grassroots' and government officials, the organizations are able to reformulate –or 'translate'– the demands of 'the people' for the government departments they work with, and vice versa.

This 'power of translation' can be even more problematic in the other type of workshops: the consultation and participation workshops. In these workshops, where the NGO seeks the opinion of 'the people', the capability of 'strategic translation' by NGOs becomes even more tricky. As the Gasela the workshop of 20 November 1997 has shown, the NGO can use its discretion, to 'consult' the community about certain topics, while leaving other topics –like the livestock issue– outside the consultation process. In other words, these moments of 'strategic translation' leave room for non-governmental organizations to reinterpret, adapt and modify the information that travels 'upwards' from the field and 'downwards' from the government. More especially in situations where 'the people' lack the background, the knowledge, or the level of education, these consultation and participation workshops can be reduced to 'going through the motions'. In such instances, the so-called 'participative process' is like a play that is enacted, while having been carefully scripted in advance. Thus, quite often, although 'participation' of 'the people' is high on the development agenda, these workshops are nothing more than seeking endorsement for intervention packages already outlined in an earlier stage by NGOs. In fact, in many instances the workshops should be understood as instruments used by NGOs, not to create close interaction and 'true participation', but, rather ensure a certain distance.

Such distance is actually quite useful when organizations create and try to maintain an image of the 'social reality in the field', as Quarles van Ufford (1993) has shown. He explained how organizations usually have to deal with the tension between organizational survival and effectiveness. In the Gasela case, between organizational prestige vis à vis the Department of Land Affairs and a sustainable option for the Gasela community. Quite often, the requirements of organizational survival and effectiveness are incompatible. According to Quarles van Ufford, *"the participants in the policy process 'manage' this tension in how they make use of knowledge and ignorance"* (p. 156).

Only in Thornhill –where members of the Thornhill Residents Association were educated teachers who have ample experience with NGOs– have I witnessed truly open and critical discussions where, in some cases, the NGO was the least influential party. In Gasela, the level of education and the amount of experience with powerful outsiders was too inadequate to ensure a critical attitude. Moreover, there were no strong leaders in Gasela who could put forward their case. As a result, it was possible for the MRA staff to neglect the livestock issue and to translate the various comments by the commissions of men, women and young people into: 'they agree with MRA's plans'. It shows that NGOs occupy strategic intermediary positions in the lines of communication between 'the field' and higher institutional levels. Especially in instances where 'the people' themselves have little autonomous contact with other outside agencies or the government, this can lead to a situation where 'the people' are quite easily misrepresented by the NGOs. The NGOs have become the gate-keepers.

However, in one sense the Monti Rural Association did ensure the increased participation of a section of the community in workshops and meetings, both in Thornhill, Gasela and other communities. In all these communities the participation of women dramatically improved, for a part due to MRA's explicit gender strategy. According to the *Annual Report January – December 1995 (1995a):*
> *"...there is an ongoing attempt to ensure that the programmes we are involved in support and create opportunities for the participation of women..."* (p. 10).

During my fieldwork I witnessed many instances where women were encouraged to speak out in workshops and meetings. Moreover, several strong women were encouraged to take responsibilities in the various residents committees. Some did very well, while in other instances, like Gasela, the female chairperson failed.

Not only are NGOs able to 'script' workshops, the frequency of such institutionalized interactions also leaves much to be desired. In 1997, for example, the Monti Rural Association conducted about ten workshops in Gasela, most of which were information dissemination workshops. Furthermore, household interviews were conducted in two consecutive weeks. On average, not counting the interviews, MRA staff were present in Gasela once every five weeks, although in some periods there would be no interaction for months on end. Moreover, there was a lack of informal contacts. Since the field staff never actually stayed on the farm for prolonged periods –let alone for the night– there was hardly any informal contact between MRA staff and the residents. Such informal contact, as has been shown by my fieldwork, can yield valuable information about sensitive topics, like the women's project.

A last disturbing issue concerns the fact that the number of people who are present in meetings and workshops is often not representative. At the crucial Gasela workshop of 20 November, where the above plans were discussed, only 53 people were present, whereby at least ten people were twenty years or younger. Considering the fact that 108 people who are said to live in Gasela are above twenty years old, not even half of that adult population was represented at that meeting. On many occasions, during my fieldwork in South Africa, I have witnessed similar problems with quorums –too few representatives present to make a democratic decision– at workshops. Consequently, so-called 'democratic decisions' are actually taken by a minority of the people concerned. This is even more problematic in areas like Thornhill where thousands of people reside and where workshops are rarely attended by more than one hundred people. As a consequence, decisions can be taken by a very small and unrepresentative group of people, frequently 'the elite'. This calls for a critical evaluation. Do intermediary NGOs actually work through democratic structures? And do they engage with, and whether they engage 'the poorest of the poor', as is so often claimed.

In conclusion one can say that a certain 'distance' was built into the relationship between MRA and the Gasela residents, because the interactions mainly took place through workshops. Although the MRA staff had quite concrete indications through their social survey that the 'social reality in the field' would not be conducive to a commercial agricultural project, they chose to ignore those clues. To achieve this ignorance, a certain amount of distance –attained through the type of research that was conducted and the interaction through workshops– became imperative. The reports produced would be the third link in the *strategic translation* chain.

The Reports
Not only the research and the workshops, but also the reports that are produced by NGOs should be considered as instruments in a political strategy. Especially in situations like Gasela, where the government institutions have little or no autonomous contact with communities, the reports prepared by and NGO can become a crucial tool. In fact, the reports to communicate with government agencies are what the workshops are in the efforts to communicate with 'the field'. A report is a locus of interaction in which NGOs have the possibility to present their version of 'reality'.

Especially in combination with the carefully scripted and translated results of workshops, these reports become important tools in political processes. Within certain limits, NGOs can use their intermediary position to 'strategically translate' both what is encountered at grassroots and in government circles. Thus, as was shown in the beginning of this chapter, although MRA acknowledged the lack of skills and problems around management capacity, the NGO was able to stress the hard 'technical facts' about soils, crops and climate in order to convince DLA that a land transfer would be the responsible thing to do. The necessary tools at the disposal of NGOs are research, workshops and reports. These instruments are crucial to intermediary NGOs and their efforts of *strategic translation*. Without these tools NGOs are bound to fail in their political battles.

The Fundamental Problem of Participation

The Gasela case has shown that the Monti Rural Association did not ensure the full participation of the Gasela farm dwellers. In fact 'participation' seemed to stand in the way of achieving the land transfer, as it could actually make political processes less manageable. If, for example, the view of the Gasela men, who regarded livestock as very important, would have found its way into the report, it would have had a devastating effect on the chances to achieve a land transfer.

This lack of participation of 'the people' in their own affairs has also been recognized by various people within MRA. Although the lack of community participation often strategically and politically suits them, it is not in accordance with the MRA view on democracy and participation. For example, in its *Annual Report January – December 1995* (1995a), the organization stated quite clearly that:

> *"MRA identified the need for supporting communities after they had acquired land. In particular, the need for proper participatory land use and settlement planning with the aim of ensuring sustainable land use practices and local land and resource administration capacity was identified"* (p. 11).

This type of commitment to the people at grassroots through participatory methods was sustained in the organization's 1997 mission statement, in which MRA is said to aim *"...strengthening communities' ability to plan and manage their own development..."*[30].

However, in order to achieve higher levels of participation, the Monti Rural Association did not acknowledge the fundamental problem, namely their need as an intermediary organization to engage in *strategic translations*. Rather, the organization sought to improve the method of interaction. Thus in 1998 MRA introduced so-called 'project control groups'.

A New strategy: Project Control Groups

One could say that the democratization wave in Africa, but especially the transition towards a democracy in South Africa did influence the NGO sector in the country to revisit its working methods. Not only did funders put the accountability issue on the agenda, also within an organization like MRA much discussion was initiated on whether the processes of transformation the NGO was engaged in actually caused the organization to drift away from the beneficiaries in the field. Especially from 1997 onwards, after the new director, Mr. Eastwood, was appointed, the functioning of the whole organization was examined in the light of the difficulties –some would term it a 'crisis'– that had been experienced in 1996. Indeed, as the 1996 evaluation, by Cole and Nyoni (1996) of the Monti Rural Association had revealed, there was an *"...absence of a clear and up to date strategic vision and framework to guide MRA activities..."* (p. 34). As a consequence, the new director used 1997 to fundamentally revisit MRA's strategies, vision, policies, procedures and working methods. In that sense 1997 and a part of 1998 was a dynamic period in which much was changed, as the Gasela case has shown with respect to the greater influence of 'the technical experts' within the organization. Besides a strong 'professionalization drive' also the organization's values and its relationship with the communities was revisited. One of the policies that the new director put in place was the abolishment of routine field trips, as he believed that many of these were unnecessary.

What was the matter with the old method of routine field visits? Field visits had stemmed from the early period when it had been very important to keep in touch with community members who were under threat of forced removal. In many of these areas outsiders never ventured, as a consequence of which 'the world' did not know about the suffering that took place. In the early days, this reporting on 'the reality in the field' in the national and international press was one of the main functions of MRA. In the nineties, on the other hand, field visits by staff, where several staff members took a MRA car to drive to one of the areas where they were somehow involved, were relatively frequent but not necessarily very 'effective' –a term from the new professionalization discourse. It should be emphasized, however, that although these visits were frequent, from the point of view of MRA, it did not necessarily mean that they were frequent from the point of view of the communities. Moreover, many of these visits were badly planned and poorly timed, resulting in a loss of productivity. Frequently, community members were not available and meetings in the rural areas failed to materialize. As a consequence, the field staff did not achieve a lot during these 'expensive' trips. Thus, although the MRA office in East London was quite often deserted all day, very little concrete work was done. To alter this situation, the new director instituted planning procedures and, more or less, abolished the 'routine field trips'. Without a clear purpose, no one was to leave the office.

Yet, in order to safeguard the contacts with communities, other options were explored. One of these options was the establishment of so-called Project Control Groups (PCGs) or Project Steering Committees (PSCs). The first community that the Monti Rural Association identified[31] for such a PCG was Macleantown[32]. As it was felt that the Macleantown case would make a good project, proper project management procedures required clear roles for both the Macleantown residents and the Monti Rural Association. Moreover, it was envisaged that the Amatola District Council, which would be involved in the planning of services in the Macleantown area, would also have to play a role. Thus, it was decided to propose the institution of a Project Control Group (PCG) in a meeting with the Macleantown residents. This PCG would consist of five members. Three delegates from Macleantown, representing different constituencies; one representative of the Amatola District Council (ADC); and, one Monti Rural Association staff member.

However, without being able to study the functioning of the PCGs, as my fieldwork ended in June 1998, it is possible to point out some areas of concern. Especially in the initial phase and during the internal MRA discussions several contentious issues emerged, that I believe could hamper 'real' participation. Yet, before going into these issues, it makes sense to study the MRA archives in order to find out whether such plans have been proposed before. Already in an internal ARA workshop in 1988[33] Jacob James suggested that *"we need community reps in ARA decision-making"*. Although everyone present also agreed that there were problems with accountability, someone related the experience of another NGO with community representatives, saying that *"...it was very difficult, [it led to] time delays and communication problems"*. Apparently, the ARA members agreed, since the whole idea to work with community representatives was not followed up. The fact that it took ten years to institute the first project control groups, indicates that the organization did not feel very comfortable to relinquish (some) control.

Although the institution of project control groups breathes the rhetoric of accountability and giving a 'voice' to the people, it raised the important issue of 'control'. After suggesting that a Project Control Group may need to be established in Macleantown the director of MRA stated that such a *"...Project Control Group can then rubberstamp the decisions..."*. *"Or change them"*, as a senior staff member replied. This obviously worried the director, who answered: *"Change them within certain limits..."*[34]. Therefore, as the management team realized that they would have to protect the position of the organization, it was envisaged that every Project Control Group would have to start with formulating its own Terms of Reference (TOR).

Thus, in my view, it was through these Terms of Reference that the Monti Rural Association would –already in an early stage– be able to have a major influence on the project. This was confirmed by a suggestion of the director at the end of the meeting, who said: *"we can bring a draft of the Terms of Reference!"*. This suggestion was indeed endorsed by everyone present in the afternoon meeting with the Macleantown representatives. On another level MRA also aimed to remain in control. By taking the initiative, the organization could strongly influence which outside agencies could be asked to sit on the Project Control Group as well.

Concluding, one can say that although participation of community members in their own affairs may potentially be brought a step forward by the institution of Project Control Groups, this solution should not be uncritically embraced. MRA will be able to exert its influence on several levels in crucial stages of the process. The organization will not relinquish its position of strategic control. On the positive side, the institution of PCGs may increase communication between MRA, other institutions and community representatives, and, thus, diminish –although not preclude– the chance that the Monti Rural Association misrepresents 'the people'. This latter element –'the people'– is yet another weak point in the whole arrangement, as it is always a certain section of the community that takes part in a Project Control Group and it is usually the NGO that decides with whom it wants to work.

Conclusion

A land sector NGO like the Monti Rural Association is an intermediary organization. Its position, mediating between 'the people at grassroots' and other institutions like government departments, ensures that its staff can engage in, what I have called *strategic translations*. Particularly in situations where government departments have little or no contact with communities, the NGOs will be able to manipulate the image of the grassroots situation that they send upwards. Moreover, these organizations also control the government messages that seep downwards. As a result, especially in situations where NGOs are held in a *market-oriented embrace* by the government, they may be tempted to portray rural communities as potentially thriving commercial farmers. In these *strategic translations*, NGO research, the interaction with rural dwellers through workshops and the presentation of research and workshop results in NGO reports are strategic tools.

The NGO research method and also NGO reports and publications, should not be regarded as neutral, independent and 'scientific'. Usually, NGO research has a strong political component, or is at least used to prove certain political points. Furthermore, the workshop, as mode of interaction, does not necessarily ensure the participation of 'the people' nor does it prevent the NGO to misrepresent them. As the Gasela case has shown, 'going through the motions' of workshops can even aid the NGO to actually facilitate a certain distance in the relationship between the NGO and 'the people'. Thus, I agree with Pottier (1997) who argues that *"participatory workshops remain structured encounters marked by hidden agendas and strategic manoeuvres"* (p.221). Consequently, the organization is insulated from information and knowledge that contradicts its plans and proposals. More important, however, it is able to insulate the government form being confronted with contradictory data.

The Gasela case has illustrated that Nyamwaya (1997) is right when he argues that such development processes are still largely controlled by government and NGO 'experts'. The participation of communities themselves, although frequently stressed by NGOs, is often minimal. When considering the question of participation, I think that that an organization like the Monti Rural Association has made a positive contribution in the development of the necessary community structures in rural areas like Gasela. In that regard MRA has positively contributed to the emergence of civil society organizations in the Eastern Cape. However, those structures remained weak and from an accountability point of view many problematic areas can still be identified. Although, indeed, the institution of Project Control Groups may seem a step forward, the initial impressions confirm my view that NGOs like MRA are not about to relinquish their intermediary and strategic positions of control. Community involvement will remain of the utmost importance, but the terms will be largely imposed by the NGOs or the government. In the case of Gasela it may ultimately lead to a land transfer, but the terms under which such a transfer will take place will determine whether the land will actually become an asset or a liability[35].

6. MRA as a 'Learning Organization'

Introduction
In this chapter I analyze and discuss the development and transformation of the Monti Rural Association as a civil society organization. As was shown in Chapter 1, the Monti Rural Association developed over a period of almost twenty years. From being a small-scale activist organization, that was involved in the overall struggle against Apartheid, it developed into a much larger and profesionalized organization in the late 1990's. Thus, broadly, one can say that MRA evolved from 'struggle' –or 'activism'– to 'professionalism'. This leads me to critically explore whether evolutionist models, that are used by authors like, for example, Howes and Sattar (1992), are useful at all. Moreover, I question whether NGOs like MRA have a learning capability, as is claimed by authors like Fowler (1997). In addition, I discuss the role of evaluations with respect to organizational learning. Are evaluations mainly exercises that legitimize future interventions, as was argued by Long and van der Ploeg (1989), or do they aid NGOs in organizational development? Furthermore, I discuss the effects of 'capacity building programmes' on organizational learning of land sector NGOs in the mid-nineties, and I examine in which manner racial issues may complicate the functioning of a South African organization.

From 'Struggle' to 'Professionalism'
When taking a bird's eye view of the Monti Rural Association from its inception in 1982 until 1998 –the end of this research project– its development seems straightforward. The organization developed from 'activism' to 'professionalism' and increased dramatically in size. The number of staff grew from two in the mid-eighties to around twenty in the late nineties, while its budget increased from a few thousand rand in the early years to over 3 million[1] rand in 1997. Moreover, an organizational metamorphosis occurred.

The organization was established during the 'struggle era' in 1982 as a voluntary organization, by Rhodes University academics. In 1984 the first full-time fieldworkers were employed, but 'the committee' of volunteers remained active. By 1991 ARA had expanded to six full-time members of staff, which justified the appointment of a coordinator. However, as a new age dawned and the organization moved to East London in 1993 it was felt that the old structure with a committee of volunteers –who were mostly Grahamstown-based academics– would no longer be adequate. As the 'freedom and consultation era' was dawning, it was thought that the organization would benefit from the involvement of people from the Border area as a whole. Therefore, the constitution was amended and a Management Board was formed. According to the Monti Rural Association Interim Report January – December 1993, *"... its membership ranges from regional civic, political and NGO leadership to a civil servant and a rural health expert, to a lawyer and an academic"* (p. 35). From then on, the day to day running of the organization was in the hands of a Coordinating Committee that was answerable to the new Board.

However, as the growth of the organization continued and a 'new realism' discourse slowly trickled down from the national level, it was decided to appoint a director in 1997. This director would manage the organization by chairing the management committee, which was still answerable to the Board. After his appointment, this director, then, proceeded to prepare the Monti Rural Association for a new century by completely restructuring the organization. Thus, in October 1998 the Monti Rural Association made its latest moves towards 'professionalism'. As a result of a lengthy sustainability drive the organization changed its legal status from being a voluntary association to becoming a Section 21 Company. Moreover, MRA purchased its own premises. In South Africa, the Section 21 legal status was designed especially for non-profit organizations, which can apply for tax exemptions, even on profit that is re-invested in non-profit activities. Organizationally, Section 21 companies are led by a Board of Directors, made up of 'outsiders' and staff members. Usually, the staff members in the Board are responsible for the day to day running of the organization.

When confronted with such a dramatic increase of an organization in size and complexity, on the one hand one encounters many progressive –and romantic– South Africans, who are inclined to equate the days of 'activism' with 'commitment' and 'sacrifice', while at the same time, equating 'professionalism' with a lack of commitment and 'self-interest'. In a National Land Committee (NLC) annual meeting in 1997, for example, a ULC[2] member of staff publicly criticized his colleagues at the NLC, equating careerism with a lack of 'true' commitment; *"...many of us are no longer activists, but people pursuing careers...".* This same rhetoric is rife within ANC ranks. According to an article in the Mail and Guardian Weekly[3] an ANC discussion document argues that the terms 'careerism' and 'factionalism' are *"...catchwords for corruption and infighting in party ranks...".* Also within MRA this topic regularly cropped up in often heated discussions about the functioning and the direction of the organization.

On the other hand, certain authors mainly assess such a development in a positive light. For example, Howes and Sattar (1992) –without any problematization– make use of so-called 'learning curves', developed by Korten (1984, p. 183-184) when they discuss scaling up efforts by the Bangladesh Rural Advancement Committee (BRAC). With respect to the development of an organization and in contrast to a *blueprint approach*, Korten describes the *learning process approach*, in which three distinct stages are identified:
- Stage 1: learning to be effective;
- Stage 2: learning to be efficient;
- Stage 3: learning to expand.

Besides the fact that these stages are said to occur consecutively, in each stage a learning curve is depicted which rises sharply over time to a maximum and, then, falls slightly to become more or less constant. Thus, according to Korten the organization first becomes effective, then efficient and, lastly, learns to expand. In the process, it is predicted that the performance of these organizations rises from a low performance at inception to a somewhat below maximum –but still high– performance at maturity. It is an early example of describing an NGO as a *learning organization*, in which *"error is treated as an essential source of information (...) in the context of lessons learned and corrective actions being attempted"* (Korten, 1984, p. 185).

Although Korten at least indicates that *"in reality* [this] *may be a very disorderly and intuitive process"* (p. 184), Howes and Sattar (1992) adopt the model with little critical reflection. Although tempting, I think that such an evolutionary and uni-directional model of organizational growth can and should be challenged. The diagrams used have an aura of the natural sciences, but as the scales are lacking and no concrete measurements of effectiveness, efficiency and expansion are available, it largely remains a freewheeling exercise. In fact, such an evolutionary model, instead of aiding us to see more, may even cause us to see less of what really happens in organizations. My research, both archival and in the field, suggests another view. Namely, of NGOs that struggle severely with their role as development organizations, where as much is unlearned as is learned over the years. And because lessons are not learned or are simply forgotten, the same mistakes can be repeated again and again. Moreover, periods of progression are followed by periods of regression and there is no indication that NGOs follow a straightforward evolutionary path.

Struggling with 'Development'

When I first visited the Monti Rural Association in 1996, the organization was in the middle of a difficult spell. The organization seemed to lack direction and vision and there were doubts as to which role MRA should be playing. Furthermore, the coordinator had just announced that she would leave the organization. About this coordinator a senior staff member later said in an interview[4]:

"...it was good that she left. She had no vision for the future...".

One of the issues that the organization particularly grappled with was the issue of 'development'. The question of whether to continue focusing mainly on lobbying, advocacy and research or whether to expand its activities as a 'development organization' in the rural areas was frequently debated. In my initial interpretation these doubts about the direction of the organization had everything to do with the new dispensation in post-1994 South Africa. As the immediate threat of forced removals was over, I believed that the organization had to revisit its aims and goals as the freedom and consultation era called for reconstruction and development.

However, only a year later, when I returned to South Africa for a fieldwork period of almost one and a half years, I discovered that the issue was much more complicated. Indeed, the transition to democracy had made questions of 'development' extra pressing, but archive material revealed that ARA had first experimented with 'development' activities in the mid-eighties, in some of the communities it worked with. Already in an early stage, questions about whether and how to become engaged in concrete improvements in communities had led to confusion, conflict and intriguing 'developmental' experiments. By discussing some of these 'experiments' during different periods in the history of the organization, it is possible to illustrate certain processes and mechanisms in MRA's organizational history.

Development in the Mid- and Late Eighties: 'development as political instrument'

Already in the 1984 the first development-related activities are mentioned in the Chairperson's Report (ARA, 1985b):

> "ARA continues to assist with projects that it has seen develop since its beginnings. Sewing projects at Wartburg and Mgwali and garden projects at Zweliginga[5] (...) with some success and some set-backs..." (p. 2-3).

However, not much is known about these projects anymore and whether they were successful at all. Moreover, it is neither entirely clear what the role of ARA was in these projects. However, a few years later, in 1987, 'development' was placed more prominently on the ARA agenda as the South African State took new initiatives to (re-)gain control over the 'black spot communities' in the Border area. According to an ARA newsletter[6]:

> "Shortly after election to the white parliament in May 1987, the MP for King William's Town announced a R12,5 million 'upgrading' programme for the seven corridor communities (...) budgeted for by the Department of Development Aid (DDA)..." (p. 6).

This 'Department of Development Aid', that also featured in the Gasela case, was a South African government department that was set up in order to assist people living in 'foreign countries' –read: bantustans– who were in dire need –read: victims of forced removals. The department was an apartheid regime instrument, which distributed resources in order to gain political control over the rural areas. It mainly supported areas and community structures, like Tribal Authorities, that collaborated with the South African regime and/or bantustan governments.

According to ARA:

> "Government moves to upgrade come packaged with an attempt to set up a local authority sympathetic to the government and willing to carry out government instructions..." (p. 6).

Thus, as the Albany Rural Association was worried about this government strategy it was decided in a meeting in February 1988 to create two types of sub-committees in the organization, namely so-called *functional committees* and *area committees*. The most important of these was the 'Development Sub-committee'. Although it derived its name from the desire to promote *self-sufficiency in* communities, it had much broader aims than the term 'development' would suggest nowadays. The role of the sub-committee was:

1. *"to make available information and expertise on the strategies of the state.*
2. *To help strengthen communities in their negotiations, and to help introduce democratically elected bodies, and to develop alternative development strategies"* [7].

Both in all internal documents and in its newsletters the organization made clear that the ARA strategy to support communities –especially the democratically elected structures– had everything to do with a political power struggle.

ARA was afraid that the State would be able to (re-)gain control of the Border communities where residents associations had been set up. According to ARA[8]:

> *"The state is clearly attempting to out-manoeuvre and side-line the Residents' Associations and to replace them with conventional political structures –tribal or community authorities. If the Residents' Associations are to survive this attack they will have to formulate clear and coherent demands and adopt well-informed positions in any dealings with state agencies..."* (p. 7).

Thus, during the struggle era, the whole issue of development was perceived to be a political tool. The State used 'development' in its strategy to gain control over the rural masses, and the NGOs, in turn, devised a counter 'development strategy'.

For ARA, nevertheless, it was still very clear that they would only play an intermediary role in development[9]. *"ARA will not get involved in setting up the projects. Role more to help communities to come to understanding of what they are able to do..."*. Thus, the staff agreed that they would only facilitate development projects. However, this was not as easy as it seemed. By donating certain resources to communities, the organization set foot on a slippery slope and, eventually, did become involved in certain projects. For example, in early 1988 ARA donated a brick-making machine to Kwelera as the residents association planned to build a pre-school. Yet, soon it emerged that there was very little progress achieved in Kwelera since, by August 1988, not a brick had been produced. This frustrated the ARA staff and in a meeting[10] it was said that ARA *"...need to put pressure on Kwelera to use their machine..."*. Furthermore, in the same meeting others suggested that pig farming could also be beneficial to the communities and that ARA needed *"...to acquire a boar on a cooperative basis..."*.

For some in the organization this went too far, as they believed that ARA was now involved in actively setting up projects. Jacob James, for example, in the same meeting remarked: *"In our initial discussions it was decided that ARA would never be responsible for projects, that ARA is just a facilitator. Are we still doing this?"*. Although this question was never really answered and the experience with getting into delivery was not particularly positive, ARA continued in the same manner. Through 'trial and error' and motivated both by the will to oppose the state and a strong desire 'to do something for the people', ARA remained active in delivery through development projects.

In conclusion one can say that 'development' in the late eighties was all about the political struggle against apartheid. 'Development' still had more to do with forming and supporting alternative and more democratic community structures, than with pure delivery. The struggle was anti-Tribal Authorities, and as a result, severe tensions surfaced in the areas where ARA intervened, usually aggravating complicated community conflicts. However, when only a few years later apartheid was on the decline, other 'development experiments' were initiated.

Development in the Early Nineties: problems in Merino Walk
In the early nineties when the threat of forced removals had abated, the Albany Rural Association made a substantial strategic shift. Several factors played a role. First, as political change was in the air, the question of what to do with the land and how to aid communities in the rural areas, which were in need of services, became urgent. Several initiatives were launched like the establishment of the Border Kei Development Forum (BKDF), with which ARA was superficially involved. 'Rural development' became a buzzword, and therefore, as Andile Kwinana explained in an interview[11], *"...at that time there was quite a lot of changing around of the organization, because in a changing environment we also had to adapt"*. Secondly, the organization believed that something needed to be done after communities successfully claimed land. ARA staff felt that they could not just walk away from the scene after a land claim was settled.

Some sort of support to plan for the future needed to be given. In an interview[12], Joy Molo, a former MRA staff member, said that with *"...some of the communities it was sort of a logical step to get into development and bringing in services"*. Thirdly, on many occasions the organization was approached by community members with requests for help to augment the situation in their areas. As is argued by MRA in Groundwork[13], where it is stated that communities in *"...an increasing number have requested development assistance from the Monti Rural Association..."* (p. 2). Fourthly, the situation in the rural areas of the Eastern Cape seemed to worsen as the early nineties were the scene of several serious droughts. As water had become a grave concern, the establishment of water projects seemed a sensible solution. Lastly, it is safe to assume that the organization itself may have worried about the immediate future. Since it was envisaged that assisting communities to access land would no longer be needed in the future, the organization battled with the fundamental question: how to survive in a fundamentally changing environment? For many, getting into 'development' was seen as a possible option. Therefore, in 1992 the decision was taken to engage in what the organization termed 'development support work'.

According to a six monthly ARA Report (1992b):

> *"ARA entered 1992 on the understanding that the year would lay the basis for development work and provide ARA with valuable experience and skills in this field (...). The work has been very intensive and has consumed a lot of ARA's time. However the approach to the work has been fairly unique. The return on this investment of ARA resources will be in generalising ARA's experience in Merino Walk, Mgwali and Mooiplaas into lessons for an approach to rural development across the Border region ..."* (p. 7).

By 1993 'this fairly unique approach' led the organization to adopt the kind of participatory discourse that fell in with the 'freedom and consultation discourse'.

The discourse coincided with moving and making a fresh start in East London and launching the more development oriented newsletter *Groundwork*. In its first edition[14] MRA is quite clear about its position with regard to development:

> *"Development is much more than getting jobs and economic growth. The process should gradually improve living conditions and address the community's physical, mental and spiritual health. This is achieved through democracy, participation, and the ability of the community to look after its own affairs and build the self-esteem of every community member.*
>
> *Domination and exploitation of the majority of the community by a specific group or by outsiders is not development. Development must benefit the whole community. In order to do this, all sectors of the community need to participate in the development process (...).*
>
> *Unity is crucial in development and all sectors of the community* **must** *participate and reach consensus on issues"* (p. 2)[15]

Clearly, this participatory discourse was not only aimed at lifting 'the marginalized', like women, it was also directed against the authoritarian tribal authorities. Additionally, just like in the late eighties, the organization declared that it would not actually deliver development:

"The MRA is not providing these communities with schools, piped water, soccer fields or tractors (...). Rather, the MRA is assisting these communities to help themselves (...), the MRA hopes to develop an approach to community development which will be appropriate to the needs and limitations of black rural communities in the Border\Kei region..." (p. 2).

However, although the rhetoric seemed well thought through, MRA did underestimate the complicated community dynamics in some of these areas. This had everything to do with the highly politicized context in the rural areas and the fact that MRA had frequently played a role in community dynamics –pro-residents associations, anti-tribal authorities– during the struggle era. As the democratic forces were gaining the upper hand in South Africa, and democratic elections were expected to take place, every intervention by organizations like the Monti Rural Association was coloured by a 'democratization drive' that was expressed in a 'freedom and consultation'-type discourse. In the quotes above, the determination of an organization like MRA to push for a 'participatory approach' is quite obvious. Achieving 'development' through 'consultation and consensus building' and through the creation of new and more democratic structures was seen as the way forward after years of local autocratic rule by elites and tribal authorities. Yet, in these early years of the transition, in which the NGO sector was almost 'drunk' with hopes for the future, it wasn't realized that certain powerful sections in communities would not give up their privileged positions without a fight. Nor was it recognized that the new community structures may become internally divided.

In those days, one of the communities MRA concentrated its work in was Merino Walk, a farm that had been invaded by part of the Thornhill Group Four community, as was described in Chapter 4. At first an integrated rural development programme was envisaged for Thornhill and Merino Walk, as described in a submission to the Province of the Eastern Cape Reconstruction and Development Programme titled *From Crisis to Reconstruction: and integrated rural development programme for Thornhill and Merino Walk* (1994c). However, in a later stage the two areas were treated more separately, especially after internal and regional tensions emerged. As Merino Walk experienced problems around water provision, toilets and agriculture, ARA helped to establish a water project, a toilet project and a garden project, amongst other things.

For each project a committee was elected. As Merino Walk had been settled mainly by 'democratic' Group Four members, who were regarded as more or less progressive by MRA, this was not one of the communities where problems around leadership were expected. However, without getting lost in the details, it is safe to say that when progress in Merino Walk became too slow, frictions arose. As a result, MRA attempted to restructure the committees on several occasions. MRA staff even attempted to form parallel structures with sections of the community whom they favoured. As a result, the organization, again, got directly involved in local power struggles. According to Albert Lobese, who had been one of the early invaders of Merino Walk and who had been employed by MRA, other MRA staff could be blamed for the mess-up in Merino Walk. *"Andile caused many problems there. He held a meeting where the leaders were not present and proceeded to elect a new committee. That caused a big conflict"*. Indeed, in its Annual Report January – December 1995, the Monti Rural Association (1995a) refers to the *"...ousted Residents Committee which was removed from office in August 1994"* (p. 39). By 1994-95 things had escalated and the situation had become extremely complex. Effectively, the community had been split in two and competition between the factions had become fierce. Both groups were now claiming the leadership and were even fighting each other to gain access to the same piece of additional land through a subsidy scheme. The situation had now become so hopeless that it prompted MRA to withdraw.

However, not only the formation of structures proved to be problematic in Merino Walk. Also the development projects itself proved hard to handle. As an example I will briefly discuss the water project. Since MRA did not have the technical expertise to establish a water project, it brokered in the help of another NGO: Land Service Committee (LSC). Although progress was extremely slow, because of the long drawn out consultative processes, eventually bore-holes were drilled, pipes were laid and engines installed. Yet, at the end of the implementation phase, when the new government had come to power, it was decided to involve the Department of Housing and Local Government. Sadly, this department had other ideas about the design and the capacity of the scheme. As Joy Molo explained in an interview:

"...eventually when government did get involved in the end, they took out the pipes that were put in by LSC and they put in new pipes. I suppose it was also an issue of engineering. Different opinions of engineers. And because you dealt with limited donor funding, the kind of service that was brought to the community wasn't..., I am not an engineer, but what I could gather is that the kinds of pipes that they laid there were not necessarily suitable to be expanded on. And the engine that you put there was a smallish engine because of the funds and in the end you needed a bigger engine because the community was growing over time".

In other words, due to limited donor funding MRA, LSC and members of the Water Committee had chosen to install lower capacity pipes and engines than the department normally deemed necessary. The work of years had, more or less, been for nothing.

As a result of these experiences the Monti Rural Association came to revisit its strategies. The staff recognized that 'development' was not their thing. Nevertheless, Andile Kwinana claimed that it was not the negative experience per se that caused a shift back to land reform. Rather, it was the realization that development work, which was incredibly labour intensive, left too little room for important land reform work that was still needed. In an interview Kwinana explained:

"Once we got hands-on experience with that type of work we realized that such work was shifting the focus of the organization away from land reform. We realized that although the development was important, other people had to do it. We still had a role to play in assisting communities to get land and in the broader policy processes around land reform. Therefore, we took a turn back to land reform..."

Moreover, Joy Molo, in hindsight, stated that it *"...was not realized by MRA, and by communities to a lesser extent, (...) that development of services is a government competence...".*

Concluding, one can say that Merino Walk became a serious failure due to both complicated community dynamics and lack of concrete development expertise in

MRA. Instead of leading to unity, the participatory ideology had caused exactly the opposite: more pronounced discord. Thus, the valuable experience that the organization had hoped to gain and a *fairly unique approach* ended in disillusionment. Nevertheless, yet other development experiments were on the cards.

Development in the Mid-nineties: the development debacle in Gallawater A

In 1993 several groups of Zweledinga residents crossed the Ciskei-South African border to occupy farms that were part of Released Area 59 (RA 59), an area of South African land that had been earmarked by the apartheid government to be added to the Ciskei. Zweledinga was a dumping ground, similar to Thornhill, for people who had left Glen Grey as they tried to avoid the incorporation in the Transkei in 1976. Just like Thornhill thousands of Zweledinga residents had not received the amount of land that had been promised to them before the move. As the Zweledinga residents were tired of waiting and eager to put pressure on South Africa to grant them the land, several farms in RA 59 were invaded.

Most of these farms belonged to the South African state. However, one farm – Gallawater A– was still privately owned by Mr. Andrew King, a white South African farmer. Land claims were submitted for most of these farms to the Advisory Commission on Land Allocation (ACLA), with the help of MRA and other organizations, like the Legal Resources Centre (LRC). For some farms these claims were successful, like Gallawater B and Langedraai. For Gallawater A, the claim was rejected. Although Mr. King's initial reaction had been to lay a trespass charge against the invaders, he withdrew it after he decided to enter into negotiations with the people of Zweledinga. Thus, with the Monti Rural Association as an intermediary, another route was tried to realize the transfer of the farm to 'the people of Zweledinga'.

As the old apartheid government had begun to make policy changes –amongst other things, it had published a White Paper on Land Reform[16]– opportunities seemed to be opening up. One such an opportunity was provided by Act 126. This *Provision of Certain Land for Settlement Act No. 126* of 1993 made it possible for rural communities to buy land that was privately owned. Through a substantial government subsidy of 80% of the purchase price such groups could access white farms. The community would have to pay 5% as a deposit and the remaining 15% over a period of five years. Thus, as this seemed an ideal opportunity, MRA and the LRC assisted the Zweledinga Residents Association (ZRA) in the whole process. By December 1995 the deal was completed and a trust was formed. Subsequently, 102 families, together paying R. 37,000 deposit, could begin to settle on the farm.

Since this was one of the first instances in South African history that a group of black South Africans took over a white-owned farm, the Minister Of Land Affairs, Derek Hanekom, attended the December 7th celebrations personally. In his speech he stated that the world would be watching the developments in Gallawater A:

> *"(...) Many are convinced that it is going to fail. I am convinced that it won't. I believe that you could be a living testimony as to what can be done once people are given the opportunity*[17]*...".*

As a present MRA gave the community a years supply of vegetable seeds, and in her speech the MRA Coordinator, Mavis Beechwood, also pointed to the responsibility resting on the shoulders of the Gallawater A trust members:

> "...the Gallawater community faces a heavy responsibility to make a success of their enterprises. There are many critics of the government's land reform programme who will be waiting to point to failure..." (p. 5).

Mr. King, the white farmer gave the community a registered breeding bullock to kick-start their livestock breeding programme. In his speech he said:

> "For you, the Zweledinga community, today is a just reward after many years of hardship and deprivation. I share your joy..." (p. 5).

However, according to Peter Nombula, the vice chairman of the Trust Committee, the whole process had taken too long:

> "...during this time, there were problems within the community –people were coming to knock on my door complaining that they want their money back (...) I did not breathe easily until the deal was finalized..." (p. 5).

Why was it then that after such a hopeful start with good intentions and high expectations, the Monti Rural Association pulled out of Gallawater A in 1998, only three years later? According to the official motivation in the MRA report (1998a) *Gallawater A: an evaluation of MRA's intervention, 1994 – 1998*:

> "...the inaccessibility of Trust members was the dominant problem. This is compounded by the fact that the current unplanned, informal situation (regarding internal rights and responsibilities) suits very powerful interests in the Trust Committee" (p. 16).

Below, I shall try to analyze how this situation could emerge, what the role of the Monti Rural Association was and what lessons the organization drew from the whole process.

Reconstruction and Development

As is clear from the speeches on the day Gallawater A was transferred to its new owners, high hopes and expectations were on everyone's lips. Although the process had taken longer than expected, the speeches rang the tone of the general atmosphere in South Africa at the time. It was a typical 'freedom and consultation' achievement. The new dispensation had also influenced the Monti Rural Association. During the period when the deal was negotiated in 1994 and 1995, the Monti Rural Association went through a major transformation. In its *Monti Rural Association Proposal 1994 – 1997* MRA (1994d) –"...*this proposal covers the period beginning immediately after the April 1994 election...*" (p. 1)– this intended transformation process was described in detail. In the 1994 proposal, which is very thorough, critical and drenched in a 'freedom and consultation' discourse, it was stated that:

> "...the Monti Rural Association (MRA) believes non-governmental organisations have a crucial role to play in the process of reconstruction under a democratic government (...) [and] "...demand-driven reconstruction accords with the process of democratization precisely because it provides an incentive for local initiative and participation..." (p. 3-8).

Moreover, the proposal oozed the kind of Gender and sustainability rhetoric that was fashionable in the mid-nineties. Thus, MRA saw the need for a greater role for rural women:

> "...*constitutional guarantees of equality for women will be largely meaningless for marginalized rural women unless reconstruction processes*

> *place such women at the centre of rural reconstruction and land reform programmes"* (p. 16).

And, as before, the organization stated its intermediary position clearly:

> *"...while not an implementing agency, MRA believes that, through its Development Support Programme, it can make a valuable and important contribution to this process of development and reconstruction in the region..."* (p. 39).

Thus, the document illustrated that 'development' had been placed high on the agenda again. This was confirmed by the strategic decisions that were taken to hire more expert staff. For example, in January 1994 an Agricultural Officer was hired to strengthen the Development Support Team.

As the proposal was well received by foreign funders, even more bold steps were taken to strengthen the organization's development capacity. One of the most significant steps was the deployment of a New Zealand volunteer –through the New Zealand Volunteers (NZV)[18]– at the end of 1994. This project manager with experience in rural resource management was envisaged to be very useful in MRA's new strategy. Moreover, it was thought that the employment of a foreign volunteer could make it easier to access foreign funds. This was argued in a letter by John Carver, the Monti Rural Association Coordinator, in which he stated that MRA was:

> *"...excited at the prospect of consolidating our relationship with NZV and hope that through such projects as we propose they will be able to lever considerable funding from their government for this and other projects"*[19].

And this is exactly what happened. In 1995 the Monti Rural Association submitted a proposal for poultry projects in Gallawater A, B and Langedraai farms to the New Zealand High Commission. In the same year the funds were awarded and received by MRA.

The idea to facilitate a poultry project in Gallawater A had several reasons. First of all, it had everything to do with the fact that Gallawater A had been a productive farm and it was thought that to continue production could be beneficial to its settlers, both from the point of view of food supply and the earning of an income. Secondly, the idea to make a commercial success of Gallawater A was more urgent than on the other farms, as Gallawater A had been purchased and 15% of the price still had to be repaid. Therefore, the idea to have an income generating project seemed a logical step. It would help the community to repay its debts. Thus, it was envisaged to divide the agricultural land in two. The one half to be farmed commercially and communally to help pay off the debts, the other half to be allocated and farmed individually. Thirdly, the idea to make the poultry project a women's project fitted in with the MRA ideology to give women a stronger role in the development of their areas and communities. Lastly, of course, the idea to facilitate a poultry project and commercial communal farming, through a New Zealand volunteer and a MRA agricultural officer, fitted in with the developmental course the Monti Rural Association had taken. There was a perceived need for *rural reconstruction*.

The Community is no Community

In the course of 1996 and 1997 it became clear that the progress on most fronts in Gallawater A was very disappointing and not as imagined on the day of the hand-over.

Within months tensions had arisen within the community. It emerged that the 'leaders' who had taken up the positions in the Trust Committee were not as cooperative as expected. While the Monti Rural Association, together with some of the – predominantly female– settlers, pushed the agenda of empowering women and introducing commercial and 'sustainable' communal farming, 'the big men' in the Trust Committee were much more interested to graze their livestock on the farm. On all levels tensions arose. Tensions surfaced between the Trust Committee and other community members, between the Trust Committee and MRA, and even within the Trust Committee. Besides a differing view with regard to farming, other major problems also arose.

First, the 102 participating families in the Trust never settled on the farm, which led to feelings of frustration on behalf of the Monti Rural Association staff. According to the report, *Eastern Cape Land reform Programme: diagnostic evaluation of the Gallawater A trust – Queenstown District*, by Mr. Wotshela (1997), only about thirty households had settled on the farm by 1997. Thus, according to MRA, which had assisted in demarcating the plots, a system of stand-pipes could not be installed. When there were hardly any settlers who would actually use the water, such an expensive project seemed useless. Only if a large percentage of the 102 families had built or were in the process of building homes, would MRA instruct the Land Service Committee (LSC), a water infrastructure NGO, to commence laying the pipes. However, some prospective settlers argued that they would not consider settling on the farm if there was not yet an adequate water supply.

Second, there were accusations that Peter Nombula, the vice chairman of the trust who had become the occupant of the large farm house in order to prevent burglaries, was acting like he owned the farm. The trust members accused him of benefiting personally from the money he collected for the telephone and the electricity expenses. However, the financial mismanagement was also caused by the fact that the trust treasurer ran a taxi business in Cape Town –1100 km (!) away. As a result, he was rarely present when the trust met. Eventually, the mismanagement led to the telephone and electricity supply being cut off. As there was now no longer electricity to operate the pump, the water supply to the farm house also came to a halt.

Third, problems emerged with enlisting the support of government departments. According to the 1995 Annual Report MRA (1995a):

> "...one of MRA's aims was to enlist the support of the Department of Agriculture and establish a relationship between the Department and the community. This has been a frustrating process, hampered by confusion within the Department about its future structure and direction" (p. 36).

As can be expected, the chaos in government did impede a smooth 'development' take-off in Gallawater A.

With regard to the poultry project, the progress was also disappointing. A group of women were given a one-week training at Mpofu Agricultural Training Centre and they were assisted by MRA and the trust to open a bank account. Furthermore MRA provided them with some basic training with regard to financial matters. In 1996 a building was identified –the former workshop on the farm– which was emptied and cleaned out in order to create room for the poultry project. However, the Monti Rural Association staff were still not convinced that these women could manage huge amounts of money. Moreover, as the rumours and accusations with regard to mismanagement of funds, property and resources by 'the big men' grew stronger, MRA came to fear that the men would influence the women to use the poultry money for other purposes. As a result, the Monti Rural Association refused to transfer the poultry project funds into the Gallawater A account. Thus, the poultry project never really materialized and when I arrived in 1997, a MRA fieldworker jokingly said: *"...I will show him the chicken project that is totally fake!"*. By then the work had effectively come to a halt. Although meetings were still held, no progress was achieved.

On the farm things got progressively worse. Even with regard to livestock –the area of interest and responsibility of the men– the situation worsened visibly. Although it had been agreed that people would pay grazing levies to the trust, no one did. Furthermore, fencing was not maintained and grazing camps no longer functioned. Additionally, the buildings on the farm deteriorated every year, as no one deemed it necessary to maintain them. By 1997 – 1998 things actually looked quite hopeless. It was not that the 'big men' had no money to spend on the farm as several members of the trust committee were members of the Zweledinga elite and successful businessmen like taxi operators. This was confirmed by the fact that these men could easily pay the heavy fines[20] incurred as their livestock was impounded when the animals invaded other farms through holes in the fencing.

MRA's Trusted Tactic: reverting to parallel structures
When the process around settlement, the poultry project and the communal farming bogged down, the Monti Rural Association tried a trusted tactic: doing business with parallel structures. It was believed that the Planning Committee, in which some of the women were represented and which had already been formed before the Trust became a legal entity, would be much more cooperative. Moreover, it was hoped that it could be of help to undermine, or at least circumvent the powerful Trust Committee. However, as could be expected, instead of improving the already tense situation, this strategy helped to worsen the situation as it led to more conflicts within the community. By mid-1997 the situation seemed hopeless: some members of the Trust Committee had left the structure, very few people turned up for meetings, no one actually knew how many of the original 102 trust families were still interested in the farm and the MRA staff who were working on the farm seemed confused, disillusioned and inclined to give up.

Field visits became more chaotic and less purposeful and the MRA staff gave many explanations for the failure in Gallawater A:
- *"People are lazy..."*;
- *"The problem is members of the trust committee not coming to meetings"*;
- *"The problem is for a great deal caused by bad MRA involvement (...). People on the team don't have planning skills and some people are not committed..."*;
- *"The problem with MRA is that we assume that they want land for development...maybe they don't..."*;
- *"People don't move because there is no water..."*;
- *"The problem is within the trust committee, which is something that we have already identified..."*;

> - *"You know what the problem is, I realize this now: at the end of the day we as MRA gave them [the Trust Committee] the opportunity (...) to mess up the others";*
> - *et cetera.*

Some of these 'explanations' had a clear circular argumentative character. Decisions could not be taken because the trust does not function; the trust does not function because people do not attend meetings; people do not attend meetings because they do not stay on the farm; people do not stay on the farm, because there is no water; there is no water on the farm, because the trust does not function. This reinforced the impression that most of the MRA staff involved in Gallawater A in the late nineties, effectively, had lost faith in the project.

Nevertheless, several strategies were tried to overcome the problems. First, in order to regain some clarity the organization sent out a questionnaire in late 1996 to find out which trust members would still be interested in settling on the farm. However, the outcome was rather predictable: the response to the questionnaire was too low to justify any conclusion. Second, the organization regularly involved new staff in the team. Besides having to do with the brain drain that took place in the mid-nineties, because of which staff left, this was also part of the strategy:

> *"I sometimes feel that they take us so much for granted, I think we need other people, (...) not necessarily people who are from the team..."*[21].

Third, MRA staff tried to set up new procedures. In order to overcome problems in the last year before the pull-out, and accomplish a re-start of the project, it was decided that a contract was needed. In my opinion a rather bureaucratic approach. Such a contract would have to ensure a cooperative trust. However, as could be expected, efforts to convince the trust committee to sign such a contract failed. Thus, the MRA team designed a last strategy to ensure a smooth relationship with the trust. MRA communicated to the trust that the Gallawater A trust members would need to formulate a formal request to MRA, signed by a large number of the trust members, in which the trust would express its appreciation of further MRA involvement. As only 37 individuals, not even belonging to different families, signed the request, the Monti Rural Association concluded that it was no longer really wanted and decided to pull out of Gallawater A.

Why Gallawater A Failed

In my analysis the role of the Monti Rural Association in Gallawater A can be characterized both as a success and as a failure. I still think that it was a significant achievement of MRA to assist the community in acquiring the Gallawater A farm. However, after the hand-over everything that could go wrong did go wrong, for which both MRA and in the Gallawater A community can be blamed.

As MRA had not been as deeply involved with the Zweledinga people as it had with the Thornhill people, its staff was not aware of the extremely complicated power struggles that were going on in Zweledinga. In an interview[22] with former staff member Catherine May, she stated that:

> *"...in Zweledinga our involvement and understanding was more nominal than in Thornhill (...). We knew what went on in Thornhill, not so in Zweledinga...".*

Like in Thornhill, MRA mainly dealt with the residents association –the Zweledinga Residents Association (ZRA)– and not with the conservative Tribal Authority. However, the ZRA was not as progressive as it seemed. By the end of October 1995 – just before the hand-over of the farm –a revealing report was published. After MRA had dealt with the community for several years, this MRA (1995b) report raised serious doubts about the non-tribal nature of the ZRA. It was stated that there were *"...doubts that ZRA is a completely non-tribal body..."* (p. 33). The fact that there were frictions between the ZRA and the new SANCO structures in Zweledinga appeared to confirm these doubts[23].

A powerful elite seemed to have taken root in the ZRA. However, the fact that MRA was dealing with the elite in Gallawater A was already known in an earlier stage. In the minutes of a 1994 meeting, for example, it was stated that *"...it would appear that it is the wealthier households who are going for Gallawater and may have the best chance of success..."*[24]. It was not thought to be a problem, and as the Monti Rural Association also had obligations in other communities, MRA did not monitor the formation of the trust more carefully. Thus, it left it to the elite to take care of things. With a better understanding and closer involvement the intervention may had a more positive outcome.

Another complicating factor was related to the lack of clarity in MRA with regard to the role it was to play. A choice for 'development' in 1994 and reverting back to land reform in 1996. This certainly did not do the Gallawater A development experiment much good. The Monti Rural Association wanted to be, but did not have the capacity nor the experience to be a successful 'development organization'. As Joy Molo, a former MRA employee, stated in an interview:

"...I don't think MRA has the capacity to deal with the conflict that you have or that you generate by introducing a more democratic and developmental approach to things. Which in itself can be a source of conflict..."[25].

However, the dynamics within 'Gallawater A community' led me to believe that a positive achievement by the Monti Rural Association would have been almost impossible.

Especially the background and analysis provided by Wotshela (1997) shows that 'the elite' that took hold of the Gallawater A trust were heavily involved in Zweledinga politics and (tribal) conflicts. Moreover, they ran businesses, 'owned' properties in several areas[26], were involved in other projects, and mainly had an interest in additional grazing land. For MRA an almost impossible point of departure. Wotshela explains that these powerful men are mostly not settled on the farm and according to Xhosa custom rely on *"...custodians and distant relatives some of whom have been placed on the farm"* (p. 17). The benefits of grazing cattle were never shared among the rest of the trust members who were the co-owners of the farm. The benefits went to the elite. Apparently, the acquisition of Gallawater A had everything to do with the power struggle in larger Zweledinga over scarce resources. Some of the Gallawater A trust committee members were also involved in the Zweledinga irrigation scheme that had originally been set up by the Ciskei. Thus, many of the conflicts that surfaced in Gallawater A, originated somewhere else, for example, in Zweledinga politics.

The most important conclusion in the Wotshela (1997) report concerns the problematic aspects of the term community. *"...It should be also noted that these families are motivated and governed by different goals and should not be treated as a "community"..."* (p. 9). This problem had severe repercussions for the work of NGOs and other intervening parties. Although many actors are aware of the pitfalls associated with the term community, it does not prevent them from being caught in the traps. The MRA staff had been aware of this problem for many years, as, for example the *Monti Rural Association Proposal 1994 – 1997* (1994d), dealing with its envisaged 'developmental course', had already warned about the tricky concept:

> *"Who constitutes 'the community'? How should land be allocated and to whom? What tenure system should underpin the allocation of land and who decides who is eligible for land?"* (p. 43).

Nevertheless, this basic mistake was repeated again and again and, thus, the settlers of Gallawater A farm were referred to as 'the Gallawater A community'. Possibly, this belief in the concept of community was reinforced in the freedom and consultation, when community rhetoric was rife. As a result, even in the MRA report (1996d) by Kwinana, about the difficulties in Zweledinga, it is still proposed *"...to revive a sense of community among the Zweledinga people..."* (p.11). As if that sense of community had ever existed...

The (im-)Possibilities of Organizational Learning

When analyzing the performance of the Monti Rural Association with regard to its 'development' activities over the past fifteen years, the similarities are striking. First, although the organization in almost every document declared that it would only play a facilitating role, it repeatedly got involved in actual 'projects', whether it was brick-making in Kwelera, or the poultry project in Gallawater A. Second, complicated community dynamics were frequently exacerbated by the projects; scarce resources were introduced in an area where power struggles over resources were prevalent. Furthermore, as an actor in these conflicts, an NGO like MRA brought its own historical baggage. Which groups had the organization supported during the struggle era, and more important, which had it opposed? Thus, in later years neutral interventions became impossible in such areas. Thirdly, the organization brought its own ideological background to the 'development' arena. For example, introducing a 'gender' and 'participatory' discourse in largely conservative communities. Moreover, such discourse would also 'contaminate' the NGO's analytical framework. A dominant 'participatory community rhetoric' complicated its interventions. However, what is puzzling is why the organization, although it was aware of many of these pitfalls, again and again got caught in these traps...

To begin with the first factor, 'getting into development', it becomes clear that an organization like the Monti Rural Association repeatedly 'wanted to do something for the people'. Achieving a land transfer was not enough. As government departments failed to assist these people who had acquired land, MRA, out of feelings of loyalty, decided that it could not leave them to their own devices. It was both a matter of compassion and prestige. These land transfers were to become successful showcases, illustrative of the possibilities of land reform. Therefore, although the organization did not have the capacity, it did what it could. Moreover, in my opinion, a factor reinforcing this behaviour has to do with a basic human characteristic: 'wanting to do something'. Being confronted with people who were in dire need, the MRA staff, again and again tried to think of ways to improve the lives of those it was concerned with. This mechanism also occurred during my own fieldwork when I often asked myself how I could 'do something' for those I encountered. Especially the fact that many staff of MRA left the organization, while others with 'fresh compassion' and an 'urge to do something' entered the organization, may account for the fact that similar mistakes were repeated. Particularly significant, in this respect, may have been the brain drain in the mid-nineties. After new staff members were appointed old ideas had a chance to resurface.

Secondly, with regard to community dynamics, I am convinced that it is very difficult for an outside agency to actually solve tensions in an area where they are not frequently present. Several factors can worsen community tensions. First, in situations where NGOs have an 'intervention history', for example during the struggle era, the neutrality of an organization is often tainted. As some groups –democratic residents associations– were supported, while others –the tribal authority– were opposed by the NGO, it became very hard to enter those communities in later years as a neutral intervening party. Especially in situations where the NGO attempted to support the less privileged, against the will of those in power –see Gallawater A– it was almost impossible to accomplish a successful intervention. Second, by not being aware of community dynamics community tensions can be exacerbated by interventions. This can lead to the domination of one group over the other as Crew (1997) has argued. *"Not recognizing conflicts between interest groups leaves control in the hands of the more powerful by default" (p. 77)*. This is exactly what happened in Gallawater A. The Monti Rural Association worked with the elite without being aware of their position in the community. As a result they were able to use their position as trust committee members to push their own agenda. In that sense the core strategy and identity of a non-governmental organization, namely its intermediary position, is full of dangers. In some situations it is the organization's strength –see the role it played in the negotiation phase of Gallawater A– while in other situations –the poultry project in Gallawater A– it reveals its main vulnerability: being dependent on the goodwill of the other parties.

In my view, however, a long and deeply rooted relationship between an NGO and a 'group of people' in which there is mutual respect and an awareness on the part of the intervening organization of the local dynamics and power struggles, may lead to a fruitful relationship. When, for example, looking at the relationship between the MRA staff and the Thornhill residents it becomes clear that an enormous amount of time and energy was invested by the Monti Rural Association to make that relationship work. As such NGOs have limited capacity and resources it may, therefore, be unrealistic to be intensively involved in more than a few communities. With each additional community the danger of superficial involvement, leading to complications, increases. Furthermore, the intervening party should go, or rather, be in tune 'with the flow'. With that I mean that the ideas and convictions –I come back to this in the next paragraph– of the intervening party should not differ too much with the ideas of the majority, or those who are in power. Without a strong majority, any intervention, whether 'progressive' or 'conservative' will fail.

This brings me to consider the last point. Usually, if not always, an intervening party –whether government, market or civil society organization– brings with it a whole set of norms, values and ideas that it wants to see realized. An NGO does not only provide 'the people' with land, it also introduces a whole package of political and social beliefs. In the case of progressive South African NGOs, such an ideological package was veiled by a 'freedom and consultation' discourse and a 'bottom-up development' rhetoric. In the case of Gallawater A and Merino Walk, for example, the 'freedom and consultation discourse' in which 'participation' was almost forced upon a group of very different people, the internal tensions that were already present were only exacerbated. Especially in the case of Gallawater A, where it first 'empowered' the elite and later realized that the 'wrong' people had been 'empowered', the forceful 'participation discourse' worked adversely. To set up parallel structures in such situations –as a way to circumvent the elite– then creates even larger problems. The elite does everything to stay in control. Instituting and working with parallel structures requires a deep understanding of community dynamics, extreme political sensitivity and an utterly reliable political judgement. As this was rarely the case, several MRA interventions successively failed. Also its 'gender ideology' and ideas about 'sustainability' added in the case of Gallawater A to the tensions that were building up. In Thornhill, however, the 'gender intervention' did have positive results as many more women became active in the structures. Again, this may have been due to the fact that those who were in power –ANC- and SANCO-aligned– were 'the progressives'.

Also the analytical framework used by non-governmental organizations is strongly influenced by this ideological background. In that sense the almost forceful 'participatory' ideology seemed to have done more harm than good. Thus, the term 'community' became central to the 'freedom and consultation' discourse. As a result, in every context the MRA identified communities, even in settings where no sense of community had ever existed. I would urge, therefore, that NGOs –and many social scientists for that matter– become more aware of the terminology they use. Especially 'community rhetoric' causes NGO staff to see unity and harmony, where, in fact, we should possibly recognize power struggles and discord.

The Role of Evaluations
With regard to organizational learning it is interesting to consider the role of 'evaluations'. Whether an external or an internal evaluation, they are both said to contribute to improved organizational performance. Thus, ideally, an evaluation exercise is part of a process of organizational learning and organizational improvement. However, some scholars are quite critical and suggest that the whole exercise should be regarded in a different light. For instance, Long and van der Ploeg (1989), in their article *'Demythologizing Planned Intervention: an actor perspective'*, have shown how an evaluation exercise usually plays a critical role in a chain of consecutive development interventions. First of all, the evaluation fulfils a role by interlinking different interventions over time, and, secondly, it aids to legitimize the role of the intervening agencies. They argue that:

> "Normally 'failures' are the starting point for the elaboration of the next rounds of interventions. (...) intervention is of course big business, not only for

firms and consultancy bureaus but also for the government agencies or NGOs involved. For all of them 'development' is a commodity with a calculable exchange value that reproduces and legitimizes particular intervention practices and interests" (p. 234-235).
Whether such mechanisms can also be detected in the Gallawater A evaluation will be explored below.

In 1998 a long-term funder requested MRA to carry out an internal evaluation of the Gallawater A intervention. As Sweden Supports Africa[27] (SSA) had funded most of the Gallawater A work and as they had been informed about the recent problems and an intended pull-out, the funder argued that an evaluation was justified. Thus, Mr. Eastwood, the Monti Rural Association Director, produced a document, titled *Gallawater A: an evaluation of MRA's intervention, 1994 – 1998*, for MRA (1998a) in December 1998. On first sight such an initiative seems laudable, as it suggests that the parties involved have a critical attitude towards the organization's work and are willing to learn from past mistakes. However, after studying the document thoroughly and keeping the work of Long and van der Ploeg (1989) in mind, several critical remarks can be made.

First of all it must be remarked that this evaluation was largely a 'paper evaluation'. Since Mr. Eastwood only became director in 1997, he studied the early phase of the intervention by studying the Gallawater A reports, a 'reported reality'. Secondly, it must be acknowledged that in an evaluation of a project, that was the responsibility of one's predecessors, it might be easier to be critical. However, the evaluation indeed yielded truly critical observations. For example, much attention is devoted to terminology:

"MRA reports over the period 1992-6 use the term "community" to denote a host of different groupings of people in Zweledinga (...):
- *the total population of Zweledinga*
- *people who have invaded the three farms*
- *people currently living on the three farms*
- *Gallawater A trust members*
- *people living on Gallawater A*
- *residents of Langedraai and Gallawater B, etc."* (p. 13).

And, according to Eastwood, MRA

"...remained strongly informed by the pre-1993 resistance work. It remained obsessed with the Zweledinga community, as though this was still a meaningful social construct in the era of land reform and development..." (p. 13).

Furthermore, Eastwood recognized a lack of understanding with respect to the tenure situation. Thus, his evaluation stated that:

"There was clearly a weak understanding in the 'Farms Team' of land rights in general and the land rights situation at Gallawater A..." (p. 13).

However, when we look critically at whether such observations will really contribute to 'organizational learning', it must, for example, be remarked that the observations with regard to the problematic nature of the community terminology were already known in MRA. Already in 1994 the term community identified as very problematic, as was discussed above. In other words, Eastwood's observations with regard to the term can and should not be judged as a 'new insight'. The second point, may be more positive. Since Eastwood's arrival at MRA, he has done a lot to make the staff aware of the need to thoroughly understand tenure legislation.

With regard to MRA's role in 'development', the evaluation argued that it took considerable time for the organization to:

> "...define its role in the development arena as land use planning. (And even then, the 1995 Gallawater A proposal went beyond the parameters of land use planning)" (p. 16).

In my analysis, this quote reflects the 'old problem' that the NGO grappled with from the early days onwards. Repeatedly, the organization had stressed that it would only facilitate development, without getting involved into the technical side of things. But as the quote reveals, again in the Gallawater A case MRA went beyond its boundaries of competence. Just like in the case of brick-making in Kwelera and the water project in Merino Walk, Gallawater A proved the impossibility of organizational learning with regard to 'development'. The organization had made the same mistake.

Nevertheless, in my opinion, besides containing a limited number of useful lessons, there is also a legitimizing component in the Gallawater A evaluation. Part of the purpose of such a document is to ensure funders that the organization has improved. Thus, the report legitimizes the direction, structure and policies of the organization which were instituted after Mr. Eastwood took over the management of the organization from Mavis Beechwood. Basically, Mr. Eastwood argued that the changes that were initiated would ensure that mistakes made in the Gallawater A project will not be repeated in the future. As the new director strongly believed in 'strategic planning', 'project management' and the distinction between 'programmes' and 'projects', these elements return in the evaluation. In order to strengthen his argument the director also made use of the HUVO evaluation of 1996 (Cole and Nyoni, 1996), which was very critical of the lack of direction in MRA before his arrival. Indeed, in my view, there was a strong need to restructure MRA after the near collapse of the organization in 1996. However, I believe that the new director sometimes put too much faith in planning, reporting, policies and procedures; a somewhat technocratic approach.

Examples of 'Eastwood-speak' in the Gallawater A evaluation are:

> "...NGOs need to be clear about the objectives of their work in order to be effective. Activities should be planned in pursuance of objectives. Objectives should not be derived from activities (...). Workshops, field trips and meetings are all a waste of time and money unless they yield measurable results..." (p. 17).

And,

> "...there should be a clear fit between strategic objectives and organogram. The organisation should be restructured in such a way that facilitates the attainment of its objectives" (p. 17).

And with regard to management,

> "...the Gallawater A case shows the necessity for adequate project management" (p. 17).

Thus, besides wanting to understand what went wrong in Gallawater A, these quotes clearly seem to legitimize the new direction of the Monti Rural Association.

Besides the fact that evaluations are used to legitimize the new direction of an organization, they are also used to explain past failures. In my opinion, this is another weak aspect of the Gallawater A evaluation, as Mr. Eastwood has misinterpreted the role of the New Zealand Volunteers[28] (NZV) volunteer in the Gallawater A project. In fact, in my opinion, he puts too much blame on the volunteer. As I have clearly shown in the section on development in the early and mid-nineties, the organization had chosen to get engaged in 'development' with the publication of the *MRA proposal 1994-1997* almost nine months before the first volunteer arrived. The fact that a volunteer was sought was a direct result of the change in direction of the organization. However, Mr. Eastwood, in the *Gallawater A: an evaluation of MRA's intervention, 1994 – 1998*, argued that it was the New Zealand volunteer who had pushed the project in a direction that was not consistent with the direction of the organization:

> *"The volunteer that worked in Gallawater A had a major impact on the drafting of the 1994[29] proposal and subsequent work for a two-year period. Unfortunately this impact was not always informed or in line with organizational trends and priorities (...) volunteers can dominate an organization rather than add value to it"* (1998a, p. 18).

As can be expected, I do not agree with the analysis of Mr. Eastwood. Although, indeed, the volunteer may have pushed an even more all-inclusive view of 'development', one cannot deny the fact that a strong and well-informed Monti Rural Association leadership had made a choice to get involved in 'development' in 1994. Part of that choice was to attract a volunteer. Although Eastwood may be right in that the NZV volunteer influenced the 1995 proposal to also include things like roads, bridges, banking and small business development support (p. 10), he is wrong to blame everything on the volunteer. MRA management had made an informed choice before her arrival.

What can be said, however, is that some in the Monti Rural Association felt that they experienced what can be termed a 'donor push' of funds. This 'donor-push' mechanism was described in an interview[30] by Eastwood's predecessor:

> *"In one or two projects donors made money available which was very difficult for us to refuse on behalf of the community..."*.

Thus, according to her, feelings of loyalty towards the community prompted MRA to take on funds to initiate the Gallawater A poultry project. However, as was illustrated above, her own predecessor had explicitly stated that an additional reason to employ volunteers from New Zealand had been to be able to access such funds...

In conclusion I would say that the Gallawater A evaluation will probably not have a substantial impact on organizational learning of the Monti Rural Association. Although the tenure lessons, may be useful, the lessons that were formulated with regard to 'community terminology' and the need to restrict MRA's role to facilitation were already known to the organization. Moreover, it was too simplistic to put so much blame on the volunteer. Rather, the evaluation became an instrument to legitimize the direction the organization had already taken from early 1997 onwards. Therefore, I would be highly critical of the final analysis that was formulated in the report:

> *"In the final analysis, Gallawater A was a bridge too far for MRA in the mid-nineties. But the experience has taught the organization valuable lessons that have strengthened it and made a reoccurrence of failures unlikely"* (p. 18).

I doubt whether those lessons were, indeed, learned. Rather, I believe that this conclusion is of the type described by Long and van der Ploeg (1989). It justifies new interventions by a better-equipped MRA and is, thus, the indispensable link between past and future interventions.

This leaves us to conclude that organizational learning is much harder than it looks. To identify a particular role with regard to 'development' may have been easy, however, to stick with that role –only to facilitate– seemed impossible. Furthermore, over a period of almost fifteen years experience with development interventions has proven one thing: it was hard, if not impossible, to achieve progress in areas with problematic community dynamics. Time will tell whether MRA will not make similar mistakes in Gasela, its new 'agricultural development project'.

The 'Capacity Building Trap'

Besides organizational learning where the skills and knowledge in an organization is improved due to 'learning through practice', there is another manner in which organizations claim to make progress. By developing the skills and building the capacity of individual staff members –sending them on courses and letting them attend educational programmes– NGOs and other organizations claim to improve. As NGOs themselves are very positive about such 'capacity building' programmes, an organization like the Monti Rural Association regularly accesses substantial funds for this purpose. The National Land Committee, for example, administers the funds for the National Capacity Building Programme (NCBP), a programme that has been set up to improve the capacity and performance of the NLC affiliates. In the *Monti Rural Association Interim Report January – July 1993* the following is stated about building the capacity of staff:

> *"This staff development programme is aimed at assisting staff to improve or upgrade existing skills while giving preference to those employees who have not had the benefit of post-matric education or training"* (p. 38).

In subsequent years much of this staff development –or 'capacity building'– work was funded by the Ford Group[31]. In this section I intend to explore whether such a capacity building programme does indeed contribute to organizational learning.

In the struggle era staff remained employed by an organization like MRA for quite a while. First, because they were committed to the struggle and the type of work and, second, many progressive people had few alternatives. Michael Ndlovu, for example, joined the organization during 1987 and only left in 1998. Therefore, when staff were trained in those early years, much of that training directly and indirectly benefited the organization or the network of National Land Committee affiliates. The fact that, for instance, Michael Ndlovu could become the chairman of the NLC in 1993, was largely due to the skills he had acquired –on the job and taking courses– during his many years with the Monti Rural Association. When he joined in 1987 he was quite intimidated by the Rhodes University academics and could hardly write his own field reports. By 1998, however, he had become a very confident personality and his skills had improved to such a degree that he was employed by the Provincial

Department of Land Affairs. In MRA's newsletter *Groundwork*[32] in which the organization bid Mr. Ndlovu farewell it was stated:

> "...when he joined the organization Ndlovu was just an ordinary activist and had no experience on the use of computers (...). Ndlovu has since grown with the organization, not only acquiring the necessary typing skills but also developing more skills in working with communities and strategic planning..." (p. 3).

Mr. Ndlovu's example does indeed seem to confirm the conviction of NGOs that the training of staff has a positive effect on the pool of skills available to an organization. However, one can question whether capacity building of staff in the mid- and late nineties had the same effect as in earlier years. At the end of the freedom and consultation era and the beginning of the new realism era South African society went through such tremendous transformation processes and upheavals that it is useful to reassess the advantages of capacity building in that period.

In this regard, one factor in particular has drawn my attention: the huge brain drain of well-trained staff in the mid-nineties. To express the magnitude of this impact it is useful to look at some figures. To begin with it is important to note that the organization expanded considerably from around six staff members in December 1993 to a staff of 18 in 1995. However, between 1995 and 1998 an immense brain drain hit the organization. Of the 18 staff members working for MRA in 1995, 11 had left –including most of the old staff– by 1996. In other words, between 1995 and 1996 more than sixty percent of the staff left the organization. As the new government was looking for new, well-trained and progressive professionals, most of the staff that left MRA joined the ranks of the state bureaucracy. It is not surprising, therefore, that 1996 has been marked as a year of crisis and confusion for the organization since most of its institutional memory left that year. In this manner, ironically, the new government for which the NGOs had fought became one of the main threats to the organizational survival of these same organizations.

This huge brain drain had another important consequence as well. As there was such a shortage of capacity within the government, especially in relatively new fields like land reform, the state not only gobbled up the well-trained staff, but even attracted people with as little as one year experience in the NGO sector. This process was subsequently reinforced by the affirmative action policies that were instituted in the mid-nineties to alter the ratio of black versus white staff in the government. As a result the state began looking for many more black professionals as well. Since decades of Bantu education had produced a large group of relatively poorly educated young people, every form of additional training was seen as a bonus. Thus, even a large percentage of the newest staff at NGOs –with relatively limited experience– could not be kept by these organizations.

Length of stay with MRA:	1 Year		2 Years		3 Years		4 Years	
New staff that left after[33]:	5	15%	11	33%	1	3%	0	0%
New staff that stayed:	2	6%	4	12%	6	18%	4	12%

Table 6.1: New staff that left MRA in the period 1994 – 1998.

These developments had disastrous effects on the staff turn-over in the NGO sector. To illustrate the increasing staff turn-over, the figures presented above in Table 6.1 show the number of years the new staff of MRA remained with the organization between 1994 and 1998. Of a total of 33 new staff members that joined the organization from January 1994 onwards 48%[34] had left again within two years. As there was such a shortage of well-trained staff in both the government and the market sector, anyone, having gained even the slightest experience, could achieve a higher status and a better paid position outside the NGO sector. Some colleagues of those who left were quite critical about this wave of 'careerism' that hit the NGOs, as the quote at the beginning of the chapter illustrated. It was almost as if a vacuum existed out there. The pull on the best staff was very hard to resist. Moreover, although it seems positive that four members of staff remained with the organization for the full 4 years, as shown in the table, two of them had notoriously problematic and persistent low skills levels. In my view, these people did not remain with MRA because of a strong sense of loyalty, rather, they could not find positions elsewhere.

Bearing these developments in mind, in my view, any training that was received by young professionals employed by NGOs in the mid- and late nineties mainly had one effect: they would leave the organization at an even faster rate than without having been trained. In other words: capacity building of staff had the opposite effect. Instead of adding to organizational learning and improving organizational performance, it reinforced the brain drain, and, thus, harmed rather than benefited an NGO. This is what I have termed 'the capacity building trap'.

Similar mechanisms took place in the communities the NGOs worked with. As the NGOs identified the 'lack of capacity in community members' as problematic –for example, because it prevented them from running local structures effectively– 'capacity building' workshops and programmes were run in these areas. However, these training programmes quite frequently resulted in the departure of the best people. In fact, often the NGOs themselves employed the most promising youngsters. In that manner the NGOs fulfilled the same 'brain drain role' opposite community structures as the government did opposite the NGO sector. In South Africa, there was such a shortage of highly trained people, that it was, on all levels, almost impossible to retain them. For the organizations concerned the situation could be very frustrating, especially since their salary scales could hardly compete with other sectors. However, when we take a broader look, it is clear that a region like the Eastern Cape, and a country like South Africa, on a meso- and macro-level did, in fact, benefit from the capacity building efforts of NGOs. In land reform, for example, a large part of the staff of Department of Land Affairs had had its training in the NGO sector.

This strange, but understandable, 'capacity building trap' has shown investments in new staff to result in a more speedy departure of those people. However, there did not really seem to be an alternative for 'capacity building'. Not training staff was no option. Only measures of contractual obligations, whereby staff are required to sign an agreement to stay for a few years when they receive training, would have been a way out. Without such measures, capacity building may actually lead to organizational decline rather than to organizational learning and improved performance.

Internal NGO Dynamics: 'racial issues'

When discussing processes of transformation in the South African context, it is hardly possible to avoid discussing the issue of 'race'. In a society that for many decades has been extremely polarized 'racial tensions' –or tensions that are interpreted by at least one party as being 'racial'– are frequently present just below the surface of any human interaction. Even in the relatively progressive NGO circles such tensions can be encountered. Especially, in times of conflict one or more parties may interpret the problem in 'racial' terms.

Here, we focus on the way in which such 'racial' tensions surfaced during the transformation of MRA. Broadly one can say that the Monti Rural Association developed from being a white organization, run by English speaking Rhodes University academics, to being a largely black organization –with 13 out of 19 people (68%) being black– in 1997. For many this is seen, and felt, as a significant development. Nevertheless, the new director, appointed in 1997, was, again, white. He himself, however, had stated during the job interview that he was of the opinion that it was time for MRA to have its first black director. It will be explored why this did not happen. First, however, I will discuss an incident that illustrates the nature of 'racial tensions'.

The Part-time Issue

In early 1997 one of the white women –a coordinator of one of MRA's units– fell pregnant. As it was clear to her that she would not be able to combine full-time work with raising a child, she asked the MRA management whether it was possible to give her a part-time contract when she would return from maternity leave. As rumours of the pending deal spread through the organization the black staff in particular got very upset. This was reinforced by all kinds of distortions inherent in gossiping: the woman concerned would work less but receive the same pay, others would have to work harder to compensate for her absence, et cetera. During my fieldwork this conflict can be marked as one of the clearest instances where racial overtones dominated the discussions. Perceived white privileges, feelings of black inferiority and pragmatic management solutions proved to be an explosive mix.

During a management meeting[35] the staff representative –a black woman– asked critical questions about the whole procedure and suggested that the organization should come up with a part-time work policy. *"How is the process, what is the principle? Maybe we should discuss it with the whole staff if we are to come up with a policy?"* In his rather formalistic answer the director explained that people have to resign if they want a part-time position. The board can then decide to advertise the new part-time position to which the old staff member –and others– can then apply. He, furthermore, said that he was aware that in the past it had only affected white women in the organization –both the media officer and the personal assistant of the director had part-time contracts– and that a black senior member of staff had told him that *"... this was not a women's issue but a racial issue"*. Therefore, the director concluded that *"We need complete transparency"*. The critical staff representative answered him and said that transparency had indeed been a problem in the past:

> *"...what is the manager's discretion? (...) should the staff only have a say after the board decision? We need guidelines! There is the race part of this issue. How can it be extended to all races? It is not clear what happens with regard to*

her salary. What about black staff, how can it be extended to people in a lower economic situation? Blacks don't have the same economic background. Rich people can afford going down in salary...".

This last remark referred to the fact that the white women all had husbands with a steady income, while most of the black women who were working for MRA were single parents. Later on in the discussion she warned:

"How does it affect the people who are left behind in the full-time jobs[36]? It creates a controversy that possibly culminates in a race issue...".

For months the issue was on the minds of the MRA staff and indeed led to heated discussions and 'racially tainted' frictions. Many of the black staff thought it was unreasonable to give white women privileges while they already came from privileged backgrounds. The white women, of course, felt aggrieved as they believed that any person –whether white or black– should have the right to work part-time. As management was intend on keeping the valuable staff member after her return from maternity leave, a pragmatic solution was found. This was made easier by the fact that the staff member was prepared to give up her position of unit coordinator. Thus, she was offered a lower position as fieldworker on her return, with a lower remuneration according to the appropriate salary scale. For a while the conflict continued to simmer with the occasional nasty comment during staff meetings, but finally petered out.

This incident and other related conflicts in the organization prompted me to discuss the 'racial issue' with many of the (ex-)staff members. As the topic of these conversations mainly concerned the situation in the eighties, in the mid-nineties and why MRA never had a black director, I will present what people have said to me, using these headings.

The Eighties
In an interview with Jacob James, one of the early, and influential, black staff members of ARA, we talked about the early days when there was still a white committee of Rhodes academics and several employed fieldworkers of whom some were black. It was a time when interactions between whites and blacks on a level of complete equality –it was still mainly a question of master servant interaction in South Africa– were still quite unusual:

"...there were no sharp tensions between the committee and the staff. However, there were some tensions between the staff with less education and the well-educated white staff. For myself this was different, as I was of a different calibre. I could match anyone on the committee(...). For someone like Michael Ndlovu, it was quite difficult to have a white boss. One could characterize the behaviour of some of the whites as a mix of sympathy and paternalism (...). I encouraged Michael to speak out, say it when he does not like certain things...".

However, in a later stage in the interview he admitted that the paternalism which had never got to him may have been a factor in his decision to leave the organization in 1992:

"I wanted to do something else, but I also started to feel some of that paternalism. I felt that problems were developing between the white and the black staff. There were slight tensions. The blacks had become more vocal and they were dependent on my guidance. This would have led to confrontations

between myself and the white management (...). We had the feeling that nothing much was done to empower the black staff within the organization...".

May Brown, also a fieldworker during the time of Jacob James explained that the whites in NGOs were, at the time, not really focused on racial issues within their own organization:

"In the early days, issues of working together were dealt with at a fairly superficial level. We got on well, had a common purpose, but I don't think that in those days there was enough of a focus on the need for black management of NGOs. That issue only emerged later as black staff got stronger and began to develop their own sense of where their organizations should be going. This process only took place in all NLC affiliates when black staff stood up and asked: 'why is all management white?'. That question had to be asked, before the change could start being put into place...".

Another old member of staff, Catherine May, in hindsight, confirmed this lack of awareness –mainly on the part of the whites– and argued that indeed ARA had been very 'white:

"...there is an acknowledgement now that MRA had been very white and very white-controlled. People like Michael had been totally –we realized afterwards– totally overwhelmed and feeling kind of inadequate when it came to talking because he felt he wasn't articulate enough because people like us were running the organization (...). Jacob, however, was very articulate, but I remember it very clearly when Michael finally told us how he just see those umlungus^{37} and just die...".

When I asked her whether there were any racial tensions in those days she said:

"...never openly although there probably was more than we thought. But it is probably one of the least fraught organizations in that sense. Maybe if you talk to Jacob and Michael they may talk about a power imbalance. But it was never open. We actually had quite good relations...".

Thus, one can conclude that although there were never real racial tensions the whites were slightly paternalistic and complacent in the late eighties, early nineties. People had to get used to working together closely.

The Mid-Nineties

According to Mavis Beechwood, the last *coordinator* of MRA before the position was changed into a directorship, 'racial tensions' in the mid-nineties had everything to do with the fundamental transformation the organization went through from a volunteer organization to an employee-based organization. *"...ARA always had a majority of black staff while the volunteers, the committee, was white...".* As there were many more volunteers, who were all white and served on the committee, the organization was, effectively white. However, during the transformation in 1993 when the committee was replaced and ARA became an employee-based organization:

"Not only was there an internal realization, also funders were raising the issue of affirmative action (...). Therefore, when recruiting new staff in the early nineties there were conscious attempt to address the issue. However, the fact that black fieldworkers were employed also had to do with the practical issue that fieldworkers had to be able to speak Xhosa (...). The tensions were not

necessarily racial, but arose when the organization was transformed from a small to a professional organization, and a management structure, policies, procedures and systems became important.

In the view of Mavis Beechwood the situation in MRA compared favourably to the tensions that surfaced in other NLC affiliates:

"In the network there was much debate on affirmative action and a lot of tensions in other affiliates. In MRA the staff always had the sense that there were issues that needed to be worked through, but that we had managed to create an open environment where at least these issues could be raised and discussed. At that time we used to pat ourselves on the back and said that although things weren't perfect, at least they were much better than in other organizations..."

However, when talking to Bongani Matsila, who spent several years in the eighties and early nineties in an ANC camp in Tanzania and joined the organization in 1994, another image appears. According to him a very fundamental transformation took place in the mid-nineties. Under Mavis Beechwood, who was the last *coordinator*, a well-educated black manager named Debby Qongwane was appointed in 1996 to ensure the reorganization of MRA after the slack period and the subsequent crisis during 1996. When Mrs. Beechwood left the organization, Mrs. Qongwane became the acting *coordinator*. A few months later, when Mr. Eastwood became the new *Director* she was appointed as *Deputy-Director*, with several management responsibilities. However, Mrs. Qongwane left within months after she was offered a better position elsewhere.

According to Mr. Matsila the interim period when Mrs. Qongwane was acting coordinator was a crucial period in the history of the Monti Rural Association for the organization's black staff:

"...it was the first time that black people felt that they are in the ownership of the organization (...). Debby was crucial, although she was there only for a short period, she opened up a gate and people went through to see the light. It was not that previously there was a suppression of views. It just was easier to deal with her. It gave us confidence to deal with a person with the same background, being a black person as well...".

Before that period, the coordinators:

"...were white and kept the culture of the organization white despite the black staff. Whites were in strategic positions...".

As Mrs. Qongwane assumed the position of acting coordinator:

"...it made a real difference. Attitudes changed and we tested the sincerity of our white colleagues".

In his view the whole power balance in the organization shifted in that period and MRA finally stopped being a 'white organization'. Subsequently, the testing of white colleagues continued after Mrs. Qongwane had left. In Matsila's view:

"...the momentum did not drop and the staff remained more radical. Since then the people were more vocal. White privileges were challenged...".

In fact, this quote sheds gives us more information about 'the part-time issue' that was discussed above. As the issue surfaced around the time that Debby Qongwane left it coincided with the period that the black staff had become extra vocal in their critique of perceived white rights. Thus, the fact it became such a serious issue in the organization may also have been influenced by this momentum.

Besides the 'part-time issue' there were also other instances when black staff indicated a degree of uneasiness with their white colleagues. But these were more superficial in nature like casual remarks and angry outbursts –*"...the atmosphere in MRA has changed, the whites are the main problem!"*. Many of these remarks had to do with a sense that they had suffered more during apartheid, and that they had been deprived of rights and resources that 'the whites' always have access to. Thus, after the transition to democracy they felt that they had to compete with whites who, in their opinion, had been given a substantial head-start. In that light a progressive gender policy, involving the right to part-time work, could be interpreted by black staff as extending privileges to the privileged.

However, in some cases it seemed just too convenient and farfetched when people interpreted a conflict in a racial discourse. According to Ms. Yako, who became a member of the new board after she left MRA and who in that capacity became aware of the most recent 'racial tensions', these tensions were mainly caused by all the new policies that were introduced by the new director, Dudley Eastwood. In her view his skin colour made him an easy target:

> *"If I would introduce the same thing that Dudley is introducing, I would have had better reception than he has. Because of the fact that he has not really been a fieldworker (...), secondly, the fact that he is also white..."*.

In her view claiming that there is 'racial discrimination' is often the easiest way to criticize someone in South Africa:

> *"...unfortunately the problem is that people –which is a natural thing that people have when they don't agree with you and they find you too powerful for them– (...) will find something that will enable them to stand up to you. And unfortunately in this country that thing is the racial thing at the moment, and it will be like that for a couple of years, if not decades..."*.

Later on in the interview she is even more bold:

> *"...you get sympathy when you say there are racial tensions in MRA: that the mainly white management is trying to dominate you. You'll get sympathy for that anywhere you go and people would tend to believe the person who is aggrieved"*.

Without denying the fact that the African population has suffered during apartheid, as a consequence of which they have been economically, educationally and socially left behind, it must be acknowledged that the 'race issue' has become somewhat tarnished as Ms. Yako has indicated. Quite frequently, in an attempt to suppress all possibilities to have a fair discussion, the so-called 'race card' is played. As a consequence it can become rather impossible to have a fair and open discussion. To turn an ordinary conflict into a race question kills all possibilities of having an open discussion. Thus it becomes harder to find a solution.

On the other hand it needs to be acknowledged that many whites in South Africa often lack a degree of sensitivity in regard to the extent of black suffering and the way it has had an impact on their social and economic position. This lack of sensitivity can cause people to overlook the consequences of seemingly neutral policies. Moreover, many of the whites are still not able to speak the local language,

Xhosa. This is often interpreted by many blacks as lacking a true interest in African life and culture. In fact, this became somewhat of an issue in MRA, especially after the tensions around the 'part-time issue'. Therefore, it was decided that all members of staff who spoke no Xhosa would have to take a language course in 1997 and 1998.

In conclusion it is clear that in order to improve the situation of the African employees affirmative action –or positive discrimination– is needed. However, it may create new tensions as it may clash with the rainbow ideology of equality and it will keep the issue of 'race' on the agenda.

Never a Black Director

The one question that remains is why MRA never appointed a black coordinator or director. About the answer to this question most actors seem to agree. In the early days of the transition it was due to a mixture of paternalism and complacency on behalf of the white committee members, and in the mid-nineties it was due to the great 'brain drain' pressure on blacks to serve 'their people' in the government. In this regard I will discuss two people, Jacob James and Joy Molo.

Jacob James, as has been shown above and in previous chapters, had been an influential fieldworker in MRA and in later years became one of the directors in the national Department of Land Affairs in Pretoria. Already as fieldworker he transcended that position as he was a visionary and someone actively involved in the underground struggle of the ANC. Nevertheless, although he was cut out for the job, no one in the ARA committee thought of offering him the position of coordinator in 1992. According to Catherine May this had to do with the attitude of the whites who were running the organization at the time and the fact that the organization was not ready yet for the market-dominated nineties. She seems to confirm the paternalistic attitude which used to irritate Jacob James:

"Jacob's leaving was also significant in the sense that we should have foreseen –I think I used to get inklings of it... It was this lack of consciousness that the new South Africa was dawning and people were not prepared to hang around in a low paid, low status position (...). But if it had been read, Jacob ought to have been offered the position as director. But he was always the 'later person' he was the fieldworker. We were more the ones doing the documentation, the kind of thinking on funding and so on. It is hard to imagine now because he is way above all of us as chief director in DLA. To some extent we were still [sigh], what is the word, giving advice to Jacob...".

Besides this somewhat paternalistic attitudes it is important to recognize that ARA had effectively not yet left the struggle era. The organization still had a flat management structure and was not ready to create the post of director with all the necessary perks. Both factors led to the departure of Jacob James in late 1992. Within weeks he had left to become a director at Kagiso Trust, a development financing institution. According to Catherine May:

"He got head-picked so quickly and given the job of director, a car, a housing allowance and you name it and he was gone. He had played a very important role as the person who had always reminded the organization of the black side of things, the constituency out there, he was like a kind of conscience...".

In the mid-nineties it was not so much the complacency –or as Mrs. May says 'lack of consciousness'– of white staff that prevented Joy Molo to become the first black director. Rather, it was the political pressure that was exerted upon black staff by their political parties. When I asked Joy Molo why she did not become the first black director in 1996, she said:

> "...I don't know, at that time...the reason was more political than anything else. I had political responsibilities...".

You were and are an active member of the ANC?

> "Yes, and at that time my responsibilities were here at the Amatola District Council. I did apply for the position at MRA but I pulled out in the end because I thought I was raising expectations that I might not have been able to deliver on".

When you applied you were already working for Amatola?

> "Yes, you see, before I was appointed to this position as CEO[38], I was the chair, a political position for a year and a half. The ANC put pressure on me to come to the Amatola District Council...".

This is confirmed by Mavis Beechwood (it was her successor that was sought):

> "I had certainly hoped and expected –I think MRA had also hoped– that Joy would become the first black director. But she had already been appointed against her will –she was not consulted about it– as the Chairperson of the Amatola District Council (...). She was put in quite a difficult position with so much political pressure. And after much deliberation she decided that she must give that appointment a while...".

Nevertheless, Mrs. Yako did continue to play an important role in MRA as Mrs. Beechwood explained:

> "...she became an influential board member in the newly appointed board of MRA".

In fact Mrs. Beechwood sympathizes with Joy Molo's decision as she said:

> "...Joy made the right move, I do not think that anyone can stay in an NGO for ever...".

In conclusion one can say that the fact the MRA, up to now, never had a black manager had everything to do with the transformation that took place in South Africa. First, it was the combination of a kind of complacency and paternalism together with the first convulsions of the brain drain that prevented Jacob James to become the first black Director and in 1996 it was mainly the role played by the ANC in the political reality of the 'new era' that prevented Joy Molo to take up a position that she was cut out for and had gladly assumed. The best people were head-hunted and used in the new government and NGOs, that until that moment had been at the vanguard of the land sector, were now perceived by many as not influential enough and of a lower status.

Concluding, one can say that this section has shown how complicated organizational dynamics can become in an arena –the South African socio-political landscape– dominated by huge disparities between social groupings. Although politicians speak of 'the rainbow nation' and preach reconciliation, the above has shown that even in progressive circles the hurt and the inequality will continue to influence many human interactions on all levels for years to come. It will be a while before one can run an organization in the South African context without referring to the term that in the human context has no biological base: 'race'.

The above has illustrated that South African whites may not always be as sensitive as they should be as there is indeed still quite a disparity between the socio-economic position of white and black staff due to apartheid. As was shown above, this can lead to a misinterpretation of a progressive policy for working mothers as being anti-black. However, it must also be acknowledged that the 'race card' is sometimes played too easily by Africans who experience a set-back. Such misuse can be counterproductive. Not only does it complicate the possibility of having a fair discussion, it may also lead to an inflation of the term, so that real cases of racism may not get the attention they deserve. Nevertheless, managers in South African organizations need extraordinary high levels of sensitivity to be able to extinguish smouldering discontent before it can develop into a serious 'racial' bush fire. Just below the surface the hurt is still there...

Conclusion

In this chapter I have looked critically at the possibilities and impossibilities of organizational learning. Specifically, I have discussed what the transformation processes entailed in which the Monti Rural Association developed from an 'activist' organization in the eighties to a 'professional' organization in the late nineties. I believe I have shown that transformation cannot be simply captured in an evolutionary model. Organizational development is the result of messy processes, involving overlapping phases that are not always clear and easily identifiable. What is especially important to note is that NGOs, like other organizations, also go through periods of regression and crisis. Much can be unlearned during the life-span of an organization. The blunders and the failures are as much part of the history of an organization as are the victories and successes. Sadly, both the failures and the victories are no guarantee for organizational learning, which is extremely difficult.

The history of MRA has revealed several mechanisms that prevent or complicate processes of organizational learning. Firstly, the fact that staff who made mistakes leave the organization makes it harder for an organization to draw the necessary lessons. Especially the brain drain in the mid-nineties constituted a massive loss of organizational memory for the Monti Rural Association. Furthermore, some mistakes, especially tied to the idea of 'wanting to do good' are made again and again, as new staff arrive.

Secondly, some issues are simply hard to deal with, which was illustrated by the complicated 'community dynamics' in most projects, and the failure of MRA to stick to its role of facilitation. With regard to community dynamics, the 'community members' are, of course, for a large part responsible for the conflicts between them. However, the examples above have shown that the introduction of scarce resources frequently increase such tensions. The same can be said with regard to the formation of parallel structures. Again, a lesson not well learned. Moreover, the history of past interventions can complicate present interventions of an NGO. MRA, for example, had a 'tainted image' in certain areas. Furthermore, forceful NGO ideology –'gender', 'sustainability', 'community participation'– frequently failed to reduce the tensions. Rather tensions were exacerbated.

Thirdly, 'evaluations', which are often presented as the ideal instrument in 'organizational learning', should be recognized for what they are. They are not primarily learning instruments but, rather, as this chapter has confirmed, instruments that help organizations to interlink consecutive interventions and legitimize new strategies or past mistakes.

Fourthly, it was shown that 'capacity building' often has the opposite effect, especially in South Africa where there is such a shortage of well-trained professionals. I have described what I call 'the capacity building trap', a mechanism where any training received by NGO staff in the mid-nineties caused them to be more attractive for other employers. Therefore, in the mid-nineties, capacity building tended to lead to organizational decline, instead of improved organizational performance. It enabled staff to leave the organization at a faster rate.

Fifthly, it was illustrated how racial tensions still exist in the South African context, as the hurt caused by colonialism and apartheid is still present just under the surface. Even in progressive circles this can seriously complicate organizational performance. Affirmative action is needed to undo the socio-economic disparities and managers in NGOs and other organizations need to stay sensitive to issues that may provoke 'racially coloured' conflicts. Sadly, such conflicts may also be provoked by people who play the 'race card' too easily.

In conclusion it can be said that it is impossible to equate 'activism' with amateurism, commitment and inefficiency, while equating 'professionalism' solely with efficiency, effectiveness and non-commitment. NGO organizational learning is not straightforward and development interventions are always messy with an outcome that is dependent on many, often contradictory, processes.

7. The Government as Praying Mantis

Introduction

After the 'act of love' the female praying mantis rewards her male partner by biting off his head. Possibly, this gruesome image aids us to grasp what took place between the new government and the NGO sector in South Africa during the upheavals of transformation. A strong and vibrant NGO sector, that fought against apartheid in the late eighties, became a 'beacon of continuity' in the mid-nineties, was eventually left largely crippled, by a government that had become firmly established in the late nineties.

In this chapter, I focus in detail on the transforming relationship between the land sector NGOs and the first democratic government in the 1990s. In broad terms the relationship transformed from great antagonism during the 'struggle era', via rapprochement and cooperation in the 'freedom and consultation era', to mild estrangement in the 'new realism era'. As was discussed in Chapter 2, the state is the most important reference point for NGOs. Thus, in my view, the so-called autonomy of non-governmental organizations, put forward by many authors, must really be seen as 'relative autonomy'. In this chapter it will become clear which interdependencies, mechanisms and processes are involved in shaping the relationship between a land sector NGO and the government in the context of the Eastern Cape in South Africa. What is important here is to realize that 'the government' as such, of course, does not exist. Although governments frequently give the impression of the contrary, 'the government' is no monolithic structure. Besides the levels of government –national, regional and local– there are big differences between ministries and departments. Moreover, even within these government structures contrary views and practices are encountered. Like in NGOs, actors in various government structures employ different strategies to achieve their goals.

Moreover, on certain levels, in particular structures, in many legislative and policy processes, spaces exist or open up, which leave room for manoeuvre for the actors involved. This can lead to interesting cooperative arrangements between those in NGOs and those in government departments. Especially during a transition period, when fundamental transformations take place such opportunities arise. Spaces can be expected to open up when everything is in flux and new modes of operation have to be explored by a government that needs to leave its 'old ways' behind. However, as such a period draws to an end, avenues of cooperation may also be expected to close again, followed by a renewed distance between the actors involved...

NGOs as a 'Beacons of Continuity'

After Mandela's release in early 1990, the progressive forces immediately began working on their plans to fundamentally change the country, in case they would have to assume government responsibility. Moreover, many exiles returned to South Africa and everywhere think tanks were established to draft policies for 'the new South Africa'. Derek Hanekom, for example, as a white ANC member, returned from exile in Zimbabwe and took up the position of Coordinator of the ANC Land and Agricultural Desk[1]. Subsequently, he became the first Minister of Land Affairs in

1994. This 'land desk', as it was popularly called, became one of the driving forces for policy development in the land sector. In addition, on all levels and in all regions coalition partners were sought to assist in these policy development processes. The ANC, and Hanekom in particular, relied for a substantial part on the expertise that had developed in the progressive non-governmental land sector, in which the National Land Committee (NLC), and its affiliates like MRA, were dominant players. These NGOs had performed an important role in putting the plight of the rural people on the national and international political agenda, but had also built an effective network of with community organizations throughout the rural areas. To put it more boldly, the ANC regarded the NLC and its affiliates as 'comrades' who had supported the 'struggle' of 'the people' and the underground ANC.

In the early years of the transition the ANC and its alliance partners –the South African Communist Party (SACP) and the Congress of South African Trade Unions (COSATU)– realized that the structural problems in the country had to be tackled with great zeal. A fundamental turnaround was envisaged which would redress the huge inequalities that had grown in the country. For this purpose, according to Mandela, the Reconstruction and Development Programme (RDP) was formulated in a process that involved widely consulting *"...its alliance partners and other mass organizations in the wider civil society"* [2]. The whole rhetoric of the RDP constituted what I have described as a 'freedom and consultation discourse', that became dominant in progressive circles. In fact, for anthropologists of development it is clear that this kind of rhetoric is quite similar to the type of discourse that is often produced by progressive NGOs in other parts of the world. Especially in the chapter *Meeting Basic Needs* the RDP oozes this kind of NGO discourse:

> *"The RDP reflects a commitment to grassroots, bottom-up development which is owned and driven by communities and their representative organisations"* (p. 15).

Why was this type of rhetoric so dominant in government circles during the first years of the transition?

First of all it is important to point to the leftist background of the alliance partners. In such progressive circles the work of progressive NGOs was usually highly valued. Secondly, many of the think tanks for policy development, that I mentioned above, consisted for a large part of 'progressives' still employed in the NGO sector, or with an NGO background. Thirdly, it should be remembered that progressive university staff, who were also engaged in devising new policy, usually had a history of close cooperation with the South African NGO sector –like the Surplus People Project– as well. Lastly, the non-governmental organizations had played a crucial role in developing the RDP, as was acknowledged in the document itself. In fact, it was almost as if these organizations would be rewarded for their efforts:

> *"Those organizations within civil society that participated in the development of the RDP will be encouraged by an ANC government to be active in and responsible for the effective implementation of the RDP"* (p. 1).

Not only would the NGOs be 'rewarded' for their efforts in the struggle as the new government proceeded to work together closely with the NGO sector, the ANC even got directly involved in setting up new NGOs.

A high profile example became the establishment of the Land and Agriculture Policy Centre (LAPC) in February 1993. As the ANC recognized that it did not have the expertise in rural issues and that there was a great lack of reliable data concerning the situation in the rural areas, it initiated the establishment of a policy research centre. It was thought that through such a centre the policy development process would be greatly aided. According to the Executive Director's report in the LAPC publication (1996) *The First Three Years: February 1993 – February 1996*:

> "There has been a critical need for policy formulation, starting with the realisation that on rural issues at least, the African National Congress (ANC) as government in waiting, was ill-prepared to deal with challenge of government. Starting with an informal network of willing volunteers, the ANC requested the establishment of a policy research centre. A research project established the basic format of a resource centre whose task would be to manage policy research and come up with policy options to be considered by the new government" (p. 3).

Such research was badly needed, and in the first three years of its existence the LAPC became a dominant actor in the land reform arena.

Very large and meaningful research projects were commissioned by the LAPC like the *Provincial Overviews* that were produced for each new province and in which most of the land sector NGOs took part. These overviews provided the government with basic information and were funded by overseas donors, like DANIDA and OXFAM. In *Land Reform Research Phase One: provincial overview Eastern Cape*, the Monti Rural Association participated together with other regional research institutions. It was the first time that these newly defined and delineated provinces were studied. Thus, this information could be used directly by the new government in the formulation of the Land Reform Programme. Although the LAPC claimed to be independent from government, the way in which this was phrased actually seemed to illustrate a degree of interdependency:

> "From its inception, the LAPC has been an independent centre, dedicated to the formation of a democratic government" (p. 3).

Although the LAPC was founded as a Section 21 company[3], many critics claimed that it was a government department in disguise. Officially the organization had an NGO label, but in practice the organization was quite intertwined with the Department of Land Affairs (DLA). Even a high DLA official, in an interview, questioned the NGO status of the LAPC. The whole set-up served to access funds and to make the best use of NGO resources as these organizations contributed to the LAPC research. After the initial three-year period, that yielded useful LAPC reports for the new government, the significance of the organization declined as most national government departments got their own act together and many of the LAPC staff left, to work for the government or become private consultants.

The Seeds for NGO Decline

As the progressive NGOs expected much of a new ANC-led government, many of the organizations decided to engage in voter education in the months before the first democratic elections in 1994. The Monti Rural Association, for example, devoted an entire issue of its rural newsletter *Groundwork*[4] to the elections in an attempt to get as many people into the voting booths. By using cartoons and by providing clear instructions and background information MRA tried to educate as many rural voters in the Eastern Cape as possible. Although, the organization did not openly urge the people to vote for a certain party, it was aware of the fact that a greater turn-out in the rural areas would result in a stronger support for the progressive parties. Thus, it is safe to assume that the ANC election victory can partly be attributed to the efforts by NGOs like the Monti Rural Association.

This good relationship between the progressive NGOs and the progressive parties was acknowledged by the first government policy documents that were produced after the elections. The role that was envisaged for NGOs was reaffirmed. In the land sector the Green Paper on South African Land Policy (1996) became one of the most influential documents that was produced. In addition to its three-pronged approach –redistribution, restitution and tenure reform– it was a document which confirmed the role NGOs would have to play:

> *"The land reform programme emphasises the key role of the non-governmental sector in supporting rural and urban development and land reform policies. Organisations in this sector have established strong links with communities involved in land struggles and have been instrumental in enabling communities to articulate their demands for land"* (p. 78).

In fact, the relationship between Minister Hanekom and the National Land Committee became so friendly that he wrote a short section for the *NLC Annual Report January 1994 – April 1995*. This also indicated that a new relationship was evolving between the government and the NGO sector:

> *"NLC is a unique nationally-coordinated and regionally-based organization with an impressive history of working towards rural justice (...). The close rapport between NLC or NLC affiliate workers and rural communities give them a keen understanding of the dynamics at work in a community (...).The NLC head office and its affiliates continue to be vital role-players in the land reform process"* (p. 27).

Such praise and recognition, from a government that urgently needed the support of the progressive NGO sector, was the rule rather than the exception in the early years of the transition.

However, this praise and recognition also contained the seeds of NGO decline. Especially since the most important asset of these organizations was human resources. As many of the brightest characters had already played a crucial role in the policy development think tanks, where they had closely cooperated with the progressive politicians of the ANC and SACP[5], the next logical step for the new government was to offer these people positions in the new administration. In the land sector it was especially the Department of Land Affairs, in which the newly appointed Minister surrounded himself with staff that came directly from the NGO sector. Hanekom's own background, having worked with NGOs in Zimbabwe and during his ANC Land Desk work, helped him to pick some of his most influential staff from the NGO sector. These people brought with them 'an NGO frame of mind'. The list of top NGO people that joined the ranks of Hanekom's national department is almost inexhaustible. For example, Jacob James and May Brown, two former high profile MRA staff members, who featured prominently in Chapter 4, joined the Minister in

Pretoria as DLA Directors. Another example is the appointment of Geoff Budlender as Hanekom's most senior civil servant. Budlender used to be the national director of the Legal Resource Centre, a chain of progressive legal NGOs MRA had closely cooperated with in their fight against forced removals and unfair detentions.

Initially, the NGOs were quite positive about this development, as they foresaw that the new government needed the support. Moreover, it was believed that having old comrades in top positions would be beneficial to the NGO sector. As was already suggested above, by the fact that the organization had invited the Minister to contribute to their 1994 – 1995 Annual Report (1995), the NLC itself stated in the same report that the organization positively assessed Hanekom and the fact that he was surrounding himself with (ex-)NGO people:

"The appointment of Derek Hanekom, former head of the ANC's Land Desk, as Minister of Land Affairs created immediate opportunities for a more sympathetic relationship between ourselves and this department. The Minister's appointment, and that of Bahle Sibisi and Joanne Yawitch as special advisors to the Minister, was another important development since both Sibisi and Yawitch came from the ranks of the NLC" (p. 6).

The above shows that both the NGO sector and the government were positive about mutual cooperation. It fitted in with the 'freedom and consultation' discourse of the early transition, where the almost euphoric feelings on both sides, of being able to make a fresh start and try new arrangements, temporarily suspended much of the critical attitude in the NGO sector towards the government and vice versa. It was a time when comrades had just assumed power and it was believed, on both sides, that cross-fertilisation and close cooperation would produce great results. It had not yet been recognized by the NGOs that this 'cross-fertilisation' was potentially rather dangerous. In fact, their fertile top soil was about to be removed, leaving them exposed and quite barren...

Local Provincial Cooperation

Besides cooperation on the national level, new institutional arrangements between the government and the NGO sector were also pioneered in the local land sector arenas. Long before the elections, for example, high profile MRA staff members joined various ANC think tanks that did pioneering work in several policy development arenas. Jacob James –MRA staff member and an ANC member– even became the convenor of the Border ANC Land Commission, while two other MRA staff members served on the core group. Moreover, MRA participated in the Border ANC Development Forum and several other cooperative arrangements as will be discussed in the next section. In all these structures MRA worked shoulder to shoulder with those who would assume political power after the elections.

Initially, in the months following the elections, so-called 'strategic task teams' were set up –building on the contacts that had evolved before the elections– in which the relevant government departments sought cooperation with the non-governmental sector. It was in this period that an eighties struggle discourse still prevailed as is shown by the fact that the newly elected politicians and the NGO staff still called each other 'comrade'. Such language is, for example, found in a letter[6] from the

Coordinator of MRA to the MEC[7] for Land Reform and Administration in the Eastern Cape –who had also worked for an NLC affiliate:

> "...Dear Cde Ezra Sigwela, (...) We believe that in various fields related to land reform, NGOs may have a valuable contribution to make (...). We would be eager to assist Strategic Task Teams in their work on the understanding that this may involve limited secondment of NGO staff..." (p. 1).

Subsequently, indeed, these task teams were formed and MRA staff participated in most Eastern Cape task teams, like the Local Government Task Team and the Land Reform Task Team. As these were, more or less, informal arrangements –the Task Teams had no formal power, but were consultative and advisory in nature– the terminology also varied. Some called them 'task teams', while others called them 'Steering Committees'. Moreover, as the transformation processes in the policy field were also continually evolving, the subject of these task teams and steering committees also changed. For example, the Land Reform Task Team became the Pilot Steering Committee, that, subsequently, became the Eastern Cape Province Land Reform Steering Committee. For the outside observer this seemed rather confusing, for the insiders these name changes were quite 'natural' and kept pace with the changes in land reform.

The institution of the task teams or steering committees can be recognized as the start of the 'freedom and consultation era' in the Eastern Cape. It was a rather euphoric time in which the hope to be able to positively change things for the better, especially for the 'disadvantaged', dominated amongst progressives both inside and outside of government. In fact, in many arrangements the distinction 'inside' and 'outside' government became blurred. For example, after the Land Reform Pilot Programme[8] was formulated in late 1994, in some provinces NGO staff were seconded to the National Department of Land Affairs to help these provinces set up the Pilot Programme.

Thus, in the Eastern Cape the Monti Rural Association seconded John Carver to the National DLA and Thornhill and environs was designated as the Eastern Cape Pilot Area. Thus, as MRA had been an important actor in Thornhill, it became an important member of the Pilot Steering Committee. From February until August 1995 John Carver was temporarily seconded and employed by DLA. However, as MRA also continued to pay his salary, and DLA refused to pay MRA directly, Mr. Carver every month handed the DLA cheque to his organization. Through such arrangements the NGOs became quite influential in certain government programmes. The distinction between government and NGO became rather vague. However, in a later stage, the NGOs paid a price as they permanently lost many of the staff they had previously seconded. For example, in 1996 John Carver left MRA to be employed by the Provincial Department of Land Affairs.

After the Pilot Programme was abandoned the Pilot Steering Committee was transformed to become the Eastern Cape Province Land Reform Steering Committee, popularly referred to as the 'Steering Committee'.

The Eastern Cape Province Land Reform Steering Committee

As I arrived in the Eastern Cape for my fieldwork I became interested to attend these Steering Committee meetings since these were typical 'arenas of struggle'[9] where new arrangements between the government and the non-governmental sector where being tried and piloted. The way in which my request to attend the meetings was dealt with by the committee members was characteristic for the openness of those initial transition years. Through my contacts with the Monti Rural Association and the Director of the East London office of the Provincial Department of Land Affairs (DLA) I was invited to come along to a Steering Committee meeting in May 1997. First, I was introduced to the people present by the Director of the East London Office of DLA and I was asked to explain my motives for being there and to explain broadly the scope of my research. Having done that I was asked to leave the room in order to give the meeting the chance to openly discuss my request. After my return the Chairman told me it had been decided that I would be welcome to attend the Steering Committee meetings as *"...the new South African government wished to be transparent"*. Moreover, it was explained to me that the Steering Committee *"...was not a statutory body but the people attended voluntarily"*. Lastly, I was told that it was expected of me to deal carefully with sensitive information. After that –as in all South African meetings– everyone introduced him- or herself. From that moment onwards, until the committee ceased to exist I was regarded as an observer who was placed on the list of Steering Committee members and who had the right to receive all relevant documents, minutes and invitations. An example of 'the new South Africa' at work.

To avoid misunderstanding, I want to make clear that such arrangements as the task teams and the steering committees, were not only instituted to facilitate government-NGO cooperation. Perhaps the most important role of these 'arenas of struggle' –'arenas of cooperation' may be a better term in the context of the South African transition– was to facilitate the cooperation and exchange of information between different government structures and levels. As the early years of the transition called for an unprecedented need of new policy in all kinds of overlapping government arenas, these steering committees were usually the loci where the different government departments were able to share ideas and experiences in relatively informal settings. Draft policy documents were shared and discussed, solutions to bottle-necks were put forward and ideas on 'fast-tracking' procedures were suggested. Sometimes the discussions were extremely detailed, at other times the discussions were much more fundamental. Moreover, at all times the NGOs were able to put forward their ideas and points of view. Some of the provincial departments that were regularly represented in the Steering Committee were the Department of Land Affairs, the Department of Housing and Local Government, the Department of Water Affairs and Forestry (DWAF), the Department of Agriculture and Land Affairs and representatives from departmental monitoring and evaluation structures. Moreover, officials of the Eastern Cape Socio-Economic Consultative Council (ECSECC) regularly attended. The NGOs that were usually present were the Monti Rural Association, The Umtata Land Committee (ULC) and the Port Elizabeth Rural Association (PERA).

An example of an exchange and subsequent clarification[10], to illustrate the type of discussions in the Steering Committee, concerned the 15,000 rand subsidy that the poor could access from the Department of Land Affairs to purchase land and build structures. This subsidy became the basis of the Land Reform Programme as it provided 'the poor' with the means to access land in a *willing-buyer willing-seller* approach. According to the Monti Rural Association representative Margaret Johnson, however,:

> "In Isidenge[11] the Department of Housing and Local Government officials stated that they would pay the whole 15,000 rand grant. We find that strange because the implication is that the Department of Housing is actually paying for the acquisition of land".

John Carver, the Department of Land Affairs representative explained:

> "At the national level the subsidies that each department provides are linked. The total sum to be accessed by the beneficiaries cannot total more than 15,000 rand. The Department of Finance and the Housing officials in East London do not seem to have the information...".

Subsequently, in the weeks following the Housing and Local Government officials who were present in the Steering Committee were able to sort this confusion out. Thus, a question tabled by an NGO served to clarify the policy and procedures in the relevant government departments. Many of such similar exchanges were witnessed by me in which government departments revisited their position and certain policies or procedures. Sometimes it took weeks or months to sort out the confusion and clarify certain issues. Frequently, it constituted true policy pioneering.

In another meeting[12] several officials of the Department of Land Affairs reported about their experiences at an important yearly national review of the Department of Land Affairs Redistribution Programme, one of the three pillars of the Land Reform Programme. According to John Carver:

> "The Minister gave us the message that we should try to be more realistic. We should make clear choices and ask ourselves when a project looks good in writing and whether that same project will still look good after 6 months, 9 months or 12 months...".

In that same discussion a phrase from the secretariat report[13] raised the eyebrows of the NGOs present:

> "...in fact increased emphasis is being placed by the Minister on quality rather than quantity and taking into account the different needs of different categories of beneficiaries..." (p. 2)

This was received very critically by the NGOs as they felt that the 'poorest of the poor', in their view the most important category of beneficiaries for land reform, were slowly being abandoned by the Minister and exchanged for economically stronger beneficiaries:

> "What about the poorest of the poor, what is the department's thinking on that category?"

The DLA Director reacted:

> "The Green Paper states that the poorest of the poor are targeted for land reform, all we are saying is that we may also allow other beneficiaries with one leg in an economic sphere".

This was followed by a plea of the NGOs not to leave 'the poorest of the poor' behind. Through such interventions the NGOs critically monitored the progress in the policy development process. Thus, as a result of cooperating closely with these organizations the government was forced to be accountable in an early policy formulation stage to civil society actors.

In conclusion it can be said that the Steering Committee served as an important forum, to exchange ideas and to get answers to various questions, for all actors involved. The NGOs devoted much of their time and energy and, thus, resources to be constructive actors in the policy development process and the government was made to be accountable in an early stage. However, in the course of 1997, as the 'freedom and consultation' era drew ended, the meetings were progressively badly attended and completely ceased at the end of the year. Nevertheless, the NGOs and the government departments stayed in touch and cooperated in projects, building upon the rapport that had been established during the Steering Committee years. However, the contact between NGOs and government became much more formalized, as the government became much more government and the NGOs became NGOs again. However, in the local government arena the NGOs continued to play a supportive role much longer, as will be discussed in the next section.

MRA and Rural Local Government: a 'beacon of continuity'
Besides contributing to the steering committee there were other institutional arrangements in which the Monti Rural Association took part. The organization operated on the level of the provincial government, but also on the district level and the lower municipal and community levels. In my opinion, the NGOs in the land sector became 'beacons of continuity' on all these levels during the processes of the formation of rural local government structures. As the government sector was completely restructured and rearranged after the transition to democratic rule, in a way, the NGOs became the 'constants'. Of course, the NGOs were confronted by great upheavals and accelerated transformation processes as well, but especially in the early years of the transition the NGOs in the land sector could act as 'beacons of continuity' as the big 'brain drain' in the NGO sector had not yet reached its peak.

Following the transition to democratic rule, the ANC leaders made it their priority to fill the vacant posts at the national the provincial level. As these were the most influential –and high status– positions it automatically caused high potential and powerful local leaders to leave the grassroots for those positions. Subsequently, the local institutional levels came to be deprived of the best people. In fact, it constituted a true 'brain drain' at the local level. Especially in areas such as the Eastern Cape, where the black population had never before assumed political nor bureaucratic responsibilities, the lack of well-trained and educated people became quite problematic as new institutions had to be formed. Both on the district level and on the municipal level it led to poorly functioning institutions. On the lowest levels, in the communities the situation was not much better. These were exactly the levels where the new government hoped the non-governmental organizations could play a useful role. And they did. The Monti Rural Association, for example, became very active in that respect in the Border area of the Eastern Cape. The constructive roles played by the organization with regard to rural local government could be captured under various headings: research, policy design and advice, and training.

Already in 1989 the Monti Rural Association –then still ARA– participated in a research project on the Ciskei where issues of local government were one area of interest. By May 1991, when the process of transition to democratic rule was on its way, MRA partook in the Local Government Policy Project (LOGOPOP) that was initiated by the ANC in order to develop policy with regard to rural local government that would serve the future government. Moreover, a MRA researcher served on the Border ANC Local Government Commission which looked at the concrete situation in the Border area of the Eastern Cape. In late 1993 the Monti Rural Association then proceeded to form a Local Government Unit to bundle all activities with regard to local government. In its *Monti Rural Association Proposal 1994 – 1997* this step was elucidated:

> "*MRA believes (...) that unless strong local government that is responsible to the needs of the people on the ground is developed over the next few years, the prospects for meaningful development and lasting peace in the region will be greatly reduced. MRA feels that as the only NGO within the region addressing the issue of rural local government, it has a significant contribution to make...*" (p. 36).

It was a political decision to vigorously support the move to democracy during a time when the balance could shift either way, since the conservative forces in the country were still strong. Through research projects and sitting on the various policy developing committees the organization was able to provide support and resources aiding the progressive forces to determine the future government's position on the shape and structure of local government.

Building upon this pre-election work, MRA took part in the Eastern Cape Local Government Coordinating Committee that was formed by the provincial authorities after the elections. According to the MRA *Annual Report January 1994 – April 1995* (1995c) this important structure comprised of:

> "*...various local government stakeholders including representation from political parties, SANCO, Regional Service Councils (RSCs), agricultural unions, traditional leaders, Parliamentary Standing Committee on Local Government and Gender Commission*" (p. 15).

It led the organization to ask itself questions with regard to their cooperative role vis á vis the government:

> "*...because policy formation in partnership with government is a new experience for NGOs such as MRA...*" (p. 15).

Especially since many staff members felt that the organization played quite a directive role. However, it was decided that this work was of the utmost importance and in line with the *Monti Rural Association Proposal 1994 – 1997* and , thus, had to be continued. According to the *Annual Report January – December 1995* (1995a), several agreements were reached in the Eastern Cape Local Government Coordinating Committee in 1995. First, the structure of rural local government in the province was designed with regard to the boundaries and the number of District Councils and Primary Local Authorities (i.e. TLCs, TRCs and TRepCs). Moreover, the framework for the establishment of District Councils with regard to budgets, personnel and infrastructure was agreed upon. And, lastly, the interest groups to participate in Transitional Representative Councils (TRepCs) –new rural local government structures with mainly a representative function in areas with too little administrative and financial capacity to have more powers devolved to them– were determined (p. 17). After this important groundwork the Committee was disbanded by the end of the year as it had achieved what it had set out to do.

As it was now clear what shape local government would take in the province, the Local Government Unit concentrated most of its energy on developing training material and on training local councillors, so that these new government officials would be instructed in the tasks they would have to perform.

Training New Local Government Officials

Following the local government elections in late 1995 the Local Government Unit of MRA started its Councillor Induction Programme. As the unit realized that covering the whole province, with their self-developed training module, would be an impossible task, it decided to train trainers first. Therefore, it brought together a group of potential training providers of two other NGOs and the government sanctioned Eastern Cape Training Board. As this proved to be a success, the Department of Local Government committed itself to coordinating activities and providing back-up support. Thus, MRA trained trainers who could each train future councillors. For the Eastern Cape government this was an ideal set-up as they themselves grappled with a tremendous shortage of capacity. Without the expertise and the resources of NGOs like MRA it would have been much more difficult, if not impossible, to get the new local government structures running in the province. Thus, as the Monti Rural Association had developed the expertise over a period of 5-6 years, it acted as a 'beacon of continuity' in the local government arena.

Not only did the organization play a crucial role by training people, but it also provided the new local government structures with well-trained staff from its own organization, as the brain drain continued. Although the local government structures benefited, this presented the Local Government Unit with its own problems in 1996 as the coordinator of the unit and another prominent staff member left MRA to take up positions in the new government. The unit coordinator, because of her local government expertise, was appointed by the ANC to become chairperson of the Amatola District council –the district with East London as capital– that played a pivotal role in the province. Again, a somewhat cynical reward for the good work MRA had delivered in the process of establishing local government structures and staff in the province. Expertise and resources, ultimately, led to organizational decline.

Nevertheless, the unit was able to continue its training work since a New Zealand volunteer joined the organization. He took it upon himself to train two counterparts within MRA who would be able to run the Local Government Unit after he would return home. The two trainers who were appointed were promising bright men from two communities MRA had worked with. This is a clear example of the 'capacity building trap' I described in Chapter 7. The government lacked capacity and appointed the coordinator of the unit as chair of the Amatola District Council and subsequently the gap left by her was filled by two bright young men who would be sorely missed in their own communities.

Examples of some of the training modules developed by MRA were *An Introduction to operating within the Statuary Requirements of Government*, *An Introduction to Local Government Finance* and *An introduction to Writing Development Projects*. Initially the unit especially targeted the emergent Transitional Representative Councils (TRepCs). However, as the unit, subsequently, became increasingly successful it also trained District Council councillors. By using the Christmas tree model whereby the unit trained its own staff and trained trainers throughout the province, and allowed anyone who attended a training course at MRA, including government staff, to use MRA training modules, the unit was able to reach thousands of new local government councillors across the whole province. Again, the organization invested much of its resources to transfer its expertise in the local government field to the new local government officials. According to a HUVO[14] evaluation (1996):

> "...*there is ample evidence to illustrate that the activities undertaken by staff from MRA's Local Government Unit made a visible and important contribution to local government policy and training in the Eastern Cape*" (p. 28).

According to the Monti Rural Association (1996b) *Annual Report 1996*, an important success in this regard was the recognition the unit received from the government:

> "...*it is significant that all courses designed to date have been accredited by the Government Training Board and conducted throughout the Eastern Cape*" (p. 28).

By accrediting the courses designed by MRA and sending the newly appointed councillors to attend these courses, the Eastern Cape government endorsed the excellent work done by this NGO.

By the turn of the century, the local government support work was continuing but the local government unit had been amalgamated with the organization's administration unit. This decision was taken as the local government arena, more or less, took its final shape[15]. Thus, MRA believed that besides its training programme it was of little use to devote much of its time and resources to local government policy development, where no longer a big impact was to be expected.

In conclusion it can be said that the organization proved to be a resource base and a 'beacon of continuity' for the new government. In the early years of the transition it contributed its resources to most policy development think tanks and after the transition to democratic rule it developed training modules, trained trainers and implemented a councillor training programme. Moreover, MRA contributed the best staff to government structures in the subsequent 'brain drain' whereby sixty percent of the staff left the organization between 1995 and 1996[16]. Financially, the organization never got in trouble as it retained most of its funders. For other NGOs, in the health sector for example, the picture became much bleaker as these NGOs not only lost staff but also lost most of their funders which transferred their funds to the now legitimate government. In the next section I explore how the NGOs and the government slowly drifted apart in the late nineties.

Lobbying 'Comrades' in the Late Nineties

During my fieldwork in 1997 I was able to study closely the so-called 'Farm worker[17] Campaign' as it unfolded in the Eastern Cape. This campaign aimed to influence the outcome of a political and legislative process to upgrade the tenure rights of farm workers. Thus, it proved to be an ideal opportunity to investigate the lobbying and advocacy endeavours by NGOs at the end of almost a decade of transformation. Since I was given the same amount of access as in the case of the Eastern Cape Land Reform Steering Committee, it meant that I could study closely the interactions between NGO staff, new government officials and the farm workers concerned in a period in which each institutional actor was withdrawing into its original niche.

I hope to show that although the organizers of the campaign –the NGOs, the government departments and the labour unions– were still quite close, as many had similar political and NGO backgrounds, the political processes at the end of the nineties had become much more formalized. Although there still appeared to be 'windows of opportunity' and 'room for manoeuvre' it became clear during the campaign that the days seemed over in which fundamental political and legal changes could be achieved. 'New Realism' had set in on most fronts and closed many avenues that had been open in the early days of the transition. True legislative pioneering had become a thing of the past. It left NGOs with a bitter aftertaste and prompted them to rethink their position vis à vis the government and their former comrades.

Background of the Farm Worker Campaign

In South Africa approximately 1,2 million farm worker households[18] –that is approximately five to six million people– live and work on commercial farms. For many the farm became their home for generations. People are born and die on farms, since they were alienated from the land of their ancestors as a result of the apartheid laws that aimed to create a cheap labour force. Although slavery does not formally exist in South Africa, many of these farm workers live and work under harsh circumstances for extremely low wages. An annual wage of US $ 200 is no exception. Most of the commercial farms are still owned by white farmers and many instances have been reported whereby these 'masters' still interfere in the most basic spheres of human life. Besides instances of corporal punishment, there are, for example, known cases when women, children and other family members were not allowed on the farm, or where workers had no rights to be visited by friends. However, the lack of rights of farm workers is most clearly illustrated by the arbitrariness of evictions. Frequently, when a farmer is faced by economic hardship or when there is friction between the farmer and his workers, farm workers are evicted from their jobs. But because the farm worker and family members are completely dependent on the farm for an income, a roof over their head and other sources of livelihood, the loss of a job has even more far-reaching effects than for an urban employee. The farm worker and his or her family members stand to lose everything.

As the new government recognized the predicament of farm workers it was decided that these people had to be protected through legislation. Therefore, in June 1996 the process to draft the *Extension of Security of Tenure Bill* was initiated. In accordance with the 'freedom and consultation discourse' the Department of Land Affairs invited the 'stakeholders' concerned to participate in the initial negotiations on what to include and exclude in such legislation. Representatives from land sector and legal NGOs, agricultural labour unions, academic institutions and white commercial farmer unions were invited to take part in the negotiations and contribute submissions. The initial negotiations did not go so well as some parties interpreted the problem in diametrically opposing ways. The commercial farmers –represented by the South African Agricultural Union (SAAU)– believed that existing labour relations legislation was sufficient to cover their relationship with workers and, thus, did not deem new legislation necessary. Moreover, they felt protected by the property clause in the constitution that was drafted to protect private (land) ownership. Meanwhile, the National Land Committee and its affiliates held that new tenure legislation should be more far-reaching in order to give farm workers ownership rights to the commercial farmland they lived on. In fact, the NLC hoped that the outcome of this tenure legislative process would have redistributive effects whereby portions of white farmland –in their view the white farms had historically been stolen from the black population– would be awarded to farm workers. As a result, the progress in the negotiations was slow.

In February 1997 the Minister of Land Affairs gazetted the first draft of the bill of which the most important hallmarks were:

- A Farmer intending to evict a worker must give two months written notice to the farm worker and the Director-General of the Department of Land Affairs of the intention to apply for an eviction order from the Magistrate Courts;
- It is illegal to evict occupiers without a good reason, unless alternative accommodation has been secured by the worker;
- An eviction is prohibited when a farm worker has occupied the farm for twenty years or longer and when he/she has reached the age of fifty-five, or when a worker has become disabled;
- When a farm worker dies, his/her family have 12 months to find alternative accommodation.

As the interested parties were so far apart in the negotiations, the first draft of the bill led to an outcry from both sides of the political spectrum.

According to the Monti Rural Association (1997d) the legislation, effectively, only regulated evictions and did not positively award farm occupiers tenure rights. Thus, it was stated that *"...the Bill's title is a misnomer: it does not extend tenure security to farm dwellers..."* (p. 3). The commercial farmers, on the other hand, felt that they lost the rights to determine what to do with their own land. According to a spokesman, *"the land tenure bill attempts to kill a fly with a sledge hammer..."*[19]. Moreover, the farmers protested the radio advertisements that accompanied the gazetting of the bill and which were meant to conscientize farm workers and make them report evictions. As the farmer uproar was very loud, the government withdrew the information campaign. On the whole the Minister was unhappy with the strong reactions on both sides and stated:

> *"The draft legislation proposes a two-pronged solution to the problem –to prevent unfair evictions and to create alternatives which provide people with independent land rights. It reflects a choice to regulate the relationship between owners and occupiers rather than upgrade the rights of occupiers*

into ownership. As such we thought it would be a relief to land owners. We know it has been a disappointment to NGOs representing landless people"[20].

In other words, the bill focused on regulating the problem of evictions, rather than awarding occupiers positive ownership rights. However, as can be expected when any new legislation is in the making, the drafting process itself and the rumours it generated led to exactly the opposite: a storm of evictions all over South Africa. Farmers chose to get rid of superfluous farm dwellers before the new legislation was enacted. As a result the government accused the farmers to have acted in bad faith and the situation got rather polarized. In that polarized situation a period started of intense lobbying from both sides of the spectrum.

The Campaign

In October 1996 the National Land Committee launched its *Land Rights for Farm Dwellers Campaign* that became popularly known as the *Farm Worker Campaign*. Besides lobbying the government at the national level and participating in the negotiations on the draft bill, the NLC stimulated its affiliates in the provinces to take up the glove. Especially since it was deemed necessary to reach as many farm workers as possible. As the draft bill came out in February 1997 there were only a few months left to make an impact. By August 1997 the bill would have to be introduced in the Parliamentary Land Affairs Portfolio Committee and subsequently passed by the National Assembly. Next, by late 1997 the bill would have to be passed by the National Council of Provinces[21] and signed by the President to become an act. In the Eastern Cape the campaign took off in May – June 1997.

One could say that the land sector NGOs involved in the campaign had three broad aims. First and foremost the progressive NGOs, pragmatically, strived to get as many positive amendments written into the bill in order to improve the rights of farm workers. Second, they endeavoured to realize a fundamental turn-around in the bill, so that, eventually, the Extension of Security of Tenure Act (ESTA) would have redistributive effects. This would help to off-set the –so far– disappointing results of the Land Reform Programme. Lastly, the campaign was meant to become the new starting point of a broad rural social movement, in order to (re-)focus political attention on the plight of the rural poor.

When Joe Porter, the NLC Chairman, came to brief the progressive forces in the Eastern Cape he stated:

"...it will be difficult to change the bill without strengthening the lobbying process tenfold and involve the farm workers (...). The political weight is not there, we should lobby the ANC to push for much more. In all provinces we should get the farm workers involved...".[22]

The meeting shared his judgement on the situation especially as someone else explained that:

"The white farmers are united and vigorous...".

Everyone present at the meeting tried to come up with the best ideas of how to make the strongest impact. Significantly, a high official of the Provincial Department of Land Affairs also attended and gave tactical advice:

"...target the members of the Parliamentary Land Affairs Portfolio Committee who will visit the Eastern Cape on the 30th of June and try to bring a group of farm workers to that meeting...".

This idea from a 'comrade' in government was embraced by the others attending the meeting. Additionally, it was decided to reach as many farm workers in the Eastern Cape as possible and to try and gather them in one large conference that would create a lot of publicity and carry political weight. At the end of the meeting a core group was put together that would drive the Farm Worker Campaign in the Eastern Cape. On that core group the following organizations and government departments were represented:

1. The Monti Rural Association (MRA);
2. The Port Elizabeth Rural Association (PERA);
3. The Umtata Land Committee (ULC);
4. The provincial Department of Land Affairs (DLA);
5. The South African Council of Churches (SACC);
6. The ANC Provincial Land Desk;
7. The Eastern Cape Socio-Economic Consultative Council (ECSECC).

A few weeks later a member of the secretariat of the Eastern Cape NGO Coalition (EGNGOC) joined the core group and became a very active member. Moreover, on an ad hoc basis, other organizations regularly attended the campaign meetings, like the Legal Resources Centre, several Advice Offices[23] in the province, and several black agricultural labour unions. For the 'moral weight' of the campaign it was significant that the churches had become involved.

When analyzing this list, several facts emerge with respect to the links with government. What is especially striking is the fact that a government department –the Department of Land Affairs– is involved in a campaign to lobby the government. In that regard, the presence of the ANC and ECSECC is also significant. The chair of the ANC Land Desk in the province had very close links with his ANC colleagues in power, as these were his old 'struggle' comrades. The significance of ECSECC needs some explanation. As was illustrated in Chapter 3, ECSECC is a provincial structure that is tailored after NEDLAC on the national level, where labour, business, government and NGO representatives come together to discuss and advise the cabinet. When ECSECC was established, only government, labour and business were represented. Subsequently, the Eastern Cape NGO Coalition joined the partnership. ECSECC is one of these advisory structures that cannot be described as a government department, nor as a non-governmental organization. Nevertheless, although it is largely financed by the government and closely linked to the Eastern Cape Premier's office, its secretariat mainly consists of ex-NGO staff and other progressives. Consequently, ECSECC is a progressive force that is generally inclined to support socially and environmentally friendly processes in the province[24]. As ECSECC, along with MRA, became the most important facilitator of the campaign, its involvement ensured easy access to the Premier's office, who originally had a farm worker background. As will be shown the ECSECC staff did everything in their power – behind the scenes– to secure a favourable outcome for farm workers. Officially, however, it kept up its appearance of representing business as well. In short, one can say that the NGOs and the government cooperated closely in the campaign.

Set-up
Basically the campaign was a five-tier campaign. First, all the organizations concerned conducted as many workshops as possible, 'deep' in the rural areas in order to reach as many of the 'unreachable' –most farm workers rarely venture into the outside world– farm workers. On a large number of farms the organizations were not welcome, and, thus, the workshops were organized on 'neutral' ground like primary school buildings. Secondly, a small delegation of about twenty farm workers from different Eastern Cape areas was assembled and brought to the Eastern Cape Legislature where they could meet with the national Parliamentary Land Affairs Portfolio Committee which was touring the country in an attempt to assess the merits and flaws of the bill. Thirdly, a large conference –the 'Capacity Building Conference'– was organized in centrally-located Grahamstown, where 450 farm workers were assembled. It involved a massive and logistically difficult operation to enable the farm workers to discuss the bill, make their voices heard and adopt resolutions. Fourthly, those resolutions, were taken by a group of farm workers and NGO staff to Cape Town where they presented their submission at a public hearing of the Parliamentary Land Affairs Portfolio Committee. Fifthly, the organizations involved tried to hold on to the Eastern Cape momentum by rallying support from high level Eastern Cape politicians, with the aim to hold a Provincial Land Summit. Another step in organizing a broad rural social movement.

In the workshops at the grassroots level emotional encounters took place with people who hardly had a history of contact with outside agencies. Some told their stories[25]:

> *"...we are a family of customs. When our extended family visits us on the farm, the farmer chases them away with the help of the police...".*

Or:

> *"...when a farmer wants to get rid of you, he causes an overload in your work. Of course you then makes mistakes. As a result he chases you away saying that you did this or that...".*

And:

> *"...we work for so little salary, some of us get only 20 rand per month[26]...".*

Moreover, an elderly man ended:

> *"...it was a good workshop, we wish other organizations would interact the way you interacted with us. Don't worry about our answers, we are not used to discuss such matters...".*

As a researcher it was truly extraordinary to witness these exchanges with people who were clearly marked by decades of oppression. In total about 1500 Eastern Cape farm workers were reached in the campaign. Quite an achievement if one takes into account how hard it is to reach this group.

When the Parliamentary Land Affairs Portfolio Committee visited the Eastern Cape, a meeting was organized in the Legislature. The portfolio committee members had just returned from a meeting with the Eastern Cape commercial farmers and appeared quite aloof and somewhat indifferent. After a presentation by a lady farm worker from Cintsa, who argued that *"...evictions should be sanctioned by a forum which had representatives from all groups, including farm workers"*, the portfolio committee chairperson stated that the problem of evictions may not be as great as portrayed by the farm workers and that hardly any figures were available about the number of evictions in the country. Thus, in their view it was of the utmost importance to set up a well-functioning monitoring system in order to be able to collect reliable data on evictions.

Rightly so, this angered Bishop David Russell of the Anglican Church, who was present at the meeting and who had fought his whole life against apartheid, *"...although I am here to represent myself, I am here to see to it that the people are heard..."*. He argued that the bill should not be called the Extension of Security of Tenure Bill, *"...because it does not provide tenure security for farm workers"*. Moreover, he accused the portfolio committee of the fact that *"...we heard two attempts from you to articulate the opinion of farmers"*. Furthermore, he stated that it was utter nonsense to collect data on evictions because:

> *"...we all know what is going on. Parliament should make a mark and make the evictions stop. Listen to what is said: Singamaxhoba okufuduswa[27]!"*.

Although everyone present was touched by the speech of Bishop Russell, the meeting left a bitter aftertaste for the delegates as they clearly felt that the parliamentarians could not as easily be influenced as they had hoped.

Nevertheless, although there was some disappointment –having friends in government did no longer seem to make a great impact– the build-up to the Grahamstown conference was taken up with energy. Organizing the conference in Grahamstown proved to be a huge task that required inputs from all organizations and government departments concerned. However, especially the Department of Land Affairs and the Agricultural Labour Unions left the work for others to finish. While DLA seemed to have other priorities and seemed quite happy that the NGOs and ECSECC did most of the work, the labour unions seemed to be chronically understaffed. Thus, most of the organizational work in the Eastern Cape was left in the hands of the three land sector NGOs –of which MRA was the most active– and ECSECC.

With regard to the topic of this chapter ECSECC is an interesting actor in this whole process. As was explained above, ECSECC is a forum where business, labour, the government and the NGO-coalition discussed, researched and advised on relevant development issues for the Eastern Cape. Its secretariat staff quite often found themselves in a dilemma as ECSECC would officially have to represent all four partners, but the staff were more sympathetic towards 'the poor' and, thus, towards progressive NGO goals. In the Farm Worker Campaign this loyalty problem was strategically circumvented. First of all, business representatives were not invited to the Farm Worker Campaign meetings as they were hostile to the idea of advising farm workers of their rights. However, as ECSECC officially represented the four parties, the ECSECC secretariat unfolded its strategy in a meeting preparing for the Grahamstown Conference:

> *"...in our proposal you will see that we have introduced the notion of a 'Capacity Building Conference'. It is an organizing conference, but we have decided to call it a 'Capacity Building Conference' because, otherwise, we can't sell it to business that we are engaged in preparing an organizing conference..."*[28].

Thus, choosing a somewhat deceptive name for the conference was a deliberate strategy to conceal the fact that the progressive staff of ECSECC together with their former NGO comrades were engaged in fighting the commercial farmers.

Moreover, in several meetings it was made clear that the Premier of the Eastern Cape was on their side as he was one of the few high level ANC politicians who *"...pushes rural issues"* and *"...the government is like a dinosaur: difficult to mobilize..."*[29]. However, it appeared that the contacts between the ECSECC secretariat and the ANC Land Desk Chair on the one side and the Premier's office on the other were mainly informal. This came to light when, in a campaign meeting, a suggestion was made that prominent politicians should publicly sign a petition, or a position statement, against evictions and for amendments to the Extension of Security of Tenure Bill with the press present. An ECSECC official remarked:

"...we can't force the politicians or embarrass them publicly, especially when a position statement is against the official government position..."[30].

At the end of the whole campaign it was clearly revealed how difficult it had actually become for the campaign staff to find a government representative who would publicly support the campaign efforts, as will be revealed below. The support from high ANC officials in the Eastern Cape remained limited to tacit support.

The Grahamstown 'Capacity Building Conference'

Nevertheless, the 'Capacity Building Conference' became a huge success, especially from the point of view of reaching and gathering so many farm workers in one place. Over 400 farm dwellers were transported to Grahamstown, a famous settler town in the Eastern Cape, where, for two days they listened to speeches and actively discussed elements of the bill in various commissions. The people slept in the dormitories of a secondary school which was in recess. There seemed to be a lot of energy in the air and songs were sung by the whole crowd:

"...Sisebenza ezifama kanzima!
Sizebenzela imali encane!"
("...We work on the farms,
we work for little money!")

In the commissions, each chaired by staff of the organizers, possible amendments to the bill were discussed with groups of about forty farm workers. However, the discussions often led to issues beyond the scope of the bill and the limits set by the convenors:

"We demand an end to oppression!"
"We should educate ourselves".
"Expropriation should be the priority of the government to make land available..."

Nevertheless, the organizers distilled a list of resolutions which began by re-stating that the farm workers still stood by the resolutions of the Land Charter taken at the Community Land Conference that the land sector NGOs had organized in 1994. Other demands in the submission read:

1. *"We demand rights to land and a moratorium on evictions (...);*
2. *Agri-villages (...) should not be used as dumping grounds by farmers (...);*
3. *The rights of women should be equal to that of men (...);*

>   4. *The prohibition on evictions should not be limited to a farm dweller having worked on the farm for 20 years (...) and having reached the age of 60 years (...);*

followed by many other technicalities and:

>   11. *"The Land Claims Commission should address farm dwellers' claims up until 1913*[31]*";*

Lastly, the submission ended with a very strong statement:

>   15. *"(...) We demand that land be expropriated and redistributed to the landless. One farmer one farm*[32]*".*

Of course, as was admitted to me by prominent staff members of the Monti Rural Association, the submission had largely been prepared by the NGO staff who organized the campaign. Although they used many of the opinions gathered on the ground during the months of workshopping and during the conference, the submission was not the original work of the farm workers.

The next day, a delegation left for Cape Town to address the Parliament. According to a MRA employee:

> *"...we expect the government to pay heed to our calls. There is no way that they will not listen to us –we are a force to be reckoned with...".*

In Cape Town the delegation addressed the public hearing of the Parliamentary Land Affairs Portfolio Committee, and that was the end of it. The waiting began and the expectations were still high.

In the mean time, the campaign core group in the Eastern Cape attempted to sustain the campaign through a series of meetings with high level Eastern Cape politicians in order to secure their support for a Provincial Land Summit and a broad rural social movement. However, it did seem as if the energy released during the Capacity Building Conference in Grahamstown and the fact that the Extension of Security of Tenure Bill was now in the last, formal stages of the legislative process – beyond the reach of the public arena– caused a loss of momentum. The people involved did not seem as motivated anymore, especially since each organization involved also had their usual activities and responsibilities to attend to which had been put on hold during the campaign. Nevertheless, a meeting with the Premier of the Eastern Cape, Mr. Makhenkesi Stofile, and with the MEC for Agriculture and Land Affairs, Max Mamase, a few weeks later, followed.

The 'New Realism Discourse' of the Eastern Cape Premier

The idea of meeting with two of the most influential politicians in the province was fuelled by a desire of the campaign staff to urge Mr. Stofile and Mr. Mamase to speak out publicly in favour of farm worker rights and against evictions. However, tacit assistance and in-chamber support proved to be one thing, public support proved to be another. The meeting with the Premier –attended by about twenty people; no press– was very well prepared and a slick multi-media presentation about the campaign was put together.

After the presentation, Michael Ndlovu, a MRA staff member, gave short speech in an informal atmosphere in which he made clear what was expected of the Premier:

> "We want to ask the government to make it clear that it does not support evictions (...). We are asking the Premier to follow the example of the Free State Premier[33] in terms of coming out very clearly to support the demands made by rural people, particularly farm workers (...).
> We get the impression that the government favours the position of organized agriculture (...). We feel that this is not right and that the government should always be biased to our position as the disadvantaged people [were the ones] who put our government into place..."[34].

It was a speech delivered among former comrades of the struggle. Although everyone present seemed to agree on the necessity to protect farm workers, only each actor's formal position –NGOs on the one side, ruling party politicians and bureaucrats on the other– left different options open for manoeuvre.

In his answer the Premier addressed his 'comrades' in a jovial manner. It was, for example, significant that he often used 'we' to express his solidarity. However, he did not give the campaign core group what they had come for. Here, I will present relatively large excerpts from his forty-five minute speech as they perfectly illustrate the growing distance between 'comrades' that remained in the NGO sector and those who had assumed government power and who got caught between competing forces:

> "Comrades, I want to congratulate the organizers with the campaign in the Eastern Cape, a province where in the mid-twentieth century people were active in the rural areas. I praise you, we have reclaimed an area where we have been pioneers before (...). I want to express my appreciation that you have actually involved the farm workers themselves (...). You have our support (...).
>
> I hear Mike saying that he wants me to emulate the Premier of the Free State. However, long before he was active I was already campaigning for these issues (...). Comrades let us make an effort at this point of time to provide sustained support (...). I agree that there is a need for the vocalization of that support (...).
>
> However, we must also intensify our lobby efforts. That is where SAAU has the upper hand to the Farm Worker Campaign. The NGOs and the churches don't go to Cape Town in order to lobby in the passages of parliament. That is where the battle is won (...). So I am saying to you comrades: get out there and lobby. Unfortunately, or should I say fortunately, we now live in a parliamentary democracy. The struggle is lost or won by what comes through the national assembly. That is why lobbying is an absolute necessity (...).
>
> The constitutional drafting process, that is where we really lost, as a matter of fact. That is why all these new acts are watered down. They cannot go beyond the property clause in the constitution. We lost that (...)".

Furthermore, he proceeded to explain that it is hard to stand up to the farmers as they have strong lawyers and vocal parliamentarians:

> "...we must be very careful not to threaten to do what we cannot achieve (...). The constitution gives our judiciary absolute autonomy. What the Supreme Court says will not be influenced by our anger or how much we disagree with

> *it (...). However, it is no license for us to do nothing. Therefore it is important that you keep us informed and abreast on these issues.*
>
> *Lastly, I want to pledge my unqualified support for this initiative (...). The idea of having a Land Summit is important. The sooner the better (...). It can help to inform us of what to do with state land in the province".*

However, in spite of his promising speech, in the following weeks the Premier never made a public statement against evictions and in favour of the campaign. His support remained tacit.

When analyzing the Premier's speech, there are several things that stand out. First, his rhetoric can be characterized as fitting in with the 'struggle discourse' of the eighties and early nineties. He calls everyone present 'comrades' and addresses people by their first name as he did with Michael Ndlovu. Obviously, the people present had a 'struggle history' together. To emphasize this, he continually spoke in a 'we-mode', as if it was still the struggle era where the enemy was clear. 'We' against 'them'. However, as a clever politician he also made it clear that his hands were tied – by the judiciary and the new constitution– and that his new position in government did not leave him much room for manoeuvre. Lastly, it became clear that the 'new realism discourse' had permeated his argument as he explained to his audience that the days of the struggle were over – *"...we now live in a parliamentary democracy..."*– and that in fact the old modes of activism, like 'mass action', were not longer suitable as they did not yield the desired results in the 'new South Africa'. In other words he said: this is how we in government nowadays do things. Under the new dispensation, and constitution, only through lobbying in the dark passages of Parliament could the ideals of the past be realized. Thus, while on the surface he maintained solidarity by employing struggle discourse terminology, he, in fact, clearly distanced himself from his former comrades and urged them to change their ways.

Nevertheless, although his analysis served his own purpose, in my view, the Premier confronted the campaign organizers with a weak spot in their campaign. Indeed, the campaign had been a campaign suited for the 'struggle era' where mass action made an impact. Lobbying parliamentarians and responsible politicians on a large scale and in a sustained manner had not taken place. In that regard the commercial farmers, and the SAAU in particular, had been much more active. They had gathered decades of parliamentary lobby experience during the apartheid era, while the progressive NGOs only had gathered 'struggle' experience. Moreover the commercial farmers represented an economic power base that yielded foreign exchange. That is why when the amended bill became an act, it became clear that the farmers had made the strongest impact. Although the progressive land sector NGOs also claimed the victory –MRA's *Groundwork*[35] came out with the headline *"Victory for farm dwellers"*– most insiders admitted to me that they had failed to achieve what they had set out to achieve.

Thus, the Extension of Security of Tenure Act (ESTA) ended up mainly regulating evictions. However, some details were positively amended. For example:

- the length of stay on the farm exempting people from evictions was reduced from 20 years to 10 years. However, the age above which evictions were illegal was increased from 55 years to 60 years;

- farmers should give 12 calendar months written notice;
- the right to evict can only be granted if an offence is committed by farm workers;
- the onus was shifted from the occupier to the farmer to find alternative accommodation.

Nevertheless, the Farm Worker Campaign organizers failed to fundamentally alter the bill. Furthermore, they failed to create an additional avenue to redistribute land through ESTA. Moreover, although the Capacity Building Conference in Grahamstown generated a lot of energy, the campaign was not sustained and, as a result, no broad rural social movement took off in the Eastern Cape.

Moreover, the organizers failed to prompt the Eastern Cape politicians to publicly announce their support and, subsequently, the Provincial Land Summit failed to materialize. In that regard the meeting with MEC for Agriculture and Land Affairs, Max Mamase, really disappointed the campaign staff as he seemed quite ignorant on the content of the Act and the only suggestion he came up with was:

"We should have workshops to popularize the Act (...). Each and every farm worker should be made aware of the Act..."[36].

In his view the land sector NGOs would have a role to play in such workshops.

Concluding, one can say that the NGOs involved largely failed to achieve what they had set out to do. However, for a relative outsider it became quite apparent that their expectations had been too high and not too realistic. They had already become somewhat side-lined by their old comrades in government, they had intervened too late in the legislative process, and had not used the suitable methods. The 'struggle instruments' employed were no longer appropriate in the late nineties. Furthermore, it became apparent that their old comrades in government merely envisaged a role for them in the 'implementation arena'. Like Mr. Mamase, the Provincial Department of Land Affairs mainly saw a future role for the land sector NGOs in the implementation of ESTA, by setting up a monitoring network in the province and by a continued involvement in the efforts to make farm workers aware of their rights. Throughout the Farm Worker Campaign the DLA staff had slowly withdrawn themselves from the core group. That was the type of relationship the 'government comrades' envisaged in the late nineties: the NGOs assisting the government departments in implementation wherever the government lacked the capacity to do the job itself. In the 'new realism era', in the eyes of the government, the non-governmental sector would be contracted to implement government policy, rather than being that critical and annoying partner in development. There was certainly government pressure on the NGOs to become what Korten (1990) has called Public Service Contractors. For the NGOs concerned it became a struggle not to fall in this trap. In the next section, another aspect of this struggle will be examined.

Trapped by the Government's 'Market-oriented Embrace'

By the late nineties, from 1997 onwards, the new government had become firmly established and a 'new realism discourse' was sweeping through the government ranks. As was suggested in the previous section, the government regained its more 'traditional' position. With that I mean that the euphoria of the early years of the transition seemed to be over. Although much of the 'freedom and consultation' rhetoric seemed to have survived –still popular were terms like 'stakeholder consultation', 'bottom-up development' and 'empowerment of the disadvantaged'– a certain 'nineties cynicism' seemed to take hold of most government officials. After years of frequently slow progress because of long drawn out consultation procedures, developing-new-policy-as-we-go-along and much legal wrangling, the government was heavily criticized by its constituents for the lack of delivery. Many of these delays –whether in housing or in land delivery– were not necessarily caused by the NGO sector, but by government departments that were not up to their tasks. The government became notorious for its general lack of capacity and the lack of progress did cause the government departments to be less enthusiastic about long drawn out consultation procedures.

With the pressure of delivery, it all seemed too burdensome. Furthermore, the longer the ex-NGO staff were active in government, the more many of them distanced themselves from the NGO sector. Some grew out to become the fiercest NGO critics, not unlike European middle-aged ex-leftists who are among the fiercest critics of their 'foolish' past. Of course, as the NGO sector was having to deal with the consequences of the 'brain drain', the sector did not exactly flourish in the late nineties. Thus, regularly, projects undertaken by NGOs from the mid-nineties onwards failed as the NGOs were no longer up to the task. Quite often, therefore, the criticism by government officials seemed well-founded. However, the NGOs not only failed to perform because the NGOs were suffering a serious brain drain, but also because the terms under which these projects were to be realized were fundamentally flawed.

As was explained in Chapter 3, the new government chose to implement the Land Reform Programme by adopting a *willing-buyer willing-seller* approach, in order not to antagonize white business. Thus, the RDP-informed *rights-based approach* –black people have the right to regain access to the most fundamental resources like water and land after decades of deprivation– became contaminated by and entangled with a *market driven approach*. Subsequently, the dominance of this thinking only increased when the macro-economic programme GEAR was launched in 1996 and a 'new realism' discourse took hold of politics. As a result, in most of the land reform projects where NGOs were employed by the government to facilitate the redistribution or restitution of land to African communities, the NGOs were compelled, by means of the terms of reference, to take into account a commercial or market-oriented component.

Thus, in my analysis, both the NGOs and the communities came to be caught in a 'market-oriented embrace' by the government, as was shown in Chapter 5. As a result of this embrace the seeds of project-failure were planted in an early stage. In fact, in most cases success was hardly possible. As the subsidy scheme was seriously inadequate[37], large numbers of households were 'forced' to pool their resources in order to buy white farms or access other tracts of land. The Communal Property Associations (CPAs) that were formed in this manner were usually not sustainable as conflicts arose over the rights to and the say over resources. Moreover, these CPAs lacked the resources to finance the necessary investments. Of course, the participating non-governmental organizations made their share of mistakes as well. Little knowledge by NGOs about the background of community dynamics, working with 'elites' and little experience with (commercial) agriculture decreased the chance of success in already difficult settings. In a research report by the Northern Action Association (NAA) –*Communal Property Associations in the Field* (1997)– these problems were identified:

> "...*this research has (...) shown that more attention should be given to the extremely complex social and institutional environment within which CPAs are being created. In the absence of a thorough understanding of this context (...) CPAs will probably not evolve as sustainable land-holding institutions*" (p. 27).

This is exactly what was illustrated by the Gallawater A case in Chapter 6. Yet, it must be acknowledged that the fundamental problems of the *willing-buyer willing-seller* approach combined with an uncritical mid-nineties post-apartheid euphoria can be said to have had the most devastating effects on these early land reform projects. It reduced the chances of success to almost zero.

In turn, these early land reform failures had a strong and detrimental impact on the relationship between the Department of Land Affairs (DLA) and the land sector NGOs, as was shown in Chapter 5, where the Gasela case was discussed. DLA, after having witnessed the initial land reform failures like Gallawater A, in which the department also played a role, became weary of transferring prime agricultural land to poor communities. DLA policy was informed by *the property clause* and the *willing-buyer willing-seller* approach in the Land Reform Programme, but it also blamed many of the initial failures on the involvement of NGOs. As a result, it took another direction, and in the case of Gasela, therefore, the department 'forced' MRA to re-write its proposal for land transfer to the community. Consequently, it became a proposal to establish an agri-village, based on commercial considerations. In that regard the case is illustrative of the tightening grip –a 'market-oriented embrace'– of the government on the land sector NGOs. Not 'rights' but 'the market' seemed to have become the norm.

Subsequently, the frictions between the Monti Rural Association and DLA increased in the Eastern Cape. In fact, it led to mild estrangement. According to MRA's (1999) *Six-monthly Report: January to June 1999*, these frictions even led to a crisis in the relationship:

> "*MRA's relationship with the provincial office of the Department of Land Affairs (DLA) remained fraught (...). For this reason we made use of a meeting between NLC and DLA in Pretoria on 26 March to table the difficulties and request national intervention. This paid dividends as the provincial office invited MRA to a bilateral meeting on 30 April. At this meeting it was decided to institutionalise bilateral meetings between the provincial office and the three NLC affiliates in the province (...).*
> *While certain differences between MRA and provincial DLA have yet to be resolved, the recent attempts to improve the relationship have certainly seen channels of communication opening up...*" (p. 4).

What made it especially painful for the MRA staff, was the fact that their former director, John Carver, who had become the Director of the Provincial DLA office, headed the department with which they experienced so much trouble. The time to rely blindly on old 'comrades' in government seemed over. Interestingly, the solution, instituting bilaterals, was reminiscent of the Land Reform Steering Committee that had been abandoned a year earlier. Thus, apparently, the loss of regular contact had increased the frictions.

By the late nineties the government had exchanged its RDP-inspired 'rights-based approach' for a GEAR-dominated 'market-oriented approach'. Government departments preferred to employ the NGOs as implementation agencies of government programmes. The NGO sector, however, was slower to react to the impact of the market and attempted to hold on much longer to their rights-based ideals. In fact, most NGOs remained determined to guard or (re-)extend their role beyond simply implementing government programmes, as the Farm Worker Campaign illustrated. Nevertheless, it seemed hard to escape the impact of the market in the late nineties. In the next chapter I will elaborate this impact further by exploring issues of sustainability, the role of donors, and the increased competition with private consultants.

Conclusion

In the 'usual' scheme of things NGOs are said to belong to civil society, while government structures belong to the realm of the state, notwithstanding overlaps and grey areas. This chapter, however, has revealed that much more fundamental shifts between the two realms took place during the storm of transformation that raged in South Africa.

During the struggle era, the two realms were, of course, diametrically opposed. A vibrant and well-developed civil society fought the state where it could. However, in the late struggle era and the early freedom and consultation days, the NGOs together with progressive politicians and returning exiles, became involved, both nationally and locally, in policy development processes. This resulted in interesting new cooperative arrangements, and new policy documents, like the RDP, that came to reflect a new role envisaged for NGOs. NGO staff took up seats in so-called 'strategic task teams', or 'steering committees', and on all levels in all fields new policies, rudimentary laws and innovative procedures were formulated, designed, and debated. Not only did the ANC stimulate NGO involvement in policy development, influential people within the party even proceeded to establish an NGO, in the shape of the Land and Agriculture Policy Centre (LAPC). Moreover, the NGO sector, in turn, proceeded to second people to government structures. In retrospect, one can say that, during this period, civil society and the state almost became one in certain fields. In the land sector civil society infiltrated the government where it could. Also during the first democratic elections progressive civil society actors became involved in aiding the progressive parties to come to power. However, instead of the situation returning to 'normal', after the elections, the boundaries increased to blur between the land sector NGOs and the government.

Not only did NGOs continue their work in the 'steering committees', they were also invited to cooperate in stakeholder forums and in more institutionalized settings like the Land Reform Pilot Programme. However, land sector NGOs even went a step further when the organizations got involved in training government personnel. As the capacity of the new government was low and confusion predominated in a sector in which nearly every law, policy and institutional arrangement came to be restructured, the government came to lean heavily on the institutional memory of NGO staff. In this period, the NGOs became, what I have called, *beacons of continuity* for a government that was about to run aground on the cliffs of transformation. Again, civil society and the state moved closer. However, like the female praying mantis, the government sector seemed insatiable as it continued to gobble up NGO personnel, being employed on a permanent basis. Not only did the Minister of Land Affairs surround himself with ex-NGO staff, also on the lower Provincial and District levels NGO personnel was offered well-paid positions. Initially, the non-governmental sector welcomed these developments as it was believed that 'comrades' in influential positions would mean easier access to the structures of power. However, as the depletion of NGO resources –especially human resources– became increasingly problematic, it was realized that the new government –like the female praying mantis– actually preyed on NGOs. Now it was no longer possible to say that civil society was infiltrating government. It seemed as if civil society had become largely emptied of its most precious resource: people. By late 1996 civil society was left largely crippled.

In the years that followed, the room for manoeuvre of 'comrades' in government became increasingly determined by the limitations set by their new positions, the new legislation, policies, and procedures that were established. The state had re-found its strength while civil society had been severely weakened. Moreover, those who had remained behind in the NGO sector became increasingly uncomfortable with their uncritical role. Moreover, as the example of the Farm Worker Campaign has shown, the NGOs increasingly had to confront the fact that their modes of operation, in lobbying and advocacy, stemmed from the 'struggle era' and were no longer suitable in the 'new realism era'. As the Eastern Cape Premier made clear, lobbying successes were no longer achieved through organizing protest marches and capacity building conferences. Thus, not only had civil society been robbed of its most precious resource, it also had to face that its modus operandi was no longer effective. The NGOs, and civil society in general, were in a crisis.

Not only had the government depleted NGO resources and become decreasingly responsive to NGO demands, also the impact of new realism progressively complicated the relationship. In my view several government departments, like the Department of Land Affairs, came to hold the NGO-sector in, what I have termed, a *market-oriented embrace*. The government had traded its RDP-informed rights-based approach for a much more dominant GEAR-informed market-oriented approach. Increasingly, the NGOs were confronted by the pressure to limit their role to implementation agents for the government. However, as the land sector NGOs did not value such a one-dimensional role, frictions occurred and a period of mild estrangement followed. Thus, the relationship had almost turned full circle. Although overlaps remained, the state and civil society –still much weakened– came to occupy positions opposite each other again.

8. The Impact of 'New Realism' and the Role of Donors

Introduction
This chapter deals with the increasingly dominant impact of the 'new realism era' on the non-governmental sector in South Africa. In the late 1990s it seemed as if the land sector NGOs were bombarded from all sides with a new realism discourse. All actors with which the land sector NGOs were dealing with were increasingly using 'the market' as a point of reference. As I have shown in the past chapters, the policy processes of government departments, like the Department of Land Affairs, became increasingly informed by GEAR. As a result of this 'market-oriented embrace', NGOs increasingly had to adapt their approach, as the Gasela case has illustrated. In this chapter I explore whether the relationship with donors had similar effects. Did donors also push the NGO sector in a certain direction? And if so, does it still make sense that NGOs are frequently described as non-profit organizations?

Moreover, other elements of the relationship between donors –especially Northern non-governmental funding organizations (NGFOs)– and local NGOs will be examined. In that relationship these Northern NGOs act as donors, since they channel Northern state and private funds to their NGO partners in the South. It is my intention to probe beyond the 'partner and counterpart rhetoric', in order to investigate what type of interdependencies have developed. Moreover, I intend to examine how these donors reconcile their fund-raising image at home, which is linked to the 'programme' that they want to see realized, with the image of 'partnership' and 'non-interference' that they normally display in Southern development settings?

Lastly, I discuss whether a certain blurring of the boundaries between private consultants and land sector NGOs can be detected. Since land sector NGOs, like MRA, increasingly took on government contracts in the mid- and late nineties, these organizations came to perform similar tasks as private consultants. Besides outright competition between NGOs and consultants, also cooperative arrangements evolved. Thus, I try to determine whether NGOs have a fundamentally different approach and whether a certain amount of cross-pollination took place in the late nineties.

The Impact of 'New Realism': MRA's sustainability drive
During the struggle era the Albany Rural Association was mainly run by volunteers and for its resources the organization was largely dependent on donor funds. According to Jack Green, one of the early committee members, the first funds came from Norway. However, as the apartheid regime was not keen on an active opposition movement, supported by foreign donors, it tried to control the flows of donor money. As a consequence, both the foreign funders and the NGOs in South Africa had to become creative in channelling the funds. Stories about foreigners carrying money-loaded suitcases across deserted borders abound. In the case of MRA the method was less spectacular. As Jack Green recounts[1]:

> "...we hosted the embassy or the consul of Norway and the money came via the Lutheran Church of Norway. But as the [apartheid] government wanted to control the money we had to make it look as if we were contracted by the Church of Norway. In that manner it was not a gift but we were paid for work

done. In the end legal complications forced the Norwegians to establish their own local organization in Cape Town called OFSC, the Organization For Social Change, in order to be able to monitor the ins and outs of the frequently changing legislation. When the state made a legal move to try to control the money, we made a counter move...".

For many years such foreign funds allowed the organization to function and to expand. It was only during the early years of the transformation that the Monti Rural Association attracted the first government funds. For example, when MRA staff was seconded to the Department of Land Affairs and when the first government contracts were carried out.

In subsequent years the importance of South African government contracts increased, especially in the 'freedom and consultation era' when ties of close cooperation between the NGOs and government developed. Nevertheless, donor funds remained vital for the organization especially as the lobbying and advocacy work had to be financed. In the late nineties the donors[2] were:

- the Organization For Social Change (OFSC);
- Sweden Supports Africa (SSA);
- Ford Group;
- HUVO and the Embassy of the Netherlands;
- Donorfund;
- Open Society Foundation of South Africa;
- Oxfam UK;
- Swiss Development Agency (SDA);
- New Zealand Volunteers (NZV);
- War on Want[3].

According to the *1997 Annual Report* the Monti Rural Association (1997c) received 79% of its income from foreign funders. Out of a total income of R. 3,143,399[4] the organization received R. 2,485,303 in grants and donations. Thus, the organization was still highly dependent on (foreign) donors in the late nineties. Therefore, the rumours that funders would pull out of South Africa after the year 2000 created much unrest and even a slight panic in MRA. Moreover, another major source of income came under attack as it appeared that Voluntary Associations would have to pay tax on interest earned. Since the Monti Rural Association annually earned a substantial sum of interest –R. 265,714[5]– on its reserve, the management of the organization also became concerned with changing the organization's legal status, to be able to apply for tax exemption. As a result, the issue of 'sustainability' came to dominate the agenda of the NGO in 1997 and 1998.

Already in the early stages of the transformation the Monti Rural Association staff contemplated the future of funding in 'the new South Africa'. For example, in a MRA Meeting in early 1994 the following issues were raised:

"A lot of foreign funders might move into bilateral funding with the ANC to fund the reconstruction development process (...). Local NGOs [are] criticised [in South Africa] on over-relying on foreign funding. Maybe raise 10% locally (...).

>   *Need to start recovering some of the costs. Difficult to recover from clients. Need to know how to price our services (...).*
>   *This costing business seems to be driving NGOs to be more market-oriented and product-oriented...* (p. 13-14)[6].

Although in those days the catchword 'sustainability' had not surfaced yet –in the 1994 Planning and Evaluation document the terms 'sustainable' or 'sustainability' were not used once!– the discussions clearly covered the same ground as in later years. In fact, early minutes of meetings and interviews with MRA staff revealed that 'the sustainability question' –how to survive if funding decreased– regularly dominated the agenda of the organization.

However, it was not until 1997, when the organization had attracted Dudley Eastwood as its first director[7] and was increasingly faced with rumours about a declining funding situation in the post-2000 era, that serious action was undertaken. A crucial first step was the organization of a Funders Summit, that was followed by a Draft Sustainability Plan and a Financial Sustainability Review. The latter was conducted by a consultant. Subsequently, the organization was fundamentally overhauled and restructured in line with the new sustainability insights. Lastly, the legal status of MRA was changed.

The Funders Summit

As it appeared, through informal contacts with donors, that the funding situation might indeed deteriorate substantially after the year 2000, the Monti Rural Association management proceeded to organize, what it called, a 'Funders Summit'. In order to gather sound information on the future of funding and attempt to harmonize reporting requirements, representatives of the donor organizations that funded MRA were invited to attend a two-day workshop in Johannesburg. The information gathered would then serve as a basis for a draft sustainability plan. In NGO-speak this was typically a *pro-active* move. Not the funders, but the funded took the initiative to meet. Amongst others, HUVO, the Dutch Embassy, OFSC, SSA and SDA attended.

During the summit the Monti Rural Association first unfolded its ideas with respect to its future direction and envisaged structure of the organization. Moreover it was explained how *"...different funders require statements at different times, e.g. quarterly, six-monthly or annually..."*[8] (p. 2), which complicated the smooth running of the organization. *"Different funders require statements at different times, e.g. quarterly, six-monthly or annually..."*[9] (p. 2). Subsequently, every funder then proceeded to elucidate what the future held in store with respect to funding MRA. Moreover, each funder clarified its reporting requirements. According to the proceedings of the workshop the Swiss Development Agency (SDA), for example, made clear that *"...SDA's support in South Africa is limited to the transition period, probably to 1999 or 2000"* (p. 5). Moreover, Sweden Supports Africa (SSA) explained that it:

>   *"...it receives money from the [Swedish] government for land reform and media work. This might be the case for a further two years. Thereafter it is unlikely to continue..."* (p. 6).

However, the Dutch Embassy and HUVO indicated that funding after the turn of the century would probably continue, although possibly only for the first years of the century.

When all donors had presented their case it became clear that MRA could, indeed, no longer rely blindly on foreign funding after the year 2000. As a result, the director concluded that although he had previously held the view:

"...that talk about the withdrawal of donors from South Africa after 1999 was exaggerated. It is now clear that this is a reality and MRA will have to plan accordingly..." (p. 13).

In fact, the MRA management returned quite shaken from the Funders Summit as they were now convinced that the funding situation would deteriorate dramatically in the years to come. Subsequently, much of the director's energy in late 1997 and early 1998 was devoted to the sustainability question.

However, with regard to the reporting requirements the summit ended on a positive note as the donors acknowledged that it was too complicated for MRA to have to satisfy funders' demands for different reporting formats and times. Together, MRA and the funders agreed that:

"...within the framework of a three year strategic plan, MRA will prepare:
- a January to June report, with a deadline of August
- an Annual report, with a deadline of March / April
- annual operational plans by the end of November of the previous year" (p. 12).

With that obstacle out of the way it was now crucial to improve the 'sustainability' of the organization.

The Draft Sustainability Plan and the Financial Sustainability Review

When discussing the issue of 'sustainability' it makes sense to determine what is meant by the term. The term became immensely popular –a 'sustainability discourse' literally conquered the development world– after the publication of the *Bruntland Report*[10] in the late eighties. It refers to a mode of production in which no –or fewer– non-renewable resources are used in order to diminish negative ecological impact. For example, with respect to energy use, 'sustainability' refers to a system whereby no non-renewable energy sources –like coal or oil– are used. It is about systems that are self-sustaining: input and output would have to be balanced. However, as with many such terms in the past it was appropriated by a variety of actors, and in the process different meanings emerged. Therefore, it is always important to assess critically who is using the term and how it is used. In this respect I agree with Escobar (1995) who is critical about the widespread appropriation of a sustainable development discourse. In that light he points out that "...*discourses do not replace each other completely but build upon each other as layers that can be only partly separated*" (p. 195).

In the NGO world a 'sustainability discourse' also became immensely popular in the nineties. Yet, as was shown earlier, the term had not surfaced in an organization like MRA before 1995. Although it came to mean different things to different NGO actors, the term frequently came to be entwined with the 'participation' and 'empowerment' rhetoric. Authors claimed that 'bottom-up' was sustainable, while 'top down' development was not. It was important to reduce the dependency of grassroots communities. However, it was often conveniently forgotten that NGO intervention could also be considered external intervention. In fact, frequently, such empowerment exercises led to an increased dependency on NGOs.

Within the Monti Rural Association the management team was quite outspoken about its use of the term 'sustainability'[11]:

> *"Organizational sustainability is much broader than financial sustainability. To be sustainable, MRA will have to be not only efficient but also effective. (...) it should be emphasized that this document is only one aspect of MRA's embrace of the sustainability challenge, namely that component which relates to financial forward planning"* (p. 1).

However, in the months that followed this rather narrow definition of sustainability, namely financial sustainability, continued to dominate the reports, plans and discussions in MRA. In this regard two remarks should be made. One, financial survival of the organization —in the new terminology: 'sustainability'— had always been an important focus of attention as it touched the core of the organization. Without financially security MRA ceases to exist. Therefore, the more recent and comprehensive sustainability rhetoric —'organizational sustainability'— would always be subordinated to the financial situation of the organization. Second, as Escobar argued, it was not that a more comprehensive sustainable development would entirely replace an 'older' 'financial sustainability' discourse. In fact, one noticed certain layers in the organization's sustainability discourse. And for a certain period at least, financial sustainability continued to dominate the agenda, especially as concern grew about the future of funding. In fact, the aim of becoming a financially sustainable organization was strongly linked to reducing its dependency on foreign funders.

After the Funders Summit had produced the necessary clarity with respect to foreign funding, MRA (1997f) produced a Draft Sustainability Plan. First, the plan reiterated the conclusion of the summit:

> *"...1999/2000 will probably be a financial watershed for the organization. Much of our current funding originates from foreign governments which regard South Africa as 'a country in transition'. The transition is scheduled to end at the turn of the century"* (p. 1).

Second, based on MRA's communications with funders and with the other National Land Committee affiliates, the plan spelled out what additional points had emerged:

> 2. *"Thus far, NGOs have not been successful in accessing the 'social responsibility' budgets of the private sector (...).*
> 3. *There are a variety of new opportunities to recover costs and/or generate income"* (p. 1).

This analysis led the organization to draw up an overall sustainability goal:

> *"MRA is on a sound financial footing going into the 21st century"* (p. 2).

As the director of the organization put it in an interview, *"...it is in the interest of funders that MRA becomes sustainable in the long term"*[12]. To achieve that higher degree of financial sustainability, the Draft Sustainability Plan mentioned four strategies: fund-raising, cost recovery or income generation, cost reduction and investment.

Fund-raising
Analyzing the Draft Sustainability Plan, it is most significant that, although it was the organization's aim to reduce its level of dependency on foreign funders, the Monti Rural Association never envisaged to become completely funder-independent. Therefore, I specifically questioned the director in an interview[13] whether the ultimate goal was to become *"...wholly independent from funders..."*? His answer was clear. *"We could never be. Only less dependent"*. In fact, he explained that there was no desire to get rid of foreign funding:

> *"We would prefer to retain our funders. We have chosen to keep our political profile. Advocacy is important and we need money for that. If that falls away, we might as well become private sector. Although I acknowledge that there are companies with morals, it is not about advocacy: 'a better life for all' (laughs)...".*

Furthermore, besides aiming to retain foreign donor support, the organization's fund-raising objectives also entailed to *"...proactively explore opportunities to access funding from South Africa sources, both corporations and the public"* (p. 3). One of the ways to become more attractive to domestic funders and the government, as outlined in the Draft Sustainability Plan, was to change the legal status of the organization into a Section 21 Company, as will be discussed below.

Cost Recovery or Income Generation
According to the Draft Sustainability Plan the cost recovery, or income generation, route would be the most important pillar of the sustainability drive. The idea was to build up a reserve *"...through contract work for government"* (p. 3). However, the organization would have to choose between two options: cost recovery or income generation:

> ***Option 1: Cost Recovery** –MRA costs its contract work (...) we cover our costs but do not generate surplus or profit. In this case, the practice would be that we would finance projects through core funding and transfer contract fees into our reserve account (...).*
>
> ***Option 2: Income Generation** –MRA costs its contract projects to cover costs and generate surplus income. In this approach MRA separates contract and core monies. We would not use core money to undertake contract work. The profits generated through contracts would be saved in the reserve account..."* (p. 4).

Although in 1997 the organization decided to pursue the cost recovery route, a year later the income generation route was adopted.

Especially since it was realized that there was only little distinction between the two. For example, the Monti Rural Association Director stated in an interview[14]:

> *"...it can be viewed as a false distinction. What is covering costs? For example, I would say: training costs should be included in project costs".*

Theoretically, only the income generation option leads to making a profit in the classical sense. However, indirectly, the building up of a reserve through cost recovery also leads to making a profit. Both amassing extra income through interest and through productive investments can be seen as for-profit activities. What was more important, however, was the recognition of management that a choice for either option would not involve a complete move to the private sector, as was stated in the Draft Sustainability Plan. *"MRA does not intend dealing with the sustainability challenge by jumping from the NGO sector into the private sector..."* (p. 4). In fact, the organization realized that it would remain dependent on funding. However, a conscious decision was taken to move away from being project funded. Core funding would leave more control in the hands of MRA.

In order to understand these options better, it may be useful to discuss what is meant by 'core funding'. Core funding refers to a donor-NGO relationship whereby the donor does not provide funds for specific projects, but where the donor provides the organization with a lump sum. This money can then be allocated by the NGO itself to organizational needs and to whatever projects it deems necessary. While project funding is rigid, core funding is much more flexible and leaves the responsibility in the hands of the local NGO.

In late 1997 the Monti Rural Association management made it clear that it would try to completely move away from being project funded. As the director indicated in a meeting in late 1997[15]:

"...we need to build up reserves so that we can survive independently (...). We want funders for core funding. We don't want project funding (...). It is a conscious decision".

According to the MRA Draft Sustainability Plan:

"...core funding is given to enable an organization to function, in order to fulfil its mission statement, not to undertake any specific work" (p 4.).

This led the Monti Rural Association to argue that the system of using core funds to run the organization, while at the same time building up a reserve, should be regarded as acceptable:

"...it is in the direct interests of MRA's core funders that we should be financially sustainable" (p. 5).

In the view of MRA management, core funding combined with taking on government contracts could not be termed 'double funding', especially since the reserve would ensure the future sustainability of the organization. Only if donors funded a specific project, while that project was also financed through (government) contracts did MRA describe it as being double funded.

Concluding, I would argue that it makes little sense to describe the Monti Rural Association as a *non-profit* agency. Although it is not the principal aim, NGOs like MRA do enter the market realm in order to make a profit. The only difference with 'true' private sector actors is that the surplus is ploughed back into the organization's other non-profit activities. In fact, the *Financial Sustainability Review Monti Rural Association* by Cannon (1997), a hired consultant, was quite blunt about these *for-profit* possibilities:

"MRA may need to reassess how it thinks of profit. Under current legislation, NGOs are permitted to generate income provided the surplus is ploughed back into non-profit activities. Thus, adding a percentage above costs which could be used for areas that will not be funded once donor funds are gone (i.e. staff development, organizational strengthening) would not be considered making a profit" (p. 8).

Thus, according to the consultant, making a profit would not be considered as such under current legislation. In my view, however, it should be recognized that making a profit is simply making a profit, whether or not it is reinvested in non-profit activities.

In the Draft Sustainability Plan other prospects for cost recovery were also explored:

> "MRA currently finances its training work through conventional funding. If possible, we should move away from this situation, to one where training projects are conducted through contractual arrangements" (p. 5).

The Sustainability Review by Cannon (1997) took the cost recovery strategies with respect to training a step further:

> "...charging some fees for services provided to communities and training groups should be considered as an option for the future" (p. 8).

Whether the Monti Rural Association will ultimately go as far as charging the communities it works with for services provided remains to be seen.

Nevertheless, the Draft Sustainability Plan suggested ways to become more market-oriented in its media strategy, by marketing its newsletter *Groundwork* internationally and *"...look into cost recovery through advertisement and other means"*. Moreover, it was believed that cost recovery in the research arena could also yield possible benefits:

> "...research undertaken for purposes other than community-based projects should be appropriately packaged and marketed for income generation purposes" p. 6).

This quote, again, poignantly made clear that a market discourse had definitely taken hold of this so-called 'non-profit' agency.

Cost Reduction

A third strategy involved improving the financial sustainability of the organization through cost reduction. By producing the same quality and quantity of work while incurring fewer costs the financial sustainability of the organization could be improved. However, the Draft Sustainability Plan suggested that there was only limited scope for cost reduction measures since *"...salaries constitute the bulk of our budget"* (p. 6). In my view this was a strange argument, because improved labour-time efficiency could, in fact, result in extensive cost reductions. This was confirmed by the Sustainability Review by Cannon (1997) which showed that the Monti Rural Association frequently underestimated the number of hours required to complete a project. Therefore *"...outside contracts taken on by MRA have not produced a profit"* (p. 6). However, one can seriously question whether it is a matter of underestimating the amount of work or whether it is a matter of not performing as efficiently as the organization expected.

Cannon also seems to disagree with the conclusion in the Draft Sustainability report that there is little scope for improvement in other areas. In fact, she states that within the Monti Rural Association *"...a culture of savings and efficient use of resources hasn't been developed"* (p. 4). Therefore she advises that *"the organizational budget needs to be shifted to a cost centre[d] approach..."* (p. 5). Moreover, management *"...should provide training to staff around costing/budgeting/planning..."* (p. 5). And it is even suggested that staff:

> "...should work with communities and other stakeholders to develop a sense of joint responsibility around budgeting and effective use of resources" (p. 5)

Although I think that shifting the onus on communities and 'stakeholders' may not be the most fruitful course of action, Cannon's analysis does point to a major shortcoming in MRA's working method: the Monti Rural Association should gain insight in its costs. Without knowing its costs, it would be never be possible to know whether MRA would have improved its efficiency.

In fact, due to the Sustainability Review by Cannon, the Monti Rural Association Director became convinced that improved 'costing' would lay at the basis of improved sustainability. In an interview[16] in early 1998 he stated:

> "The cost recovery versus income generation debate is momentarily suspended until we know our costs. That is the most important step now: learning how to calculate our costs...".

In 1998, therefore, much work was done to improve insight in the organization's costs. Through improved costing tendering would become more lucrative.

Investment

The last strategy in the financial sustainability drive was to find a productive use for the huge reserve that the Monti Rural Association was aiming to build up. In the Draft Sustainability Plan it was formulated that *"...the target range (...) is that MRA build up reserve monies of R2m-R3m*[17] *over the next three years..."* (p. 5). This reserve of about 3 million rand would provide the organization with a buffer of one year organizational survival if all funding would cease. Moreover, in case of 'only' reduced funding –or a shift to project funding– the reserve spin-offs would aid the organization to sustain its lobbying and advocacy work. In other words, the reserve could be used productively in order to make money. This additional budget could then be used to keep the political profile of the organization and, thus, retain a degree of independence.

As it was thought that it would be irresponsible to keep the reserve money in the bank, the Monti Rural Association management came up with investment options in its Draft Sustainability Plan. This clearly involved more *for-profit* activities:

> "...with the building of the reserve account, we are now in a position to consider a range of investment options. The guideline in this regard is that we should not select options that carry a high risk. We should rather opt for investments that are 'safer' even if this implies that returns will be lower. The one large investment that MRA will undertake is the purchase of business premises..." (p. 6).

Of the investment options the purchase of business premises appeared the most pressing. Since the organization annually spent R. 120,334[18] on rent it would mean a great reduction in recurrent costs once it owned its own premises. In a Board meeting[19] the Director of MRA exclaimed: *"We are throwing away 11,000 rand per month! This is useless!"*. The Board agreed, but a Board member warned: *"...we are custodians of taxpayers' money, whether local or foreign, we should make a sensible purchase...".* After a suitable building was identified, and the funders were consulted, the Monti Rural Association went ahead and purchased its own building in late 1998. This would also provide the organization with a secure fixed asset if the financial situation would deteriorate in the future. Other productive investment options were also explored, which I will discuss below.

With regard to the Draft Sustainability Plan and the Sustainability Review I would argue that a concern for financial survival prompted the organization to enter the market realm and cross the non-profit/for-profit boundary. Thus, contrary to the non-profit myth, an organization like MRA would no longer be able to survive in the cut-throat 'new realism' era without opting for contracts and seriously considering certain marketing tools and investment options. In order to complete the sustainability drive the organization's next step involved restructuring and changing its legal status.

Restructuring

Already in the period in which the Draft Sustainability Plan and the Sustainability Review were prepared, MRA management set out to sketch the structural consequences of the sustainability drive. During several management and staff meetings in 1997 much of the preliminary work was accomplished and in a crucial Staff Meeting in early 1998[20] the new plans regarding the structure of the organization were presented to the staff. First the director drew the old structure of the organization on the blackboard:

3 Programmes:	5 Units:
• Rural Development	• Finance & Administration
• Land Reform	• Land Use Planning
• Local Government	• Land Rights
	• Research
	• Local Government

This was followed by a sketch of the new structure he envisaged:

6 Methodologies:	6 Programmes:	3 Units:
• Institution Building	• Land Use Planning	• Land Use Planning
• Development Facilitation[21]	• Restitution	• Land Rights
• Networking and Brokering	• Redistribution	• Finance and Administration
• Research	• Tenure	
• Information Dissemination	• Land Administration	
• Advocacy	• Gender	

First, the director explained that all the Monti Rural Association projects, programmes, campaigns and other activities would be subject to the organization's mission statement. Any lucrative contract that would fall outside the realm of the mission statement would not be considered by the Management Team. This issue had presented itself in an earlier meeting in 1997[22] when a member of staff asked the director: *"...what if tenders (...) do not agree with our mission statement?"*. The director's answer was unequivocal: *"No, then we don't take it up..."*. The mission statement, which had been in place since 1996, would continue to guide the organization in face of the challenges that lay ahead[23]:

> *"MRA is committed to addressing the social and economic needs of rural people, particularly the marginalized and women, by means of a fair and*

equitable distribution of land, and the development of effective community land management.

MRA strives to pursue this objective by:
- *assisting communities to lobby for access to land and resources;*
- *strengthening communities' ability to plan and manage their own development;*
- *promoting security of tenure; and*
- *contributing to the building of effective local governance and the formulation of policies responsive to community needs at all levels of government".*

Anything beyond the scope of the organization's mission would not be considered.

That is why the Monti Rural Association management was extremely critical when it was confronted with a document[24] from the National Land Committee Executive in which it was suggested that the NLC proposed:

"...to set up a business wing which operates as a separate entity from the NLC but is in some way accountable to it. A company can be set up that manages finances, manages the selling of our skills and investigates investment opportunities..." (p. 4).

The MRA Director communicated to the NLC executive that he disagreed strongly, even more so because he was told that such a company could do things that fell outside the National Land Committee Mission Statement. In an internal MRA meeting[25] the director said:

"We as MRA believe that we can become sustainable, we do not need another company for that. It is plainly crazy to have a company do things for you that you cannot do yourself...".

As the NLC executive was heavily criticized by most affiliates, the plan never materialized. However, in my opinion it is significant that it was even suggested, as it was proof of the deeply penetrating nineties rhetoric.

Besides resolving some management and staffing issues by reducing the number of units, the new MRA structure reflected a more systematic and detailed approach with regard to programmes and methodologies. An expanded subdivision in the programmes and more clarity on the organization's methodologies would impact positively on project management and planning, which were also announced. Most significant, while not reflected on the blackboard, however, was the decision to divide the bulk of the projects between so-called *community-based projects* and *programme projects*. This typology directly resulted from the sustainability drive. Community-based projects would mainly be financed through (government) contracts, while programme projects, which reflected the political profile of the organization and involved the classical NGO work, would be financed through the organization's own resources –the core funding. The community projects would be targeted at specific communities, while the programme projects would *"...either aim to influence agrarian reform policy and implementation, or to improve MRA's capacity to meet programme objectives"*[26]. In other words, the community projects were the development projects, while the programme projects involved lobbying and advocacy activities –to influence government policy– and building the capacity of the Monti Rural Association to accomplish those tasks.

Linking this idea to the sustainability drive the director explained[27]:

> "Some of the community-based work should become sustainable. Programme work or lobbying and advocacy will always need financial support. Without that type of work we might as well become private sector...".

Thus, by restructuring the organization two objectives were achieved:
1. to become more sustainable and market-oriented;
2. to retain a political profile.

By restructuring and implementing project management and a planning, monitoring and evaluation cycle, 'the market' definitively entered the core of the organization. However, I think that the Monti Rural Association management and staff must be commended for the fact that, in every public debate or internal discussion the (political) role of the organization as NGO was emphasized and debated. Most MRA staff understood that remaining true to the mission statement was crucial. Everyone realized that without its political profile, that involved a strong lobbying and advocacy role, the Monti Rural Association would be 'reduced' to becoming a private consultant. In this respect the new director, Dudley Eastwood, played a critical role. He combined a firm believe –in my view, sometimes too firm– in 'systems', 'planning', 'structure' and 'policies' with the conviction that some of the 1980's political drive would have to be recaptured. Therefore, although the market impacted strongly on the organization, the Monti Rural Association strongly guarded itself against taking this 'final step'. The sustainability drive, however, had one other structural implication: changing the legal status of the organization.

Changed Legal Status

As an important step in the lengthy sustainability drive, the Monti Rural Association considered to change its legal status. Being a Voluntary Association the organization examined the possibilities of becoming a Section 21 Company, not-for-profit. In South Africa, this legal status was designed especially for non-profit organizations, and, thus, as a contractor, the South African government also favoured such Section 21 companies. Therefore, in the light of decreasing foreign funding it made sense to the management of the organization to adapt MRA to the local funding requirements by increasing MRA's legitimacy, as was proposed in an internal discussion document[28]:

> "...it is important to look beyond the present, and project into the future. It seems to be generally true that South African stake-holders favour Section 21 Companies above Voluntary Associations. If the funding situation changes such that MRA is more reliant on domestic donors, or if we need to increase the amount of income generation work that we undertake, it would be appropriate to upgrade our status" (p.2).

Although the legal status of Section 21 Companies was especially designed for *non-profit* organizations, the 'non-profit' label can lead to confusion. Especially since it conceals the fact that these NGOs can apply for tax exemption on *for-profit* activities, as long as the profit is reinvested in non-profit activities. It seems rather contradictory: a legal status designed for *non-profit* organizations in order to secure tax exemption on *for-profit* activities. In my view, this, again, exposes the non-profit myth for what it is.

Although I left South Africa in mid-1998, I did attend many of the preliminary discussions that preceded the move to become a Section 21 Company. According to MRA's auditor[29], remaining a Voluntary Association, would lead to three areas of concern as such an association is not a legal persona:

1. If MRA staff members make a mistake or commit an offence as a result of which they get sued[30], the organization, the director, or the Board could be held personally liable;
2. As a Voluntary Association it is difficult to purchase a building, a vehicle, or sign a lease. There is no such problem with a Section 21 company;
3. A Section 21 company can apply for tax exemption; a voluntary organization must pay taxes on profits or interest.

Since the organization was about to purchase business premises, it became imperative to proceed with the metamorphosis. Furthermore, the reserve was annually yielding an increasing amount of interest and it would be advantageous not to hand it over to the tax collector.

However, organizationally, a Section 21 Company would be much more rigidly organized than a Voluntary Association. First of all there is a fixed structure:

MEMBERS
I
BOARD OF DIRECTORS
I
EMPLOYEES

The Board of Directors would be made up of executive and non-executive members –MRA staff and outsiders[31]. With respect to the members the auditor explained that a membership of 80-100 people would be required:

"These would be a broad range of people interested in seeing that land reform takes place in the Eastern Cape (...). The structure is not very different from the old Albany Rural Association structure, where there were members of interested individuals and a Board".

According to the director *"...we would have to go on a big membership drive to recruit people from the government, members of beneficiary communities and funders...".* It was significant that the director mentioned the government so prominently. However, two months later –after several quarrels with government departments about Gasela and Thornhill– he suggested in a meeting[32] that the membership would be recruited from:

- communities;
- funders;
- the private sector; and
- interested persons.

Moreover, he stressed that becoming a Section 21 Company would also provide an opportunity to increase MRA's *"public accountability"*. This democratization argument was in line with the ideas that had matured in MRA with respect to instituting Project Control Groups (Chapter 5) where community representatives would get a say in MRA projects. However, it was also striking that the director explained the benefits of having a membership with the *"...analogy of shareholders...".* This, again, confirmed how a 'market-speak' had pervaded the land sector NGOs.

Finally, in October 1998 the Monti Rural Association went ahead to change its legal status by becoming Section 21 Company. Was MRA now ready for the 21st century?

Concluding Remarks Sustainability

In my communications with the Monti Rural Association in the year 2000 several points struck me. When looking back on the sustainability drive in late 1997 and early 1998 particular issues emerge. First, as the restructuring process seemed successful, within a year the organization also came to regard the sustainability issue increasingly in perspective. For example, already in May 1998 the director realized that if government contracts were not forthcoming, it would be hard to reach the targets it had set for contract work. Thus, the organization itself again would have to be more pro-active in using its core funds to undertake the work MRA deemed necessary[33]:

"...I am more comfortable than in April. I have realized that sustainability is something secondary (...). We employ 22 people who should be working. We try not to be in conflict with sustainability...".

Second, by the year 2000 it had become clear that MRA had gone a step further and had become even more involved in the market. In the Monti Rural Association's Sustainability Plan (2000), for example, it was explained that out of the 3 million rand raised for the reserve *"...the lion's share –approximately R1½ million– has been earned through investment banking..."* (p. 2). This was followed by a statement at the end of the report. *"...MRA has R1 million invested off-shore in various five-year portfolios"* (p. 9). Again, this exposes the *non-profit* myth for what it is and proves the extent to which a new realism market discourse had pervaded the NGO sector.

Last, to end on a positive note, the anxiety caused by the Funders Summit did have positive effects. The organization was able to fundamentally restructure and put in place the necessary policies, systems and procedures that were beneficial to functioning in a much more market-oriented world in the late nineties. In late 2000 the Monti Rural Association reaped the benefit of the sustainability drive when they were awarded an award by the South African NGO Coalition. Not only were they presented with an award for their lobbying and advocacy work for a 'new' community, but the organization also received the Katlego award for 'Financial Sustainability'. This yielded much positive press attention and seemed to confirm that the Monti Rural Association had become one of the most financially sound NGOs in South Africa. This could prove to be an asset in the quest for new funders.

Donors: Partners or Bosses?

As it was revealed that, in spite of increased market involvement, the Monti Rural Association remained dependent on donor funding, this section will explore the changing relationship between the organization and its funders. In Chapter 2 I was argued that it is necessary to state clearly which type of donors one is dealing with. The funders that I am discussing below are, what I call, Northern non-governmental funding organizations (NGFOs). I focus on these organizations because the Monti Rural Association is mainly supported by Northern NGFOs. The relationship between funders and funded has always been controversial. Thus, in this section I cover three topics. First, I discuss the types of funding available and the extent to which NGOs have a choice between funders. I critically discuss Fowler's (1997) 'high quality versus 'low quality' distinction. Second, I will look at the issue of dependency. Can one refer to the relationship as a 'partnership'? What are the implications with respect to 'donor accountability'? Third, I focus on the 'programme' of funders. What is their intention? Why are they sometimes uncomfortable about their aims?

'High Quality' and 'Low Quality': a problematic distinction
In Fowler's (1997) opinion it makes sense to distinguish between donor funds as being either 'hot', or 'high quality', or 'cold', or 'low quality'. In his view, the funders disbursing 'low-quality' money push Southern NGOs to become mere service providers. 'High quality' funds, on the contrary, can –and according to Fowler should– be used to gain a higher level of autonomy from the government and the 'official aid system'. He identified only a relatively small group of Northern NGFOs that disburses these 'high quality' funds. In this section I try to examine how these 'high quality' funders operate. Moreover, I attempt to discover if their modus operandi fundamentally differs from other types of funding agencies.

Although Fowler's terminology is not used by an organization like the Monti Rural Association, the NGO is very much aware of the different types of funding. As was illustrated above, MRA has consciously moved away from 'cold money', or 'project funding'. The reason for this is that core funding offers more flexibility and shifts the responsibility to the NGO. Thus, the organization nowadays prefers 'core funding', as the director explained in an interview[34]. *"We say to funders: this is our mission. If by fulfilling our mission statement we help you to fulfil your mission statement: give us money..."*. Only if the 'high quality' funding would decrease substantially *"...we might have to ask ourselves whether we want to consider funders like USAID. So far, we have managed with politically correct funding"*. Fortunately, the Monti Rural Association, in the late nineties, had a reputation that was relatively impeccable, especially in comparison with other NGOs. This gave the organization the chance to choose between alternative core funding sources. Moreover, these high quality funders were open to suggestions as the funders summit has shown. One problem, however, with these high quality funders is that they themselves are usually highly dependent on Northern government funds. For example, HUVO, a Dutch co-financing funder is for more than 90% dependent on government funds. These are largely funds acquired through the Dutch Co-Financing Programme[35]. The Co-Financing Programme was introduced as the Dutch government became increasingly hesitant to fund politically problematic regimes. By disbursing the money through several civic actors –HUVO, NOVIB and other Dutch co-financing organizations– civic to civic funding could be achieved. Thus, the Dutch government could never be accused of supporting rogue states, nor could these states accuse the Dutch of directly funding opposition groups.

However, in the mid- and late nineties, when South Africa had left its rogue state status far behind, bilateral state-to-state funding became acceptable again. As foreign governments could now support the legitimate government, the NGO sector – especially the health and education sector– in South Africa was confronted with dwindling foreign government support. As equitable land reform was generally deemed important, the land sector was not as critically affected by the dwindling of foreign government funds in the mid- and late nineties. However, as described above, the sword of Damocles hung above the land sector with respect to the post-2000 period. Yet, in 1997, the Monti Rural Association was faced with a completely contradictory situation. Not a shortage of funds, but outright competition between direct and indirect Dutch government funding caused tension, frustration and confusion. As the restructuring[36] of Dutch development cooperation entailed a vigorous decentralisation of tasks, the Dutch embassies were given the power to identify suitable development projects. As a result, outright competition arose between the embassies -directly disbursing government development cooperation funds –and the Dutch Co-Financing Organizations– indirectly disbursing Dutch government funds. Thus, in South Africa and more specifically in the Eastern Cape – as this was the Dutch provincial focus area– a serious conflict occurred between the Dutch Embassy and HUVO, with MRA in the middle.

In February 1997 the Monti Rural Association was visited by a delegation from the Dutch Embassy and offered a direct funding relationship, whereby the embassy staff uttered negative remarks about the added value of HUVO. In a fax to the HUVO[37] representative in Harare the MRA Director wrote:

> *"...the delegation raised the possibility of their having a direct funding relationship with us. I was asked what value HUVO adds to the relationship...".*

HUVO, of course, felt betrayed by the embassy and a dispute followed between the two Dutch institutions. An anonymous Dutch source explained that the restructuring of Dutch development cooperation:

> *"...led to much tension between the embassy and the Dutch Co-Financing Organizations, as both wanted to cooperate with the same local partners. This led to 'counterpart grabbing'[38]. HUVO accused the embassy of 'stealing' MRA...".*

After several months of tension the Monti Rural Association wrote the Dutch Embassy that, following discussions with HUVO:

> *"...given the long and mutually beneficial relationship between HUVO and MRA, MRA's preference would be for a continuation of the current relationship between the two organisations...".*

However, the embassy then put pressure on HUVO and a compromise was found whereby both Dutch institutions would 'share' the Monti Rural Association, as was revealed in an internal MRA meeting[39]:

> *"...Dudley reported that MRA has received a letter from HUVO proposing a joint arrangement where HUVO funds us 100,000 Dutch Guilders and the Embassy 250,000 Dutch Guilders. This is, from MRA's point of view, a very agreeable arrangement...".*

Yet, although the conflicts were finally resolved, it took the two Dutch institutions forever to come to an agreement. By late April 1998 (!) the Monti Rural Association had still not been given the green light:
> "The HUVO/Dutch embassy grant is the only contract that is outstanding. We have been advised not to contact the embassy, but to continue to pressurize Hans Bos at HUVO"[40] (p. 3).

This example shows the type of absurdities caused by direct and indirect Dutch funding in a context that has changed from authoritarian to democratic rule. Although both types would be characterized as 'high quality' by Fowler (1997), it left the Monti Rural Association in a vulnerable position. Thus, an 'excess' of funding possibilities can also lead to difficulties for the funded. Outright competition between funders can put an NGO in a difficult spot. Although the organization initially did not mind accessing new 'high quality' funds through the Dutch Embassy, it did not want to offend the funder with which it had developed a long-standing relationship. Whether these relationships can indeed be regarded as a 'partnership', as the funders frequently claim, will be explored in the next section.

NGO Dependency and Donor Accountability

In my view the relationship between funders and funded will always have to be interpreted in the light of a degree of dependency. The funded, of course, are especially dependent on funders for finances, whether they are 'high quality' or not. But, as the above example has shown, funders are also dependent on their 'counterparts' for success and recognition, which can lead to funder competition. The funded are usually very much aware of being dependent, while the funders on the other hand frequently disguise the fact that there is a certain amount of inequality in the relationship. Funders use terms like *"our local partners"*, *"our counterparts"* and even in official letters[41] *"...dear friends..."*. However, this egalitarian and amicable tone often contrasts with the more formal and directive top-down practices of funders. Frequently, such top-down pressure leads to excessive NGO accountability to funders, even to 'high quality' funders. To illustrate this I discuss several, relatively well-documented, incidents that occurred between HUVO and the Monti Rural Association and which reveal a certain unevenness in the relationship. First, however, it is important to emphasize here that the relationship between HUVO and the Monti Rural Association has generally been described from both sides as good and constructive. These conflicts are not unique, similar differences have also occurred between MRA and other high quality funders.

It is useful to note that HUVO reformulated its South Africa strategy during the Freedom and Consultation era. The funder saw a need to establish a more business-like approach to their 'partners' in South Africa[42]:
> *For HUVO this implies revisiting its 1987 country strategy in order to prioritize future areas of support, against a background of new development actors inside South Africa..."* (p. i).

Moreover, it valued increased professionalism in the South African NGO sector:
> *"HUVO intervention aimed at the performance of the NGO sector itself will therefore have to assist in overcoming its present weaknesses, so that services*

> *will be provided on the basis of proven professionalism and at the request of clients"* (p. 17).

Thus:

> *Support will be provided in areas of (...) internal organizational/financial development and management, in conjunction with programme development..."* (p. 17).

Therefore, HUVO began to commission evaluations in the mid-nineties, in order to assess the NGOs the funder worked with. However, before discussing the first evaluation the Monti Rural Association was ever subjected to, I will first briefly describe the problems that emerged around the signing of a contract between MRA and HUVO.

When, in 1995, the HUVO head-office in The Hague overruled a contract signed between MRA and the HUVO office in Harare, the Monti Rural Association felt betrayed. As a result, the relations between the two organizations soured. As the coordinator formulated it: *"the source of tensions lay in the manner in which MRA's contract had been unilaterally reformulated"* (p. 2)[43]. Especially the fact that the revised contract offered by The Hague implied a budget reduction angered MRA. Therefore, for months, MRA management deliberated whether the revised contract should be signed or not. The organization even contemplated taking legal action to pressure HUVO to honour the first contract. In a fax[44] to the Harare office the MRA management blamed HUVO and its top-down behaviour for the situation that had arisen:

1. *"MRA believes that the rescinding of a contract should be a negotiated process, particularly as the mistake was made by HUVO and the new contract is less advantageous to MRA in financial terms than the existing one (...).*
2. *MRA believes that HUVO's mistake will be a costly one for MRA and that HUVO have not given due consideration to the effect this will have (...).*
5. *MRA and HUVO have enjoyed a long standing and very positive relationship. The lack of consultation and discussion around rescinding an existing contract does not seem to reflect the spirit of this relationship nor take into account MRA considerable disadvantage in the current situation".*

Although HUVO did indeed acknowledge having made a mistake, the funder did not increase the amount in the new contract. After much consultation the Monti Rural Association finally gave in and signed the revised contract. Nevertheless, it did approach the Dutch Embassy in order to ask them to put some pressure on HUVO. That also failed to prompt HUVO to increase the funds available and relations remained strained for a while. In my opinion, this incident sheds some shocking light on the quality and moral standing of such a 'high quality' funder. Possibly, Fowler (1997) has exaggerated their exceptionality.

It was in this atmosphere of strained relations that in 1996, after years of working together, HUVO commissioned an evaluation of the Monti Rural Association. The evaluation had nothing to do with the tensions around the new contract, but resulted from the HUVO strategy intended to forge a new and more 'professional relationship' with its 'counterparts'. Nevertheless, the evaluation caused the relationship to sour even more. Especially as the evaluation took place in mid-

1996, MRA's crisis year when some of its most high profile staff had just left the organization.

A few days after the evaluation, in a letter[45] to all the other National Land Committee affiliates, the MRA Coordinator wrote:

"MRA is presently in the middle of an external evaluation process commissioned by HUVO. The interviews with MRA staff and other bodies with whom we work have just been completed. We now await the evaluators' report and the workshop where the report will be presented to MRA. Let's just say that the evaluation process to date will not make it into 'MRA's Top Ten Hit Parade of Pleasant Experiences'...".

Moreover, in a Board Meeting[46], the coordinator reported that:

"...the evaluation had seemed satisfactory until, on the last day, the evaluators expressed strong dissatisfaction at what they perceived to be an unwillingness on the part of MRA to co-operate...".

Furthermore, just before the evaluation report was completed the Monti Rural Association management issued an "*...assessment of the external evaluation...*"[47], in order to inform the board about the problems encountered during the evaluation process. In it the MRA Coordinator used some harsh words to criticize HUVO:

*"...MRA unwittingly lost control of the process (...) MRA came to feel that the external evaluation was indeed **external** –something that was happening to MRA and not **with** MRA.*

(...) the fact that HUVO never explained how they intended to use the results of the evaluation placed MRA in a vulnerable and somewhat defensive position.

(...) HUVO had an unequal say in the appointment of both evaluators (...)" (p. 1-2).

This second bad experience with HUVO within a year caused an extra strain on already troubled relations between the Monti Rural Association and its funder. Only when after the evaluation HUVO made it clear that it would continue to support MRA, despite the critical points that had surfaced in the evaluation report, did the relationship slowly improve again. Furthermore, as the first resentment waned within the Monti Rural Association, the evaluation report was used as a basis to restructure and improve its level of operation. As this was exactly what HUVO had envisaged the cooperation improved further.

However, in 1998, HUVO, again, acted in an authoritarian fashion. In an unusual move the Executive Director of the entire organization in The Hague –not the Harare Regional Office– sent a 4-page letter[48] to *"...all HUVO' Counterpart Organizations in South Africa...".* Again, an amicable tone *–"Dear Friends..."–* disguised the directive content of the letter. It outlined how HUVO intended to initiate cooperation with a locally based but Northern-owned donor consortium called Donorfund. It was envisaged that *"...Donorfund will start to manage the existing portfolio of HUVO' funded counterpart organization in South Africa"* (p. 2). This would ultimately result in *"...a complete transfer of HUVO programmes to Donorfund"* (p. 2). Finally, the letter closes with a call *"...to react to our plans and voice any comments..."* (p. 3). Nevertheless, it appeared as if HUVO and Donorfund had already progressed to the final stages of the agreement. For an 'objective' outsider as well as for MRA, this type of funder behaviour contrasted strongly with the 'partner rhetoric'. Within MRA the incident led to some irritation, especially since the organization had had bad experiences with Donorfund in the past.

In my opinion, these examples illustrate how the relationship between a funder and the funded is always flawed. Despite the rhetoric of funders about equal partnerships, the funder remains in charge of the money. Even so-called 'high quality' funders repeatedly seem to operate in a relatively 'top-down' fashion. As was shown above, a 'high quality' funder like HUVO could take the liberty to just annul a contract. Thus, even when taking into account that funders are also dependent on the funded, the relationship remains unequal. Especially incidents, as described above, led to periods of increased preoccupation with funders, in order to keep them satisfied. This can lead to an accountability shift from 'grassroots' to funders, especially since the communities have no monetary instruments at their disposal to demand attention. However, notwithstanding this criticism, an organization like MRA is much more positive about funders that provide core funding, as it is much less rigid and leaves much of the responsibility in the hands of the organization, compared to project funding.

In the next section I look at 'programme' of ('high quality') funders.

The 'Programme' of Funders: assistance or meddling?

It makes sense to discuss the programme of donors in South Africa, because both the donors and the NGOs they supported came, quite unexpectedly, under rather heavy attack from the ANC in 1997. Based on a report by staff of the United States House of Representatives –reviewing the USAID programme in South Africa– in which it was said that USAID used its funds to support groups in South Africa which critically monitored and lobbied the government, President Mandela (1997) lashed out to the non-governmental sector. In his speech to the 50th National Conference of the ANC, he strongly criticized the NGOs for not being 'real' NGOs and undermining the government of South Africa:

> *"...many of our non-governmental organizations are not in fact NGOs, both because they have no popular base and the actuality that they rely on the domestic and foreign governments, rather than people, for their material sustenance.*
>
> *As we continue to struggle to ensure a people-driven process of social transformation, we will have to consider the reliability of such NGOs as a vehicle to achieve this objective"* (p. 6).

And:

> *"This has also created the possibility for some of these NGOs to act as instruments of foreign governments and institutions that fund them to promote the interests of these external forces"* (p. 12).

Of course, it is clear that Mandela's speech should be analyzed in a political light. For example, a degree of 'scapegoating' served him well to deflect attention away from the underachievement of the alliance in delivering on the election promises. However, he does seem to have a point in that foreign donors, frequently, do have 'a programme'.

Usually, such a programme is officially about strengthening civil society or stimulating 'democracy'. However, the line between 'strengthening' and outright meddling is sometimes hard to draw. That this frequently leads to fuzzy NGO-speak will be shown here. Of course Mandela's definition of what constitutes 'a real NGO' can and should be challenged. I, for one, do recognize that most intermediary organizations without members are the 'real NGOs'. The ANC's rhetoric of a 'people-driven' process, in fact, disguises the generally top-down fashion in which the party elite deals with contentious issues. In that respect the party does not differ much from the type of non-governmental organization that is criticized by Mandela.

In this section I focus on the Sweden Supports Africa (SSA), an amalgamation of Swedish local groups dedicated to development cooperation. According to the local SSA representative in the Eastern Cape, the organization receives 80% of its funding from the Swedish government, while 20% is raised locally in Sweden. It has a strong-voiced programme: *"...we are fighting against imperialism..."*[49] (p. 1), and it aims to:

> *"...support people in the developing countries in their aspirations for economic and social levelling, economical and political independence and a democratic development of society"* (p. 1).

Moreover, in regard to South Africa, the organization *"...supports the transformation from apartheid and the building of the new democratic South Africa"* (p. 1). However, when I talked to Agneta Bornholm, the local SSA representative in East London, it emerged that critically discussing 'the programme' of a Northern NGFO was not so easy. It may be that Mandela's speech had left an impression that caused the SSA staff to be extremely cautious. On the other hand, Bornholm's narrative[50], in my view, illustrates precisely the dilemmas of funders, since every funder does have a 'programme' and is established to realize as much of that programme as possible.

With respect to the accusations in Mandela's speech the SSA representative suggested that it referred primarily to practices by an NGO from *"...a very big country..."*. In her opinion USAID and the Peace Corps had indeed been (ab-)used by the American government to influence policy in developing countries. In response to this remark I asked her: *"Doesn't Sweden have a programme to promote democracy?"* She answered defensively:

> *"Yes..., but don't forget that we are not there to enforce our type of democracy. We don't say: 'this is the way to do it'. We are here to support organizations that want to build democracy in South Africa themselves. They have their own goals and objectives (...). We are not there to influence them on how democracy should take shape. We don't say it has to be the way we do it in Sweden. But of course, in discussions with them, we can give a lot of examples of how it works in Sweden. But, I mean, we are not enforcing that to be their model. It can be used as an example. Therefore we invite people to come to Sweden. That is part of our programme, so that they can see how things are done in Sweden".*

This led me to remark:

> *"But there is a political agenda in Sweden, as your country is committed to democracy"*.

She then explained how the Swedes had, indeed, been very supportive of the fight against apartheid. I then inquired: *"Does the political agenda of SSA overlap with the political agenda of the South African government?"*. Again, her answer was somewhat hesitant:

> *"Yes..., to come back to the Mandela speech, if the policy of the states that he has in mind differs a lot from what he would like to achieve in South Africa, then of course it is very sensitive.*
>
> *(...) as long as the influence comes from an equivalent perspective, then it is not too bad. But still, it is not our wish to impose or to sell a Swedish type of democracy, the way that it is set up. The basic rules when it comes to democracy, yes, but not the structures...".*

In my opinion, this conversation clearly illustrated the sensitivity of the 'programme' of a progressive funder in the local development context. Although the organization did have clearly stated objectives, especially intended to gain support in the Swedish context, stating these aloud in the South Africa context would have endangered their consultative and participatory approach in which they first have to listen to what their 'partners' say. In fact, these Northern NGFOs are fundamentally Janus-faced. Speaking unambiguously in Sweden to raise funds, while at the same time having to operate cautiously in the South African context in order not to offend their 'counterparts', nor the political leadership.

NGOs and Private Sector Consultants: eroded boundaries?

As this chapter has illustrated, land sector NGOs have increasingly been influenced by the new realism market discourse. Therefore, it makes sense to explore how these NGOs differ from the private consultancy firms that are active in the land sector. Has an increasingly dominant market eroded the boundaries between the two?

First, I would like to discuss a phenomenon typical of the new realism era in the late nineties. Besides leaving the affiliates of the National Land Committee to join the under-capacitated government, ex-NGO staff also proceeded to set up new consultancy firms. In the NGOs they had gained experience with government contracts and the tendering process and recognized that, especially in the land sector, the government had so little capacity to implement its policies that there was ample work for both NGOs and consultancy firms. Therefore, in the mid- and late nineties many such consultancy firms sprung up. Usually their work largely overlapped the type of work carried out by land sector NGOs. Thus, these firms competed with the old NGOs –and their former comrades whom they left behind– for government contracts.

When looking at the distinguishing features between consultants and NGOs, it is evident that NGOs are informed by their mission statements. Moreover, NGOs usually occupy a niche that is usually defined by their historical links with certain communities. Without a mission statement and this historical 'baggage' the new consultants are usually much more flexible. However, it is not that these new consultants –some call them *rainbow consultants*– do not adhere to any principles. As Kwinana, who established *Ilanga*, explained: *"As consultants we do not have a mission statement. However, we are bound by a certain set of values that we have taken with us from the NGOs...".* The most significant difference, of course, concerns the mode of financial survival. For NGOs like MRA, that rely largely on core funding, their market-oriented activities are of relatively limited importance. For a consultant this is, of course, an entirely different matter. As is explained by Mr. Kwinana[51]: *"I have to deliver a product. In the end there must be a product. We cannot raise too many questions..."*. More specifically, *"With regard to development, the emphasis of NGOs is on 'the process', while our emphasis is on the product..."*. Therefore, according to Kwinana, *"...strategic alliances between NGOs and consultants are ideal"*. In such an alliance the NGO would guard the process and the quality, while the consultant would make sure that a product is ultimately delivered.

To learn whether the approach of NGOs does indeed differ from the approach of consultants it is useful to focus on the Thornhill Development Project.

MRA as Lead-Agent

Throughout the project –the last leg of the Eastern Cape Land Reform Pilot– the Monti Rural Association, an NGO named Land Service Committee (LSC) and French and Associates, a consultancy firm, cooperated closely in the Thornhill Consortium. Although it must be said that French and Associates is not a new consultancy firm like Ilanga, the firm has ample experience in more progressive land sector projects. What makes this case especially interesting is the fact that the Monti Rural Association was the so-called 'lead agent' of the consortium. MRA took on the role of sub-contractor opposite LSC and French.

Besides being the lead-agent in the project and, thus, shouldering the main responsibility, MRA carried out an extensive social survey in Thornhill and in Zola and Phakamisa, where part of the Thornhill community had moved. In addition, the Monti Rural Association facilitated a difficult process that yielded the establishment of a communal property trust. This legal entity would ultimately be able to access and manage additional farmland that would be transferred to the community. Moreover, French conducted a technical settlement survey, in which the lay-out, land-use and density of the settlement was mapped. Lastly, Land Service Committee produced a water supply and sanitation resource evaluation and an evaluation of Thornhill's groundwater resources. Eventually, the information was brought together and the organizations produced the *Thornhill Development Plan: a development framework for Thornhill, Zola and Phakamisa settlements* (MRA, LSC & French, 1997).

For MRA it meant a useful experience as it confronted the organization with the intricacies of tendering, costing and consultancy firm dead-lines. It revealed that the Monti Rural Association still experienced serious shortcomings with respect to more market-oriented activities. As a result the MRA staff would sometimes have to ask advice from the consultancy firms it worked with. For example, in an internal MRA meeting[52], the MRA leader of the project said:

> *"...our 150 rand per hour rate does not cover our expenses. Let's find out what consultants do. Our rate has not been recently reviewed. It has been 150 rand for two years already. We only get 22,000 rand for this past half a year. That is very little..."*.

Many such examples followed and as the Monti Rural Association was the lead-agent, the organization experienced major difficulties to complete its task, which resulted in exceeding costs and major delays. In actual fact, it proved to be both a learning experience and a night-mare for the organization. For one, the project cost much more than it generated. Therefore, when the project was finally completed a sigh of relief was heard in the organization. In a MRA meeting[53] the director exclaimed:

> *"The Thornhill report is finally submitted! You can look at it in my room. We finally reached the end of the pilot. Thank God!".*

In an interview with Dick French[54] –the consultant in the consortium– he discussed his experiences while pointing to the thick final version of the Thornhill Development Project report on his bookshelf:

> *"This is an amalgamation of the reports on the project. I mean this is excellent work, first class, it's better then I've ever seen as a consultant. You know, the trouble and time it takes actually to bring the whole thing together. That must have cost a considerable amount, it should be on their budget, I am sure.... So with core funding from other sources, of course, they are able to do this. But certainly as a consulting business I would never have been able to afford it in the tight budget that was available to do this type of work. That's very impressive".*

Thus, this consultant did confirm the belief held by NGOs that they produce higher quality work than consultants. Although not referring to French, some NGO staff[55] were quite blunt in this respect: *"Consultants generally do a rush job, they are not committed. An NGO takes longer, but then some say we are not as efficient...".* Also government departments, who hire consultants, are often critical about the quality of the work of these private firms. However, in my view, it is time to expose the myth, prevalent in NGO circles, that working longer on a project automatically entails a higher level of quality. In several instances I have noticed that the quality of NGO work is simply used as an excuse for inefficiency. In actual fact core funding can lead to a certain amount of complacency, as there is less need to adhere to budgets and deadlines.

This is view is confirmed by Dick French, who did add some critical remarks, particularly with respect to the delays in the project:

> *"...it is easy to criticize, but I think the difference we feel between an NGO and (...) a consultant is that an NGO is very people-oriented, but very much softer on management and business discipline and time frames, things like that. So where consultants would have said we had deadlines set by Land Affairs to have this* (taps on the report) *finished by a certain date, MRA finished six months later...".*

For the consultant, a six-month delay can, for example, really lead to serious financial problems:

> *"...you wait six months to get payment because the other elements [in the consortium] had not done their part of the work, so you couldn't actually submit the total invoice. That's a bit difficult to work, to get used to...".*

In several instances in the past French had to mortgage his house in order to survive such lulls. However, in the Thornhill project, the Monti Rural Association could help out due to its core funding reserves:

> *"...but then, after a meeting with MRA they agreed in certain instances to pay us out of their funds, because they knew they would perhaps be a little bit late, you know, we had help from that side".*

MRA staff seemed to hold similar opinions with regard to their lack of experience as lead-agent. For example, in a MRA meeting[56] a senior member of staff remarked:

> "...we are not a consultant, we didn't have experience in budgeting, therefore we under-budgeted (...). French, [however], is always coming with receipts. We should learn how to budget. We are simply not used to budgeting because of our core funding...".

Naturally, Dick French also identified access to core funding as the most crucial difference between the NGO sector and the private consultants:

> "...there is a obviously a feeling of the fact that consultants are very money-orientated, and we tend to always worry about the budget and invoices and payment. And I think the NGOs find it difficult to reconcile with that, to get used to that. I think they are, with their core funding, (...) actually in a privileged position where they are able to concentrate totally on their work and their financial manager gets the money eventually. Fine, but for us, unfortunately, we have to live the other way around...".

Other consultants are more critical as they accuse the NGO sector of false competition. Since NGOs frequently vie for the same government contracts as consultants, it is said that their core funding could allow them to ask a lower price for their services. In the eyes of the consultants this is not fair, since they do have to charge the full price in order to survive financially.

However, the argument that core funding leads to false competition was strongly contradicted by the data revealed by Mavis Beechwood[57] –nowadays a senior Department of Land Affairs official and a former Coordinator of MRA. She explained that in the land sector the private consultants, actually, have absolutely nothing to fear from the NGO sector. In fact, due to a continued lack of capacity in the government there is an ever-increasing amount of work:

> "Nowadays, 90 % of our work is carried out by private consultants. The quality of the work is not always as good as the NGOs (...). The NGOs miss a huge opportunity!"

As the last remark indicates, Beechwood and other government officials are quite critical about the National Land Committee affiliates:

> "The NGOs leave a huge gap. They rely too much on their old ties, that is communities they historically developed ties with(...). If NGOs are unwilling or unable, we make the private sector, the consultants, rich".

Not only do NGOs seem to lack the capacity to take on more contracts, Beechwood also identified a certain amount of complacency within the NGO land sector:

> "There is a lack of new initiatives. We as DLA only manage land reform, we don't have the manpower to do it on our own. We bring in outside facilitators. However, the NLC affiliates do not take it on in great numbers...".

I believe Beechwood indeed does have a point. There are certainly affiliates –MRA is not one of them– that could be much more productive. The whole transformation process has left these affiliates in a bad state: little political profile, badly managed and inefficient. However, even if all affiliates were in excellent shape, it should be recognized that there is only a small number of NLC affiliates. Moreover, these organizations are simply too small. As a result, the land sector NGOs could never take on the ocean of available government contracts.

Nevertheless, it is often these same problematic organizations that complain about the fierce competition caused by the emergence of consultants. In my opinion, however, the increased competition by consultants has generally benefited the NGO sector in South Africa. It honed their commercial qualities which increased their chances of survival in the late nineties. For example, in the case of the Monti Rural Association, the whole sustainability drive was positively influenced by the experience gained as lead-agent in the Thornhill Consortium and what was learned from working with private consultants.

In conclusion, I would like to remark that the impact of the market has indeed caused the boundaries between NGOs and consultants to erode. However, the boundary has not completely disappeared. Despite being employed by the government and even making direct and indirect profits there are NGOs, like MRA, that have done their utmost to safeguard the organization's NGO identity. Through core funding MRA was able to adhere to its mission statement, retain its political profile and continue its lobbying and advocacy work. Other NGOs, however, failed to do this and have become much more like private consultants, though not as successful.

Conclusion

In the 'new realism era' the market became increasingly dominant in South Africa. As land sector NGOs feared the substantial decline of funding in the post-2000 period, an increasing pressure was felt to become more 'sustainable'. In this process the interaction with government departments, foreign donors and private consultants had a marked impact. Therefore, the Monti Rural Association, restructured, purchased its own business premises and changed its legal status to become a Section 21 Company. Furthermore, MRA carried out government contracts, tested cooperative arrangements with the private sector and even built up an off-shore investment portfolio. Thus, it is clear that NGOs can no longer be described as *non-profit* agencies. Nevertheless, although the organization engaged in *for-profit* activities, in my opinion, it managed to avoid becoming a private sector firm through a continued dependence on foreign funding. The organization remained an NGO.

In this regard there is a continuing need for 'high quality' funders –the Northern Non-Governmental Funding Organizations– to support the non-governmental sector in South Africa. Especially the so-called core funds supplied by these donors aided the Monti Rural Association to adhere to its mission statement. Thus, in spite of an increasingly dominant market, the organization was able to (re-)strengthen its political profile through intensified lobbying and advocacy activities. The organization became both more market-oriented –more financially 'sustainable'– and at the same time regained some of its political qualities that it had lost during the crisis in the mid-nineties. However, as I have shown, it is important to recognize that this donor dependency can give rise to an accountability shift to funders. Not only when reports are due, but especially when tensions occur between the donor and the NGO.

Furthermore, it should be realized that these donors, that are described as 'high quality' donors by Fowler (1997), do not treat their 'partners in the South' as equal partners. Although the fact that these Northern non-governmental funding NGOs (NGFOs) provide core funding is appreciated, these organizations frequently operate in a similar 'top-down' fashion as other funders. They are simply another link in the chain between 'top-down' funding arrangements in which Northern governments play a dominant role. Furthermore, it was shown that these organizations are essentially Janus-faced. They have 'a programme' to gain support and generate funds in the North that demands clarity and outspokenness. However, in the development context of the South such unambiguous and explicit programmes frequently create tensions. Especially in polarized political contexts this requires a more diplomatic –read concealing– donor discourse, or outright fuzzy 'donor-speak'.

9. The Implications of Freedom

Introduction

As I am critical of what I have called 'NGO literature', this research project is an attempt to move beyond the umpteenth theorization of *"what a real NGO is"*. As the 'NGO' label has become largely meaningless, I distance myself from approaches, normally produced by 'development anthropology insiders', that try to capture such organizations in ideal-typical descriptions and fancy acronyms. Instead, this book is based on an actor-oriented and ethnographic approach in order to understand and describe a 'real organization' active in the South African land sector in the 1990s. As the title of the book –*The Implications of Freedom: the changing role of land sector NGOs in a transforming South Africa*– suggests, it is an effort to understand the dynamic interplay between the transformations that took place in NGOs and in the rest of South African society.

I concentrated my research efforts on the role of the Monti Rural Association in South African land reform for several reasons. First, South Africa as a country seemed an interesting case, since few contemporary societies have experienced such a fundamental transformation in one decade. Second, the choice to focus on the land sector was informed by the large disparities in South African land ownership. Since these inequalities had to be redressed and NGOs were playing an active part in the process, it provided an ideal setting to study the dynamic interplay between civil society, the state and the market. Finally, I decided to focus on this particular NGO, as it was a relatively well-functioning organization with an interesting history. Originally the organization had been established by academic activists in the early eighties to publicize and fight forced removals of black rural communities. By the late nineties it had evolved into a professional land sector NGO that had become a dominant player in Eastern Cape land reform.

The research has focused on the activities, the people, the processes, the policies and the interactions within the Monti Rural Association, but also, as a matter of course, on the relationships with other actors in the state, civil society and the market. Moreover, to achieve the necessary depth, I attempted to (re-)introduce the *historical*, the *political* and *socio-economic* dimension, as case studies should be placed in a dynamic context. The result is, what I have termed, an *embedded tale* about a land sector NGO, operating in the Border Region of the Eastern Cape in South Africa.

After discussing the benefits of this *embedded tale* I explore what conclusions can be drawn from this case study concerning the myths about NGOs prevalent in the 'NGO literature'. Furthermore, I will examine what agendas for future research may be drawn up to further improve our understanding of the role of non-governmental organizations. Lastly, I will share my more personal observations about the role of land sector NGOs and the apparent failure of land reform in South Africa.

An Embedded Tale

In my opinion one cannot begin to understand the role of NGOs without taking into account the historical dimension. Simply looking at an organization or an intervention in the present tells us too little. Thus, it is crucial to embed and interpret cases historically, as a longitudinal view can provide us with insights that an a-historical approach cannot uncover. Secondly, it is important to try and understand the political context in which such organizations have developed since an NGO like MRA can be imagined as a small spider in several institutional webs that link and cut across local, regional and national levels. In addition, it is crucial to analyze the political aspects of NGO interventions themselves. Thirdly, is crucial for social scientists to be aware of the socio-economic dimensions of development interventions. In the case of South Africa, for example, it was argued that it is not possible to understand the changing role of NGOs without being aware of the impact of the RDP and GEAR.

In my opinion the 'NGO literature' and 'development anthropology' approaches concerned with implementation usually do the opposite. They largely ignore the historical, political and socio-economic context as was shown in the Lesotho case, presented by Ferguson (1990). Long and van der Ploeg (1989) have also argued how an excessive concern with implementation may lead to the boxing in of time and space. Therefore, it becomes crucial to embed the role of NGOs and the development interventions they are engaged in, by studying, analyzing and describing the context they operate in. This context is best studied by employing a multi-level, multi-sited and multi-vocal actor-oriented approach. As I was convinced of the impossibility to understand the role of NGOs in the South African context without studying and analyzing national, regional and more local developments, the research was conducted on all levels. While the research principally focused on the meso-level of operation of the NGO –the provincial level and the district level–, it also took place on the national level and the more local community levels. Although, in my opinion it is heuristically useful to distinguish a macro-, meso- and micro-level, we should be careful not to lose sight of the overlaps, contradictions and inter-relatedness. It is exactly this inter-relatedness of the story of the greater South African transformation and the transformations that took place on other levels, that fascinated me.

An important element in this research project involved the unravelling of the complex history of the Monti Rural Association. By studying the archives, from old annual reports to minutes of meetings and correspondence with funders and government departments, it was tried to piece together the changes that took place over the years. Furthermore, (ex-)members of staff were interviewed about their experiences in different periods. As a result, it was possible to gain insight into the fundamental transformations that took place over the years, which ultimately resulted in the manner in which the Monti Rural Association functioned in the late nineties. This revealed an organization that still had the same name[1] as a few years earlier, but had fundamentally changed on many fronts. However, perhaps more important, the research revealed that organizations such as MRA do not evolve from 'activism' to 'professionalism' in a teleological manner. It is not a matter of straightforward evolution. Rather, this historical approach has shown that processes of organizational learning and un-learning go hand in hand. The development of organizations involves periods of progression, but also of regression. Organizational learning and development is a complicated process, since much of what is learned at one stage may be unlearned in another. Thus, a more longitudinal analysis may reveal that mistakes are repeated again and again.

Beyond focusing on its organizational history, it is also necessary to study how the history of an organization like MRA is entwined with the histories of communities the organization has been involved in. Especially in Chapter 4 it was illustrated that the history of the Monti Rural Association and the history of 'the people' of Thornhill can hardly be separated. Without understanding the history of Thornhill it would be more or less impossible to understand the history of MRA, and vice versa. However, in turn, it is also difficult to understand the history of a community like Thornhill without grasping the regional political struggles that took place in the Eastern Cape. Especially in the South African context where reasons for conflicts are frequently explained in 'racial' or 'ethnic' terms, it is useful to be aware of this political dimension.

Thus, it was shown that the developments leading to the massive 'dumping' of people in Thornhill, in the late 1970s, can largely be explained by the power mongering of Lennox Sebe, the first ruler of an 'independent' Ciskei, and the political struggle for power of the Herschel chiefs. In addition it was shown that 'the people' were not simply 'victims', as many had good reasons –a shortage of land– to leave Herschel. Moreover, this more politically-oriented history of Thornhill has revealed that many factions –whether tribal or non-tribal in nature– battled with each other over the years. It is a story of changing coalitions and allegiances. Such an analysis has also aided to reveal the political dimension of NGO interventions. This case of the Monti Rural Association, for example, has shown that aiding rural dwellers to set up residents associations in the eighties, had everything to do with the overall struggle against apartheid, as some of the MRA staff were linked to the underground ANC. Again, this illustrates that such 'micro-struggles' were influenced by the major political developments in South Africa and vice versa.

This research project has illustrated the interdependencies between 'small politics' and 'large politics' and between 'national history', 'regional history' and 'local history'. Histories are interrelated and national political and socio-economic developments have shaped local developments and vice versa. It is clear that there is not **one** all-encompassing history, but a series of partially overlapping histories. Therefore, I have also tried to reinterpret recent national South African political history, from the perspective of the 'progressive forces'. In my opinion, this can aid to improve our understanding of the transformations that occurred in South Africa over the past two decades and the way in which these transformations impacted on the role of NGOs.

Beyond Apartheid and Post-apartheid
I chose to analyze recent South African history from the perspective of the 'progressive forces' that fought apartheid and ultimately took over the government in 1994. When studying the upheavals of transformation, it increasingly appeared that one had to move beyond the scheme of 'apartheid' and 'post-apartheid', as it ignored the extraordinary period of transition. Therefore, in order to understand the complex changes that took place in South Africa, I proposed to identify three consecutive eras: the 'struggle era' in the 1980s; a 'freedom and consultation era' between 1993 and 1996; and a 'new realism era' after 1996. Although I have dated these periods in South African history quite precisely, I am the last to argue that there are no overlaps.

The 'struggle era' ended when the interim constitution was approved by Parliament on 18 December 1993. From that moment on it was more or less certain that apartheid was defeated. It marked the beginning of a new era of 'freedom and consultation'. It was a time of euphoria and of a firm belief in the possibilities of reaching consensus and solving problems through consultation. In this period Mandela preached reconciliation, and the ANC (1994) and its partners published the Reconstruction and Development Programme (RDP). It was a time of great transformations and a fluidity of the boundaries between the state and civil society. For NGOs it seemed a period of unlimited opportunities, but as it turned out, also of grave threats. However, by June 1996 the 'freedom and consultation' era ended when the National Party quit the Government of National Unity and the new Minister of Finance produced the neo-liberal macro-economic Growth, Employment and Redistribution (GEAR) strategy. This marked the beginning of the 'new realism era'. For 'the progressive forces' the honeymoon was over and the time of delivery and a harsh confrontation with the limitations and possibilities of the world market had begun.

These national political developments impacted strongly on society, but were, in turn, also influenced from below. Each era came with its own political discourse, that influenced actors, and, thus, shaped NGO interventions. However, people were always able to use elements of previous discourses as well. In Chapter 7, for instance, it is shown how politicians, nowadays, can eclectically make use of these discourses whenever it suits them. The speech of the Eastern Cape Premier that is described, for example, contained 'struggle' elements to express his solidarity with the NGOs and farm workers, 'freedom and consultation' elements to stress his commitment to an open government and 'new realism' elements to convince the NGOs that their modes of lobbying were no longer appropriate in the late nineties.

To round off, I would argue that an *embedded tale* is an attempt to ground cases in their context and link levels of analysis, whereby both the interdependencies and the inherent contradictions are revealed.

The Storm of Transformation: chaos and continuity
The upheavals of transformation that engulfed South Africa during the 1990s led to great confusion. The 'progressives' entered legitimate politics; a new constitution was drawn up; black areas were reintegrated in white areas; apartheid bureaucrats were replaced by 'rainbow' bureaucrats; democracy replaced oppression; the apartheid legislation was largely scrapped; most government policies and procedures were reviewed and altered; new provinces emerged; new local government structures were established, et cetera. For all actors concerned it proved to be a time of bewilderment, leading to great opportunities for some and grave threats for others.

For social scientists this period of rapid change meant a historic opportunity. Not only did the NGO sector display great openness towards critical research, also government departments were very accessible, as the Rainbow Nation advocated complete transparency. As a result, a foreign researcher could attend –and participate in– several 'freedom and consultation'-type forums, thus witnessing 'the new South Africa' in action. The extreme nature of these transformations was revealing and as the whole institutional environment was in flux it proved easier to recognize the mechanisms of change in NGOs themselves.

Consequently, this research project did not result in a standard portrayal of NGOs in a, more or less, stable institutional environment, as is normally the case in the 'NGO literature'. In such studies organizations are frequently objectified, while the institutional environment is assumed to be unchanging. In South Africa, however, nothing remained what it was. NGOs, government departments, politicians, bureaucrats, private consultancy firms and 'the people at grassroots': all actors performed in a play, although someone seemingly had lost the script. At times one actor seemed in charge, at other times a complete 'democracy' –read chaos– reigned.

For the social scientist it was fascinating to watch that the model of state-civil society-market seemed to become completely fluid. As was shown in this book, NGO personnel was seconded to government; NGOs became active in voter education; government staff cooperated with NGOs to advise them how to best lobby the same government; and NGO staff left the NGO sector to establish private consultancy firms. In other words, boundaries blurred and in some instances the NGOs became government and vice versa. Significantly, however, an organization like the Monti Rural Association actually became a *beacon of continuity* for the new government during the early phase of the transition. MRA set up training programmes for local government staff, MRA staff participated in many of the steering committees that designed new policies and, for example, the Eastern Cape Land Reform Pilot Programme was established in Thornhill and environs because of the fact that MRA had developed close ties with this community during the 'struggle era'. Thus, in my opinion, it is safe to say that the implementation of land reform, in the early years of the transition, was to a large extent facilitated by the NGOs affiliated to the National Land Committee.

During this transition period the NGO sector contributed much of its human resources. The institutional memory in the land sector was largely located in the minds and hearts of the people in NGOs who, for almost two decades, had devoted their energy to the land struggles. Ultimately, it was exactly this resource that was targeted and incorporated by the first democratic government. This caused a massive brain drain, which left the NGO sector essentially crippled after the mid-1990s, while the state had gained in strength. However, this institutional memory was not lost for South Africa. It only meant that the people had traded in civil society for the state, where they continued to shape land reform. However, the state hunger was not easily stilled. Thus, an increasing number of 'rainbow' bureaucrats was needed when affirmative action policies were adopted, which meant that anyone with only the slightest bit of training gained in NGOs could be used. Hence, I described, what I have termed, the *capacity building trap* in the mid-nineties. In that period NGO capacity building led to organizational decline rather than to organizational upliftment, because the extra training caused people to leave the NGO sector more rapidly instead of building up the sector's capacity.

Looking back, I would argue that civil society was very strong in the eighties as the struggle against apartheid intensified. Of course, as was shown in Chapter 2, other scholars may argue that civil society was weak in those days because the majority of South African citizens were, in fact, not citizens, and had few civil rights.

Hyden (1996), for example, argued that former colonial states in sub-Saharan Africa were not conducive to the development of civil society:

> "...civil society presupposes the existence of a public realm in which there is a clear delineation of rights and obligations between individual citizens, on the one hand, and the state on the other" (p. 103).

However, authors like Kasfir (1998) and Lewis (2002) have shown that such a prescriptive and normative use of the term *civil* society creates difficulties in the African context. They, in fact, argue for a more inclusive definition that leaves room for a wider group of actually existing organizations and associations. In my opinion the South African case unmistakably shows that substantial civic activity and a momentous social movement against the apartheid rulers destabilized the regime. Thus, in my opinion, a strong and brutal autocratic state was challenged by an increasingly strong civil society. When the apartheid regime was finally toppled in the early nineties, the new government lacked experience and capacity and was initially quite weak. By the mid-nineties, during the 'freedom and consultation era', substantial overlaps between state and civil society developed, whereby the boundaries between the realms increasingly blurred. However, by the late nineties, civil society was in crisis. Not only had the NGOs been deserted by the best staff, also other civil society organizations were battling with apathy and a dwindling membership. The most obvious example is the South African National Civics Organization (SANCO) that used to have an immensely active membership during the struggle years. By the late nineties it had lost a substantial part of this membership and it struggled to define its position in society. This was made more difficult as prominent members of the organization became influential politicians. In the Eastern Cape, for example, Max Mamase, a leading SANCO figure, was given a high position in the provincial government. Was this the co-opting –or the rewarding– of civil society by the state? Whatever the mechanism, it did seriously harm the critical monitoring abilities of civil society.

This example is, in fact, exemplary of the specific problems experienced in South Africa during the late nineties. As Wood (1997), Abrahamsen (2000), Kasfir (1998) and others have argued, citizens need a well-functioning state. In a balanced society, the interplay between the state, civil society and the market does not produce one overly dominant realm. Normally, therefore, the performance of civil society benefits from a well-functioning state. State structures, policies and procedures are needed for the state to be lobbied effectively. However, in the late nineties, as the state had finally regained some of its strength, and a strong civil society was needed to lobby and critically monitor that state, civil society had largely withered. The state praying mantis had bitten off the head of its civil society partner.

In conclusion, I would argue that the land sector NGOs in South Africa developed from being a strong anti-state bastion during the 'struggle era' to being a cooperative comrade during the 'freedom and consultation era' in the mid-nineties, when the boundaries between the state and civil society temporarily blurred. By the late nineties the NGO sector was left largely crippled and a period of mild estrangement followed as NGOs and the state each seemed to retreat into their original niche. After discussing these upheavals of the South African transformation it is now time to focus on some of the myths about NGOs.

NGO Myths: a revealing case study

Authors like Farrington and Bebbington (1993), Edwards and Hulme (1992), Fowler (1991, 1997), Ball and Dunn (1995) and Bratton (1990) have contributed to what I have called the 'NGO literature'. It is this body of development literature that has tended to produce numerous myths about NGOs. These NGO myths will be discussed here to show what aspects must be reconsidered as a result of the of the Monti Rural Association ethnographic case study.

Autonomy and Independence

As this case study has shown, we must really question the NGO myth that portrays these organizations as 'independent' or 'autonomous'. Indeed, the Monti Rural Association is to a certain degree independent, as it can make decisions to support certain communities or join campaigns like the Farm Worker Campaign. However, this label of independence can also impede our observations, as it may obscure the webs of interdependency an intermediary organization like MRA is entangled in. In fact, the intermediary quality of the NGO sector is both its strongest asset and its Achilles heel. As an NGO is less bound by the laws of hierarchy and procedures prevalent in government departments, nor hampered by the decision-making procedures common in membership-based organizations, it is able to operate with relative flexibility and speed on many levels and in different arenas at once. Most importantly, however, an NGO can engage in, what I have called, *strategic translations* in order to reach its goals. It can make use of the spaces it identifies, especially when other actors –like the state and communities– do not communicate directly. Thus, NGOs may strategically shape the pictures that are relayed.

In my view, therefore, the Gasela case illustrated the significant dependence on more powerful actors in government, rather than confirming the NGO's independence. Since the government owned the land that the Gasela community desired, both MRA and the Gasela rural dwellers were highly dependent on the Department of Land Affairs (DLA) to make a favourable decision. As a result, the NGO came to be caught in DLA's 'market-oriented embrace', which encouraged MRA to paint a picture of Gasela as a potentially thriving agri-village. This made little sense as the community history had shown that these rural dwellers –a rural proletariat?– lacked the necessary agricultural background.

Especially in schemes where NGOs are contracted by the government, the degree of dependency on government can be extensive. To limit such ties of dependency, however, NGOs usually seek support by donors. Yet, there is an inherent contradiction in the fact that in order to overcome being excessively dependent on governments, NGOs become increasingly dependent on (foreign) donors. Particularly, when NGOs are funded to undertake specific projects, the donors have a large say in the running of such projects. Therefore, NGOs like the Monti Rural Association prefer core funding, as it provides them with some room to decide more freely in what (political) activities –like lobbying and advocacy– the money is invested.

When we consider the so-called independence of the NGO sector we also have to discuss the dependence of NGOs on the communities they support. Although NGOs usually recognize the fact that the term *community* is flawed, as it disguises competition for power and resources by different groups or individuals, the organizations repeatedly get caught in the same trap as the term is simply too convenient. As a result of labelling groups as a 'community', the Monti Rural Association has, on numerous occasions, underestimated the tensions in these groups. For example, the interventions in Merino Walk, Gallawater A and Gasela all revealed how such dynamics and conflicts were repeatedly underestimated and ignored by MRA. Consequently, development interventions were frustrated and sometimes even broke down completely. Another problem with regard to community dynamics and the success of interventions is related to history of previous interventions. As land sector NGOs in South Africa often stick with the communities they have worked with from the days of their inception, these organizations can become the 'victim' of their previous interventions. For example, during the struggle against apartheid NGOs had both hidden and exposed agendas when they pushed the establishment of residents associations in the rural areas. In fact, the choice to back the 'progressives' actors in communities automatically involved a choice to oppose the tribal authority structures which were linked to the oppressive bantustan regimes. Thus, although in my view sympathetic, such interventions usually reinforced discord in areas marred by conflict. When in such communities the Monti Rural Association engaged in development interventions in later years, it was always confronted with a section of 'the people' whom they had turned against during the struggle. These people usually had not forgotten MRA's past role and were generally quite negative about these new interventions. In other words, an image that was created during a past intervention can haunt an NGO in the present and the future.

Related to this issue is the fact that the choice to work with the wrong group of people can also have its repercussions, like the Gallawater A case has exposed in Chapter 6. Frequently, except in small areas with little hierarchy, NGO staff is inclined to work with the leaders, elites or better educated people in a community. Not only do these elites present themselves as leaders, in many instances it is also most convenient for the NGO staff to interact with people who, for example, speak English and have some grasp of organizational processes. However, fairly regularly, such leaders are already involved in conflicts, as the Gallawater A case has revealed. If NGOs are not aware of the extent of such conflicts, these projects can blow up in their faces. When, in order to find a solution in such situations, NGOs then proceed to set up parallel structures, as was done by MRA in Gallawater A and Merino Walk, the problems are usually exacerbated. For the Monti Rural Association eventually only one option was left open: a total withdrawal from the area.

Participation, Accountability and Democracy

Two other NGO myths are strongly related: the myths of participation and accountability. Indeed, from a more superficial point of view, it seems that NGOs are more keen to involve 'the people at grassroots' or 'the poorest of the poor' than other development actors from the state or the market that employ 'bottom-up approaches'. However, the Monti Rural Association case study has revealed that there are several fundamental problems in such participatory approaches. As a result, one can seriously question whether NGOs are indeed the 'agents of democracy' they are frequently portrayed to be. Firstly, problematic 'community' dynamics, as described above, may impede a balanced involvement of all sections of the population in an area. Secondly, it must be realized that many areas are simply to big for participatory approaches. In an area like Thornhill, for example, with approximately 15,000 residents, it is hard to involve everyone in community decisions. Although MRA normally attempts to reach as many people as possible, it has proven to be extremely difficult to drum up more than 200 people in the community hall. For routine meetings, usually not more than 30 people turn up, which is not enough to make a quorum. Even if the representatives that do attend aim to consult their supporters, it must be strongly doubted whether the decisions taken at such poorly attended meetings have any democratic value. Normally, the intervening party –whether NGO, private sector, or government agency– holds the trump cards. These agencies draw up the agendas for the meetings and have a greater say in what is discussed. If such meetings are then used to be accountable to 'the people', 'democracy' in action is, of course, inherently flawed.

It is interesting that such flaws can be more easily detected when research is conducted beyond the dynamic interactions that take place between an NGO and a community. In fact, this research project has revealed that it is worthwhile –if not crucial– to undertake ethnographic research in communities when the NGO is absent. During the absence of the intervening parties much can be learned about the relationship between the local community and the NGOs. By only attending the dynamic workshops and meetings between an NGO and the community, we, as social scientists, may get a distorted view concerning the relative importance of an NGO. Thus, we may develop a kind of road-side bias –we could call it *the workshop bias*– as a result of which we fail to see what is beyond the first row of houses. Therefore, in order to understand NGO interventions, we should remain behind –for a few days at least– when the NGO has left.

With regard to the participatory rhetoric of NGOs, it is necessary to discuss the methods of interaction these organizations frequently employ. Although meetings may generate some true debate, usually 'the workshop' is much more flawed. In my opinion, so-called *participatory workshops* are regularly carefully scripted in advance. For example, I have witnessed many instances where the participatory outcome was already known before the workshop had even started. This confirms the view of Pottier (1997), who has argued that participatory workshops are structured encounters, marked by hidden agendas.

What I must remark, however, is that this is not always necessarily problematic, because NGOs may be quite aware of what kind of intervention is needed. Moreover, in many instances it does not seem to make sense to ask 'the people' what they want, as 'the people', because of their poor educational background, can hardly make an informed choice. For example, I attended a workshop in Thornhill where 'the people' had to decide what kind of a pit latrine toilets they wanted installed in their settlement. They were shown fancy technical drawings and elaborate plans, but, of course, the technical NGO expert, by advising them of the advantages and disadvantages of certain designs was able to steer them in a certain direction. Cynically argued, such workshops involve just going through the participatory motions, to give the people the feeling that *"they own the process"*[2].

Another aspect of participation, or the lack thereof, concerns the fact that 'the people at grassroots', have little or no influence over the strategic direction taken by the NGO that intervenes in their community. This research has revealed that the Monti Rural Association has struggled with this issue from the early years of its existence. Although there were always proponents within the organization who believed in a more profound involvement of community members in the running of the organization, this never truly materialized. Only recently have so-called *project control groups* been set up which are aimed to ensure greater community involvement in the running of projects. However, as I have shown, the NGO professionals are not keen to relinquish their positions of control. Also with regard to recently becoming a Section 21 Company, for which the MRA has engaged in a membership drive, the NGO professionals seem determined to remain in control of their organization. They set the agendas and control the funds. In my opinion, therefore, more research is needed to reveal to what extent the participation rhetoric of the NGO sector makes sense.

Voluntary Organizations that are Value-driven
Another persistent NGO myth overemphasizes the voluntary character of the sector. Of course, as MRA history has illustrated, the voluntary character of the organization in the early years was very clear. And even today, some of the board members are volunteers. However, it has also become obvious that organizations like MRA have become increasingly run and staffed by professionals. Thus, the voluntary component in 21st century land sector NGOs in South Africa is very, very limited. Yet, what must be stressed is that increased professionalism not necessarily automatically involve decreased commitment, as is often claimed by disillusioned ex-activists. At the same time, the case studies have revealed that 'professionalism' cannot be simply equated with 'better', or more 'efficient' or 'effective'. In my view, organizations do not follow evolutionary paths as is often argued in the 'NGO literature'. Rather, contradictory processes can take place in an organization and periods of regression and processes of unlearning may occur as other types of knowledge are prioritized. An ethnographic approach can uncover such inconsistencies, contradictions and paradoxes that frustrate processes of organizational learning. Consequently, failures may occur again and again, even in highly professionalized organizations.

Related to the discussions concerning professionalism is the modern NGO myth that non-governmental organizations are purely 'value-driven' and not 'self-serving'. Indeed, superficially, most NGOs, that are established to fight some cause or support a disadvantaged section of society, will not contradict such a myth. However, as with every organization, business or government department, people have to get paid, budgets have to be passed and organizational dynamics have to be sustained. In the case of MRA it has been revealed that a certain concern for its long-term survival prompted the management of the organization to engage in a sustainability drive during the late nineties. Although it must be acknowledged that the restructuring process was meant to improve organizational performance in delivery, there was clearly a self-serving component as the management feared a complete collapse of funding in the post-2000 era. Again, it must be reiterated that being to a degree self-serving, does not mean that values do not play a role in NGOs. In my opinion, therefore, Korten (1990) was wrong when he indicated that on the one extreme one finds Voluntary Organizations that are value-driven, while on the other extreme one finds Public Service Contractors in which values play no role. The Monti Rural Association case illustrated that it is possible to combine political values, moral values and societal values with an increased drive towards professionalism.

Non-Profit and the Role of Donors
The last myth I want to touch upon concerns the 'non-profit' label that is frequently associated with NGOs. Especially the American literature normally portrays the NGO sector as the 'non-profit sector'. However, as I have argued in Chapter 2 this label is problematic as it obscures the fact that NGOs, like any other institution, are increasingly confronted with the dominance of the market. With regard to MRA it was also illustrated that a 'new realism' discourse has progressively penetrated the South African land sector NGOs. It cannot be denied that for-profit activities have been added to their repertoires, although it is still obvious for the NGOs that for-profit activities must be reinvested in non-profit activities. Not only has this impact of the market led to a market-rhetoric in which grassroots communities are described as 'clients', NGOs have also engaged in actual investment activities. For example, the Monti Rural Association now holds an off-shore investment portfolio, not for the sake of making money, but in order to sustain the organization. These developments, in my view, make it highly questionable to still describe the NGO sector in the early 21st century as the non-profit sector.

Nevertheless, although land sector NGOs have increasingly entered 'the market', the Monti Rural Association case has illustrated that (foreign) donors remain of the utmost importance. Basically, an organization like MRA will cease to exist as an NGO when these funders pull the plug. Only through funding –preferably core funding– are these organizations able to retain their political profile and a degree of 'independence'. According to the MRA management, the core funds provide them with the possibility to remain politically active and to reinforce their lobbying and advocacy activities. However, it has also been revealed that the relationship with Northern non-governmental funding organizations may get strained as these donors, increasingly, relay the professionalization and management pressures they are under from Northern states to their counterparts in the South.

Although Northern non-governmental funding organizations usually present themselves as 'partners in development' of Southern NGOs, this 'counterpart rhetoric' can prove to be quite hollow. There is usually a clear 'top-down' element in the relationship as the donor controls the money. As illustrated in Chapter 8, this can sometimes lead to excesses, like unilaterally rescinding a contract or announcing that another organization will handle future contracts. Thus, these Northern NGFOs are sometimes as technocratically 'top-down' as the Northern states that provide them with the funds. Moreover, this research project has shown that these organizations are essentially Janus-faced. They have to balance an image created to raise funds in the North with a neutral, largely non-political image in the South, in order not to offend their 'counterparts', nor the political leadership.

Are these Lessons Universal?
The question now remains whether the observations made in this case study can be generalized. In order to get a clearer picture, I conducted literature research, visited

similar land sector NGOs in South Africa and attended the four-day Annual General Meeting of the National Land Committee (NLC) –the umbrella organization of land sector NGOs– in 1997. From my conversations with members of staff of these other NLC affiliates, it emerged that these NGOs faced similar issues and problems as the Monti Rural Association had faced in the 1990s. Therefore, I am convinced that the experience of the Monti Rural Association during the storms of transformation generally applies to all the land sector NGOs in South Africa. For example, these organizations all faced severe brain drain problems and management problems in the mid-nineties and struggled with their participatory approaches. In comparison, it must be acknowledged that the Monti Rural Association, although it experienced a severe crisis in 1996, is usually recognized by the National Land Committee as a positive example. For example, at the turn of the century both sister affiliates in the Eastern Cape –the Port Elizabeth Rural Association (PERA) and the Umtata Land Committee (ULC)– were disaffiliated by the National Land Committee due to mismanagement.

In addition, I have spoken to and interacted with other NGO umbrella structures, like the Eastern Cape NGO Coalition. This helped me to piece together a picture of the situation in health and education NGOs, that have faced similar brain drain problems in the mid-nineties. However, the problems in these sectors were exacerbated by extreme declines in funding. As Northern governments and donors began to transfer their funding to the now legitimate government, after the first democratic elections, many non-governmental organizations faced bankruptcy.

Whether or not the MRA case study can be simply generalized, or extrapolated, to the rest of the world I cannot say for sure. Yet, I believe that this case study can aid other social scientists, but also people within NGOs in other regions of the world, to become more sensitive to similar problems in non-governmental organizations. For example, I am convinced that the fundamental issues concerning the 'participatory approaches', the ambivalent relationship with the state, the doubts with regard to NGOs being the 'agents of democracy', and the dependence on donors can be encountered everywhere. Moreover, as other authors have also pointed out on numerous occasions, there are inherent flaws in the terminology employed by NGOs. Whether 'community', 'empowerment', 'bottom-up', 'the poorest of the poor', 'grass-roots', 'the household': such 'NGO-speak' is encountered everywhere. As such a rhetoric clouds our understanding, I believe that there is a need for more research. We need to move beyond the myths and improve our understanding of the functioning of 'real' organizations out there.

Agendas for Future Research

When pondering agendas for future research several things come to mind. First, it would of course be of great value if many other detailed ethnographic studies about NGOs would be conducted in different regions of the world. Such *embedded tales* about NGOs would help to build a large and rich data-base about non-governmental organizations in different fields, regions, contexts and societies. Not only is such a database valuable because of its documentary character, but it may also serve well-founded comparative research, which contrasts with the shallow examples often encountered in the 'NGO literature' (e.g. Bebbington and Farrington, 1992). Such rich ethnographic studies can help us to move beyond many of the NGO myths that are still prevalent and create a more realistic picture of NGOs. Thus, for example, questions may be answered about the difference between NGOs that function opposite authoritarian regimes and NGOs that function in full-fledged democracies; or about the difference in 'participatory approaches' between Southern African and South American land sector NGOs. In addition, I want to remark that such research into the role of NGOs will teach us more about different civil societies. However, this should also be complemented by research into other types of civil society organizations, because indeed, as Lewis (2002) has argued, *"there is a rich theoretical tradition of thinking about civil society, but far less empirical work available"* (p. 581).

Second, I would urge the donor community, and especially Northern non-governmental funding organizations (NGFOs), to open its doors for critical 'anthropology of development' endeavours. Donors have to move beyond employing 'development anthropologists' –'relative insiders'– in order to give an integrated development project a socially acceptable flavour. In my opinion it would be of great use –to learn more about all types of NGOs– by employing ethnographic research methods. An fascinating theme is to study the Janus-faced character of NGFOs. It would be interesting to uncover the political 'webs of dependency' these organizations are engaged in, by employing historically- and politically-oriented research methods. What, for example, are the relationships of Oxfam-family organizations with the Northern states? How independent are they? To what degree are they influenced by the political discourses that originate in the Northern ministries of development cooperation? What is the role of informal contacts in these relationships? I believe that such studies can further our understanding about the overlaps between civil society and the state in the North.

More importantly, it would be useful to discover more about the relationship between Northern NGFOs and the Southern NGOs they support; from the point of view of these funding agencies. As this research project has explored the relationship between Southern NGOs and their funders from the vantage point at the receiving end, it would be complementary to initiate similar research projects from the other vantage point. It would, for example, be interesting to look at the congruence between the 'partner rhetoric' in Northern funder reports and fund-raising pamphlets, and the manner in which the staff in such organizations, de facto, speak about and deal with their 'counterparts'. Moreover, it may be revealing to witness the way in which staff review Southern NGO reports or grant applications –the 'reported reality'. How do they assess the rhetoric in such documents? In addition it would be interesting to observe staff during their evaluation missions in order to learn how they interact with their 'partners in the South': how they value the trips into the communities and what they think about the model projects that they are shown. However, it remains to be seen whether such organizations, that are highly dependent on their public image, would be willing to take the risk of tolerating a critical anthropologist.

Third, I would argue to initiate more community-based research projects that specifically focus on the decision-making procedures in communities and the participatory approaches and accountability strategies of NGOs. This is particularly relevant because these themes are entwined with issues of democracy. In my research it was, for example, exposed how the participation of community members in their own affairs was flawed. It would be useful to discover whether other communities experience similar problems, as Pottier (1997) has also argued. Since I have shown that community structures and the role of community representatives are usually contested as well, it would make sense to design research projects that trace exactly how decisions are taken within communities. It would be valuable to then trace such decisions that are taken forward by the NGOs that support and discover how they are ultimately dealt with by the relevant government departments. In order to determine the extent to which 'democracy' works, it is important to chart exactly who is involved in *the production of* decision-making. In this regard it is also valuable to find out more about the roles of elites. Who is left out of decision-making and how communities deal with contested issues?

A last issue is especially relevant in the South African context. As land sector NGOs have been partially responsible for setting up Communal Property Associations (CPAs), much more detailed research is needed on the functioning of these structures. Although I am aware of at least one such project, undertaken by Chris de Wet of Rhodes University, I believe that many more projects should be initiated and funded. As the *willing-buyer willing-seller* approach of implementing land reform in South Africa has produced such entities, it is crucial to determine whether the land has become an asset or a liability for the beneficiaries involved. Is it possible to manage a farm with one hundred rural families? How are decisions taken? How are the financial burdens and the proceeds shared? Without first answering such fundamental questions it is, in my view, irresponsible to continue establishing such structures in land reform across South Africa.

Observations about Land Sector NGOs and Land Reform in South Africa

To end this book I want to share my personal opinion about land sector NGOs and land reform. However, let me first make some remarks about the results of this research project. Although the book might seem overly critical about the role of land sector NGOs, it must be stressed that much of this critique is the result of engaging in an academic debate. In debate with the 'NGO gurus' it was necessary to critically examine the myths about NGOs. However, by doing so an impression might have been created that not much of what the Monti Rural Association did was 'good'. However, this *embedded tale* is not about 'good' or 'bad'. It is about gaining understanding, and in the process showing that failures as well as successes are an inherent part of NGOs and civil society. Thus, the failures do not warrant the conclusion that NGOs are useless.

Land Sector NGOs

Let me begin to say something about the Monti Rural Association and the other affiliates of the National Land Committee that I have come to be acquainted with in the mid- and late nineties. First of all these NGOs must be commended for the role they played in the struggle against apartheid. These organizations were crucial in publicizing the extent of the suffering that was caused by forced removals. They were the first organizations to 'go out there' to interact with the 'victims' and relay their stories to the world. Subsequently, the NLC affiliates became active during the establishment of new land reform policies, procedures and government institutions, for which they should also be praised. However, my interaction with these organizations in 1996, 1997 and 1998, took place in another period. It was a period of crisis, decline, but, in the case of the Monti Rural Association, also a period of reconstruction and reconstitution. I would say that MRA actually exited the tunnel stronger and better-equipped to deal with land reform in the 21st century. Sadly, however, other affiliates, more or less, collapsed. Not only did MRA set course on a path to increased 'professionalism' but also a conscious strategy was mapped out to recapture some of its political profile that seemed to have been lost by late 1996.

It is exactly this political role which is, in my view, indispensable for NGOs. Therefore, what I have found most impressive was the ability of these organizations to sink their teeth in a certain problem, issue or community and bring that problem to the attention of others. In such an agenda-setting role NGOs can put issues on the local, regional or even the national agenda. A recent example is the research MRA conducted in Chata, a rural area that was subjected to betterment (Chapter 3) during apartheid. After extensive research the organization argued successfully with the Department of Land Affairs that communities, which were the victims of betterment, also deserved to be eligible for restitution. Thus, when the South African government agreed, a huge precedent was set, which opened up new avenues for the land restitution programme. For this project the Monti Rural Association received an NGO award[3].

An NGO campaign that I witnessed during my research was the Farm Worker Campaign. Although not as successful, it was invigorating to witness the civic energy released by such efforts. It was moving to attend such interactions with farm workers, that were conducted deep in the rural areas. Besides the fact that the commitment and effort of the MRA staff was impressive, it was especially touching to see the reaction of old farm workers, who had never before been taken seriously or listened to. In my opinion, organizations that achieve such results have every right to exist and deserve to be funded. Nevertheless, as I uphold my criticism with respect to the problematic nature of participation and consultation, mechanisms should be explored to improve these interactions. It should be attempted to increase democratic control and accountability to the people they are meant to serve. These organizations can be –and should be– the 'civil society catalysts' that are indispensable for a healthy democracy. Sadly enough the Farm Worker Campaign also illustrated the current weakness of the land sector NGOs, as it proved, on the whole, too little too late.

Overseeing South African land sector NGOs and the state they were in during the late nineties and taking into account the news of the demise of some NLC affiliates, it must be remarked that there is still much to worry about. In a land sector where government, which is seriously understaffed and under-equipped, relies on other implementation agents, there is too little NGO capacity to aid the rural poor. There are simply too few organizations like the Monti Rural Association and the work that is taken on is a drop in the ocean. Not only are the number of NGOs that have remained active too few, also the lack of well-trained staff and management capacity in some of the affiliates is worrying. Thus, the work in land reform is increasingly undertaken by private consultants. And although some of these are 'rainbow consultants', land reform is too crucial for the development of a stable society to be left largely in the hands of the private sector. In my opinion it is time that NGOs do their utmost to set up new subsidiaries, training programmes and try to convince funders to support new initiatives. In this respect it is absurd that there is still talk amongst donors of pulling out of South Africa, as the transition is said to be almost completed. Society benefits from a strong state that is critically monitored by a strong civil society. Thus, there is a need for organizations like the Monti Rural Association, and funders should aim to invest more, rather than less.

Land for the Landless
By spending time in the former bantustan dumping grounds and other rural communities in the Eastern Cape, it has become absolutely clear to me during my fieldwork that more drastic measures are needed to achieve progress in South African land reform. The destitution of much of the rural population is still substantial. There is a lack of Infrastructure, there is little prime agricultural land available, there are problems with erosion, access to services is problematic and there are hardly any economic opportunities to support the people in their daily needs. If we take into account that, at the same time, wealthy white communities still live in luxurious circumstances, it is clear that these rural people deserve something better. The least they deserve is a well-functioning land reform programme. In the early nineties 63% of South Africa's land surface was in the hands of approximately eighty thousand white farmers. On the other hand fourteen million (!) 'blacks' lived on 13.7% of the worst land, as was shown in Chapter 3. This was roughly the point of departure for the Department of Land Affairs in 1994. If we look back and assess what Mandela and Mbeki have achieved with respect to land reform, one can only conclude that the programme has failed dismally. By late 1999 only a few hundred restitution claims had been resolved, the redistribution process was simply much too slow and little progress had been achieved in tenure reform. Of course, the rainbow coalition may claim that it battled with the bureaucratic apartheid legacy. As a result, so many new procedures, policies and legislation had to be (re-)invented, that it was hardly possible to achieve more progress. In fact, as a highly placed official told me the Department of Land Affairs had underspent its budget by about 80%, during the early years of the transition. However, in my view, the lack of progress should also be blamed on fundamentally wrong choices that were made from the start. If such huge disparities are not corrected within the next decades, South Africa will always remain the scene of widespread social unrest.

In my opinion the new administrative approach in restitution, introduced in 1999, has indeed improved results, mainly by settling relatively small urban claims through financial compensation. Nevertheless, there are still huge challenges ahead, principally in the rural areas. I am, furthermore, apprehensive about the future of redistribution, as I do not believe that Land Redistribution for Agricultural Development (LRAD), which was launched in 2001, is the solution. It is still too slow, and I have serious doubts whether the land will be transferred to 'real' farmers. The recent developments with regard to tenure reform are even more worrying. The Communal Land Rights Bill and the Traditional Leadership and Governance Framework Bill, which were both tabled in 2003, propose to strengthen and revive the Tribal Authorities, which are remnants of the colonial and apartheid-era oppressive machinery. It will be an enormous setback for democracy and the potential emancipation of women, which is quite incomprehensible in a country that only ten years ago hailed democracy and its progressive constitution. Hopefully, the democratic forces will eventually prevail.

In my opinion, the ANC should have fought much harder to make expropriation a viable option. Although the party succeeded to include a section in the constitution that would allow expropriation for public purposes –including land reform– the responsible politicians have waited too long to investigate this option more seriously. Only recently, in 2001 has Thoko Didiza, the new Minister of Land Affairs in the Mbeki cabinet, tried to expropriate white land[4]. However, the uproar that was caused was so huge that the expropriation attempt was more or less aborted. An important reason for the uproar however, had little to do with the act of expropriation as such. The farmer was primarily offended by the limited amount of money that was offered to him in compensation. Although I understand that land reform has not been designed to make white farmers rich, I am convinced that when negotiations are handled properly it is possible to settle such cases satisfactorily.

In my view, widespread expropriation that is responsibly handled, is the only solution to achieve serious progress in the land sector. However, South Africa should be careful not to emulate Zimbabwe, where politically motivated divide and rule tactics and government-instigated violent attacks against farmers and farm workers are prevalent. In my opinion, some basic rules should be observed. First, the government should ensure that the relatively small group of economically successful commercial farmers have nothing to fear; as long as they abide by the laws of the land. However, even this group can be stimulated to experiment more with, for example, share-equity schemes[5], as some have already done. Moreover, expropriation measures should first be applied to those farmers who own more than one farm. Furthermore, many of the other farms are so large that large tracts of land are, more or less, unused. These portions of land could also be targeted. Although I agree with the analysis of the National Land Committee analysis that most land was once robbed from the original owners, I think that it is unfair not to pay adequate compensation, as many contemporary farmers once bought the land they now farm. Moreover, these entrepreneurs need capital to start new businesses, which may ultimately benefit South African society. Thus, the state should enter into negotiations with white farmers' organizations to agree upon rules that determine the height of the compensation. In keeping with the 'freedom and consultation discourse' this may lead to a form of 'negotiated expropriation'.

What is also important is that the people selected to receive prime agricultural land should be screened. Only proven farmers should receive high quality land. Others, who also have the aim to farm may be given the chance to prove themselves, but should be monitored accurately. If they fail to establish themselves –say within five years– others should be allowed to take over. However, to most rural dwellers – the majority of which are **not** potential farmers– only a residential plot with a reasonably sized garden should be awarded, in order to provide tenure security, but not waste prime agricultural land. Furthermore, to support serious emergent farmers, small-scale, slightly subsidized, but commercially oriented agricultural resource centres should be established across the country. Here farmers may get advice, inputs and credit for a reasonable fee. It is important that no large bureaucratic extension schemes should be established, as such schemes have failed almost everywhere in the world. What I find worrying in this regard is that the Eastern Cape Province plans to revitalize the old bantustan irrigation schemes. In my opinion these prime examples of corruption and inefficiency will never produce the desired result.

Lastly, I believe that the resources and staffing of the Department of Land Affairs, handling restitution, redistribution, tenure reform and 'negotiated expropriation' should be substantially increased. Highly positioned Department of Land Affairs officials explained to me that only a few hundred officials across the country were handling land reform in the late nineties. This means that there is very little human capacity allocated to land reform in South Africa. In comparison, Japan after World War II appointed 36,000 officials to carry out land reform and realize the transfer of 30 million pieces of land (Cloete, 1992). Although such large numbers of staff may neither be realistic nor required in the South African context, I believe that the current number is simply not enough. It is time that the dispossessed are finally granted access to the land they have been waiting for...

Appendix 1: Methodological Notes

Before commencing my fieldwork in 1997 I chose to visit South Africa in 1996 to investigate which research location and which organization would be most suitable for a prolonged fieldwork period. A crucial determining factor was the willingness of such an NGO to cooperate with as little reservation as possible. During this exploratory visit two organizations expressed their interest to cooperate: the Monti Rural Association in the Eastern Cape and the Northern Action Association in Gauteng. I chose to conduct the research in the Eastern Cape, as it had been earmarked by the Dutch government as area of focus, since it was one of the poorest provinces South Africa. Moreover, the Eastern Cape proved interesting as it encompassed two former homelands. Furthermore, it appeared that both the non-governmental and the governmental sector in the province were characterized by a great openness. I order to ensure a degree of academic distance, I became a visiting research fellow at the Institute of Social and Economic Research (ISER) of Rhodes University at the campus in East London.

The actual fieldwork covered a period from early 1997 to mid-1998. I spent most of the first year with the Monti Rural Association and the institutions that the NGO dealt with. Initially my strategy involved a participant observation –'fly on the wall'– approach. I attended internal meetings, went along with staff on field trips to communities, and attended meetings with government institutions, other NGOs, consultants and funders. I was amazed by the general level of openness shown towards me. A certain amount of 'freedom and consultation' euphoria persisted and nearly everyone –both inside and outside the NGO– was willing to tolerate this relative outsider taking notes. This openness was still greater in the more informal settings, like conversations during lunch breaks and parties. As a result of the many opportunities to exchange ideas, I conducted very few formal interviews with staff of the Monti Rural Association. Only with the director of the organization and some of the longer serving members of staff I held interviews. During the first year I also spent time at the provincial Department of Land Affairs, where an ex-coordinator of MRA was in charge. He was very cooperative and helped to open many doors for me in government circles. As a result I could witness many different Eastern Cape interactions on many levels. Besides taping and minuting these interactions I also kept a private and a professional diary.

The choice of concentrating my research efforts in certain communities while relatively ignoring others was mainly influenced by the activities of the MRA staff that took place in 1997 and 1998. As a result, Thornhill, Gasela, Gallawater A and the Farm Worker Campaign feature prominently in this thesis. In my view these examples of MRA involvement give an excellent picture of the strengths and weaknesses of land sector NGO involvement in South Africa. Obviously, to improve my understanding of MRA interventions I also studied background material and reports that had been produced by the organization. However, what was disappointing, was the poor state of the archives within the organization. Since the mid-nineties many files had become incomplete as staff and outsiders had repeatedly failed to return material that had been used. However, it was possible to find some of the relevant material at the Cory Library of Rhodes University where many of the older files had been stored[1]. However, the oldest archival sources (1980 – 1983) within the organization seemed to lost. Nevertheless, when at the end of the year I did a thorough search of the building, I discovered boxes with archives from the early years in a tiny boarded up kitchen where junk was stored. These contained minutes of the first meetings ever held, early reports and newspaper clippings from that activist period. Very valuable stuff. In addition, I was given permission to look into and copy some of the donor correspondence in the Administration Unit. Furthermore I was given the opportunity to access and copy most of the computer files of the organization. Together this material gave me the opportunity to study the –near complete– reported reality of the organization from 1980 through to 1998.

This interest with old documents resulted from a profound feeling that I had developed at the end of 1997. Although it was still interesting and useful to be present in the organization, I felt that it was now necessary to take a more active role as a researcher. In order to accomplish this I took three crucial steps. The first involved gaining historical depth. Besides gathering the archival material I also attempted to track down important ex-members of staff of the organization who had been active during the early years. These people –in Grahamstown, Queenstown, Cape Town, Pretoria and East London– were then interviewed about their past involvement, their present work –usually in the land sector– and their perception of MRA's work today. Besides getting a better understanding of the early years, this strategy provided additional access to all kinds of institutions, especially government departments, where these people had become employed.

The second step was to seek contact –independently from MRA– with leading figures in institutions that the Monti Rural Association regularly dealt with. Thus, I interviewed prominent staff members of other land sector NGOs, more technical NGOs, private consultancy firms and a local donor in the province. It improved my insight in the cooperative arrangements the Monti Rural Association was involved in. In addition I attended the five day National Land Committee Annual General Meeting in 1997, where the NLC affiliates gathered, which improved the comparative element in the research project.

Thirdly, and most importantly, I realized that there was a danger of getting a distorted view of the role of land sector NGOs in the rural areas. As I had only visited communities when the NGO staff went on field trips and conducted dynamic workshops, the project could possibly suffer a dynamic bias. Pondering this dilemma I came up with the idea that in order to study the role of NGOs in these rural settings it was also important to study the absence of these organizations. For the purpose of my research I chose two very different locations: Thornhill and Gasela. Thornhill being an immense area with thousands of inhabitants and Gasela being a small farm with approximately thirty ex-farm worker households. Thus, in 1998 I spent a total of one month in these rural communities. This was very revealing as 'the silence', the general lack of NGO activity and problematic community dynamics became strikingly apparent.

A last methodological note is almost obligatory for the social scientist. I refer, of course, to the 'insider'/'outsider' perspective, that is also related to the development anthropology/anthropology of development discussion. Although I have attempted to completely immerse myself in the daily activities of the Monti Rural Association in order to become a 'relative insider' during my fieldwork, I strove to remain a 'relative outsider' with regard to my 'academic integrity'. Finding this balance was often difficult and proved to be an almost daily challenge. Sometimes the balance tipped one way –when MRA asked me to help conduct a workshop together with staff of the organization– at other times the balance tipped the other way –when I did independent research. Although on one level it is a pragmatic problem –how far do I go in immersing myself– I believe that on another level it is mainly an attitudinal issue. With this I mean that although one can decide to cross the boundary with regard to participating actively in NGO activities, it is crucial to keep a critical mental distance. Therefore, it also important to continually question one's own role as researcher. One thing I found difficult concerned feelings of guilt. Mainly because I was always critically scrutinizing my 'colleagues' who were basically trying their best to improve the lives of 'disadvantaged groups'. While their work was often difficult and testing, 'playing' the critical 'outsider' frequently seemed too easy.

In the South African context it is hard ignore the 'racial' component of one's stay. Although apartheid has officially been abolished it is still very much a part of people's lives. Therefore, being a white Dutch male meant having to be aware of 'racial' and gender sensitivities. This was one of the reasons to study Xhosa, in order to convey the message that I was willing to learn about people's backgrounds. Generally this effort seemed to be appreciated. In the rural communities it was also very helpful to speak and understand some Xhosa. Moreover, being introduced by the right people –the NGO or government staff– also helped to take away a certain suspicion. I believe that although some people found it a little confusing that I wanted to stay in their communities overnight, the idea was welcomed. Certainly, I was truly amazed by the fact that black South Africans were so friendly towards 'whites', taking into account what they had experienced during apartheid. I also found it surprising that, as an anthropologist, one tends to become a local confidant. Many people felt free to unburden themselves, even about the most sensitive topics. Being a male did not seem to be a problem either, as women did not seem inhibited and were as open as the men in my conversations with them.

After my fieldwork it was just me and my computer, the reports, the archives and my informants on tape and in notebooks. When I sent the Monti Rural Association a draft version of the thesis, the director was initially upset and even felt personally aggrieved by some of the passages. His reaction included, what he called 'factual errors', 'interpretation differences' and 'personal hurt'. Especially the first category contained useful corrections of mistakes (dates, land law interpretations et cetera). With regard to the second category some differences could not be resolved. However, he wrote me: *"I'm sure that we will disagree on certain issues, but that is to be expected in any case"*. In the last category I did effect some changes, as I had no intention of hurting people personally. Although the line of argument was not fundamentally altered, I did alter the phrasing here and there. Still, the Monti Rural Association thought it wiser to revert to pseudonyms, as the organization was afraid that its reputation would be damaged by certain critical passages. This I did, and when I presented the dissertation to them during a visit in 2002, their reaction was friendly and positive.

Appendix 2: Archival Sources, Formal Interviews & Taped Exchanges

Archival Sources
1. Community files in the Monti Rural Association archive.
2. Monti Rural Association archive at the Rhodes University Cory Library in Grahamstown.
3. MRA Media Officer computer files 1992 – 1997:

- Media 1;	- Media 5;
- Media 2;	- Media 6;
- Media 3;	- Media 7;
- Media 4;	- Media 8.

4. Computer files of the Personal Assistant to the MRA Director 1994 – 1998:

- Board;	- Mancom;
- Gallawater;	- Mavis[1];
- Ecngoc;	- Qcm&staf;
- Funders;	- Wordpfct.

5. Computer files of the ex-Coordinator of MRA, John Carver 1988 – 1994:

- Ara88;	- Ara92;
- Ara89;	- Ara93;
- Ara90;	- Ara94.
- Ara91;	

6. Funder correspondence files present in the filing cabinet of the Administration Unit.
7. Copies of the earliest ARA files discovered in the boarded-up kitchen on the second floor: material 1980 – 1983; minutes of meetings, newspaper clippings et cetera. Several seemingly incomplete files from the period 1984 – 1987.

Formal Interviews & Taped Exchanges
This list comprises taped and minuted **formal** interviews and taped workshops and meetings. However, the bulk of the fieldwork material consists of notes of field visits, meetings and more informal conversations not listed here.

1. **Staff and ex-members of staff of the Monti Rural Association**

Interview	Dudley Eastwood, MRA Director	29.04.97
Interview	Michael Ndlovu, senior MRA staff and one of the first ARA fieldworkers	11.12.97
Interview	John Carver, ex-MRA Coordinator	06.12.97
Interview	Catherine May, ex-ARA research staff	23.01.98
Interview	Dudley Eastwood, MRA Director	03.02.98
Interview	Joy Molo, ex-MRA staff and member of the MRA Board	04.02.98
Interview	Bongani Matsila, senior MRA staff	17.02.98
Interview	Jack Green, ex-ARA senior committee member	28.01.98
Interview	Albert Lobese, ex-ARA fieldworker and leader of Group 4 in Thornhill	01.02.98
Interview	Albert Lobese, (see: above)	06.02.98
Interview	Andile Kwinana, ex-MRA researcher	07.02.98
Interview	Mr. Informant MRA 1[2], member of the MRA Board	02.03.98

Interview	Mr. Informant MRA 2, Chair of the MRA Board	08.04.98
Interview	Jacob James, former ARA fieldworker	13.04.98
Interview	Mrs. Informant MRA 3, MRA VSA volunteer	01.05.98
Interview	Dudley Eastwood, MRA Director	18.05.98
Interview	Mr. MRA 4, ex-member of ARA Committee and ex-senior staff of the Land Claims Commission in East London	28.05.98
Interview	Mrs. Mavis Beechwood, ex-MRA Coordinator	20.07.98
Interview	Mrs. May Brown, one of the first ARA fieldworkers	04.08.98
Interview	Dudley Eastwood, MRA Director	19.06.98

2. Workshops and Field visits

Field visit Gallawater A	meeting MRA and Gallawater A Trust	10.05.97
Field visit Mgwali	meeting MRA and Mgwali Quitrenters	15.05.97
Field visit Gallawater A	meeting MRA and Gallawater A Trust	17.05.97
Field visit Gallawater A	meeting MRA and Gallawater A Trust	23.07.97
Farm Worker Campaign	meeting of the Campaign Staff and the Premier of the Eastern Cape	05.09.97
Field visit Gallawater A	meeting MRA and Gallawater A Trust	10.09.97
Interview	Mr. Informant Galla 1, former progressive leader in Mgwali	21.04.98
Interview	Peter Nombula, Vice-Chairman of the Gallawater A Trust Committee	15.06.98

3. Interviews with MRA partners

Interview	the Director of Nkuzi (prospective NLC affiliate)	17.09.97
Interview	Agneta Bornholm, Sweden Supports Africa[3] representative	18.02.98
Interview	Dick French, French & Associates[4]	20.02.98
Interview	Informant P 1, senior member of staff of the LSC	09.03.98
Interview	Mr. Informant P 2, senior Member of ECNGOCO	22.05.98
Interview	Mr. Informant P 3, Director of the ULC	31.05.98
Interview	Mr. Informant P 4, Senior Member of ECSECC	02.06.98
Interview	Mr. Informant P 5 and Mr. Informant P 6, senior staff members of the PERA	17.06.98
Interview	Mr. Joe Porter and Colleague Mr. Informant P 7 Chairperson and Vice-Chair of the NLC	03.08.98
Interview	Mr. Informant P 8, Dutch Embassy	04.08.98

4. Formal Interviews in Gasela

Interview	Mrs. Informant G1, resident	24.02.98
Interview	Mr. & Mrs. Vukhapi, residents	24.02.98
Interview	Jim Dabani, retired Gasela leader	25.02.98
Interview	Mr. & Mrs. Informant G 2, residents	26.02.98
Interview	Xolani Dubeni, former Chair of the GRA	26.02.98
Interview	Vuyo Yako, vocal resident	27.02.98
Interview	Mr. & Mrs. Informant G 3, elderly couple	27.02.98
Interview	Mrs. Informant G 4, resident	27.02.98
Interview	Mrs. Nolindili Bhatyi, Chairperson of the GRA	26.03.98
Interview	Mrs. Informant G 5, ANC Women's League member	27.03.98
Interview	Mr. Nomphelo Mbutana, Secretary of ANC Women's League	28.03.98
Interview	Mr. Mbulelo Mfene, member of GRA and local ANC Branch	29.03.98

Interview	Mr. Nakase, Stutterheim Councillor	28.05.98
Interview	Mr. Lindile Msukwini, Secretary GRA and local ANC Branch	15.05.98
Interview	Group interview with 6 young Gasela men	22.05.98

5. Formal Interviews in Thornhill

Interviews	Albert Lobese (see MRA list)	
Interview	Mrs. Mnyamani, secretary of the TRDC	04.03.98
Interview	Mr. & Mrs. Kwinini, member of the TRDC Settlement Sub-Committee	04.03.98
Interview	Mr. Frank Tikile, Thornhill SANCO Officer	05.03.98
Interview	Mrs. Mayingisa and Son Mr. Mayingisa, members of the breakaway Group 4	06.03.98
Interview	Mr. Informant Thh 1, the 'imposter Chief B.'	06.03.98
Interview	Mr. Sipho Teka, Chairperson of the TRDC	07.03.98
Interview	Mr. Sipho Teka, Chairperson of the TRDC	03.04.98
Interview	Mr. Informant Thh 2, local Thornhill councillor	04.04.98
Interview	Mr. Informant Thh 3, acting Chairperson of the ANC, Ntabethemba Branch and two sons and neighbour	05.04.98
Interview	Mrs. Informant Thh 4, local councillor living in Zola	05.04.98
Interview	Mr. Lungisile Qakaza, Vice-Sec. of TRDC and youth activist	06.04.98
Interview	Mr. Thh 5 and Mr. Thh 6, critical conservatives	06.04.98
Interview	The Thornhill Chiefs and councillors	25.05.98
Interview	Zandisile Teka, prominent Thornhill ANC member and first Chair of the TRDC	05.06.98
Interview	Mrs. Kwinini, member of TRDC Settlement Sub-Committee	05.06.98
Interview	Mr. Frank Tikile, Thornhill SANCO Officer	05.06.98

References

Abdelrahman, M.M. (2000) *State-Civil Society Relations: the politics of Egyptian NGOs*, Dissertation ISS, The Hague, the Netherlands: Shaker Publishing.
Abrahamsen, R. (2000) *Disciplining Democracy: development discourse and good governance in Africa*, London: Zed Books.
African National Congress (ANC), The (1994) *The Reconstruction and Development Programme: a policy framework*, Johannesburg: Umanyano Publications.
Albany Resettlement Association[1] (1983a) *Albany Resettlement Association Newsletter*, No. 1, Grahamstown: ARA.
Albany Rural Association (1983b) *Albany Rural Association Newsletter*, No. 2, Grahamstown: ARA.
Albany Rural Association (1985a) *Albany Rural Association Newsletter*, No. 3, Grahamstown: ARA.
Albany Rural Association (1985b) *Albany Rural Association Chairperson's Report 1984*, Grahamstown: ARA.
Albany Rural Association (1988a) *Albany Rural Association Newsletter*, No. 9, Grahamstown: ARA.
Albany Rural Association (1988b) *Albany Rural Association Newsletter*, No. 10, Grahamstown: ARA.
Albany Rural Association (1988c) *Albany Rural Association Newsletter*, No. 11, Grahamstown: ARA.
Albany Rural Association (1988d) *Albany Rural Association Newsletter*, No. 12, Grahamstown: ARA.
Albany Rural Association (1988e) *Albany Rural Association Newsletter*, No. 15, Grahamstown: ARA.
Albany Rural Association (1989) *Albany Rural Association Newsletter*, No. 20, Grahamstown: ARA.
Albany Rural Association (1990) *Albany Rural Association Newsletter, No. 22*, Grahamstown: ARA.
Albany Rural Association (1992a) *Albany Rural Association Newsletter*, No. 29, Grahamstown: ARA.
Albany Rural Association (1992b) *Albany Rural Association Report August – December 1992*, Grahamstown: ARA.
Anonymous (1989) 'Ethnicity and Pseudo-ethnicity in the Ciskei' in Vail, L. (ed.) *The Creation of Tribalism in Southern Africa*, London: James Currey.
Ball, C. and Dunn, L. (1995) *Non-Governmental Organizations: guidelines for good policy and practice*, London: The Commonwealth Foundation.
Bank, L. (1997) 'Town and Country: urbanisation and migration', in *SA Labour Bulletin*, vol. 21, number 4, august 1997.
Bayart, J.F. (1986) *Political Domination in Africa. Reflections on the Limits of Power*, Cambridge.
Bayart, J.F. (1996) *The State in Africa: the politics of the belly*, London: Longman.
Bebbington, A. and Farrington J. (1992) 'NGO-government interaction in agricultural technology development' in M. Edwards and D. Hulme (ed.) *NGOs, Making a Difference: NGOs and development in a changing world*, London: Earthscan.
Bebbington, A. and R. Riddell (1997) 'Heavy Hands, Hidden Hands, Holding Hands? Donors, intermediary NGOs and civil society organisations' in D. Hulme and M. Edwards (ed.) *NGOs, States and Donors: too close for comfort?*, London: McMillan Press.
Beinart, W. and Colin Bundy (1987) *Hidden Struggles in Rural South Africa*, London: James Currey.
Bernstein, Henry (ed.) (1996) *The Agrarian Question in South Africa*, London: Frank Cass.

Bierschenk, T. (1988) 'Development Projects as Arenas of Negotiations for Strategic Groups: a case-study from Benin', in *Sociologia Ruralis*, p. 146 – 160, Vol. 28 2/3, Wageningen.

Binsbergen, W. van (1993) 'Sociaal-wetenchappelijke aspecten van niet-overheidsorganisaties in Afrika', http://come.to/vanbinsbergen.

Blair, H. (1997) 'Donors, Democratization and Civil Society: Relating Theory to Practice' in D. Hulme and M. Edwards (ed.) *NGOs, States and Donors: too close for comfort?*, London: McMillan Press.

Boonzaier, E. (1988) ''Race' and the race paradigm' in *South African Keywords: the uses and abuses of political concepts*, by E. Boonzaier and J. Sharp (ed.), Johannesburg: David Philip.

Boonzaier, E. and J. Sharp (eds.) (1988), *South African Keywords: the uses and abuses of political concepts*, Johannesburg: David Philip.

Bosch, Margarita (1997) 'NGOs and Development in Brazil: Roles and Responsibilities in a 'New World Order' in D. Hulme and M. Edwards (ed.) *NGOs, States and Donors: too close for comfort?*, London: McMillan Press.

Bratton, M. (1990) 'Non-Governmental Organizations in Africa: can they influence policy?' in *Development and Change*, Vol. 21: 87-118, London: SAGE.

Buckle, Tony (1995) 'Land Relations and Social Dynamics: reflections on contemporary land issues in South Africa, with particular reference to the Eastern Cape', in Tony Lemon (ed.) *The Geography of Change in South Africa*, Chichester: Wiley.

Buhlungu, Sakhela (1997) 'Flogging a Dying Horse' in *SA Labour Bulletin* (vol. 21, number 1).

Bundy, C. (1988, 1977) *The Rise and Fall of the South African Peasantry*, Cape Town: David Philip.

Bureau of Information (1991) *White Paper on Land Reform: a summary and background study*, Pretoria: Government Printer.

Cannon (1997) *Financial Sustainability Review Monti Rural Association*, East London: the Monti Rural Association.

Chambers, R. (1992) 'Spreading and Self-improving: a strategy for scaling-up' in *Making a Difference: NGOs and development in a changing world*, by Edwards, Michael and David Hulme (ed.), London: Earthscan.

Charsley, S. (1982) *Culture and Sericulture: social anthropology and development in a South Indian livestock industry*, London: Academic Press.

Charton N. and G. R. kaTywakadi (1980) 'Ciskeian Political Parties', in *Ciskei: economics and politics of dependence in a South African homeland*, edited by N. Charton, London: Croom Helm.

Cleary, Seamus (1997) *The Role of NGOs under Authoritarian Political Systems*, London: McMillan Press.

Cole, J. and Nyoni, P. (1996) Evaluation Report on the Monti Rural Association for the period 1994 – 1996, commissioned by HUVO, the Netherlands, unpublished.

Commission on Restitution of Land Rights (2003) *Land Restitution in South Africa: our achievements and challenges*, Pretoria: Office of the Chief Land Claims Commission, http://land.pwv.gov.za/restitution/

COSATU (1996) *A Draft Programme for the Alliance*, www.cosatu.org.za/docs.

COSATU (1999) *Special Congress: Composite Resolutions, Alliance Programme*, www.cosatu.org.za/congress/cong99/all-res.htm

Cousins, Ben (ed.) (1994) *Issues and Options for Institutional Change for Rural Development, Agriculture and Land Reform: Volume 1, Summary and Overview*, Johannesburg: LAPC, Policy Paper 9.

Cousins, B. (1996) 'Livestock Production and Common Property struggles in South Africa's Agrarian Reform' in Henry Bernstein (ed.) *The Agrarian Question in South Africa*, London: Frank Cass.

Cousins, B. (2002) 'Reforming Communal Land tenure in South Africa: why the draft Communal Land Rights Bill is not the answer', in *ESR Review (Economic and Social*

Rights in South Africa Review), Cape Town: Community Law Centre, University of the Western Cape.

Cousins, B. and A. Claassens (2003) 'Looming Land Disaster', in *Mail & Guardian Weekly*, http://www.mg.co.za/Content/l2_ca.asp?sa=4.

Cox, Aidan and Antonique Koning (1997) *Understanding European Community Aid*, London: ODI, Brussels: European Commission.

Crais C.C. (1992) *The Making of the Colonial Order: white supremacy and black resistance in the Eastern Cape, 1770-1865*, Johannesburg: Witwatersrand University Press.

Crew, E. (1997) 'The Silent Traditions of Developing Cooks' in *Discourses of development: anthropological perspectives*, Grillo, R.D. and R.L. Stirrat (ed.) Oxford: Berg.

Dawson (1992) 'Mobilization and Advocacy in the Health Sector in Peru', in *Making a Difference: NGOs and development in a changing world*, London: Earthscan.

Department of Finance (1998 (1996)) *Growth, Employment and Redistribution: a Macro-economic Strategy*, www.polity.org.za/govdocsa/policy/growth.html.

Department of Land Affairs (1996) *Green Paper on Land Policy*, Pretoria: Department of Land Affairs.

Department of Land Affairs (1997) *White Paper on South African Land Policy*, Pretoria: Department of Land Affairs.

Department of Land Affairs (1999a) *Restitution Figures*, Internet: http://land.pwv.gov.za/Restitution/new_stats_rest(graph).htm, 19.11.'99.

Department of Land Affairs (1999b) *Annual Report 1998*, Internet: http://land.pwv.gov.za/98%20Annual%20report/Chapter3.html and (...)/Chapter3.html, 22.11.'99.Department of Land Affairs (1999c) *Land Reform in South Africa*, Internet: http://land.pwv.gov.za/briefin2.htm, 22.11.'99.

Department of Land Affairs (2003) *Communal Land Rights Bill*, Internet: www.land.pwv.gov.za/legislation_policies/bills.htm, 24.11.03.

Donaldson, A., Segar, J. and r. Southall (1992) *Undoing Independence: regionalism and the reincorporation of Transkei in South Africa*, special issue of *the Journal of Contemporary African Studies*, Volume 11, No.2, 1992, Grahamstown: Institute of Social and Economic Research.

ECSECC (1997a) *Eastern Cape, a statistical snapshot*, Bisho: ECSECC publication.

ECSECC (1997b) *The Extension of Security of Tenure Bill: source material*, Bisho: ECSECC, unpublished.

Edwards, Michael and David Hulme (1992) *Making a Difference: NGOs and development in a changing world*, London: Earthscan.

Escobar, A. (1991) 'Anthropology and the Development Encounter: the making and marketing of development anthropology', in *the American Ethnologist*, Vol. 18, No. 4, 1991, p. 658 – 682.

Escobar, A. (1995) *Encountering Development: the making an unmaking of the third world*, Princeton: Princeton University Press.

Farrington, J., Bebbington, A. with K. Wellard and D.J. Lewis (1993) *Reluctant Partners? non-governmental organizations, the state and sustainable agricultural development*, London: Routledge.

Ferguson, J. (1990) *The Anti-Politics Machine: 'development', depolitization and bureaucratic power in Lesotho*, Cambridge: Cambridge University Press.

Fisher, Julie (1998) *Nongovernments: NGOs and the Political Development of the Third World*, West Hartford: Kumarian Press.

Fowler, A. (1991) 'The Role of NGOs in Changing State-Society Relations: Perspectives from Eastern and Southern Africa' in *Development Policy Review*, Vol. 9: 53-84, London: SAGE.

Fowler, Alan (1997) *Striking a Balance*, London: Earthscan.

Fox, Roddy (1995) 'Regional Proposals: their constitutional and geographical significance', in Tony Lemon (ed.) *The Geography of Change in South Africa*, Chichester: Wiley.

Gardner, K. and D. Lewis (1996) *Anthropology, Development and the Post-modern Challenge*, London, Pluto Press.

Gardner, Katy (1997) 'Mixed Messages: contested 'development' and the 'Plantation Rehabilitation Project' in *Discourses of development: anthropological perspectives*, edited by R.D. Grillo and R.L. Stirrat, Oxford: Berg.

Grillo, R.D. (1997) 'Discourses of Development: the view from anthropology in *Discourses of development: anthropological perspectives*, edited by R.D. Grillo and R.L. Stirrat, Oxford: Berg.

Grillo, R.D. and R.L. Stirrat (ed.) (1997) *Discourses of development: anthropological perspectives*, Oxford: Berg.

Hailey, J. (2001) 'Indicators of Identity: NGOs and the strategic imperative of assessing core values', in *Debating Development: NGOs and the future*, Oxford: Oxfam.

Hardin, G. (1968) 'The Tragedy of the Commons', in *Science*, 162(1968):1243-1248.

Haren, J. van (unpublished) *Democratization and Civil Society in South Africa: NGOs and multiple interests in low cost housing*, unpublished conference paper, CERES Summerschool 2001, Wageningen.

Hargreaves, Samantha and Ann Eveleth (2003) 'The Land Redistribution Programme: advancing real reform or delaying it?' *Development Update*, Vol. 4, No. 2, 2003: Interfund and the NGO Coalition, http://www.interfund.org.za/vol4no22003.html.

Heaton, C. (2003) *Order and Disjuncture in the Practice of Development Relations: 'bracketing' identities in an NGO setting in Nepal*, EIDOS workshop paper, London: 25-28 sept. 2003.

Hilhorst, D. (2000) *Records and Reputations: everyday politics of a Philippine Development NGO*, Thesis Wageningen University, Wageningen: Ponsen en Looyen.

Hobart, M. (ed.) (1993) *An Anthropological Critique of Development: the growth of ignorance*, EIDOS, London: Routledge.

Howes, M. and M.G. Sattar (1992) 'Bigger and Better? Scaling-up strategies pursued by BRAC 1972-1991' in *Making a Difference: NGOs and development in a changing world*, by Michael Edwards and David Hulme (ed.), London: Earthscan.

Hulme, David and Michael Edwards (1997) 'NGOs, States and Donors: An Overview' in D. Hulme and M. Edwards (ed.), *NGOs, States and Donors: too close for comfort?*, London: McMillan Press.

HUVO[2] (1993) *Revised HUVO Strategy South Africa 1993 – 1996*, The Hague/Harare: HUVO.

HUVO (1995) *Jaarverslag 1995*, Den Haag: HUVO.

Hyden, Goran (1996) 'The Challenges of Analyzing and Building Civil Society' in *Africa Insight*, Vol. 26, No. 2.

Kasfir, N. (1998) *Civil Society and Democracy in Africa: critical perspectives*, London: Frank Cass.

Kessel, I. van (2000) *Beyond Our Wildest Dreams: the United Democratic Front and the transformation of South Africa*, Charlottesville and London: University Press of Virginia.

Korten, D.C. and R. Klauss (1984) *People-Centred Development*, West Hartford: Kumarian Press.

Korten, David C. (1990) *Getting to the 21st Century: voluntary action and the global agenda*, Kumarian Press, Connecticut.

Land and Agricultural Policy Centre (1995) *Land Reform Research Phase One: provincial overview Eastern Cape*, working paper 24, Johannesburg: LAPC

Land and Agricultural Policy Centre (1996) *Regional Overview of Land Reform-Related Issues in the Eastern Cape Province*, Johannesburg: LAPC.

Letsoalo, E.M. (1987) *Land Reform in South Africa: a black perspective*, Johannesburg: Skotaville Publishers

Levin, R. and Daniel Weiner (1996) 'The Politics of Land Reform in South Africa after Apartheid: perspectives, problems, prospects' in Henry Bernstein (ed.) *The Agrarian Question in South Africa*, London: Frank Cass.

Lewis, D. (2002) 'Civil Society in African Contexts: reflections on the usefulness of a concept' in *Development and Change* 33(4): 569-586, Oxford: Blackwell Publishers.

Long, N. (ed.) (1992) *Battlefields of Knowledge*, London: Routledge.
Long, N. and J.D. van der Ploeg (1989) 'Demythologizing Planned Intervention: an actor perspective' in *Sociologia Ruralis*, Vol. 29, 3/4: 226-249, Wageningen.
Long, N. and J.D. van der Ploeg (1994) 'Heterogeneity, actor and structure: towards a reconstitution of the concept of structure' in *Rethinking Social Development: theory, research and practice*, edited by D. Booth, London: Longman.
Lund, Susan (1992) *An Overview of Development Needs, Initiatives and Challenges in the Transkei, Border and Eastern Cape: towards a process of re-formulating NOVIB project policy in South Africa*, The Hague: NOVIB (unpublished).
Mamdani, Mahmood (1996) *Citizen and Subject: contemporary Africa and the legacy of late colonialism*, Princeton: Princeton University Press.
Mandela, N.R. (1994) at his inauguration as President of the Democratic Republic of South Africa, Union Buildings, Pretoria May 10 1994. ANC speeches: the internet.
Mandela, N.R. (1995) *Long Walk to Freedom*, London: Abacus.
Mandela, N.R. (1997) *Political Report of the President, Nelson Mandela, to the 50th National Conference of the African National Congress: Mafikeng December 16, 1997*, Johannesburg: Mathibe Printing & Publishing.
Manona (1980) 'Ethnic Relations in the Ciskei' in *Ciskei: economics and politics of dependence in a South African homeland*, edited by N. Charton, London: Croom Helm.
Manona, C. (1997) 'Tribal Authorities and Civic Associations' in Chris de Wet and Michael Whisson (ed.) *From Reserve to Region: apartheid and social change in the Keiskammahoek District of (former) Ciskei: 1950-1990*, Grahamstown: ISER, Occasional Paper No. 35.
Marcus, T., Eales, K. and A. Wildschut (1996) *Down to Earth: land demand in the new South Africa*, LAPC, Durban: Indicator Press.
Maylam, P. (1986) *A History of the African People of South Africa: from the early iron age to the 1970s*, Cape Town: David Philip.
Ministry for Provincial Affairs and Constitutional Development (1998) *White Paper on Local Government*, Pretoria: Ministry for Provincial Affairs and Constitutional Development.
Ministry for Provincial and Local Government (2003) *Traditional Leadership and Governance Framework Bill*, Internet: http://www.gov.za/bills/, 24.11.03.
Minnaar, Anthony (1994) 'The Dynamics of Land in the Rural Areas: 1990 and onwards' in *Access to and Affordability of Land in South Africa: the challenge of land reform in the 1990s*, Pretoria: HSRC Publishers.
Monti Rural Association, the[3] (1993a) *Groundwork*, Vol. 1, No. 1, East London: The Monti Rural Association.
Monti Rural Association, the (1993b) *Groundwork*, Vol. 1, No. 5, East London: The Monti Rural Association.
Monti Rural Association, The (1993c) *Monti Rural Association Interim Report January – July 1993*, East London, The Monti Rural Association.
Monti Rural Association, the (1994a) *Groundwork*, Vol. 2, No. 3, East London: The Monti Rural Association.
Monti Rural Association, the (1994b) *Groundwork*, Vol. 2, No. 2, East London: The Monti Rural Association.
Monti Rural Association, The (1994c), *Submission to the Province of the Eastern Cape Reconstruction and Development Programme, From Crisis to Reconstruction: and integrated rural development programme for Thornhill and Merino Walk*, East London, The Monti Rural Association.
Monti Rural Association, The (1994d), *Monti Rural Association proposal 1994 – 1997*, East London, The Monti Rural Association.
Monti Rural Association, The (1995a) *Annual Report, January – December 1995*, East London: The Monti Rural Association.

Monti Rural Association, The (1995b) *A preliminary investigation into land-related issues in Zweledinga and some of its neighbouring Hewu settlements in the former Ciskei, January 1994 – April 1995*, by L. Wotshela and W. Beinart, East London: The Monti Rural Association.

Monti Rural Association, The (1995c) *Annual Report, January 1994 – April 1995*, East London: The Monti Rural Association.

Monti Rural Association, the (1996a) *Groundwork*, Vol. 4, No. 1, East London: The Monti Rural Association.

Monti Rural Association, The (1996b) *Annual Report 1996*, East London: The Monti Rural Association.

Monti Rural Association, The (1996c) *Gasela, proposal to the Department of Land Affairs*, East London: the Monti Rural Association.

Monti Rural Association, The (1996d) *Land Tenure in Zweledinga: pieces of the puzzle*, by Andile Kwinana, East London: the Monti Rural Association.

Monti Rural Association, The (1996e) *MRA's Assessment of the External Evaluation: report to the Board*, East London: The Monti Rural Association.

Monti Rural Association, The (1997a) *Strategic Direction 1997-1999*, East London: the Monti Rural Association.

Monti Rural Association, The (1997b) *Report on Gasela November 1997*, East London: the Monti Rural Association.

Monti Rural Association, The (1997c) *'97 Annual Report*, East London: The Monti Rural Association.

Monti Rural Association, The (1997d) *Briefing Document*, East London the Monti Rural Association

Monti Rural Association, The (1997e) *Groundwork 1997*, Vol. 5, No. 3, East London: the Monti Rural Association.

Monti Rural Association, The (1997f) *Draft Sustainability Plan*, East London: the Monti Rural Association.

Monti Rural Association, The (1997g) *The Legal Status of MRA, a discussion document*, East London the Monti Rural Association.

Monti Rural Association, The (1997h) *Groundwork 1997*, Vol. 5, No. 4, East London: the Monti Rural Association.

Monti Rural Association, The (1998a) *Gallawater A: an evaluation of MRA's intervention, 1994-1998*, East London: the Monti Rural Association.

Monti Rural Association, The (1998b) *Groundwork 1998*, Vol. 6, No. 2, East London: the Monti Rural Association.

Monti Rural Association, The (1998c) Six-monthly *Report, January to June 1998*, East London: The Monti Rural Association.

Monti Rural Association, The (1999) Six-monthly *Report, January to June 1999*, East London: The Monti Rural Association.

Monti Rural Association, The, LSC & French (1997) *Thornhill Development Plan: a development framework for Thornhill, Zola and Phakamisa settlements*, East London: prepared for the Department of Land Affairs, October 1997.

Murray, C. (1996) 'Land reform in the Eastern Free State: policy dilemmas and political conflicts' in Henry Bernstein (ed.) *The Agrarian Question in South Africa*, London: Frank Cass.

National Department of Agriculture (2001) *Land Redistribution for Agricultural Development*, http://www.nda.agric.za/docs/redistribution.htm

National Land Committee, the (1995) *Annual Report: January 1994 – April 1995*, Braamfontein: Media unit of the National Land Committee.

National land Committee, the (1996) 'Milder models of land reform' in *Land Update*, Braamfontein: Media unit of the National Land Committee.

Nauta, W.W. (2001) *The Implications of Freedom: the changing role of land sector NGOs in a transforming South Africa*, Amsterdam: PhD dissertation Vrije Universiteit.

Nauta, W.W. (2001) 'How to Transfer and Manage a Public Resource?', in *Everyday Governance of Land in Africa*, APAD Bulletin no. 22, Münster: Lit Verlag.
Nauta, W.W. (2003) *Researching NGOs : the benefits of an embedded tale*, EIDOS workshop paper, London: 25-28 sept. 2003.
Nel, E. (1997) 'The Local Economy: no hope for the poor?', in *SA Labour Bulletin*, vol. 21, number 4, august 1997.
Northern Action Association, The[4] (1997) *Communal Property Associations in the Field*, Johannesburg, NAA.
Nuijten, M. (1992) 'Local Organization as Organizing Practices' in *Battlefields of Knowledge,* edited by Long and Long, London: Routledge.
Nuijten, M. (1998) *In the Name of the Land: organization, transnationalism, and the culture of the state in a Mexican ejido*, Wageningen: proefschrift.
Nuijten, M. and Van Gastel, J. (2003), *The Reinvention of Ownership at the Dutch Ministry of Development Cooperation:an anthropological/organizational approach to the construction of a policy model'*, EIDOS workshop paper, London: 25-28 sept. 2003.
Nyamwaya, D. O. (1997) 'Three Critical Issues in Community Health Development Projects in Kenya' in *Discourses of development: anthropological perspectives,* edited by R.D. Grillo and R.L. Stirrat, Oxford: Berg.
Peires, J.B. (1992) 'The Implosion of the Transkei and Ciskei', in *African Affairs*, 1992, volume 91, p.365-387, London.
PLAAS (2003) *Press Release: redistribution and LRAD Programme*, Cape Town: UWC.
Pottier, J. (1997) 'Towards an Ethnography of Participatory Appraisal and Research' in *Discourses of development: anthropological perspectives,* edited by R.D. Grillo and R.L. Stirrat, Oxford: Berg.
Quarles van Ufford, Ph., Kruijt, D. and T. Downing (ed.) (1988) *The Hidden Crisis in Development: development bureaucracies*, Amsterdam: Free University Press.
Quarles van Ufford (1988) "The Hidden Crisis in Development: development bureaucracies in between intentions and outcomes" in *The Hidden Crisis in Development: development bureaucracies*, Quarles van Ufford, Ph., Kruijt, D. and T. Downing (ed.), Amsterdam: Free University Press.
Quarles van Ufford, Ph. (1993) 'Knowledge and Ignorance in the Practices of Development Policy' in Mark Hobart (ed.) *An Anthropological Critique of Development*, an EIDOS publication, London: Routledge.
Quarles van Ufford Ph. and A. Kumar Giri (Forthcoming) 'A Moral Critique of Development: in search of global responsibilities', London: Routledge.
Ramphele, M. (ed.) (1993) *Restoring the Land: environment and change in post-apartheid South Africa*, London: The Panos Institute.
Rifkin, Jeremy (1998) 'Foreword' in Fisher, Julie (1998) *Nongovernments: NGOs and the Political Development of the Third World*, West Hartford: Kumarian Press.
Robinson, Mark (1992) 'NGOs and rural poverty alleviation: implications for scaling-up' in M. Edwards and D. Hulme (ed.) *NGOs, Making a Difference: NGOs and development in a changing world*, London: Earthscan.
Robinson, Mark (1997) 'Privatising the Voluntary Sector: NGOs as public service contractors?' in D. Hulme and M. Edwards (ed.) *NGOs, States and Donors: too close for comfort?*, London: McMillan Press.
Saunders, C. and N. Southey (1998) *A Dictionary of South African History*, Cape Town: David Philip.
Skalník, P. (1988) 'Tribe as colonial concept' in Emile Boonzaier and John Sharp (ed.) *South African Keywords: the uses and abuses of political concepts*, Cape Town: David Philip.
Southall, R. (1992) 'Introduction: rethinking Transkei politics' in *Undoing Independence: regionalism and the reincorporation of Transkei in South Africa*, special issue of *the Journal of Contemporary African Studies*, Volume 11, No.2, 1992, Grahamstown: Institute of Social and Economic Research.
Sparks, A. (1995) *Tomorrow is Another Country*, London: Heinemann.

Stapleton, T.J. (1994) *Maqoma: Xhosa resistance to colonial advance*, Johannesburg: Jonathan Ball Publishers.
Stats SA (1996) *The Eastern Cape*, internet:
www.statssa.gov.za/census96/HTML/press/Part009.html
Strathern, M. (ed.) (2000) *Audit Cultures*, London: Routledge.
Surplus People Project (1983a) *Forced Removals in South Africa: the SPP reports, vol.1 General Overview*, Cape Town: The Surplus People Project.
Surplus People Project (1983b) *Forced Removals in South Africa: the SPP reports, vol.2: The Eastern Cape*, Cape Town: The Surplus People Project.
Sweden Supports Africa[5] (1994) *Programme for the SSA*, Stockholm: SSA.
Switzer, L. (1993) *Power and Resistance in an African Society: the Ciskei Xhosa and the making of South Africa*, Pietermaritzburg: University of Natal Press.
Vail, Leroy (ed.) (1989) *The Creation of Tribalism in Southern Africa*, London: James Currey.
Verschoor, G. (1992) 'Identity, Networks and Space' in *Battlefields of Knowledge*, edited by Long and Long, London: Routledge.
Verschoor, G. (1998) *Tacos, Tiendas and Mescal: an actor-network perspective on small-scale entrepreneurial projects in Western Mexico*, Wageningen: proefschrift.
Villareal, M. (1992) 'The Poverty of Practice' in *Battlefields of Knowledge*, edited by Long and Long, London: Routledge.
Vries, P. de (1992a) 'Plunging into the Garlic' in *Battlefields of Knowledge*, edited by Long and Long, London: Routledge.
Vries, P. de (1992b) *Unruly Clients: a story of how bureaucrats try and fail to transform gate keepers, communists and preachers into beneficiaries*, Wageningen: proefschrift.
Walzer, M. (1995) 'The Civil Society Argument' in R. Beiner (ed.) *Theorizing Citizenship*, New York: State University of New York.
Wellard, K. and Copestake, J.G. (ed.) (1993) *NGOs and the State in Africa: rethinking roles in sustainable agricultural development*, London: Routledge.
Westaway, A. 'Headmanship, Land Tenure and Betterment Planning in Keiskammahoek, c. 1920 – 1980', in C. de Wet and M. Whisson (ed.) *From Reserve to Region: apartheid and social change in the Keiskammahoek District of (former) Ciskei: 1950-1990*, Grahamstown: Occasional Paper 35, Institute for Social and Economic Research, Rhodes University.
Wet, C. de and M. Whisson (1997) *From Reserve to Region: apartheid and social change in the Keiskammahoek District of (former) Ciskei: 1950-1990*, Grahamstown: Occasional Paper 35, Institute for Social and Economic Research, Rhodes University.
Wood, G. (1985) 'The Politics of Development Policy Labelling' in *Development and Change*, Vol. 16: 347-373, London: SAGE.
Wood, G. (1997) 'States Without Citizens: the problem of the franchise state' in D. Hulme and M. Edwards (ed.) *NGOs, States and Donors: too close for comfort?*, London: McMillan Press.
Worden, N. (1995) *The Making of Modern South Africa*, Oxford: Blackwell.
World Commission on Environment and Development (1987) *Our Common Future*, New York: Oxford University Press.
Wotshela, L. (1997), *Eastern Cape Land reform Programme: diagnostic evaluation of the Gallawater A trust – Queenstown District*, Internal Report Department of Land Affairs, East London.

Newspapers and other media:
Business Day, (10.11.03) *NLC and PLAAS advertisement*
City Press (21.06.87) *Torture over our Report.*
Daily Dispatch (07.01.77) *Disease kills 10 border babies.*
Daily Dispatch (17.01.77) *Thornhill: SA aid R250,000.*
Daily Dispatch (21.01.77) *Sebe to blame for Thornhill – Mabandla.*
Daily Dispatch (06.03.91) *Marais Slated after Thornhill Meeting.*

Daily Dispatch (09.04.97) *Groundwork Dicey in bill that pins down farmers.*
Mail & Guardian Weekly (1999) *When we were kings...*, internet edition:
    http://www.sn.apc.org/wmail/issues/990423/NEWS30.html

Other Sources:
Proceedings of Meetings Regarding the Excision of Glen Grey and Herschel: 24th and 25th April, 1975, East London: Monti Rural Association Archives.

Endnotes

1. An Embedded Tale

[1] The name Monti Rural Association (MRA) and its predecessor Albany Rural Association (ARA) are pseudonyms.

[2] This is based on the ARA and MRA newsletters, editions of *Groundwork*, plus archival material (see appendix). The South African and Eastern Cape events in this chapter are loosely based on several sources: Worden (1995), Sparks (1995), Mandela (1995), Saunders and Southey (1998), SABC television and the Mail & Guardian Weekly.

[3] By presenting the history of the organization in a, more or less, chronological order, the impression may be given that the author has an evolutionary and teleological outlook. This is not the case.

[4] Terms like 'community', 'grassroots' or 'household' are not value-free. However, the author does use them as they are frequently actor terms.

[5] Botha's nickname: 'the Great Crocodile'.

[6] Sadly, the apartheid history of South Africa forces us to employ terms and concepts that were crucial to the regime then, but still carry weight in present-day South Africa. Although it would be more correct to place these terms between inverted commas –to indicate that these terms are contested– I have decided to avoid this to keep the text more readable.

[7] UDF's Secretarial Report, February 1986, quoted by van Kessel (2000, p. 37).

[8] Surplus People Project (1983a) *Forced Removals in South Africa: the SPP reports, vol.1 General Overview*.

[9] Grahamstown is situated in the Albany District.

[10] ARA minutes, 04.09.82.

[11] In the Department of Political Science at Rhodes University.

[12] Eastern Province Herald, Thursday, October 7, 1982.

[13] The South African legal system offered opportunities to fight or delay the implementation of apartheid policies.

[14] These are all pseudonyms.

[15] Albany Resettlement Association (1983a) *Albany Resettlement Association Newsletter*, No. 1.

[16] Albany Rural Association (1983b) *Albany Rural Association Newsletter*, No. 2.

[17] Albany Rural Association (1985a) *Albany Rural Association Newsletter*, No. 3.

[18] ARA Minutes 10.02.88.

[19] Jacob James in an internal workshop: ARA minutes: January 1988.

[20] Albany Rural Association (1988a t/m e) *Albany Rural Association Newsletter:* No. 9, 10, 11, 12 and 15.

[21] Albany Rural Association (1989) *Albany Rural Association Newsletter*, No. 20.

[22] Albany Rural Association (1990) *Albany Rural Association Newsletter*, No. 22.

[23] Albany Rural Association (1992a) *Albany Rural Association Newsletter*, No. 29.

[24] Leader of the homeland of KwaZulu.

[25] These semi-independent black states like KwaZulu-Natal, the Ciskei, Transkei, Bophuthatswana and others were never recognized internationally as they were understood to be part of the apartheid regime. This was often demonstrated when crises led to interventions by Pretoria.

[26] These security forces that were responsible for destabilization through instigation of violence in the country, especially on the Rand around the mining hostels and in KwaZulu Natal, were referred to by Mandela as 'the third force'.

[27] The term 'volksstaat' is an Afrikaans term that refers to the wish for 'a homeland' where the Afrikaner people can establish their own state.

[28] 'Ethnicity' in South Africa is a contentious term with a long (colonial) history. For example Boonzaier (1988) argues that terms like 'culture', 'ethnicity' and community have in many instances the become the substitute for the politically incorrect term 'race'.

[29] The South African constitution; Bill of Rights, Section 25.

[30] During Mandela's reign Thabo Mbeki was Deputy President.

[31] Monti Rural Association, the (1993a) *Groundwork*, Vol. 1, No. 1.

[32] Monti Rural Association, the (1993b) *Groundwork*, Vol. 1, No. 5.

[33] Ibid.

[34] Formerly the National Committee Against Removals (NCAR).

[35] Monti Rural Association, the (1994a) *Groundwork*, Vol. 2, No. 3.

[36] Monti Rural Association, the (1994b) *Groundwork*, Vol. 2, No. 2.

[37] Prof. William Beinart, nowadays Rhodes Professor of Race Relations, Oxford University.

[38] Act 126.
[39] Monti Rural Association, the (1996a) *Groundwork*, Vol. 4, No. 1.
[40] Cole, J. and Nyoni, P. (1996) Evaluation Report on the Monti Rural Association for the period 1994 – 1996.
[41] HUVO: Humanisten Voor Ontwikkelingssamenwerking; this is a pseudonym.

2. Critical Reflections on NGOs

[1] Although many authors choose to present these figures, I will not do so because of definitional problems and sketchy statistical data.
[2] E.g. Farrington and Bebbington (1993), Edwards and Hulme (1992), Fowler (1991, 1997), Ball and Dunn (1995), Bratton (1990); authors like van Binsbergen (1993), Wood (1985, 1997) and Bierschenk (1988) are the exceptions to the rule.
[3] Translation from Dutch: "monsterlijke termen".
[4] Although Southern Europe is often treated in a similar fashion by Northern European scholars.
[5] Translated from Dutch: *"... het is een actorenbegrip uit een bepaalde politieke cultuur... "*.
[6] He is, amongst others, inspired by Blaney and Pasha (1993, cited in Lewis 2002).
[7] Kasfir builds on the work of Putnam (1995): 'Bowling Alone: America's declining social capital', in *Journal of Democracy*, 6, 1, 65.
[8] My emphasis.
[9] Although I use the term 'anthropology', in my view the term 'sociology' can be used interchangeably.
[10] He attributes the distinction to Charsley (1982, cited in Grillo 1997).
[11] See: Appendix 1 for methodological notes.
[12] These homelands became part of the Eastern Cape Province in 1994.

3. Land and Politics

[1] 122 million hectares.
[2] Afrikaans term which means 'farmers'; descendants of originally Dutch speaking settlers.
[3] An area, furthest south in the Eastern Cape, where the city of Port Elizabeth is situated nowadays.
[4] The oral history of the Xhosa is apparently problematic for historians. According to Switzer (1993) *"the oral genealogies of Xhosa chiefs are difficult sources to interpret when it comes to chronicling Xhosa history"* (p. 38). As a consequence, Tshawe, who is said to be the founder of the Xhosa royal lineage and who must have lived in the seventeenth century, is hard to place in any historical context, according to the author. Nevertheless, most historians agree on the fact that Phalo (1715-1775), as a descendant of Tshawe, was an important king, whose sons, Gcaleka and Rharhabe, came into conflict with each other. As a result, the Xhosa kingdom experienced a major schism. The followers of Gcaleka became known as the Gcaleka and largely stayed in what later became known as the Transkei, and the followers of Rharhabe became known as the Rharhabe, who moved further south-west across the Great Kei River. The Gcaleka did not encounter as much turmoil as the Rharhabe who moved further south and encountered other Xhosa, Khoikhoi groups and, eventually, whites from the Cape, who were trekking north.
[5] According to Switzer (1993) there is disagreement among historians about what the Mfengu actually are. Some argue that they were just a collection scattered refugee Xhosa groups and named 'Fingo' by the British settlers, while others believe that they were made up of other Nguni groups had fled during the Mfecane, the expansion of the Zulu kingdom.
[6] In 1860 British Kaffraria even became a separate crown colony for a short period of time until it became part of the Cape Colony in 1866.
[7] Stapleton's (1994) more politically-oriented explanation begins by stressing the fact that Xhosa society should be understood as depending on their particular form of pastoralism. According to Stapleton (1994) two distinct forms of cattle-holding were of importance. *"Firstly, wealthy individuals, such as chiefs, lent their cattle to poorer men who cared for the animals in exchange for milk and calves. Under this (...) system, the owner could repossess his cattle at any time. Secondly, the majority of cattle were in the possession of homestead heads who could exercise independent control of them"* (p. 172). Through (the threat of) repossession, the chiefs and other important figures could exercise their control over commoners. However, by developing large herds, subordinate chiefs could break away from the dominant chief and start their own chiefdom. According to Stapleton, the British, in an attempt to undermine this power of the chiefs proceeded to put a ban on repossession in the late 1840s. When, as a result, some chiefs did begin to collaborate with the British, commoners, in order to protest this collaboration started to kill their chiefs' cattle. Thus, in Stapleton's analysis the cattle-killing should be understood as a political act by commoners, who wanted to overthrow their chiefs. The

aristocracy, in turn, issued a ban on cultivation in order to bring their subjects to their senses. By not cultivating the commoners would have to keep relying on the cattle, which would make it harder for them to kill the livestock. In Stapleton's view this combination of factors led to the devastating impact of the cattle killing.

[8] An example of one of the first Christian Xhosa intellectuals was Tiyo Soga (1829-1871), who became the first Xhosa minister of religion after he had been educated in the well-known Eastern Cape Lovedale mission station and trained in Scotland. He was a writer and a composer and translated texts into Xhosa.

[9] Nevertheless, the apartheid regime remained very influential behind the scenes and frequently interfered when things did not go their way. However, in some instances – e.g. the pro-ANC stance of Bantu Holomisa, ruler of the Transkei after a coup – homeland leaders did prove to be able to operate somewhat independently.

[10] It is important to note here that the term 'Mfengu' applies both to African groups that were settled east of the Fish River by the British and other groups that settled in the more northern parts like Herschel.

[11] According to Maylam (1986) the Transkei government revenue was for 50% dependent on the South African state in the 1960s, while in the 1970s it had reached a staggering 80%.

[12] In his 1992 article, Jeff Peires, a distinguished historian and one of the early activists in the Monti Rural Association, reveals that he was the Anonymous author of the 1989 article *Ethnicity and Pseudo-Ethnicity in the Ciskei*.

[13] In 1937 Hewu was added by carving it out of the Queenstown District.

[14] After it had been named Broederbond (!) first.

[15] Beinart and Bundy (1987) discuss several early twentieth century popular protest movements in the Eastern Cape. With its long history of struggle against colonial domination, the Eastern Cape was a region where popular protests thrived. For example, they discuss 'the anti-dipping movement' –the protests against compulsory dipping of cattle– which emerged in the Eastern Cape region in the first decade of the twentieth century. Furthermore, they show how groups of women also became active in the Eastern Cape. Women organized boycotts in the early twenties against local traders who kept prices too high, and against schools in the mid-twenties, because the teachers played a role in the detested compulsory land registration. In the 1920s and 1930s another development caused much anxiety for the white regime, when the ICU, the Industrial and Commercial Workers Union, became a mass-based black political movement in South Africa. In fact, the authors show that the Eastern Cape population has always played a dominant role against oppression.

[16] After the second democratic elections in 1999, Thabo Mbeki replaced Hanekom by Thoko Didiza, who is said to be more concerned with the plight of black emergent commercial farmers than with the plight of the poorest and landless.

[17] This is higher than the amount of 63,455 claims mentioned above. One of the reasons is that the NGO sector has successfully lobbied to get other types of cases included in the Restitution Programme. For example, the Monti Rural Association lobbied effectively to get betterment areas in the Eastern Cape (e.g. the Chatha community) included.

[18] The South African constitution; Bill of Rights, Section 25.

[19] The NLC had been critical during the process of consultation that resulted in the Green Paper on Land Policy. They were concerned with the fact that the interim constitution seemingly blocked all avenues leading to expropriation. According to NLC's annual report of 1995 *"... of particular concern is the clause which stipulates that expropriation is permissible only for 'public purposes' –a term which has been interpreted in other countries to exclude land reform"* (1995, p. 5). Thus, the progressive land sector NGOs and the ANC fought to get the expropriation clause adapted. In its final version, therefore, it is stipulated that *"the public interest"* included land reform.

[20] In 1999 this was increased to R. 16 000 (± $ 2600).

[21] 5 people per household.

[22] Although 'the young' were generally more pro-democracy than 'the old', the author is aware that it is impossible to draw clear-cut generation differences.

[23] Mail & Guardian Weekly 23.04.1999.

[24] Some estimate it to be 400000.

[25] Both DOA and DLA are part of the Ministry of Agriculture and Land Affairs.

[26] Around the turn of the century both other NLC affiliates – ULC and PERA – were disaffiliated for lack of administrative control and under-delivery.

[27] However, the intention to cooperate more closely was often mentioned.

4. MRA and the Dumped People of Thornhill

[1] The author is aware of the fact that the word 'tribe' is a contested term. Peter Skalník (1988), for example, declares it 'a colonial category' (p. 68). I use it here because the people in Thornhill have used it to describe themselves.
[2] These numbers are contested as the Surplus People Project Report (1983) shows. Chief Malefane is cited to have put the figure at 32 000 in mid January 1977 with 8 000 more to come, while two months later two Ciskei ministers are cited to have put the figure at 43 000, while another Ciskeian official is cited to have put the figure at 50000. One complicating factor in this discussion is the number of migrant workers who are away most of the year.
[3] *Restoring the Land*, edited by M. Ramphele (1993), p. 46.
[4] See: proceedings of the Herschel meeting under References; Other Sources.
[5] One day before the Proclamation of the excision decision regarding Herschel and Glen Grey, on Friday 25 April 1975, by the Ciskei government.
[6] Roof-sheet that was taken off their original home in Herschel and transported to Thornhill.
[7] The Daily Dispatch, 07.01.77.
[8] The Daily Dispatch, 17.01.77.
[9] The Daily Dispatch, 21.01.77.
[10] South African English for erosion ditch.
[11] Whittlesea was a Ciskei administrative centre, while Queenstown was a South African administrative centre.
[12] ARA minutes, 04.09.82.
[13] Eastern Province Herald, 07.10.82.
[14] Albany Resettlement Association (1983a) *Albany Resettlement Association Newsletter*, No. 1.
[15] Albany Rural Association (1983b) *Albany Rural Association Newsletter*, No. 2.
[16] Because of the political repression.
[17] Bisho was the capital of Ciskei; see: Chapter 4.
[18] Jacob James was originally from Queenstown and knew that his home was observed by the security police.
[19] May Brown was another ARA field worker who was on the run for the security police for her political activities.
[20] South African English for pick-up truck.
[21] City Press, 21.06.87.
[22] 1989 Fieldworkers report, John Carver.
[23] The new province where Johannesburg and Pretoria are situated.
[24] BOCCO was later amalgamated into the South African National Civics Organization SANCO).
[25] One South African Ministry that Group Four was forced to deal with was the Ministry of Development Aid, as they were responsible for 'foreign policy' regarding the homelands.
[26] Daily Dispatch, 06.03.91.
[27] South African word meaning: mini-bus.
[28] Joy Molo is nowadays CEO of the Amatola District Council, the district in which the Monti Rural Association is most active.
[29] In the late nineties he became the chairman of the Thornhill Reconstruction and Development Committee (TRDC).

5. Strategic Translations in Gasela

[1] Based on this chapter the following article was published: Nauta, W.W. (2001) 'How to Transfer and Manage a Public Resource?', in *Everyday Governance of Land in Africa*, APAD Bulletin no. 22, Münster: Lit Verlag.
[2] The South African word for barbecue, and a white national pass-time.
[3] Excluding 2 extended households.
[4] Approximately $ 55 000.
[5] The isiXhosa term 'Ukulima' is usually translated by Africans into English as 'to plough'. An English term which captures the meaning more fully is 'to cultivate'.
[6] The round 'traditional' African mud huts with grass roofs.
[7] Afrikaans for boss or master.
[8] In a generator shed the sign 'MOOIFONTEIN departement van ontwikkelingshulp' can still be found, used to patch up a hole in the wall of the shed.
[9] A black area located within a white area; see: Chapters 3 and 4.

[10] South African National Civic Organization: the 'umbrella' organization of South African civics or residents organizations.
[11] See MRA Gasela archive. Fax dated 28-10-1993.
[12] See MRA Gasela archive. Letter ref: 6/2/2/d/63/0/0/6.
[13] This was a so-called 'stakeholder meeting' in the offices of MRA. However, no Gasela residents were present. Only the institutions that in one way or another dealt with Gasela.
[14] Meeting at the Monti Rural Association office on the 14th of August, 1997.
[15] Act 31 of 1996: this act protects people with informal rights to land from evictions during the period 1996-1998 when new legislation will be drafted and enacted.
[16] Used in the meaning of small subsistence plot.
[17] Weeds.
[18] Nakase's Transitional Rural Council.
[19] IsiXhosa meaning: "I don't know".
[20] Source: MRA (1997b, p. 24); the original table in the MRA report contains information on more crops. However, as these are the crops that the organization recommends, information the other crops is left out.
[21] In an excellent chapter, *The Bovine Mystique: a study of power, property, and livestock in rural Lesotho[21]*, Ferguson (1990), for example, has shown how complicated the relationship of people with their livestock can be. For instance, when he asked them to choose between receiving a gift in the form of cash or receiving one in the form of cattle, many Basotho preferred the cash, even if the amount was much less than the value of the cow. According to Ferguson this is because people cannot freely exchange a cow that was received as a gift for cash. Selling animals is not a private and simple economic act. Rather, it is an (extended) family matter. Cash lies much more beyond these cultural control mechanisms.
[22] A meeting on 25 November 1997.
[23] Bisho was the capital of the Ciskei, built by the apartheid regime, ten kilometres outside the 'South African' town of King William's Town.
[24] Brigadier Oupa Gqozo ousted the Ciskeian ruler Lennox Sebe in 1990 and subsequently became an even worse tyrant.
[25] The Monti Rural Association (1998a) *Gallawater A: an evaluation of MRA's intervention, 1994-1998*.
[26] MRA evaluation and planning meeting, Cintsa, July 12-15 1993.
[27] Advisory Commission on Land Allocation: see text above.
[28] Strategic planning meeting of the Land Rights Unit, 03.11.1997.
[29] This research project in the village of Mgwali would possibly become a 'tenure test case' through which the government would learn about the intricacies of tenure issues and overlapping land rights.
[30] The Monti Rural Association (1997c) *1997 Annual Report*.
[31] Macleantown meeting 11.09.1997.
[32] A community MRA had supported in the early nineties by helping them to submit one of South Africa's first land restitution claims, which had failed dismally and had led much frustration for the Macleantown residents.
[33] Minutes ARA Internal Workshop 1988.
[34] Macleantown meeting 11.09.1997.
[35] In my communications with MRA in early 2001 I have learned that – with heavy involvement of MRA – the Gasela residents have successfully started farming the land. For this involvement MRA has received a Katlego award from the South African NGO Coalition.

6. MRA as a 'Learning Organization'

[1] Monti Rural Association '97 Annual Report, Total Income: R. 3.143.399 (U.S. $ 525.000); Total Assets: R. 2.633.688 (U.S. $ 440.000).
[2] Umtata Land Committee, which was disaffiliated from the NLC in 1999.
[3] www.mg.co.za/mg/za/news.html: 11.07.2000.
[4] Interview with Bongani Matsila, 17.02.98.
[5] This is spelled wrongly. Should be: Zweledinga.
[6] Albany Rural Association (1988) *Albany Rural Association Newsletter*, 10.
[7] ARA Minutes 24.02.88.
[8] Albany Rural Association (1988) *Albany Rural Association Newsletter*, 10.
[9] ARA Minutes 24.02.88.
[10] ARA Minutes 24.08.88.
[11] Interview 07.02.98.

[12] Interview 04.02.98.
[13] Monti Rural Association, the (1993a) *Groundwork*, Vol. 1, No. 1.
[14] Ibid.
[15] My emphasis.
[16] Bureau of Information (1991).
[17] Monti Rural Association (1996a), *Groundwork*, Vol. 4, No. 1, page 1.
[18] This is a pseudonym.
[19] Letter to the Ministry of Water Affairs and Forestry, July 27 1994.
[20] According to Wotshela (1997, p. 15) Mr. Nombula claimed to have paid about R. 2000 on pound and transportation fees over a period of 13 months.
[21] According to MRA's Agricultural Officer during a field trip 10.05.1997.
[22] Interview 23.01.97.
[23] Normally a residents association would align itself with SANCO.
[24] Meeting re Gallawater Trust, Langedraai, July 18 1994. My emphasis.
[25] Interview 04.02.98.
[26] 'Straddling', the mechanism whereby families who are moved to new land retain a property in the old settlement seems to have been part of the problem. Someone like Rex Nombula, who actually lived in Gallawater A, built a house on Langedraai farm and retained his house in greater Zweledinga, where he was also politically active.
[27] This is a pseudonym.
[28] A New Zealand organization.
[29] Apparently this is a typographic error. It should be 1995.
[30] Interview with Mavis Beechwood, 20.07.98.
[31] R. 51 379 in 1995.
[32] Monti Rural Association (1998b) *Groundwork* Vol. 6 Number 2 March/April 1998.
[33] Data based on MRA Annual Reports '94, '95, '96 and QCM's '97 and '98
[34] 16 members of staff: 5 people left after one year, 11 people left after two years.
[35] Management Committee meeting, 21.05.97.
[36] Similar remarks are heard in the Netherlands by childless workers who criticize the fact that their child-bearing colleagues get too many perks, like the newly instituted 'parental leave'.
[37] Umlungu is a Xhosa word – often somewhat derogatory – meaning white man.
[38] Chief Executive Officer.

7. The Government as Praying Mantis
[1] Short Hanekom biography on the ANC web-site: www.anc.org.za/people/hanekom.html.
[2] See the preface of the RDP document (ANC, 1994).
[3] A legal construct most suitable for non-governmental organizations.
[4] Monti Rural Association, the (1994b) *Groundwork*, Vol. 2, No. 2.
[5] Naturally, many people working in the NGO sector were themselves members of the progressive political parties as well.
[6] Letter dated July 20, 1994; MRA archive.
[7] Member of the Executive Council: the provincial equivalent of minister in the national executive.
[8] See: Chapter 3.
[9] Term used by Prof. Norman Long (1992, p.271) in *Battlefields of Knowledge*, to describe loci of interaction where different 'life worlds' meet.
[10] Steering Committee meeting 26.06.97.
[11] A community MRA has worked in.
[12] Steering Committee meeting 29.05.97.
[13] Eastern Cape Land Reform Steering Committee Secretariat Report, 25 May 1997.
[14] HUVO: a high quality Dutch funding organization, one of the main funders of the Monti Rural Association.
[15] Nevertheless several contentious issues remain, of which the position of 'traditional' leaders with regard to local government is, by far, the most explosive issue as is illustrated by the political wrangles preceding the local government elections of 2000.
[16] See: chapter 7.
[17] The campaign was popularly called 'Farm Worker Campaign'. However, a more correct term for 'farm worker' would be 'farm dweller' as the legislation also meant to address the rights of the dependents of farm workers. In some NLC documents, for example, the term the *Land Rights for Farm Dwellers Campaign* can be encountered.

[18] Figures according to the *White paper on South African Land Policy* (1997).
[19] Article in Eastern Cape newspaper *The Daily Dispatch*, 09.04.97.
[20] Eastern Cape Socio-Economic Consultative Council (1997b) *The Extension of Security of Tenure Bill: source material*.
[21] The National Council of Provinces has a similar function as the First Chamber in the Netherlands or the House of Lords in the United Kingdom.
[22] Briefing organized by MRA and ECSECC in Bisho, 03.06.97.
[23] Advice Offices, often aligned to churches, provide the rural poor with advice on government and legal matters; usually understaffed and resource-poor.
[24] This assessment concerns ECSECC in the period 1996-1998.
[25] MRA workshop near Qomga, 01.06.97.
[26] 3 US$/month.
[27] *"We are the victims of being chased away!"*.
[28] Farm worker Meeting at ECSECC, 20.06.97.
[29] Farm worker Meeting at ECSECC, 03.06.97.
[30] Farm worker Meeting at ECSECC, 16.07.97.
[31] The date of the first discriminatory land act: the Natives Land Act of 1913.
[32] The Monti Rural Association (1997e) *Groundwork, Vol. 5, No. 3*.
[33] The Free Sate Premier had made various strong public statements against evictions and for farm workers rights.
[34] Meeting with the Premier in the ECSECC building in Bisho, 05.09.97.
[35] The Monti Rural Association (1997e) *Groundwork*, Vol. 5, No. 3.
[36] Meeting between the Farm Worker Campaign staff and the MEC For Agriculture and Land Affairs Max Mamase in his office, 12.11.97.
[37] Households could access a maximum of !5 000 rand – later increased to 16 000 rand – for the acquisition of land and/or to erect structures or facilitate improvements.

8. The Impact of 'New Realism' and the Role of Donors

[1] Interview with Jack Green in Queenstown, 28.01.98.
[2] The organizations that are discussed in detail are 'protected' by pseudonyms.
[3] The Monti Rural Association (1997c) *1997 Annual Report*.
[4] Total income: about US $ 525 000. Donor funds: about US $ 415 000.
[5] Interest: about US $ 45 000.
[6] MRA Planning and Evaluation Meeting, East London 17 – 21 January 1994.
[7] Before, the organization was led by a Coordinator.
[8] Proceedings of MRA's current and potential Donor Partners held at the offices of the National Land Committee, Johannesburg 9 and 10 June 1997.
[9] Proceedings of MRA's current and potential Donor Partners held at the offices of the National Land Committee, Johannesburg 9 and 10 June 1997.
[10] World Commission on Environment and Development (1987) *Our Common Future*, New York: Oxford university Press.
[11] The Monti Rural Association (1997f) *The Draft Sustainability Plan*.
[12] Interview with Dudley Eastwood, 03.02.98.
[13] Ibid.
[14] Interview with Dudley Eastwood, 03.02.98.
[15] Quarterly Content Meeting, October 1997.
[16] Ibid.
[17] approximately US $ 500000.
[18] Approximately US $ 20000.
[19] Board Meeting, 30.03.98.
[20] Staff Meeting, 22.01.98.
[21] In the *'97 Annual Report* 'Development Facilitation' was changed into the more general term 'Facilitation'.
[22] Quarterly Content Meeting, October 1997.
[23] *'97 Annual Report*.
[24] National Land Committee (1997) Proposal to the Executive on Strategic Funding Issues, unpublished.
[25] MRA ManCom Meeting, 25.11.97.
[26] Ibid.

[27] Interview with Dudley Eastwood, 03.02.98.
[28] The Monti Rural Association (1997g) *The Legal Status of MRA: a discussion document*, 6 June 1997.
[29] Board Workshop, 17.03.98.
[30] In the NLC network a staff member of one of the affiliates offended an opponent in a publication and the organization got heavily fined in 1997.
[31] In June 1998 it was decided to reduce the Board from ten members to seven: four non-executive members and three executive members.
[32] MRA Staff Meeting 27.05.98.
[33] Interview with Dudley Eastwood: 18.05.98.
[34] Interview with Dudley Eastwood, 03.02.98.
[35] HUVO (1995) *Jaarverslag 1995*.
[36] The Dutch term: het 'herijkingsproces'.
[37] Fax from MRA to Toto Ndebele, HUVO, 11.03.97.
[38] This quote is translated from Dutch, the Dutch term used is: "counterparts afsnoepen".
[39] MRA Mancom meeting minutes, 22.09.97.
[40] MRA Mancom meeting minutes, 28.04.98.
[41] A HUVO letter: *to all HUVO' Counterpart Organizations in South Africa*, 16.02.98, Number: 535/SA/INTE/160214/KC/jw.
[42] HUVO (1993) *Revised HUVO Strategy, South Africa 1993 – 1996*, The Hague/Harare: HUVO.
[43] Ibid.
[44] Fax by the MRA Coordinator to the HUVO Regional Office in Harare, 26.03.96.
[45] Letter from Mavis Beechwood to the Exec Members of the National Land Committee, 12.06.96.
[46] MRA Board Meeting, 27.06.96.
[47] Monti Rural Association, The (1996e) *MRA's Assessment of the External Evaluation: report to the Board*.
[48] Letter from HUVO' Executive Director to all South African Counterpart Organizations, 16.02.98, number: 535/SA/INTE/160214/KC/jw.
[49] Supports Africa (1994) *Programme for the SSA*.
[50] Interview with SSA representative Agneta Bornholm, 18.02.98.
[51] Ibid.
[52] MRA Mancom meeting, 22.09.97.
[53] MRA Mancom meeting, 21.01.98.
[54] Interview with Dick French, 20.02.98.
[55] Meeting with Thandi Jack, 20.05.97.
[56] Quarterly Content Meeting, 25.06.97.
[57] Interview with Mavis Beechwood, 20.07.98

9. The Implications of Freedom
[1] Obviously the Monti Rural Association also went through several name changes, as described in Chapter 1.
[2] This type of 'rainbow speak' was frequently encountered in the South African NGO sector.
[3] Each year the Katlego awards are presented by the South African NGO Coalition.
[4] The Mail & Guardian Weekly, February 13, 2001: www.mg.co.za/mg/za/news.html.
[5] In such schemes workers receive shares in the farm, so that they benefit from economic success.
[1] As MRA cleared much of its storage space during my stay at the organization, I was asked to transport a fresh load of archival material to Cory Library.

Appendices
[1] This is a pseudonym. The sub-directories 1994 and 1995 contained in this directory contain most of the MRA files of the ex-coordinator of MRA Mavis Beechwood.
[2] People who are not mentioned by name (pseudonym) in the thesis will be called *Informant*.
[3] This is a pseudonym.
[4] This is a pseudonym.

References
[1] The names Albany Resettlement Association (ARA) and Albany Rural Association (ARA) are pseudonyms.
[2] The name HUVO is a pseudonym.

[3] The name Monti Rural Association (MRA) is a pseudonym.
[4] The name Northern Action Association (NAA) is a pseudonym.
[5] The name Sweden Supports Africa (SSA) is a pseudonym.

Wissenschaftliche Paperbacks
Politikwissenschaft

Hartmut Elsenhans
Das Internationale System zwischen Zivilgesellschaft und Rente
Gegen derzeitige Theorieangebote für die Erklärung der Ursachen und die Auswirkungen wachsender transnationaler und internationaler Verflechtung setzt das hier vorliegende Konzept eine stark durch politökonomische Überlegungen integrierte Perspektive, die auf politologischen, soziologischen, ökonomischen und philosophischen Ansatzpunkten aufbaut. Mit diesem Konzept soll gezeigt werden, daß der durch Produktionsauslagerungen/Direktinvestitionen/neue Muster der internationalen Arbeitsteilung gekennzeichnete (im weiteren als Transnationalisierung von Wirtschaftsbeziehungen bezeichnete) kapitalistische Impuls zur Integration der bisher nicht in die Weltwirtschaft voll integrierten Peripherie weiterhin zu schwach ist, als daß dort nichtmarktwirtschaftliche Formen der Aneignung von Überschuß entscheidend zurückgedrängt werden können. Das sich herausbildende internationale System ist deshalb durch miteinander verschränkte Strukturen von Markt- und Nichtmarktökonomie gekennzeichnet, die nur unter bestimmten Voraussetzungen synergetische Effekte in Richtung einer autonomen und zivilisierten Weltzivilgesellschaft entfalten werden. Dabei treten neue Strukturen von Nichtmarktökonomie auf transnationaler Ebene auf, während der Wiederaufstieg von Renten die zivilgesellschaftlichen Grundlagen funktionierender oder potentiell zu Funktionsfähigkeit zu bringender, dann kapitalistischer Systeme auf internationaler und lokaler Ebene eher behindert.
Bd. 6, 2001, 140 S., 12,90 €, br., ISBN 3-8258-4837-x

Klaus Schubert
Innovation und Ordnung
In einer evolutionär voranschreitenden Welt sind statische Politikmodelle und -theorien problematisch. Deshalb lohnt es sich, die wichtigste Quelle für die Entstehung der policy-analysis, den Pragmatismus, als dynamische, demokratieendogene politisch-philosophische Strömung zu rekonstruieren. Dies geschieht im ersten Teil der Studie. Der zweite Teil trägt zum Verständnis des daraus folgenden politikwissenschaftlichen Ansatzes bei. Darüber hinaus wird durch eine konstruktiv-spekulative Argumentation versucht, die z. Z. wenig innovative Theorie- und Methodendiskussion in der Politikwissenschaft anzuregen.
Bd. 7, 2003, 224 S., 25,90 €, br., ISBN 3-8258-6091-4

Politik: Forschung und Wissenschaft

Klaus Segbers; Kerstin Imbusch (eds.)
The Globalization of Eastern Europe
Teaching International Relations Without Borders
Bd. 1, 2000, 600 S., 35,90 €, br., ISBN 3-8258-4729-2

Hartwig Hummel; Ulrich Menzel (Hg.)
Die Ethnisierung internationaler Wirtschaftsbeziehungen und daraus resultierende Konflikte
Mit Beiträgen von Annabelle Gambe, Hartwig Hummel, Ulrich Menzel und Birgit Wehrhöfer
"Die Ethnisierung der internationalen Wirtschaftsbeziehungen und daraus resultierende Konflikte" lautete der Titel eines Forschungsprojekts, das diesem Band zugrunde liegt. Es geht um die Themen Handel, Migration und Investitionen. In drei Fallstudien werden die Handelsbeziehungen zwischen den USA und Japan, die Einwanderung nach Deutschland bzw. Frankreich und das auslandschinesische Unternehmertum untersucht. Die Ergebnisse des Projekts sehen Hummel und Menzel in den späteren Ereignissen bestätigt: Ethnisierende Tendenzen können sich in der Handelspolitik und der Investitionstätigkeit von Unternehmen nicht durchsetzen, während die Ethnisierung im Bereich der Migration andauert.
Bd. 2, 2001, 272 S., 30,90 €, br., ISBN 3-8258-4836-1

LIT Verlag Münster – Berlin – Hamburg – London – Wien
Grevener Str./Fresnostr. 2 48159 Münster
Tel.: 0251 – 23 50 91 – Fax: 0251 – 23 19 72
e-Mail: vertrieb@lit-verlag.de – http://www.lit-verlag.de

Theodor Ebert
Opponieren und Regieren mit gewaltfreien Mitteln
Pazifismus – Grundsätze und Erfahrungen für das 21. Jahrhundert. Band 1
Das grundlegende und aktuelle Werk eines Konfliktforschers, der über Jahrzehnte in pazifistischen Organisationen, in sozialen Bewegungen und in Gremien der Evangelischen Kirche gearbeitet hat. Ebert breitet in anschaulichen Berichten und doch in systematischer Ordnung die Summe seiner Erfahrungen aus und entwickelt Perspektiven für eine Welt, die mit der Gewalt leben muss, doch Gefahr läuft, an ihr zugrunde zu gehen, wenn sie auf die Bedrohungen keine neuen, gewaltfreien Antworten findet.
Aus dem Vorwort: "Es gibt eine pragmatische Befürwortung des gewaltfreien Handelns in innenpolitischen Auseinandersetzungen durch eine Mehrheit der Deutschen, und dies sollten wir als tragenden Bestandteil der Zivilkultur nicht gering schätzen. Doch die Frage, wie man mit gewaltfreien Mitteln regieren und sich gegenüber gewalttätigen Extremisten durchsetzen kann und wie man sich international behaupten und Bedrohten helfen kann, ist bislang kaum erörtert worden... Dieses Buch soll klären, was unter politisch verantwortlichem und doch radikal gewaltfreiem Pazifismus zu verstehen ist, und wie mit gewaltfreien Mitteln nicht nur opponiert, sondern auch regiert werden kann."
Bd. 3, 2001, 328 S., 20,90 €, br., ISBN 3-8258-5706-9

Theodor Ebert
Der Kosovo-Krieg aus pazifistischer Sicht
Pazifismus – Grundsätze und Erfahrungen für das 21. Jahrhundert. Band 2
Mit dem Luftkrieg der NATO gegen Jugoslawien begann für den deutschen Nachkriegspazifismus ein neues Zeitalter. Ebert hat sich über Jahrzehnte als Konfliktforscher und Schriftleiter der Zeitschrift "Gewaltfreie Aktion" mit den Möglichkeiten gewaltfreier Konfliktbearbeitung befasst. Von ihm stammt der erste Entwurf für einen Zivilen Friedensdienst als Alternative zum Militär.
Aus dem Vorwort: "Wer sich einbildet, auch in Zukunft ließe sich aus großer Höhe mit Bomben politischer Gehorsam erzwingen, unterschätzt die Möglichkeiten, die fanatische Terroristen haben, in fahrlässiger Weise. Jedes Atomkraftwerk ist eine stationäre Atombombe, die von Terroristen mit geringem Aufwand in ein Tschernobyl verwandelt werden kann. Wir haben allen Grund, schleunigst über zivile Alternativen zu militärischen Einsätzen nachzudenken und die vorhandene Ansätze solch ziviler Alternativen zu entwickeln."
Bd. 4, 2001, 176 S., 12,90 €, br., ISBN 3-8258-5707-7

Wolfgang Gieler
Handbuch der Ausländer- und Zuwanderungspolitik
Von Afghanistan bis Zypern
In der Literatur zur Ausländer- und Zuwanderungspolitik fehlt ein Handbuch, dass einen schnellen und kompakten Überblick dieses Politikbereichs ermöglicht. Das vorliegende Handbuch bemüht sich diese wissenschaftliche Lücke zu schließen. Thematisiert werden die Ausländer- und Zuwanderungspolitik weltweiter Staaten von Afghanistan bis Zypern. Zentrale Fragestellung ist dabei der Umgang mit Fremden, das heißt mit Nicht-Inländern im jeweiligen Staat. Hierbei werden insbesondere politische, soziale, rechtliche, wirtschaftliche und kulturelle Aspekte mitberücksichtigt. Um eine Kompatibilität der Beiträge herzustellen beinhaltet jeder Beitrag darüber hinaus eine Zusammenstellung der historischen Grunddaten und eine Tabelle zur jeweiligen Anzahl der im Staat lebenden Ausländer. Die vorgelegte Publikation versteht sich als ein grundlegendes Nachschlagewerk. Neben dem universitären Bereich richtet es sich besonders an die gesellschaftspolitisch interessierte Öffentlichkeit und den auf sozialwissenschaftlichen Kenntnissen angewiesenen Personen in Politik, Verwal-

LIT Verlag Münster – Berlin – Hamburg – London – Wien
Grevener Str./Fresnostr. 2 48159 Münster
Tel.: 0251 – 23 50 91 – Fax: 0251 – 23 19 72
e-Mail: vertrieb@lit-verlag.de – http://www.lit-verlag.de

tung, Medien, Bildungseinrichtungen und Migranten-Organisationen.
Bd. 6, 2003, 768 S., 98,90 €, gb.,
ISBN 3-8258-6444-8

Harald Barrios; Martin Beck; Andreas Boeckh; Klaus Segbers (Eds)
Resistance to Globalization
Political Struggle and Cultural Resilience in the Middle East, Russia, and Latin America
This volume is an important contribution to the empirical research on what globalization means in different world regions. "Resistance" here has a double meaning: It can signify active, intentional resistance to tendencies which are rejected on political or moral grounds by presenting alternative discourses and concepts founded in specific cultural and national traditions. It can also mean resilience with regard to globalization pressures in the sense that traditional patterns of development and politics are resistant to change. The book shows the that the local, sub-national, national, and regional patterns of politics and development coexist with globalized structures without yielding very much ground and in ways which may turn out to be a serious barrier to further globalization. Case studies presented focus on Venezuela, Brazil, the Middle East, Iran, and Russia.
Bd. 7, 2003, 184 S., 20,90 €, br.,
ISBN 3-8258-6749-8

Ellen Bos; Antje Helmerich
Neue Bedrohung Terrorismus
Der 11. September 2001 und die Folgen. Unter Mitarbeit von Barry Adams und Harald Wilkoszewski
Die terroristischen Anschläge des -11. September 2001 haben die Weltöffentlichkeit erschüttert. Ihre weitreichenden Auswirkungen auf die Lebenswirklichkeit des Einzelnen, den Handlungsspielraum der Nationalstaaten und das internationale System stehen im Mittelpunkt des Sammelbandes. Er basiert auf einer Ringvorlesung, in der sich Wissenschaftler der Ludwig-Maximilians-Universität München aus den Fächern Amerikanistik, Jura, Geschichte, Politik-, Religions-, Kommunikations- und Wirtschaftswissenschaft mit den geistigen Hintergründen und den Konsequenzen des Terrorismus auseinandersetzten.
Bd. 9, 2003, 232 S., 19,90 €, br.,
ISBN 3-8258-7099-5

Heinz-Gerhard Justenhoven; James Turner (Eds.)
Rethinking the State in the Age of Globalisation
Catholic Thought and Contemporary Political Theory
Since Jean Bodin and Thomas Hobbes, political theorists have depicted the state as „sovereign" because it holds preeminent authority over all the denizens belonging to its geographically defined territory. From the Peace of Westphalia in 1648 until the beginning of World War I in 1914, the essential responsiblities ascribcd to the sovereign state were maintaining internal and external security and promoting domestic prosperity. This idea of „the state" in political theory is clearly inadequate to the realities of national governments and international relations at the beginning of the twenty-first century. During the twentieth century, the sovereign state, as a reality and an idea, has been variously challenged from without and within its borders. Where will the state head in the age of globalisation? Can Catholic polilical thinking contribute to an adequate concept of statehood and government? A group of German and American scholars were asked to explore specific ways in which the intellectual traditions of Catholicism might help our effort lo rethink the state. The debate is guided by the conviction that these intellectual resources will prove valuable to political theorists as they work to revise our understanding of the state.
Bd. 10, 2003, 240 S., 19,90 €, br.,
ISBN 3-8258-7249-1

LIT Verlag Münster – Berlin – Hamburg – London – Wien
Grevener Str./Fresnostr. 2 48159 Münster
Tel.: 0251 – 23 50 91 – Fax: 0251 – 23 19 72
e-Mail: vertrieb@lit-verlag.de – http://www.lit-verlag.de

Politics and Economics in Africa
Series Editors: Robert Kappel and Ulf Engel
(Universität Leipzig)

Jedrzej Georg Frynas
Oil in Nigeria
Conflict and Litigation between Oil Companies and Village Communities
"Oil in Nigeria is destined to become a standard reference work on the Niger Delta and a template for future legal studies. Its relanvace extends beyond Nigeria and it deserves a wide readership." (African Affairs)
"An important study of the interplay among multinationals, local legal systems, and activists for human rights and the environment." (Foreign Affairs)
"I would highly recommend this book to everyone interested in understanding the complex story of the oil industry in Nigeria, the role of both the state and the oil companies and the impact of oil exploration on local communities in the Niger Delta." (Journal of Modern African Studies)
"The autor's approach is lateral and the narratives made clear with illustrations and conclusions, are compelling and revealing." (Social & Legal Studies)
"This carefully researched book ... is of interest not only to specialists in Nigeria, but to anyone seeking to understand how international relations of diplomacy and business have adapted to the brave new world of privatisation." (Stephen Ellis, African Studies Centre Leiden)
Bd. 1, 2000, 288 S., 25,90 €, br., ISBN 3-8258-3921-4

Ulf Engel
Die Afrikapolitik der Bundesrepublik Deutschland 1949 – 1999
Rollen und Identitäten
Gibt es angesichts der Vielschichtigkeit der afrikapolitischen Beziehungen Bonns eine übergreifende Klammer für die Interpretation der westdeutschen Afrikapolitik? Auf der Basis einer als "empirischer Konstruktivismus" bezeichneten Wissenschaftsmethode werden in dieser Arbeit vier Interpretationsdimensionen bemüht: Rollen, Normen, der Prozeß der Normenaneignung und das Verhältnis von Identität und Paradigmenwechsel. Dabei steht die Frage im Vordergrund, wie sich afrikapolitische Identitäten konstituieren, reproduzieren oder verändern. Einem Überblickskapitel zu den dominanten politischen Paradigmen der Bonner Afrikapolitik folgen Fallstudien zur Anwendung der Hallstein-Doktrin gegenüber Tanzania (1964–65), zur Beteiligung der Bundesrepublik an der UN-Sicherheitsratsinitiative 435 zur Lösung der Namibiafrage (1973–83), zur im Rahmen der Europäischen Politischen Zusammenarbeit betriebenen Sanktionspolitik gegenüber Südafrika (1985/86) sowie zur Politik in Zentral- und Westafrika unter den Vorzeichen regionaler französischer Hegemonie, mit besonderer Berücksichtigung von Togo (1956–67 bzw. 1991–94).
Bd. 2, 2001, 344 S., 25,90 €, br., ISBN 3-8258-4709-8

Barbara Praetorius
Power for the People
Die unvollendete Reform der Stromwirtschaft in Südafrika nach der Apartheid
Seit Anfang der 90er Jahre steht die südafrikanische Stromwirtschaft vor der Herausforderung, sich an die neuen gesellschaftlich-politischen Bedingungen am Kap anzupassen. Reformbedarf ergibt sich sowohl aus den historischen Ungerechtigkeiten als auch den exklusiven, von der Apartheid geprägten politisch-institutionellen Strukturen. Bereits frühzeitig begannen die neuen gesellschaftlichen Akteure mit breiten Konsultationsprozessen, in denen nach Lösungen für die Unterelektrifizierung, Strukturmängel und die fehlende Transparenz und Partizipation in der sektoralen Steuerung gesucht wurde. Die Autorin recherchierte diese Reformprozesse für die Zeit von 1990 bis 1999 während mehrerer Forschungsaufenthalte in Südafrika. Sie analysiert den Verlauf der sektoralen Koordinationsprozesse aus einer handlungstheoretischen Perspektive im Kon-

text des Systemwechsels zur Demokratie. Die Dynamik der sektoralen Verhandlungen lässt sich so aus dem Zusammenwirken von politisch-institutionellem Rahmen und dem strategischen Handeln politischer Akteure wie dem ANC, den Gewerkschaften, den Kommunen, den Regierungsinstitutionen und der Stromwirtschaft selbst erklären. Es zeigt sich, dass der zunächst formulierte Anspruch einer partizipatorischen und transparenten Entscheidungsfindung nur bedingt durchgehalten wird; er weicht vielmehr einer erneuten Zentralisierung der politischen Strukturen und Steuerungsmechanismen.
Bd. 3, 2000, 312 S., 25,90 €, br.,
ISBN 3-8258-4772-1

Afrikanische Studien

Werner Biermann
Tanganyika Railways – Carrier of Colonialism
An Account of Economic Indicators and Social Fragments
Bd. 9, 1996, 150 S., 19,90 €, br.,
ISBN 3-8258-2524-8

E. Adriaan B. van Rouveroy van Nieuwaal; Werner Zips (eds.)
Sovereignty, Legitimacy, and Power in West African Societies
Perspectives from Legal Anthropology
Bd. 10, 1998, 264 S., 19,90 €, br.,
ISBN 3-8258-3036-5

Beat Sottas; Thomas Hammer; Lilo Roost Vischer; Anne Mayor (Hrsg./éd.)
Werkschau Afrikastudien – Le forum suisse des africanistes
Bd. 11, 1997, 392 S., 24,90 €, br.,
ISBN 3-8258-3506-5

Hans van den Breemer; Bernhard Venema (eds.)
Towards Negotiated Co-management of Natural Resources in Africa
Bd. 12, 1999, 368 S., 25,90 €, br.,
ISBN 3-8258-3948-6

Lilo Roost Vischer; Anne Mayor; Dag Henrichsen (Hrsg./éd.)
Brücken und Grenzen – Passages et frontières
Werkschau Afrikastudien 2 – Le forum suisse des africanistes 2
Bd. 13, 1999, 480 S., 25,90 €, br.,
ISBN 3-8258-4398-x

Fred Krüger; Georgia Rakelmann; Petra Schierholz (Hg.)
Botswana – Alltagswelten im Umbruch
Facettes of a Changing Society
Bd. 14, 2000, 224 S., 15,90 €, br.,
ISBN 3-8258-4671-7

Deutsch-Madagassische Gesellschaft e. V. (Hg.)
Madagascar: Perspectives de Développement
Croissance de la Population et Croissance Economique contre Sauvegarde de la Nature
Bd. 15, 2000, 344 S., 20,90 €, br.,
ISBN 3-8258-4807-8

Joe L. P. Lugalla; Colleta G. Kibassa
Urban Life and Street Children's Health
Children's Accounts of Urban Hardships and Violence in Tanzania
Bd. 16, 2003, 176 S., 20,90 €, br.,
ISBN 3-8258-6690-4

Christoph Haferburg; Jürgen Oßenbrügge (Eds.)
Ambiguous Restructurings of Post-Apartheid Cape Town
The Spatial Form of Socio-Political Change
Bd. 17, 2003, 200 S., 20,90 €, br.,
ISBN 3-8258-6699-8

Eva-Maria Bruchhaus (Ed.)
Hot Spot Horn of Africa
Between Integration and Disintegration
Bd. 19, 2003, 208 S., 19,90 €, br.,
ISBN 3-8258-6835-4

LIT Verlag Münster – Berlin – Hamburg – London – Wien
Grevener Str./Fresnostr. 2 48159 Münster
Tel.: 0251 – 23 50 91 – Fax: 0251 – 23 19 72
e-Mail: vertrieb@lit-verlag.de – http://www.lit-verlag.de